AS I REMEMBER HIM
The Biography of R.S.

BOOKS BY

HANS ZINSSER

RATS, LICE AND HISTORY
AS I REMEMBER HIM
The Biography of R.S.

AS I REMEMBER HIM

The Biography of R.S.

BY

HANS ZINSSER

BOSTON
LITTLE, BROWN AND COMPANY
1940

THE ATLANTIC MONTHLY PRESS BOOKS
ARE PUBLISHED BY
LITTLE, BROWN AND COMPANY
IN ASSOCIATION WITH
THE ATLANTIC MONTHLY COMPANY

PRINTED IN THE UNITED STATES OF AMERICA

To the memory of R.S., without whose constant coöperation and criticism this book could not have been written

CONTENTS

AS I REMEMBER HIM
The Biography of R.S.

CHAPTER I

Introductory apology

"But why in thunder," asked my friend the novelist, "should anyone want to write a biography of R.S.? Biographical study should be reserved for men and women who have been intellectually or politically distinguished, have influenced the course of human thought or destiny, and from whose accomplishments or errors the world can derive profit. The records of the lives of great men are a sort of historical histology in which the microscope is centred on a single significant unit of a period, disclosing the forces which shaped the unusual variant and his influence upon his generation. Or, as in such relatively recent studies as the *Education of Henry Adams* or Brooks's *New England*, the subtle atmosphere of an era is clarified by filtration through the minds of superior individuals in a manner unattainable by the grosser methods of macroscopic history."

He had learned a certain medical vocabulary from me which he took great pride in displaying.

"Now this R.S.," he continued, "what after all distinguishes him from thousands of others? He contributed his little farthings to scientific medicine. He went to war like ten million others. He wrote poetry that wasn't read — possibly, to do him justice, because it was published in the *Atlantic Monthly*. He made a nuisance of himself in countless academic controversies. He had so little intellectual self-control that he reacted like an Aeolian harp to every wind that blew,

missing what little chance he had of giving out a really significant note in anything. And when he died, the world had
no unusual reasons to mourn him.

"If you want to enter the biographical racket, why don't
you do as Ludwig and Maurois do? Pick some great man who
has been well written up, and compile a nice, modern, and
exciting version from the education of the near-illiterate adult.
Or take up somebody who has really made an impression
on our civilization, such as Aimee McPherson or Jimmy
Roosevelt."

I explained to my friend that the very things he criticized
were my motives for wishing to write about R.S.

For some years before his death, which occurred quite
recently, I had been much thrown with R.S. by common
professional interests, and he attracted me largely because
he seemed so typically a child of his time. Born and brought
up in the nineteenth-century traditions which prevailed
until the Great War, he never succeeded in adjusting to
the social and political turmoil which, since then, has
shaken the foundations of a private and public life that had
seemed permanently established in a reasonably stabilized
world.

He appeared a noticeably average representative of that
educated middle class which lived its maturer years through
this transitional period, nostalgically conservative, yet trying
hard to fall in with the spirit of the times; eventually realizing that, as far as he and his fellows were concerned, their
main contribution must be to carry over into the new era
something of the precious past which most other people
seemed intent on completely destroying. And I felt that the
education and thoughts of a reasonably intelligent, average
person might give a more accurate picture of these times than
any biographical record of the distinguished and brilliant who

might, because of their genius, belong to any age while representing none in particular.

In spite of my novelist's discouraging remarks, therefore,
I suggested to R.S. himself that I write his biography, and
explained — more or less as I have tried to in the preceding
paragraphs — why I should like to do so. He objected, and to
my surprise his opposition was not based, as I had expected, on
modesty. Indeed, he was hurt. He seemed to believe that he
was quite a remarkable fellow and, if a biography were to be
written, it should be a serious one. But he didn't like the idea
of biography for a number of other reasons.

"First of all," he said, "I wouldn't tell you some of the most
interesting things about me, because I'm ashamed of them.
Look at Rousseau. Everyone gloats over the *Confessions*.
If he hadn't written them, people would occasionally read
the *Contrat Social* and the *Nouvelle Héloïse*, and realize his
intelligence instead of using him for psychoanalytical genius-
snooping.

"Me," he said ungrammatically, "I have been like most
other people, both a hero and a coward; an idealist and a
humbug; a Galahad and a sensualist. Virtue and the Devil
have been constantly rolling over each other within me. '*Tras
la Cruz esta el Diablo*' — behind the Cross is always the Devil,
as Cervantes said. Taking it by and large, I had more fun
when the Devil was on top, and I have often been thankful
that Martin Luther was such a bad shot with the ink bottle.
But I am far from considering myself hopelessly wicked for
that reason. For after all, man made the Devil in his own
image, and if there were no Devil we should have to invent
one. Yet I shouldn't like that to go into a biography — certainly not with documentation.

"Besides," he continued, "I'm a doctor. And I'm sick of
books by doctors and about doctors. It's a racket. The whole

publicizing of culture is a racket. Everybody's a little educated nowadays, and they're all hungry for easy culture — medicine, philosophy, mathematics, chemistry, literature. They want books about books. Of course you can't blame them. People are too busy to read Goethe or Voltaire or Cervantes or Kant. Can you see the average reader poring over 'Zweitens der Grundsatz dass Realitäten (als blosse Bejahung) einander niemals logisch widerstreiten, ist ein ganz anderer Satz von dem Verhältnisse der Begriffe, bedeutet aber weder in Ansehung irgend eines Dinges an sich selbst (von diesem haben wir keinen Begriff) das mindeste.' He can get it much more easily from Will Durant or Alpern or Fuller. It's more fun to read Van Wyck Brooks in a hammock than Emerson, or Ludwig than Goethe. They want it in hypodermics or like liver extract."

I quote this only as an example of how he was apt to run on at the slightest provocation — always, I may say, including in his reasonable talk a lot of things about which he knew practically nothing at all. This was at the same time his defect and his charm, for — often — the more illogical and excited he was, the more he illustrated the confused reaction of his class to the things going on in the modern world. He became what Rachilde calls a "cerveau enflammé."

I quieted him by telling him that I had no idea of writing about him as a doctor. "The medicine," I said, "is purely incidental. I have no thought of making you the excuse for another Odyssey in Wonderland, like Victor Heiser's, or a Science and Health, like Dr. Carrel's. I should like to write about you and your reactions more or less as Henry Adams wrote about himself: the times filtering through your personality — you yourself an example of your kind of people.

"You see," I fortified my point, "Henry Adams was an American, blood and bone of him. You represent the recent stock. It would be amusing to contrast the reactions of a relatively parthenogenetic American with those of the immediate post-Iroquois strain."

At this juncture he broke into a tirade about the advantages of being an outsider. He quoted Samuel Butler. He then started on the Anglo-Saxons in America, who regarded everyone who lived among them without Anglicizing his name as something inferior. I let him run down. But I did get him interested.

Through the ensuing years, there was a tacit understanding between us that he would write, for my perusal and editing, his recollections and thoughts. The responsibility of connecting them into an acceptable sequence was to be mine, and I was to be permitted to write — in the third person, of course — any additional information which I could gather from our frequent conversations. I was also to have complete possession of any papers he left behind, and I fell heir to notes and keepsakes, unfinished articles, poems, and even a Rabelaisian series of unfinished fairy tales, that he would otherwise have destroyed. But, faithful to our friendship, I have suppressed many things that I know he would not have liked to see in print and which, indeed, were often disgraceful.

The greater part of this book, written in the first person, is almost unedited from the pen of R.S. himself. In consequence, it is in places badly written, and sometimes vague and discursive. The smoother writing, in the third person, is my own.

My friend the novelist, like many others of my literary acquaintances, questioned my ability to accomplish so difficult a task, since I had published only one non-medical book, which is now printed in the Blue Ribbon series, together with the *Complete Dog Book* and *The Sexual Life of Savages*. And, of course, I am considerably intimidated by the modern insistence on what is called "craftsmanship" by professional writers. But I took courage from Sainte-Beuve's remark: *"Rien ne m'est pénible comme le dédain avec lequel on traite souvent des écrivains du second ordre, comme s'il n'y avait place que pour ceux du premier."*

I approached my task with modesty, therefore, hoping that I might acceptably convey in this study the portrait of a representative of that generation, now rapidly disappearing, — like the T-model Ford, — whose lives bridged the transition from horses to gasoline, from gaslight to electric bulbs, from Emerson and Longfellow to T. S. Eliot and Joyce, from stock companies to the movies and the radio, etc., etc. — in short, from Victoria to Mrs. Windsor.

If there appears, in this account, occasional confusion of subject and sequence, this — apart from my possible ineptitude — is due to very reluctant coöperation by R.S. and to the fact that, although in his science he had some excuse for calling himself a specialist, he was one of those people on whom all controversial questions of the time acted like horseflies on a half-broken mule. The work of the last year, however, was much facilitated by the fact that his doctors persuaded him to stop drinking.

CHAPTER II

Westchester County autumn: in this short chapter, R.S. speaks of his parents, their marriage, and their death

AUTUMN is the season which, more than any other time of the year, brings back to me the bittersweet pageant of the past. In the Hudson Valley in the days before motorcars, — when my horse's feet went slushing through fallen leaves which a gust of wind brought blowing and tumbling across the roads, — the swamp maples turned first, and then the other trees and bushes, with the wild vines making bright cardinal patches across the great rocks; and the hills, gaudy and carnival-like in the noon sunshine, would grow sombre with a majestic mournfulness as the short afternoons chilled into dusk. The sweet, acrid wood smoke hung in the air as I rode past a farmhouse, and at home, when the saddle was off and a forkful of hay pitched down to the blanketed mare, there would be a log fire in the big stone fireplace that smoked just enough to let one smell the wood. There would be a cold supper, a bottle of wine, and the affectionate banter of intimacy. And, before bedtime, a stroll to the stable — warm and dark — with the beloved smell of horses and hay; a stamping and a turning of heads in the stalls when the lantern light swung around the shadows of the beams, with perhaps a barn swallow waking from sleep and fluttering into the rafters. Then back under cold stars hung low in a brightly black sky, with just chill enough to send one off to bed with a jump from the opened window to the blankets.

It was in the autumn that my father died. I was sitting beside his bed, waiting. He had looked into the eyes of death for two years; at first, a little frightened and shocked. But as the sense of inevitableness became a habit, and pain more constant and severe, he complained only of the cruel slowness with which death comes — so long after his coming is announced. He died at night and — as I have seen it so often — his mind cleared during the last hours. When the end finally came, there was a pressure of my hand, and a smile. The smile remained to soften the lines of suffering in his face when he was dead, and I found myself sitting there beside him, with the first light of day creeping into the windows — feeling, for the moment, utterly alone in a world which I had never imagined without him.

He had no belief in God. He had no hope of immortality. And in these negations he did not weaken during the months of agony. If he shed a tear, it was for the sorrow of leaving us who loved him so deeply. He believed that man's immortality lies in the offspring of his body and mind, and wanted no consolation for what he accepted as the inevitable destiny of all living things.

When he died, my mother's life was over. She had met him, a gay student of twenty-two, with the black-red-gold ribbon — later for a historic moment the colors of the German Republic — across his breast. She was the daughter of a disgraced political dissenter in the Black Forest, a lawyer who would neither do homage to the political powers nor shave off the beard that proclaimed his allegiance to a defeated cause. The man of her heart went to America, to the promised land where there was still room for all the free spirits whose wings were clipped at home by bigotry and political oppression. The English love liberty, Heine has said, as a legitimate wife — not too caressingly, but with a sense of ownership and protectiveness; the French, he said, love her as a mistress — always to be wooed in order to be retained. The Americans, my father added, treat her like a familiar drudge — so sure of her that they may abuse and neglect her. She will grow old and feeble in time, and will perhaps die altogether. He did not live long enough to know how nearly his prophecy was to be fulfilled. For, in his day, liberty in America was young and vigorous. And up to the end of his life the words "freedom" and "liberty" had a sense of solemnity for him. He loved Abraham Jacobi and idolized Hans Kudlich, who said: ". . . *Ihr Deutsche! haltet die Nacken steif!*"; and he wanted to be buried next to Carl Schurz in the Sleepy Hollow Cemetery, where he now lies.

He came to America with pockets almost empty, but with the help of an older brother, already in full career, soon turned his chemical training to good use. But it was no sudden affluence; and, meanwhile, the dark-eyed girl in the Schwarzwald was having a hard time. Her mother had died — the father a little later; there was hardly any money. She went for a while as a governess to France and taught a little Monsieur de Something de Something very little German, in return for which she perfected her French, confirmed her instinct for social formality, and lost a great deal of national prejudice. But I can imagine her often, on autumn evenings, wandering in the château garden thinking wistfully of the merry young chemist who was so sad on leaving her, and who had said that he would never stop loving her, wherever he might be.

And then something happened that seemed like a miracle. A letter came, like the answer to a wish in a fairy tale.

The young chemist had written home. Home was a schoolmaster's house on the Rhine, in a village conveniently located for harboring refugees at night, when they tapped on the kitchen shutters after the children were asleep — or were supposed to be. Often they were not, as my father told me, and they would lie in their beds in the attic, wide-eyed and alert, listening in silent excitement to the sounds of hurried meals and furtive departures below.

The broad-shouldered old schoolmaster was alone now — his wife dead and all the seven birds flown from the roost into the wide world. Four sons — a doctor, two merchants, and a chemist — in New York; three daughters married, one of them in America. He spent long evenings in his garden — a lonely old man — thinking of the past, and hoping for letters. "I am now in a position to marry her," the young chemist wrote. "But it is two years since we have seen each other and we were then very young. Does she love me enough to journey almost a quarter of the circumference of the world, to settle in a new, strange, and curiously unfriendly country, with no one but myself to be home to her?"

On a happy day the letter came to her from the old schoolmaster, whom she had never seen. "The boy loves you and wants you to marry him," it said. "You may think you are still in love with him and, being a brave girl, you may have courage enough to go to him and fulfill your promise. But you are very young and very lonely, and neither of us can tell how these two years among the clever Yankees may have changed him. But if you think you are sure of your feelings, I will take you to him myself. And if we find him the same warmhearted and high-spirited boy we knew and loved, I will see you married to him before I come back. If not, you shall return with me to the Rhine, for I have sore need of a daughter."

They met in the city of her birth — Freiburg im Breisgau. The old man arrived with a heavy bag of long-hoarded gold pieces. America was much farther away then than it is now, and the schoolmaster was a very old man. But he was also a very gallant one: flirted with his son's girl all the way over; rolled her in blankets; tucked her in at night; brought her all the simple things he could afford — in short, it was a sort of pre-honeymoon.

That's how my father and my mother were finally brought together. No parson, however; a justice of the peace at the City Hall and a party in the little wooden house near the chemical factory, with Asmus, the mining engineer-poet, Onkel Fritz, the musician-doctor, and all the jolly half-homesick exiles for whom America was a great adventure where their talents and training had full play but where, in some respects, their freedom was like that of the desert. To the Americans of their own class and culture, though there were plenty of them, they had no easy access, and with the others they wanted little contact. So for many years they remained in a sort of cultural oasis of their own, — socially and intellectually self-sufficient, — waiting perhaps a little arrogantly for this country to seek them out, instead of exploring. We spoke German at the table until my father's death. Sunday-evening dinners were patriarchal reunions of a clan, imposed by a custom of affectionate reverence, with open house for waifs for whom talent or science or music or sheer loneliness had loosened the latchstring.

These exiles had no complaints to make of their new home,

and they became politically Americans with a speed and thoroughness surprising to all who did not understand their fervid admiration of our institutions. But when they had left behind all the things they had hated at home, they rediscovered in their own hearts the love for the many other things they missed in their new surroundings.

Now he was dead. And after fifty-two years of journeying together my mother's life was over. She wanted to go back to Westchester County to the house where they had spent so many happy years. We younger ones had a little farmhouse not far from the home place, in one of the narrow valleys through which the brooks run down to the Hudson. To this she came, with two maids and her chauffeur.

Maids were different in those days, and chauffeurs were usually old men and recent coachmen. They were not birds of passage and servants. They had little pay compared with to-day, but their place of service was their home. They stayed a long time, and there was affection in their relationships. My mother was a benevolent tyrant. Her maids were praised and scolded, supervised, bullied, and petted. My mother knew about their families, their small brothers and sisters, and their troubles. They stood in awe of her a little — but loved her a great deal. Now, in her affliction, they cherished her with humble devotion.

She wanted to be alone and, with them, she was alone — and taken care of. We brothers took turns visiting her. One of us came to see her each day, driving up from New York. We would find her sitting on the lawn in front of the house, silently knitting — a pitifully small and shrunken figure against the blazing grandeur of the autumnal hills. At a suitable distance, on one side, sat Anna, her maid; just far enough to be out of the way, but near enough to hear when she was spoken to. Somewhere, near by, John the ex-coachman was busy, tinkering at some useless task, in order to be within reach. Thus, when I came, I would find her, wrapped in a fur coat, sitting — with the dignity and poise of great sorrow — among the falling leaves.

She roused herself when we came and chatted reminiscently, and took great pleasure in our coming. But we whom she had loved so dearly for ourselves were now obviously only what was left of him. Her life was over, and in two weeks she followed him. Gradually, she had grown more feeble for no physically noticeable reason. She seemed to die of his death.

CHAPTER III

He speaks of his birth and childhood, and since he seemed to derive a nostalgic satisfaction from this, I allowed him to run on — though he introduced much that is quite irrelevant

1

MY birth fell into the period intermediary between the methods of Dr. Slop and the modern aseptic obstetrics — "twilight sleep," prenatal and after care — which have made childbirth a not too unpleasant interruption between a dinner party and the hunt races. In May 1847, Semmelweis had introduced chlorine water into the wards of the Vienna hospitals, and the deaths in childbirth had dropped within a year from 12 per cent to 1.2 per cent. The horrors which Dr. Holmes describes in his eloquent essay were recent and dreadful memories. To be sure, there was not yet any intelligence about birth control and — in this sense — I cannot escape the belief that to some extent I really should not have been born. For there were eight years between me and my next older brother. Of course when I came I was not, for that reason, unwelcome; for my parents were intrinsically good and tender of heart.

Yet it is a strange and terrifying thought that a human life — long and adventurous, full of joy and sorrow, effort and disappointment, pregnant with possibilities for good and evil, for suffering, for vice and virtue — should be begotten more or less accidentally, for no particular reason except the enchantment of an early harvest moon.

In the famous letter received by the late Professor Wheeler, Wee-Wee, the King of the Termites, commenting on the inferiority of human society to that of his own species, says: "And owing to the absence of eugenics and birth control, and to your habits of fostering all weak and inefficient individuals, there is not even the dubious and slow-working apparatus of natural selection to provide for the organic fixation of castes through heredity." Wee-Wee is quite right, and among termites this last offspring would not have been in the planned order of society and might well have been omitted without serious loss.

At any rate, there I was; and, thanks to the newer obstetrics, my mother had not too much discomfort of me, and I was rendered neither imbecile nor paralyzed by the procedures of passing — in the words of Goethe — through that arch under which all candidates for immortality must pass.

Incidentally, the slowness of the progress which this science of obstetrics made through the ages to arrive even at the point which it had reached at the date of my birth is extraordinary. The Greeks had a kind of midwife. Only difficult cases called for a physician, but — strangely enough in a race so athletic — Simon Magnetes records that three out of every five childbirths were difficult ones. In the oldest sculptures, according to Haeser, the habitual position during birth was a "kneeling" (probably squatting) one; and this seems a habitual phenomenon among aboriginal races, often retained long after their removal from primitive surroundings. While riding the Roosevelt Hospital ambulance, not yet too old to blush while performing professional service, I encountered several instances of emergency childbirth in the San Juan Hill negro district, in which the prospective mothers refused to move from the squat in a dark corner of the room. In one case, in order to do my duty of holding back the head, I was forced to lie in an awkward position on a very dirty floor, while performing my probably quite unnecessary functions. But I was young and compassionate, and there was in my heart that pride of devotion which suppresses disgust and ennobles service. Fortunately, the night was bitter cold, and I had a thick overcoat to spread beneath me. But I remember well the difficulties I had kicking a little dog away from my legs, and my worry at being helpless to stop the first-born — a lovely naked pickaninny of three — from looting my ambulance bag while all this was going on. It was done in the dim light of a gas flame; but within the hour we were all — including the little bag robber — riding merrily to the Sloane Maternity in the ambulance.

But to come back to obstetrics: in this art the Greeks did not advance beyond the skill of the ancient Hindus. The latter already had midwives, — four to a case, — knew quite a lot about the stages of pregnancy, tied off the umbilical cord, hung it about the neck of the child, and actually (Susruta) described abnormal positions *in utero*, recommending "version" in certain cases, to pull down the legs.

In the second century, Soranus of Ephesus wrote a considerable work on diseases of women, in which he included much crude and — to our modern minds — murderous advice about manipulatory aid in first deliveries. Incidentally, living in Rome at the time of Pliny and Trajan, Soranus may be regarded as the first advocate of birth control reliably on record, giving advice which — in principle — is not so unlike that which is now prohibited in the United States mails.

But we are talking about my own birth, and not writing a history of obstetrics. By the time I was born, bacteriology had begun to reveal the principles which made obstetrics — as indeed all other forms of surgery — humane and relatively safe. The rest was technique. And obstetrics had advanced almost as much, if not more, by the principle of noninterference as by safeguarding procedure. Before Semmelweis, it is likely — though we have no statistics to prove it — that fewer women would have died if midwives and doctors had been prohibited by law from coming near the prospective mother until just before delivery of the placenta. Some of the women whom I attended as ambulance surgeon, and who came through quite robustly, had had their babies either by themselves or with the sympathetic and, fortunately, timid "assistance" (in the French sense) of a policeman or a streetcar conductor long before I arrived. In one case a policeman — himself a father, as he later told me — had tied off the cord with a shoestring. One poor girl, — I recall her with the reminiscent tenderness of my youthful compassion, — ashamed of having a baby without a husband, had taken a room in an obscure boardinghouse, with the intention of hiding her disgrace and remaining alone until it was over. When the crisis came, her nerves gave way and she called for help. I well remember the miserable hallway, the indignant drudge of a landlady, — with bare arms, broom, and mobcap, howling the respectability of her hovel, — the dim hall bedroom, and the agonized, lovely young thing on the dirty bed. It all went well. I don't know what became of her afterward. The Sloane nurse told me later that she left the hospital quite happy, with a frail baby in her arms.

But she never did give her right name, and was "O.W." (out of wedlock) on the records.

There is not, in our present society, any greater example of hard luck than that of having an illegitimate baby. The only imaginably greater misfortune might be having illegitimate twins or triplets. The one case of that kind I can think of, though of course it must have happened often, is that of Robert Burns's second love, the patient Jean, who actually did have illegitimate twins — later legalized, though not until, I believe, there had been one or two (I'm not sure) "love children" from other attractive girls in between. And, of all things, this had to happen in Scotland. What a man! Not because he produced the children, but because he could keep right on writing poetry. Indeed, it seemed to stimulate him.

About other obstetrical adventures I may have more to say in later chapters of this narrative. To the sensitive young disciple of medicine, these experiences are perhaps the most profoundly stirring in his education as a human being.

To come back to my own birth: with a knowledge of the circumstances and the state of the science at the time of my entrance into this turbulent planet, it is not difficult to reconstruct just what happened.

Having thoroughly dried me, old Dr. Gulecke slapped me vigorously on the buttocks, leaving across them the scarlet imprint of four bony fingers, thereby stirring me, as was intended, to the indignant protest that filled my lungs with their first sweet air. It brought a healthy flush of anger to my little wrinkled face; but — nothing perturbed — the doctor turned me over to reassure himself as to the kind I was and, wiping his brow with the reverse side of the towel with which he had dried me, handed me to Frau Schultz.

It was, no doubt, an amazingly casual and prosaic performance. There was no rustle of angel wings, there were no strains of heavenly music; but for the tired girl in the next room — who looked then just like the faded photograph that I have on the desk before me — a miracle had been performed that stirred her lips in grateful prayer. And when the competent Frau Schultz — having rolled me and smeared me, dabbed and swathed me — laid me, with a last professional and totally unnecessary wipe of the nose, in the waiting arms, she hugged me to her breast and went immediately to sleep.

Frau Schultz, I am sure, began to tidy up, and the doctor to fasten his cuff links, long before they gave a thought to my poor father, who was pacing up and down on the floor below in his wrinkled clothes, anxiety and a feeling of guilt struggling for mastery within him.

Then the doctor — as they always do — drove away with the air of a worker of miracles.

2

The minds of little children are like rolls of cinema film on which long series of uncoördinated impressions, gathered by the senses, are caught. Usually most of these fade completely in later years. It is only here and there, in the earlier years, that an experience impresses itself with sufficient coloring to remain as a memory in later life.

My earliest reminiscence goes back to when I must have been between one and two years old. It was like a vaguely remembered dream until I found later, in speaking of it, that it was based on fact. I remembered clouds in a blue sky, against which the spars of a ship were swinging to and fro, and at the same time I heard a little tune sung with German words: —

Schlaf', mein liebes Kind.
Draussen bläst der Wind.
Hör! des Nachbars Hündchen bellt!
Alles schläft in der weiten Welt. . . .

I can't remember any more of it. Later, I learned that I was taken abroad as a baby, and that my father often sat on the deck of the old *Moselle*, which still had masts and spars for emergency rigging, and sang me to sleep on his lap with the little song.

As a boy, I would often — especially before going to sleep at night — hear him singing again, see the swinging spars against clouds scudding through a blue sky, and go to sleep happily. And a warm wave of affection floods my heart even now for the young, blond man whose love enclosed me while he lived and whose hand I have felt caressingly on my head throughout my life, whenever I was in need of comforting.

At times the dead are closer to us than the living, and the wisdom and affection of the past stretch blessing hands over our lives, projecting a guardian care out of the shadows and helping us over hard places. For there are certain kinds of love that few but the very wise fully understand until they have become memories.

3

Our dog, a mongrel poodle, was an important part of my life then, as dogs have been more or less ever since. He had not been ruined by too much social life. Let a dog know too many people, and he turns out badly. Bring him up in a family where he is always about with a few companions, shares house and board, lies by the fire, runs with the children, steals in the kitchen, and sleeps under a bed, and you have — at five or six — a wise and affectionate and altogether lovable dog. The same principles apply to people, as Isaac Newton well knew, because it is said that, when he was first asked to join the Royal Society, he declined — saying that he was afraid it "might increase the circle of his acquaintances."

When I lay awake in the very early mornings the birds would begin to chirp in the vines that grew along the wall under my window. They were only humble city sparrows, but they made a merry confusion of sound. And when my mother came in to bid me good-morning, she always said: "Did you hear your birds?" She gave me the birds as my own, as Anatole France's mother gave him the rose on the wallpaper. And ever since I have thought of the early morning sparrows as my own particular property.

The walk in the Park was the event of the mornings. I was accompanied by the dog, on a leash, with a fine green collar, and we were both in the care of the "Rothe Anna," a faithful, deep-chested, redheaded girl from the Schwarzwald. The dog, being on a leash and thereby protected, made brave growling jumps at squirrels and birds, and I ran ahead, pulling a little express wagon or rolling a hoop. With other children I had little association on these walks, because my English was distinctly foreign. I do remember hitting another small boy over the head with the shaft of the express wagon one day, but have forgotten the preliminaries. It was the earliest example of a great many similar episodes that, in later life, gave me the reputation of having a quick temper; though, as I think them over, they can all be explained by the fact that — not growing very big — I was quarrelsome merely to keep up my self-respect.

Anna always straightened out any difficulties the dog or I

got into, and brought us home happy. She was a good Catholic and worried a great deal about my irreligious upbringing. So, on our walks, she often entertained me with stories of saints; and once, just as we were standing under a big elm in the Mall, she pointed upward and said: *"Der liebe Gott wohnt dort droben."* For a long time, I believed that God lived in an elm tree in Central Park, and often I would stand under it and gaze upward, hoping to get a glimpse of Him.

4

Onkel Fritz was a doctor. Of course, I had known him from the beginning in the impersonal way in which a very small boy would become interested in a shaggy head from which a single sharp and kindly blue eye gazes at him. Little children and dogs have no sense of good looks or ugliness; and it was not until much later that I realized with some surprise that the rest of the world thought Onkel Fritz an unusually unprepossessing person. By that time he had passed his fiftieth year, and gray threads had begun to accentuate the blondness of his unbrushed hair and patchy beard. While not exactly fat, he was broad and stout, which made him look smaller than he was; and he was always very untidy. His most noticeable feature was his one sharp and humorous eye, of a very light sky-blueness; and most interesting to me was a deep scar which went up diagonally from the other — the blind one — for an inch and a half across his forehead, so deep and adherent to the bone that I could press my finger into it when he held me on his knee — unless he had, as was usual with him, shoved his glasses up from his nose, over his eyebrows. This was a habit of his, and he seemed to me always to be shoving his gold-rimmed spectacles out of the way in this manner, whenever he wanted to look at something. The scar, he always told me, was the result of his falling on a rake when he was about as big as I was. Later, when I found out that he had acquired it in a duel with heavy sabres, he admitted the duel, but said that he had had to fight the Czar of Russia because he had stuck his tongue out at him at a court reception. This scar of Onkel Fritz's made him a hero to me, and I often imagined him, with his spectacles on his forehead, dressed just as he was then, in striped trousers, a black coat, and stiff collar, — and, most illogically, with the to-be-acquired scar already in place, — slashing away at a frantically parrying and terrified Czar who was jumping about in an ermine cape, with a crown on his head.

The reason I loved Onkel Fritz so early in my life was mainly, I believe, because he took me seriously. The ladies and gentlemen to whom I was often embarrassingly introduced at afternoon *Kaffee* had the habit of making themselves and me ridiculous with baby talk and silly questions, calling me *kleiner Mann*, and hiding their essential lack of interest under an assumed delight in my resemblance to my parents and similar rubbish. Onkel Fritz made me a contemporary. He was no more "grown-up" with me than he was with the dog. He seemed to realize that we were both of us sensible and intelligent people, and that conversation with me was more profitable than the idle talk of the others about the coffee table.

5

Whenever I look at an Italian primitive, my feet begin to hurt. The reason for this is that, as a small boy of ten to fourteen, I was often taken along on excursions through Italy in the company of this Onkel Fritz, who felt it his duty to form my taste, as he called it.

Onkel Fritz, whose polyphemoid appearance I have just described, was an odd character. A successful dermatologist and syphilographer in New York in the 1860's and 1870's, he retired from practice at a relatively early age, bought himself a house and garden in the lovely *Kurort* Wiesbaden in Hessen-Nassau, and devoted himself to playing the fiddle and collecting folk songs. I lived with him while I was sent to school for one year in Wiesbaden, and remember him most vividly either pacing the upper hall in his Jaeger underwear, practising Kreutzer *études*, or lying late in bed in a sunny room lined with bound volumes of music, reading scores and apparently hearing the silent notes as he read. Later in life he took up old paintings and became professor of art and curator in the small but excellent local "Museum." His trips to Italy with us were therefore, in a manner, professional, and he being by instinct a pundit, and the rest of the family having become quite skillful at getting out from under, mine was the helpless mind which he determined to improve.

I was of value to Onkel Fritz in two respects on these travels, a nuisance in all others. My chief usefulness — one from which I myself gathered considerable enjoyment — was in regard to keeping other travelers out of the second-class compartments in which four of us managed almost invariably, thanks to me, to occupy the space intended for six. Bribery of the conductor was often quite adequate. But when this appeared impracticable, the same result could be achieved with my help by one or the other of two systems. One — the most satisfactory to me — was to ornament my face and forehead heavily and not inartistically with the red and blue crayons which I carried for the purposes of juvenile sketching, until I presented the appearance of a horrid little boy all broken out with smallpox or leprosy. Then, when we arrived at a station with eager second-class passengers milling about for vacancies, I stuck my head out of the window. This, to the accompaniment of considerable virtuosity in distorting my childlike features into grimaces of great suffering, — an accomplishment in which I took pride, and often practised before a mirror, — quite successfully protected us on most occasions, though it once led to embarrassing attentions from a traveling physician. Onkel Fritz's other method was to train me to loud and heartbroken weeping during our stops at stations, a subterfuge which, while not as regularly effective as the former, still saved us from many a crowded and unpleasant journey.

The other function in which I was useful to Onkel Fritz was in this matter of old paintings. I take it for granted that he knew a great deal about them, and I am sure that he had much genuine pleasure from them. But his enjoyment was infinitely enhanced by the act of explaining and displaying his learning. The impulse to educate my taste, to start me in the right directions of appreciation, was — though in itself not entirely insincere — yet subsidiary, I believe, to the didactic passion. But it was hard on my feet, and all I gained from it artistically at that time was an aversion to Giottos, Fra Angelicos, Lippo Lippis, and such, which lasted until I returned to these galleries in later life — when, strangely enough, I found that deep in long-unexplored crevices of my mind there lingered memories of the good old man's enthusiasm which gave me understanding I should not have had without him.

CHAPTER IV

R.S. speaks of his earliest religious impressions and
of his school days. But since the school in which he
spent eight years was presided over by a Jew, he
wandered off into a diatribe on anti-Semitism. I tried
to divert him from this dangerous topic, because I
feared it might ruin the book. But there was no
stopping him

In assembling material for the preceding chapters my problem was chiefly that of selecting from a mass of notes and
conversations those episodes in the childhood of R.S. which
I believed might best illustrate domestic environment and
personal relations. Since it is obviously difficult to create a
complete picture by this method, it has seemed advisable,
from time to time, to fill out the background of these disconnected sketches with explanatory information.

It is apparent that family life, habits, language, and cultural
influences, during the childhood of R.S., remained essentially
German. But it should be understood that the Germanicism
of this family was that of the Rhineland and the Black Forest,
a variety which penetrating historians like Sorel, Brinton, and
others have recognized as clearly differentiated from that of
Prussia, the Central States, and Austria. For the Rhineland
and the southern border provinces had long been under the
influence of French thought and political doctrine. They had

been frequently invaded and had "felt deeply the republican propaganda of the French Revolution." There had even been a Jacobin Club at Mainz during that time, and the aspirations toward civil liberty then fostered were never again completely lost. Moreover, many of the peasantry were landholders whose general outlook was more like that of the French post-revolutionary peasant proprietors than that of the more feudally governed people of the rest of Germany and of Prussia. In consequence, as we shall see in a later chapter, the political storms which broke after 1830 swept over these regions more violently than they did over the eastern provinces. Families emigrating to America from the Rhineland, therefore, fitted immediately and with complete contentment into those free political institutions for which they had unsuccessfully struggled at home. Yet, though thus politically acclimatized from the very beginning, they long remained culturally and socially isolated from Americans of their own class and educational level. This was due partly to their own conceit and lack of social adaptability and, in part, to the provincialism of the American upper classes, who at that period seemed quite unaware that there were cultivated people among foreigners who immigrated and kept them at arm's length. R.S., who spoke no English until he was ten, though eventually completely absorbed into the life of America, always felt himself — probably because of this early social isolation — to some extent an outsider. This may explain much about his later reactions.

1

My mother was brought up in a convent in the Black Forest. In girlhood she had been a pious Catholic. But something happened to her faith early in her married life. Was it that she was carried away by the tide of the new world of scientific skepticism into which she had entered, or was it passive acquiescence, unwillingness to be out of harmony with her surroundings? Probably, being almost altogether heart and not at all a logical person, she concluded that love was enough and that ritual was unessential for what she valued in religion. At any rate, she made no active objection to the complete omission of any kind of religious instruction for her unchristened boys.

In later years, however, I often wondered whether we had not, all of us, — my father included, — taken too much for granted. Much later, thinking about this, I remembered hearing her express horror when Voltaire was mentioned (probably reminiscence of the convent, for she was essentially an unlearned person), and her unwillingness to read either Strauss or Renan when I offered them to her. At any rate, at that time it never occurred to any of her family — at least it was never expressed — that she might have been silently faithful through all those years, with so complete a trust in the goodness of a reasonable God that she felt content, for herself and for her children, to dispense with the forms, so long as the true spirit of her own Christianity could be instilled into their daily lives in feeling and in action.

I suspect that this may have been the case; for I alone, being by many years the youngest and, therefore, most intimately her companion, had occasion to be with her in moments when — with no one but a beloved child to observe her — she relaxed into expressions of that longing to believe that God exists which is the source of faith.

I remember how, on several occasions, in the cold and noisy city dusk of Christmas Eve, unknown to anyone else, my mother took me to the Cathedral of the Paulist Fathers on

59th Street. In her victoria, drawn by the two dapple grays
I so admired, we drove through the crowded streets. All about
us, in this neighborhood of tenement houses, tired-looking and
poorly dressed people were hurrying homeward with packages
under their arms; shop windows were bright; and the man
with the long stick was going about lighting the gaslights on
the lampposts. At the corner, under the elevated railroad,
August the German coachman was left to walk the horses,
while my mother took me by the hand and led me up the stone
steps and through the padded swing doors into the church.
It was chilly and dim in the great Gothic vaults, but the altar
was brightly lighted; here and there were a few poor, old,
drudgy-looking women and a shabby man or two, kneeling
with bowed heads in front of wicker chairs placed in rows.
There was a little chapel on one side, where there were candles
burning below a high crucifix, with red, spreading spots on
the hands and feet of the Saviour who hung suspended from
it. And over a small altar there was a large picture of the
Virgin.

Here Mother would sit, and draw me close against her lap.
She did not pray — at least, not audibly — and she did not
speak; and I was too subdued to move or to say anything by
a sense of frightened, but still gentle awe. Perhaps I shared
her feelings more than I then could comprehend. For, in later
years, I found myself going into Catholic churches — Saint-
Sulpice, Chartres, my childhood's Saint Paul's, even the Cathedral in Boston's South End — to sit for a few moments as
I used to sit with her, silently and with no realized purpose,
except perhaps to feel again the uncomprehended, mystical
solemnity which held me peacefully quiet, so many years ago
on Christmas Eve, with my body pressed against her knees;

and to remember how she softened for me the shock of being again suddenly in the bustling ugliness of the cold and sordid street, held me close to her and kissed me before entering the carriage to drive home.

2

I was the youngest of four sons, and, as I have said, there was a gap of eight years between me and my next older brother. As a result, I was much spoilt, and my mother, wishing to keep me near her as long as possible, delayed sending me to school until my eleventh year. Meanwhile, I was reasonably well taught by tutors, male and female, both in this country and during a winter at Pallanza on Lago Maggiore; but eventually it became obvious that, by this method, I should develop into an incurable sissy.

The choice of a school was not easy in those days. The public schools, to which a man of my father's democratic convictions was inclined to send me, were not good enough, and the prospects there even of learning to speak grammatical English were nil. He had solved the problem in the cases of two older brothers by sending them abroad to live with my uncle and attend the *Gymnasium*. In my case, he abandoned this idea in deference to my mother. But he had looked into the possibilities of the New England boarding schools which were then being started in more or less acknowledged imitation of the English public schools. It did not take him long to decide that this was not what he wanted for me. These institutions were scholastically much superior to public schools — though not nearly as much so as he thought they should have been. The boys were an attractive lot, as a rule, but were sent to these schools as much for snob appeal as for other advantages.

And, throughout, there was a deep Anglo-religious atmosphere that my father believed had no place in secondary education, and which repelled him. After taking me to visit one of these institutions over the week end and attending the compulsory chapel services, he said: "When I sat there, listened to a medi-aevally stupid sermon, and saw all the medicine men going through their ritual exercises, I felt that if any of our family went to a place like that, both your poor grandfathers would roll over in their graves."

As a matter of fact, I am inclined to think that my father's superficial judgment of these schools had some prophetic value. Primarily conceived to fill the needs created by the failure of public education to maintain standards under the pressure of the mass immigration of culturally neglected European stock, they soon began to represent instruments of a class differentiation absurd in its incongruous aping of British traditions. In an age during which education in all enlightened countries was being progressively emancipated from church control, they introduced Episcopalian, often High Church management. They borrowed from English school customs their most pernicious practices of fagging and hazing, while failing to take from their prototypes the excellently rigid educational program in mathematics and classical literature. Their underpaid teachers fell far below the scholastic standards established by Arnold and others in England, often combining such duties as the teaching of fundamentals with coaching of the baseball nine or the football team. Though conceived at first for the training of sons of the established well-to-do bourgeoisie, their foundation fell into our period of Gargantuan commercial expansion, and they were soon overrun by the new plutocracy, a class never exceeded in history for its confidence in the power of money. With a magnificent opportunity to develop out of this vigorous and competent stock the rudiments of a true democratic aristocracy of learning, tolerance, and sense of public obligation, they succeeded only in encouraging class barriers based purely on economic standards, without any of the intellectual and spiritual differentiations which justify such distinctions. They made practically no contributions to American national education, either in method or in content. That the original purposes of such schools can be successfully accomplished without the social and religious hocus-pocus has recently been demonstrated by a few exceptional institutions — notably Exeter — and even by a few public high schools in regions less subjected to immigrant pressure. To be just, it must be admitted that a slow transformation is now in progress. Under the influence of inside opinion, as the plutocracy — by several generations of substitution of cigarettes for chewing tobacco — is developing, if not into an aristocracy, at least into a liberal patrician group, these schools are undergoing changes; and with wisdom and weakening of the snob appeal, they may yet become important experiment stations for secondary education and point the way for public institutions less favorably situated. In my youth, however, they were in their worst reactionary phases, and I believe that my father's judgment was a wise one.

For one winter session, when my parents were traveling in Europe, I had been sent to a *Fremdenschule* in Wiesbaden. This institution was organized particularly for the education of the sons of English families resident in Germany who wished to have their boys prepared for Oxford and Cambridge. The teaching, therefore, was sound; the instructors largely English university men of the typical Arnold tradition. What I remember most vividly of that school is my introduction to the British scholastic habit of physical chastisement. A bad recitation or an impertinent answer brought a prompt and vigorous box on the ear, and a cane was under the teacher's desk. The first time this was applied to me, I fell into an hysterical rage, as did another American boy similarly treated. We were spared repetition, and it still remains a matter of amazement to me that the British boys didn't seem to mind it. For this reason, or perhaps from a sense of national solidarity, it was on them that all the lickings were thereafter concentrated. They didn't even appear to feel humiliated, and, contrary to what might now be psychoanalytically predicted, these docilely supported beatings had no influence — certainly no immediately noticeable Rousseauan influence — on their characters. One boy, to whom I exhibited contempt at a moment when the welts must still have been painful, gave me the worst fight of my quarrelsome boyhood — in which I came off very much second-best. All that the canings seemed to do to these English lads was to make them amazingly resistant to pain in that part of the body where the back loses its honest name. It is not impossible that this habit, early inculcated in the British ruling classes, of knowing when they were licked, taking it with docility on the least vulnerable part of the body, yet remaining unhumiliated thereby and ready to rise when opportunities for resistance were more favorable, has had profound influence on English foreign policy. It is only lately that the umbrella has become symbolic of this attitude.

On our return to America, my father — who had given the matter much study — decided to send me to a private school in New York in which he believed that the system of German secondary education was competently followed. It was run by a distinguished scholar and pedagogue, a German Jew, Julius Sachs.

Julius Sachs! Oh, the terror of him! Large and well-paunched, he had a head like the marble Jupiter that, weighing a hundred pounds or more, perches precariously on the high shelf over my head. Was he a Jew? The little I had no idea. He was the ruling spirit that presided over the house in 59th Street to which, every morning, I carried my small *Ranzen* (dogskin knapsack, with white and black spotted hair on the flap), filled with Latin grammars and arithmetic books, getting into the door just as the bells clanged loudly to tell me I was a few minutes late.

From the time I woke up with the sun in my eyes until I entered the schoolhouse doors each morning, my behavior was governed by the instinct to delay the evil hour. Washing and dressing were performed with a deliberate slowness not justified by a too meticulous attention to crevices of the ears and fingernails. There was a good deal of gazing out of the window; making the faucet squirt by holding the thumb over the spout; swimming paper boats in the bathtub; doing dumbbell exercises; or lunging at the doorknob with an old foil. Then, at breakfast, the oatmeal had to be made into an island surrounded by a sea of milk; the eggshell had to be tapped with the spoon to a tune before it could be picked off the top of the egg; the glass of milk, just mulattoed with a tinge of coffee to make it "grown-up," was carefully scrutinized and often refused by reason of a "hex" — that is, a film of coagulated milk — which had to be fished out. Mother was patient and helpful. Father almost not — but too much amused to show irritation. At any rate, the little pea jacket adjusted, the flowing tie pulled into place, the *Ranzen* packed with books, a paper of sandwiches, and an apple, the journey to school was eventually begun, with a kiss and a shove out of the door.

It was amusing either to step on all the cracks between the pavement stones or — at other times — to jump over them. Puddles had to be leaped into, to make splashes. Encountered dogs were always of interest. My father, indulgent in these matters, had often said: "If a boy and a dog meet in the street and neither of them pays any attention to the other, they are both a little queer."

As the school was approached, other boys converged. It was of interest, and often of profit, to compare exercises and answers to problems. Finally, as the fatal hour drew near, there was nothing to do but to enter, in a state of mind compounded of apprehension, loathing, and a certain amount of arrogant courage. Dr. Sachs, who knew his pupils, often called me "Fabius Maximus Cunctator" — which shows the kind of man he was. Julius Sachs — Jew, German, schoolmaster, and noble scholar! I often think of him when I ponder this question of anti-Semitic violence that we had thought was settled in the Middle Ages — as we thought until 1914 so many other things, political and social, had been finally disposed of.

3

In his *Rabbi von Bacherach*, Heine lets Jäckel, the fool, say: "It is an important business, for if Abraham had really slaughtered Isaac and not the billy goat, there would now be more billy goats and not so many Jews in the world." Jews were an important influence in my education. It is a curious paradox in the history of the Teutonic race that, although there is an almost instinctive inclination to anti-Semitic prejudice in them, there is — on the other hand — no race upon which the influence of Jewish thought and genius has had a more profound effect.

My father once told me that in the 1840's, in a village along the Rhine, a boy had thrown a stone at a Jew. The missile did not hit the Jew but it broke a windowpane; and the Jew was made to pay for the damage, because, if he hadn't dodged, the pane would not have been broken — the playful brutality of healthy children maltreating a cat.

Yet, in this very setting, Jews were taking a more significant part in the molding of national thought — political, literary, philosophical, and musical — than anywhere else in the civilized world. Heine, the lovable, detestable, arrogant, idealistic, materialistic, German-hating, German-loving exile, often expressed his nostalgic love for a fatherland which treated him badly — not because he was a Jew (he was baptized in his youth, and professed himself a Christian), but because his patriotism was too intellectually dangerous. He felt and considered himself a German — witness his verses: —

> *Und als ich die deutsche Sprache vernahm*
> *Da wurd mir seltsam zu Mute.*
> *Ich meinte nicht anders als ob das Herz*
> *Recht angenehm verblute.*
>
> . . . . . .
>
> *Seit ich auf deutsche Erde trat*
> *Durchströmen mich Zauberkräfte.*
> *Der Riese hat wieder die Mutter berührt*
> *Und es wuchsen ihm neue Kräfte.*

In later days, I heard another exile — not a Jew, but an ex-Chancellor of the Reich — express the same belief in the essential soundness of the soul of a people temporarily subjugated by an hysterical "racialism" born of political and economic fear. Germany, thou owest much of thy national soul to thy Jews, who — as in no other nation in the history of the world — have striven to become citizens of the Western world under thy reluctant wings! English Jews became Lords and Chief Justices, French Jews became bankers and cabinet ministers, German Jews became Germans.

Julius Sachs and his staff were learned men, and most of the boys who went to the school were the children of cultivated German-Americans, Jewish or gentile, who — though race-conscious to a moderate degree — were not arrogantly so, certainly not sufficiently so to have it make any difference whatever. I mention this in order to testify to the fact that since my earliest youth I have seen much of Jews. And in later life I have had Jewish friends, pupils, and colleagues — some of whom I have respected and loved, others of whom I have detested, just as it has happened with other people. Once, even, I was very fond of a Jewish girl. She was lovely, and she pinned a rose on my coat one night when we were beginning to look deeply into each other's eyes. Then she didn't let me see her again and, within six months, married one of her own race, now a judge. She had a lot more brains and foresight than I had. She still has, and I hope she remembers me as affectionately as I do her.

Thus I have had every reason to keep a warm spot in my heart for the Jews, and I look with puzzled distress upon the subtle growth of anti-Semitic feeling in our own country. It frightens me, because infinitely more dangerous than the most serious imagined injury that could accrue to society from the Jews is the destructive injury we must inevitably inflict upon all that we cherish in the progress of the world by allowing intolerance and cruelty to determine our treatment of minorities. As Heine said, concerning this question: "Be entirely tolerant or not at all; follow the good path or the evil one. To stand at the crossroads requires more strength than you possess."

There is probably not an intelligent, kindly gentile to-day who is not puzzled and is not trying, if he is honest with himself, to probe his own prejudice; to ask himself: "Why?" The day for a religious answer is long past. To understand it without religious implications usually leads to the trivial analysis of Jewish social and business habits, their "unethical" competitive spirit, and their "egocentric determination to get ahead." By these traits, H. G. Wells believes, they step up the competitive tempo until it becomes uncomfortable for the rest of us. "You may repudiate . . . the Nazi methods," he continues, "but that does not close the Jewish problem for you." He sees the root of the evil in Jewish solidarity. "Why do they refuse to be men among men? . . . Come out of Israel!" he cries.

But, we may ask, have they been allowed to "come out of Israel"?

Renan, who has given the matter the same deep thought that he gave to other things, says in his *L'Antichrist*: "Ça ne peut être sans raison que ce pauvre Israël a passé sa vie de peuple à être massacré. Quand toutes les nations et tous les siècles vous ont persecuté, il faut bien qu'il y ait à cela quelque motif. Le juif jusqu'à notre temps s'insinuait partout en réclamant le droit commun; mais en réalité le juif n'était pas dans le droit commun; il gardait son statut particulier. . . . Il voulait les avantages des nations sans être une nation, sans participer aux charges des nations. Les nations sont des

*créations militaires . . . elles sont l'oeuvre de paysans et
de soldats; les juifs n'ont contribué en rien à les établir.
Là est le grand malentendu impliqué dans les prétentions
israélites."* [1]

There was probably some truth in this when it was written.
Since then — certainly in America and in France — the Jews
have taken an energetic part in political and professional life,
no better and no worse in effect than that of other groups,
feeling and voting and working according to their social and
economic positions rather than as Jews.

The points made by Renan seem to me to have lost strength
in direct proportion to the degree in which the Jews have been
allowed to "come out of Israel."

My friend L., far and away the most distinguished of my
professional colleagues, himself a Jew, believes that the solution lies in an absorption of the Jew into the national life,
which shall distribute Jewish participation into all layers of
social and economic activity. Physical absorption will be an
inevitable and less essential consequence. L. says, in agree-
ment with Renan, that the differences between Jew and
gentile — which he freely acknowledges as existing — are attributable to the fact that "our race, unlike the English, German,
and French, has for centuries lacked that backlog of a peasantry

[1] "It cannot be without good reason that this poor Israel has passed its
life as a people marked for massacre. Since all nations of all ages have per-
secuted you, there must surely have been some motive for this. The Jew,
even up to our own time, insinuated himself everywhere [into our civilization]
demanding equal rights; but, as a matter of fact, the Jew did not subject
himself to equality; he retained his own particular position. . . . He wanted
to possess the advantages of nationality without being a nation, without
participating in the obligations [responsibilities] of nations. Nations are the
creations of military power . . . they are the results of the labors of the
peasants and of the soldier; the Jews have contributed in no way towards
their establishment. This is the great misunderstanding implied in Jewish
pretensions [claims]."

from which, annually, the over-commercialized and over-intellectualized urban populations are rejuvenated."

To pretend that we do not discriminate against the Jews in this country is mere self-deception. Let us be honest. We discriminate in our colleges, in our clubs, and in our hotels. And many quite commonplace people, when they associate intimately with Jews whom they admire, rarely fail to be conscious of their tolerance. As long as this prejudice exists, the problem is not solved — certainly not for the proud and sensitive Jew, the cultivated and high-minded Jew, whom we should accept on terms of absolute equality. Complete sympathetic friendship, without any sense of separateness, is something that has happened to most of us with individual Jewish friends, to prove — to me at least — that the so-called "Jewish traits," other than the physical, are not inherently racial, somatically hereditary, but conditioned by the treatment the Jews have received. The problem, instead of remaining insolubly racial or religious, has resolved itself into the not simple, but soluble one of social adjustment. Here, as in France, if ever before in the world, combined efforts of Jews and gentiles might at last bring this wandering Israel to harbor.

When R.S. had arrived at this point, he seemed extremely well satisfied with himself. I could see that he felt rather noble, and believed he had made a distinct contribution.

"I take it, then," I said, "that you are having no difficulty in suppressing that insidious germ of anti-Semitism that occasionally invades your consciousness and of which you are so afraid."

"I refuse," he replied with some heat, "I utterly refuse to allow myself to yield to any such illogical, inhumane, and pernicious prejudices. I believe with my best Jewish friend,

Heine, that if the Jews disappeared from the world and I found that somewhere there existed a surviving specimen of this people, I would travel hundreds of miles to examine him and to press his hands in reverence for the services his race has rendered."

He was silent, and sat long in contemplation. I could see that he was thinking, with emotion, of his many Jewish friends. Then, suddenly, with that characteristic and honest self-contradiction which made him so sympathetically amusing to me, he exclaimed: —

"Oh, Joseph, Jacob, Abe, Milton, Sidney, Rebecca, Isidor, and Lydia! How I love and honor you! You have been my sisters and my brothers. How much I owe you in kindness and friendship! But why, oh why, have you such terrible uncles and cousins and aunts?"

"Well," I thought, "here is the problem in a nutshell."

"But the cousins-and-aunts question may eventually be solved, just as the Joseph, Jacob, and Rebecca one is now. Let's not make ourselves unhappy about it. And at any rate, even these cousins and aunts can say — as old Börne did: 'Jésus-Christ? Je le dis en parenthèse — il était mon cousin.' "

CHAPTER V

Of college and the rising of the sap: higher education of various kinds

---

1

WERE I writing an autobiography, instead of this disconnected series of thoughts and impressions, I might describe the early years of my college course at Columbia, during which — largely because of the imbecile fraternity system which entangled me before I had learned my way about the buildings — I went far toward becoming an objectionable and ignorant young blighter. The group into which I was at first thrown were bawdy and idle; we worked as little as we dared; we drank and spent hours playing pool in the Buckingham Barroom. The only thing that saved me from worse pitfalls was the complete lack of sophistication with which I had come to college and which, though it exposed me to some ridicule and the occasional contempt of my ribald associates, saved me from crossing thresholds from which there is no complete spiritual returning. Before this could happen, I had the good fortune to attract the attention, by some verses I had sent to a college paper, of a group of more mature students, among whom was Frederick P. Keppel. His friendship has been one of the great satisfactions of my life, but of the services his affection has done me that first one was the most far-reaching; for he drew me into the group of young enthusiasts who were at that time sitting at the feet of George Edward Woodberry.

Woodberry was at that time best known for his poetry. I say "at that time" because, as I judge him now, I believe that his ultimate place — a high one in American letters — will rest on his prose writings, his critical essays, and his *Taormina*, all of which combine distinction and color of style with great learning and a sensitiveness to beauty which mark him as a poet writing prose. Woodberry was of the tradition of Shelley, Wordsworth, and Coleridge. His mind was deeply saturated with European culture and the art of Greece and of Italy. But he added to this, especially in his later verse, a purely American note — an enthusiasm for the equality of men, optimism for the realization of the ideal life by the evolution of American democracy. He was an intensely American poet, without trying to break away by studied eccentricities of style or content from the continuous stream of the European traditions which inspired him and which, flowing through his spirit, gathered the emotion and the inspiration of his Americanism. If his poetry is not as great as it might be, it is perhaps because of a certain sentimentality and emotional lushness which sprang from an inherent softness in his character, and which I did not recognize until much later. But there are passages in the *North Shore Watch* (for which James Russell Lowell called him the American Shelley), in the *Roamer*, and in a few lyrics and sonnets, which will again be read and loved when the present vogue for incomprehensibility and brutality in verse has run the course of other decadent periods.

Philosophically, Woodberry was a Platonist. He was deeply influenced by Greek idealism, not only in the sense in which Plato "ascribed the highest form of existence to ideals and abstractions," conceptions of beauty, truth, and love; but in the artistic sense as well — the idealism which, as Professor Waldstein discovered, manifests itself by the representation of the ideal type rather than the particular portrait. Woodberry's own work was conceived in this spirit, but he fell short, it seems to me now, as Gilbert Murray falls short, by too much ornamentation, by too emotionally softening the austere Greek standards, as though — as a learned lady has said — one planted rambler roses round the Parthenon, obscuring the cold majesty of its lines.

Whatever may be the eventual position of Woodberry in American letters — an estimate which I am not competent to make — he was unquestionably one of the greatest teachers this country has seen, inspiring with his own passionate sincerity and sensitive perceptions a large and diverse group of young men, few of whom, whatever their subsequent occupations, ever lost entirely the imprint of his personality. His life turned out to be a deeply tragic one, and the last time I saw him (I took my young son to call on him) he was sitting in the little ancestral farmhouse at Beverly, isolated from the world, a poor and very sad old man. I reflected upon how much I owed him — how the whole course of my life and thoughts had been lighted by the sparks from his spirit, and how I was only one of fifty and more for whom he had done the same thing. I tried to tell him this, and I like to think that it made him happier to hear it acknowledged with grateful affection.

The one thing his teaching needed to make it still more effective was a contemporary Irving Babbitt to counterbalance him, to give us hardness of soul to discipline the emotions Woodberry aroused in us. For his influence, good as it was, left me, at least, with vague yearnings for aesthetic abstractions, with almost a disdain for the discipline of reason, trusting for guidance — as his beloved Shelley recommends in *The Defence of Poetry* — in the adequacy of emotions nobly exercised. This state of mind, a sort of *Weltschmerz*, a romantic being-in-love with the "ideal" as Woodberry presented it, had incalculable moral value at the time. It was built, however, on a foundation of feelings and dreams, enthusiasms and exaltations. As far as we thought about religion at all, we were attracted to the mysterious, the miraculous, and the poetry of Christian thought, without being able to accept supernatural authority. We were in the position, attributed — I believe wrongly — by some satirist (I think it was Durant) to Santayana, of believing that "there is no God and the Virgin Mary is His Mother." Yet, though it was a period of intellectual confusion, it was a happy one, and it created for many of us a mental atmosphere of aesthetic values that followed us through life and helped us over many hard places where reason failed.

The destinies of man are guided by the most extraordinary accidents. In my sophomore year, while in the Woodberrian poetic exaltation, and feeling much of the time like a young Shelley, I threw a snowball across the campus at a professor emerging from the Natural Science Building. It was a prodigious shot, a good hundred yards, I think. I hit him in the ear, knocked his hat off, and had time to disappear around the corner. I had nothing against him. It was an impulse, and a happy one, because I became guiltily conscious of him, thereafter, and eventually I took one of his courses as a sort of apologetic gesture. He happened to be both an anthropologist of note and a philosopher, and it was he who awakened in me the realization of the philosophical implications of scientific fact. There were great teachers of science at Columbia in those days, and the junior year — largely owing to the inspiration of the man whom I had hit in the ear — found me, without cutting loose entirely from the Department of Comparative Literature, feeling as though I had suddenly entered a new world of wonders and revelations, on the top floor of Schermerhorn Hall under the reign of Edmund B. Wilson and Bashford Dean.

2

These men and their assistants, Calkins, Strong, and McGregor, were direct spiritual offspring of the magnificent group of biologists that followed in the wake of the Darwinian period. They had known Haeckel and Huxley. Weismann, Dohrn, the Hertwigs, and Tyndall became our household gods. And Wilson and Dean, and, to a lesser degree, Osborn, were a new experience in professors. They were highly trained specialists, but their minds swept the horizon. And though they stood in the first rank of scientific accomplishment and were cultivated gentlemen, they had time for their elementary students — a combination that one must search for to-day with the lantern of Diogenes. Their laboratories became my home, and even more than the courses themselves I remember the afternoons of puttering when Dean or his faithful McGregor puttered with us and, with that greatest art of the gifted teacher, made us feel like younger colleagues rather than raw students. To be sure, I did not fail here as elsewhere to get into trouble — notably on the day when, for the benefit of a pedantic fellow student whom I did not like, I pretended I had caught hydrophobia from a dog brain, and started to bark and bite this colleague — now hysterical — in the leg. But the astute Oliver Strong, who came on the scene just as my victim, trying to escape, had upset an incubator, instead of disciplining me academically had other students hold me down and poured a bucket of sea urchins down my neck. But, apart from interludes of this type, my career in this department became as deeply satisfying and stimulating as that under Woodberry.

My college education, to make a long story short, then consisted of Woodberry, Wilson, and Dean — thus again affirming the truism that one is trained by men and not by curricula. The remark about the superb educational value of sitting on a log with Mark Hopkins on the other end of it is quite correct in principle — though from what I have read of that gentleman's philosophical views and information, I should have picked someone else for my log.

3

During my third year at college came the sinking of the *Maine* and the Spanish War. It affected Americans in many different ways. There was no great excitement except among those who were by temperament jingoes, and a large proportion of the conservative population considered the war unjustified and imperialistic. By some of the group with which I was associated at Columbia the war was dismissed as an episode of little importance, while others rushed to join the militia or the naval reserve. As for me, I had no philosophical views whatever about the justice or otherwise of declaring war on Spain, but I was carried away by the prospects of being a soldier for no reason more sensible than a craving for excitement. After much argument with my father, who took the position that the trouble would be over before I had learned to stand at attention, I finally persuaded him to sign his consent to my enlistment papers to the local cavalry unit, Squadron A. I could ride and I could shoot, but I had no idea whatever of the meaning of military discipline. I was very proud in my uniform, although — being slight and small for my age, though tough and hard — my sabre came almost to my collarbone. I did get an enormous thrill out of riding forward to face the enlistment officer from Washington and taking the oath of allegiance.

All that summer I drilled. One troop of the Squadron had already left for Camp Alger, and the rest of us were waiting in the hope that we might be sent as replacements, since the boys of the original troop were coming down like flies with typhoid fever. The most notable fact of our Spanish War was the unbelievably miserable sanitary supervision of the camps and the consequent enormous incidence of enteric fevers. It was during this time, it was said, that a high official of the War Department, not a professional man, came to inspect one of these camps and — shown the water supply — filled a glass, held it up to the light, and said: "This water looks all right to me." It was also during this time that Victor Vaughan and his colleagues of the Army Medical Corps discovered the immense importance of flies in the transmission of typhoid bacilli from open latrines to food. It is interesting to remember that the great Belisarius, who was perhaps — apart from being a notable strategist — one of the earliest commanders of troops to realize the importance of sanitation, knew about this fly business, or — according to Procopius — suspected it sufficiently to include it in his precautions.

I never got to the front, and at about the time when our first troop landed in Puerto Rico and we were daily expecting orders to join them, the war ended and my father was grateful in a manner that I did not fully appreciate until my own son was seventeen years old and war was swinging by a thread like the sword of Damocles over the head of an anxious world.

I stayed in the Squadron after the war and proudly became one of the bodyguard of Theodore Roosevelt when he was inducted into the governorship of New York. I was still a private, having been demoted from the eminent position of Troop Bugler, which had appealed to me because I could ride behind the captain on a white horse and transmit his commands by a variety of raucous blasts. I did fairly well in the Armory, but unfortunately just before the Dewey parade, in which I had imagined myself prancing proudly down Fifth Avenue in front of our cavalcade, I blasted a number of sour notes at a drill. The captain, a kindly man, ordered me to his dressing room after dismissal and asked me to blow an intricate series of commands as he directed. The result was that he said: "If you could blow as well as you can ride, we might have a successful parade; but as things are, half the troop will be charging while the rest will be doing a left turn."

Instead, therefore, of proudly bugling my squadron through the parade, I was told off to a detail consisting of a sergeant and twelve privates who were to escort Theodore Roosevelt from his residence to his place in the parade. This was my first close view of the man who later became one of my chief admirations and whom I came to know just before the beginning of the World War, when he discussed the "hyphenated Americans" problem with me and booked me as Sanitary Inspector of the division that was never to be organized. This first meeting, however, gave me the most characteristic view of him that I was ever to have. We rode to his house, leading with us a spare horse carrying a brand-new, yellow, Western stock saddle and a bridle wonderfully embossed with silver studding. We dismounted and I held Mr. Roosevelt's horse beside my own. We waited about ten minutes, and while we were drawn up at attention in rigid military form, the sergeant was beginning to worry about how he could find our proper place in the parade. Suddenly the front door opened, Mr. Roosevelt appeared in a frock coat and a high hat, rushed down the high stoop straight to the horse I was holding, mounted, and tearing the bridle out of my hand was off at a clatter down the street toward Fifth Avenue and around the corner before we could mount and follow. He found his own place, but we never caught up with him again. But that was the sergeant's worry.

My fellow privates in the Squadron were all members of well-to-do families and almost entirely college men. There came a time, after two years of service in this unit, when — going through that period of socialistic and radical emotion which comes to many young men — I had myself transferred to what I thought was the toughest outfit in New York. I wanted to get intimately acquainted with the underprivileged — and I did. It was my first experience of the depths to which coarseness, vulgarity, and smut can attain. Being a medical student at this time, I had a venereal clinic in the lavatory after every drill and learned a vocabulary which prepared me for later experiences with sheepherders in the Rockies, and with fishermen on the Banks. I was too inexperienced at the time to realize that language is a matter of habit and that the bestial implications of the words used had little bearing on the characters of the men of this class who used them as clichés.

Wishing to be a thorough democrat, I attended the dances and picnics which were the social life of my new companions and found — another lesson of sociology learned — that the mothers, wives, and sisters of these men were about ten tiers above them in decency and gentleness.

My final performance in this military unit was not to my credit. We were reviewed by the Governor, who passed our parked battery in a victoria with a stovepipe hat held above his head. The arrangement was that after he had passed each gun by about a hundred yards, the lanyard was to be pulled and his progress thus marked by a series of cannon shots, going off at regular intervals, far behind him. When he came opposite the gun of which I was the cannoneer, I was overcome by one of those impulses half compounded of nervousness and a perverted sense of humor. I pulled my lanyard, and the blast of black powder burst under the nearest horse's belly. The last I saw of the Governor was a cloud of dust and a heavily rocking carriage. The things that our very fat Major said to me exceeded in force and in imagination anything I ever heard from a quartermaster. I would have been court-martialed, but my enlistment was up anyway.

I got out of the army with much pleasure, little knowing that I was to spend almost two full years in it later on.

4

At the end of my third year at college the treasures unlocked for me by Woodberry and by my teachers of science made the world seem a happy and a rich land for exploration. My head was full of moonshine and hope, and I was ready for adventure. I took a job for Professor Osborn, to help dig for fossils on the western edge of the Staked Plain. The books I had with me in my bag testify to the incongruous jumble of badly insulated ideas that were joggling through my head: I had a *Golden Treasury*, a copy of Dana's *Geology*, and a Bible — which I had made up my mind to read through, from beginning to end. The Bible furnished me not only some instruction, but a great deal of amusement. I recall particularly a story in Genesis about the Jews, when they were at war with a tribe they failed to conquer in open battle. So they sent their priests among their enemies, to convert them with all the rites that go with conversions to Judaism. And then it said: "On the third day, when they were sore," they descended upon them. This, and similar stories, have made the Old Testament as dear to me as Rabelais's five books. But in spite of the ribald pleasure I had from the lusty history of the ancient Jews, I soon found myself — with no lighter literature to turn to — captivated by the magnificent cadences of the language and the *maestoso* of the poetry of the Psalms. The Bible alone was worth the trip, for I might never have read it, as I did then, against the background of the majestic desolation of the desert and under conditions of physical frugality which have always brought out the best there is in me.

My boss was Collins, a Protohippus expert and a worthy citizen, with some learning, a great enthusiasm, and a long Western experience which had made him a genius at finding his way in mountains and in desert, without being able to tell anyone else how he did it. I was quite the opposite, and usually when I rode out of sight of camp it took me all day to get back. Sometimes they had to look for me.

The other member of our three-man expedition was a cowpuncher by the name of Chipman, the son of a rancher who lived near Clarendon, fifteen miles from the single-track railroad that ran north and south through the panhandle.

We got along together pretty well, largely because Collins was an extraordinarily patient individual, and the cowboy was a little crazy, — possibly from long stretches of lonesomeness, — with a lunacy that expressed itself by long silences, sometimes lasting all day, and complete oblivion of his surroundings.

We had a team, which he drove, and some saddle horses. The cowboy would sit on the box of the truck that carried our outfits, hours on end, driving through the hot desert; brooding most of the time, but occasionally, remembering some dance he had attended, he would hang the lines over the brake bar, take out a jew's-harp, and play. All by himself, he would impersonate a Western dance. He would play a snatch on the jew's-harp; then shout commands to the dancers: "Swing your partners!" or "All form a circle!"; then dance with his heavy boots against the dashboard, while he took up the jew's-harp again.

Meanwhile Collins, who rode behind, would sing to himself — usually hymns or, rather, the same hymn over and over again. His favorite was: —

> Are your garments spotless?
> Are they white as snow?
> Are they washed in the blood of the Lamb?

He would sing it once, then hawk and spit, and sing it over again.

This sort of thing, going on hour after hour, together with the heat, the long stretches of wide desert, with here and there a few mesquite bushes or some yucca plants, would get on my nerves; and I would ride way off on the horizon, where I could just keep the general direction. When I stayed near them, or when we made camp and cooked our food, the little habits — like Collins's hawking or the expression on the cow-puncher's face — would make me nasty; and if I wasn't murdered on the expedition, it is very largely because of the fact that Collins was at heart a very kind man, and the cow-puncher most of the time didn't understand what I was driving at.

We were out three months. My job was taking care of the horses, and at night hobbling one of them and letting the others run, before I turned into my blankets under the open sky. In the morning, I unhobbled the captive horse and drove in the others. On these rides I would often run into a herd of antelope and tire my horse for the day, racing after them. I also helped to search for signs of fossils when we reached the escarpment, and to dig with a pick and shovel when we located something. We did get a Protohippus tooth, besides some mastodon heads, and camel and turtle bones. And so, from the point of view of the Museum, the undertaking was a success. Meanwhile, I learned a good deal of geology, read my Bible, and grew tough, brown, and thin as a leather strap.

Before we started into the desert, Collins left me with the horses at a ranch near the Oklahoma border, — then Indian Territory, — while he made a ten days' trip to look at some reported fossil pits north of us. During that time, I had nothing to do but see that the horses were grazed and watered, go out with my shotgun for prairie chickens, and hunt jack rabbit on some of the rancher's horses.

Jack-rabbit coursing was better fun than anything else I have ever done, except drag hunting. There was a herd of tough young Western horses from which I could choose, and the rancher's son and I would go out with a couple of mongrel greyhounds to start the rabbits. Then we would gallop hell-bent for leather across the prairie. There was nothing to look out for except gopher holes and mesquite bushes. The rabbits would run at incredible speed, and whenever the hounds got near them would double off at an angle, the dogs shooting way ahead on the wrong course. It was at this point that the rider was useful, standing up in the stirrups and changing direction until the hounds caught up again. It was exciting — and so joyful that I shouted at the top of my lungs while I was riding.

On these rides, the rancher's daughter would often join us. She was a nice young girl of about seventeen, and her name was Mary. Mary had a hard life. The ranch buildings consisted of a dugout, which was both living room and kitchen for the rancher, his wife, the son and daughter mentioned, and an unbelievably dirty six-year-old boy, whose nose was always running. The older brother, a boy of nineteen, slept in an old wagon bed about a hundred yards from the house, and Mary slept in a lean-to next to the chicken coop. I made myself at home under a mesquite bush on the hill above the dugout.

The only available literature for this family was a Sears, Roebuck catalogue, which was happily thumbed in contemplation of imaginary purchases, few of them ever achieved.

Mary worked hard, helping her mother, tending the vegetable garden, feeding the chickens, boiling food for the pigs, patching overalls, darning socks, and doing any little chores that were to be done; while her father was out mending fences, and her mother was usually sleeping in the sun. Mary had never had any companionship or fun, and what seemed incredible to her, apparently, was the fact that I was respectful, and carried her saddle for her, saddled her horse when we went out after jack rabbits, or showed her any little courtesy that was perfectly natural and unexaggerated, but of which she had apparently had no experience whatever. She was being courted, nevertheless, because on Sunday a couple of young cowboys came riding in, turned out their horses, and prepared to stay for the day.

The entertainment consisted of sitting in a circle in the dugout — the whole family, the two boys, and I, the stranger — in utter silence. Every now and then, one of the visitors would get up and perform a feat of strength. One of them chinned himself on the door with one hand. Then the other got up and leant over backwards, until the top of his head touched his heels. There were various exhibitions like this, and between tricks there would be occasional and widely separated remarks, chiefly dealing with cattle, hogs, grain, and horses. At night, after a tremendous meal of corn, cabbage, and pork, the cowboys caught their horses and rode off.

I spent ten days on the ranch, riding with Mary whenever there were no chores to be done, and telling her about New York. She was thirsty for news of the big places, and I am quite sure that half the true things I told her she didn't believe, while she took as gospel some of my wildest cock-and-bull stories. When finally our expedition left, and we were riding away, Mary sat by the chicken-coop door, weeping bitterly. I wrote a very bad sonnet about her.

CHAPTER VI

The background of an agnostic. A discussion of religion quite devoid of philosophical value

THE children of Catholics are usually Catholics; the children of Methodists, Methodists; the sons of poor Jews are Jews, and those of rich Jews often Episcopalians; those of Episcopalians are not infrequently bankers and stockbrokers, and so forth and so forth. It can hardly be said, then, that philosophical convictions of a religious nature are accidental or engendered by revelation or by grace. Yet, somehow, the thoughtful individuals of whatever denomination — unless suffering a complete early petrification of the spirit — learn to mold the essential principles common to all the religions to their own eventual spiritual needs; that is, granted they belong to that small percentage of our modern commercial society who remain conscious after the age of sixteen of such things as spiritual needs. The molding, its direction and ultimate form, depend on many things, chiefly the forces of intellectual environment. In our time, an era of intensification of the pressure of scientific discovery upon theological doctrine, there has been an extraordinary mutual approximation between the final beliefs of those who started as devout believers and have moved in liberal directions, and those who — starting as agnostics — end by scratching their scientific heads in perturbed desire for a faith.

In both cases, this is commonly known as the much be-written and be-argued struggle between science and religion, a struggle which after each battle leads to a sort of philosophical peace of Versailles and must be fought all over again with each advance of human understanding. Yet, unlike the more worldly controversies, this war grows less and less virulent with every armistice, and except in such regions as Central Africa and Tennessee, science and religion are beginning to join hands.

R.S. was brought up an agnostic. The philosophical confessions in which he traces his development from childhood to his final conclusions might have been more appropriately dealt with in a later chapter of this book. I place them here, however, because their later direction was deeply influenced by his family antecedents, and because in discussing them he goes back into family history.

1

Having always been a creature of impulse rather than reflection, I am aware of the fact that what I call my own religious experiences are quite without philosophical value. I set them down, nevertheless, such as they are, because — representing the reactions of a mind lacking both the talent and the taste for metaphysical speculation — they are more likely to form an "average type" experience than would those of a trained philosopher. I take courage to enter upon this subject from the fact that even great thinkers have, on occasion, taught us not to take the philosophers as seriously as they take themselves. "Se moquer de la philosophie," says Pascal, "c'est vraiment philosopher." And another, nearer my heart, Montaigne, declared: "Philosopher ce n'est aultre chose que s'apprester à la mort."

So I am in no manner philosophizing in the technical sense,

because I have always been mortally afraid of professional philosophers who take delight in showing how childish the views of the rest of us are when we poach on their professional preserves, the universe. Lately, only, I have read a much praised book of reflections by a Columbia professor of philosophy who seems very learned in the things that have been said by other philosophers, but almost cheerful about his own ignorance of mathematics or the other sciences which it serves. That seemed to me even less helpful than the arrogance of the others, for surely metaphysics cannot rationally begin except where "physics" — in the sense of general scientific observation — ends, and philosophical thought must constantly shift, with changes in its underpinnings of scientific knowledge. Philosophical speculation that does not take off from a broad knowledge of contemporary science would appear to be what Bacon calls the "distemper of learning, when men study words and not matter."

I know that anything I may say has been better said many times. Real philosophers, however, are also very often repetitious, and get away with it because so many of them can say old things in such an incomprehensible manner that, by the time one has reread a sentence five or six times, one takes so much pleasure in thinking that one has comprehended the thought that one forgets how old it is. I commend to disdainful professionals the — to me — comforting book of Wahle, *Die Tragi-Komödie der Weisheit*, which begins with the words: *". . . hier sollte Jubel ertönen darüber dass die Menschheit sich von der Philosophie befreit hat"* (At this point [in his book] we should rejoice that mankind has liberated itself from [academic] philosophy), and after four hundred and fifteen jolly pages ends by saying: *"Und so nimmt die trugfreie Kritik alle die philosophischen Gestaltungen . . . knetet sie in zwei Kügelchen, und nimmt sie in die Rechte und in die Linke und wirft die zurück in das Wasser der Täuschungen. . . ."* (And thus sane criticism takes up all these philosophical complexities . . . molds them into two little balls, holds them in the right hand and then in the left hand, and tosses them back into the waters of confusion [deceptions].) And I recall having read that the ancient Greeks, with all their reverence for philosophy, at times applied the word σπουδογελοῖος or "serio-comic" to some of their philosophers. This gives me courage to proceed, if only with the purpose of tracing the course by which one modern individual of average intelligence tossed for a long lifetime between headlands where the sweet voices of sirens lured him to comforting mysticism and the cold, open seas of stark reason; and, nearing the end of his voyage, he was still unable to find harbor in either direction, but was content — with agnostic modesty and reverence — to let the currents of forces he could not comprehend carry him to his destined anchorage.

2

As I have said before, I was brought up without any religious preconceptions. Of my mother's vestigial Catholicism I have spoken in another place. My father's family belonged to that group of early nineteenth-century agnostics who were, more than they realized, under the influence of French rationalism. The conquest of Germany by Napoleon had brought to that disunited country the stimulus to national unity which is often wrongly attributed to Fichte and his *Reden an die Deutsche Nation*. As a matter of fact, this pressure for freedom did not effectively express itself in Germany until the Spanish, the Tyrolese, the British, and the Russians had begun to break the stranglehold of the great Pan-European on the continent. Once thoroughly infiltrated with French thought, Germany absorbed with extraordinary eagerness the spirit of the conquerors; and French jurisprudence, education, and philosophy transformed its intellectual life and helped to plant the germs of 1848. But even this uprising did not gather force in Germany until the signal had been given by the proclamation of the French Republic on February 24 of that year. Smothered by the force of Prussian efficiency in those fateful months, the immediate flowering was suppressed, but the seed was too strong to die.

A more learned scholar than I may some day write an important chapter of cultural history by analyzing the profound intellectual and spiritual debt which nineteenth-century Germany owed to France. Must France again render this service to Germany ninety years later? By tenuous and often subterranean channels, the thought of the Encyclopaedists, of Voltaire, of Rousseau and of Diderot, of Condorcet and of Ampère, had been trickling eastward for fifty years and, in the wake of the French Revolution and of the Napoleonic conquest, liberalism and the enthronement of pure reason in all human affairs took a strong hold on the minds and imaginations of German academic youth. The immediate consequences became apparent in the universities, especially in the sciences, which began that golden age of German learning which has now again been temporarily slowed by political disease. Berzelius, Wöhler, Liebig, Mayer, Von Baer, Schleiden, Schwann, Von Mohl, Max Schultze, and, later, Kirchhoff, Helmholtz, and a host of others laid foundations of experimental science which, apart from their direct importance in discovery, exerted far-reaching effects upon philosophical thought. Enthusiasm for science in its youthful vigor, coupled with growing skepticism and distrust of theological doctrine, bred — just as in France, though fifty years later — an exaggerated faith in the eventual triumph of pure reason. It was not only in the sciences, of course, that this new energy developed, though in these it was most obvious. It was the age, as well, of Winckelmann, of Lessing, of Herder, and of the great idealistic philosophers. And Goethe lived through most of it. But I cannot help thinking that the scientific developments gave impulse to the whole movement. For whatever one may believe, with Babbitt and less distinguished but more peevish modern critics, philosophical and theological thought can never afford to neglect the fundamental discoveries of science, which eventually, also, must influence art. Art is usually not influenced by scientific ideas until these have overcome initial uncertainties and doubts and have gained permanent momentum. But eventually all experience previously recorded is the common material of both, and the method of treatment determines whether the result is art or science.

The spirit of this age of my German grandfathers was one of growing philosophical materialism which, in the thoughtful, took the form either of frank agnosticism or of a sort of unitarianism originated by a school of revolting young theologians, one of whom, — Schünemann-Pott, — a man in his philosophy not unlike Emerson, brought the movement to America. Schünemann-Pott was one of a considerable group of Lutheran preachers who organized what they at first called "Free Religious Societies," the impossible though noble purpose of which was the "honest adjustment between faith, belief and reason." Their first conference was held in September 1847, at Nordhausen. Branch societies were formed throughout Germany, sometimes openly, more often under cover. At first mildly tolerated, they were soon so deeply involved in the general revolutionary movement that they were driven from town to town, the preachers often imprisoned, and their meetings broken up. Yet Germany was still a mosaic of small states and, by dodging from border to border and into some of the free Hanseatic cities, the Society kept alive into the eighteen-fifties. Schünemann-Pott came to America in 1853, when his last refuge at Lübeck became uncomfortable. Though hounded out of organized existence, these Societies left a deep and lasting impress on German thought. It is my guess that this influence is still hotly smoldering in the German people and will burst into flame again when propagandized fear and hatred give way to sanity.

The "Freie Deutsche Gemeinde" which these men founded abroad and brought to America became, according to the degree of liberalism of individual leaders, exceedingly free Christian communities or "ethical culture societies" of the sort carried on for many years by Felix Adler in New York. In view of the present situation in Germany, it is interesting to note parenthetically that the group collected under the leadership of this high-minded Jew included — almost equally — German-Americans and Jews, drawn together by a common cultural background. It would be inaccurate to say that there was no race consciousness whatever. But what there was was utterly submerged by cultural solidarity. For the differences of race between them were more than offset by the political and philosophical like-mindedness which had led them to revolt in Europe and to seek citizenship in this then free country.

When in 1859 the *Origin of Species* was published, nowhere did the Darwinian ideas take root so rapidly and so deeply as in Germany, where they found their apostles in Haeckel, Weismann, Dohrn, the Hertwigs, and others who carried them to the German people as Huxley, Lyell, and Romanes carried them to the English. It is a fascinating story, this intellectual *Sturm und Drang* in the German youth of that period, and if one studies it, — even superficially, — one is strongly impressed by the intellectual and spiritual interdependence of England, France, and Germany. One gains the conviction that, given half a chance, reasonable freedom from the economic hardship and the propaganda which breed misunderstanding and political perversion, science and intellectual coöperation might again draw them all together, at least sufficiently to act as brakes on international greed. One cannot, of course, hope ever to eliminate entirely the avarice of commercial competition between modern nations largely composed of shopkeepers. But the little average butter-and-eggs men who compose the bulk of populations want nothing more than to be left alone to the enjoyment of their nether senses, and the big fellows — the international, super-butter-and-eggs men — might, in the end, be held reasonably in check by a growing educated class under the leadership of intellectuals civilized to the appreciation and admiration of scientific discovery, spiritual nobility, or artistic distinction, wherever or by whom produced. How different the world would be to-day if Hitler could get a kick out of the Psalms, if Mussolini could see himself with the eyes of Voltaire, or if Mr. Roosevelt had taken Lawrence Henderson's course on Pareto! Or would it?

3

The atmosphere of my youth, then, was entirely irreligious in the doctrinal sense. My father had not been baptized; neither had the doctor, my Onkel Fritz; neither were my brothers and I. The tradition of no formal relationship to any established church has now extended through four generations, unbroken except where isolated members of the recent clan — with affluence and social position — began to send their children to St. Paul's and Groton and acquired Episcopalianism together with Cadillacs and broad a's.

My father was a frank agnostic. His prophet was Goethe. He was quite exasperating in his ready citation of *Faust* on all occasions. As a rule quite unexacting in his personal habits, there were two things on which he insisted. Being a fat man in his later years, and hating to reach behind to button on his suspenders, he demanded a set of permanently attached suspenders for every pair of breeches he owned. His other idiosyncrasy was a copy of *Faust* for the pocket of every coat he possessed. He bought small paper editions, and had them bound in soft black leather. Whenever, at table after dinner over the wine, or anywhere else, anyone made any remark whatever which was meant to be clever or original, his hand would slip into his pocket and he would say — often with an irritating grin: "*Das steht alles im 'Faust.'*" Sometimes he would then insist on reading the passage, which he readily found. It was a long time before I could read *Faust* without a feeling of annoyance. We rarely talked religion with my father, but there is a great deal of metaphysics in this tragedy which, as Goethe wrote to Wilhelm von Humboldt, had been conceived by him in his youth and had matured in his mind for over sixty years. There is in it the complete evolution, almost biographical, of Goethe's own development: his gradual consciousness of the futility of knowledge alone to reconcile the spirit to human existence; his groping for understanding (*Am Anfang war das Wort; der Sinn; die Kraft; die That*); his search for release in worldly pleasures, and the acute suffering from the awakening conscience, where Faust — returning from the Brocken — sees the injury he has done. And then the final tragedy. There is still, even at the end of the first part, unresolved confusion, and the thing is unfinished, and left for the second part — which I never did understand. So I, too, was left confused — suspended in metaphysical mid-ether, as it were. But still there was a liberal education in *Faust* — absorbed unwillingly and with much exasperation from my father's little black books.

It is not unlikely that, in an intellectually rudimentary way, every thoughtful person who is not conditioned to a religious faith from youth and beyond the exercise of reason travels along the same paths that carried Kant from his *Critique of Pure Reason*, in which — as Heine said — he slew God, into the *Critique of Practical Reason*, in which he found he could not get along without Him. "*Der alte Lampe muss einen Gott haben, sonst kann der arme Mensch nicht glücklich sein.*" It is the development which we see again and again in our most distinguished scientists — men who arrive at the conception of an eternal ordering force not as the result of theological doctrine, literally accepted, not from the arguments of Thomas Aquinas, but in consequence of study of the laws that govern the universe and the inescapable conviction that science — though it may eventually describe the operation of these laws

— will never penetrate into first causes or conceive the purposes behind them.

From what I have said, it is clear that I was in the intellectually enviable position of being able to approach these problems without that conditioning in youth which, for the large mass of Christians, stigmatizes doubts of creed or critical appraisal of doctrine as reprehensible or even sinful; and which automatically inhibits later contemplation except from theologically fixed premises. My mind was not, in the liquid state of childhood, poured into a mold and allowed to harden into one or the other of the ingots of Christian denomination which, whatever their minor differences of pattern, all hold through life, unmalleable in the fires of reason, the basic form of unquestioning faith.

Whatever may be the practical disadvantages of this for one living in a world where social adherence to organized religion is a criterion of respectability and moral worthiness, there can be little question of the intellectual advantage of discovering for oneself, in the unspoiled enthusiasm of adolescence, the beauties of Christ's teaching; and, later, to develop by the process of reason, based on the contemplation of fact, the conviction of an orderly universal force of which we are a part; and thus to discover for oneself what Santayana means when he says that "nothing would be as beautiful as Christianity, if not taken too literally."

Yet I had experienced, even as a child, during those visits to the Cathedral on Christmas Eve, leaning against my mother's shoulder, that mysterious reverence that is the origin of religious feeling. Call it merely an emotional reaction to the solemn beauty and tranquillity of the dim church; but, even so, it was of a kind with later reactions, the vague yearnings — both painful and keen with happiness — that come in rare moments: gazing from mountains into valleys, or looking up at the stars; or the quick rush of love or pity at the sight of misery or sorrow; the release from material things, the spiritual elevation from which spring — untaught and instinctive — those unexplained organs of the mind, conscience, compassion, charity, and sense of justice — in short, Kant's Categorical Imperative. I realized this only much later, as I became convinced that my sciences could not and would never explain those ethical forces which compel the spiritual evolution of the mind even as physicochemical forces energize the manifestations of organic life; and I knew that our intellectual competence as human beings, transitional forms in evolution, would never attain the insight to formulate the surely existing thermodynamics of the spirit.

4

It is from the study and experience of science that all my subsequent ideas which might be dignified by the adjective "religious" were derived. A particularly strong impression was made upon me by my first not too complicated course in physical chemistry in its exposition of the simple yet marvelous mathematical relationships of ionic concentrations, electric conductivity, freezing and boiling points, and osmotic pressures. The laws of conservation of matter and of energy in the inorganic world, and the carrying of these laws into the regulating mechanisms of life processes, followed. I lived through an era in which the various branches of science began to flow together, and in which what may be broadly called physiology is, as predicted by Claude Bernard, being founded more and more upon physicochemical processes. It is needless to follow this development in detail. It has been done so much better than I can do it by many men, notably by my friend Lawrence Henderson, in his *Order of Nature*. Moreover, my experience is that of innumerable others who, after long apprenticeships in the experimental sciences, have come to identical conclusions, at least as far as essentials are concerned.

Pasteur's feeling that "we can only kneel" in the face of the incomprehensible is actually nothing less than a reverently expressed confession of agnosticism. His Catholicism was the adherence to an ethical system of morals and submission to the eternal order which probably he would not have undertaken to define anthropomorphically. This surely is the case with two of my most intimate professional friends, both of them among the great bacteriologists of all time; one of whom became a Catholic at thirty, the other about a year before he died, at sixty-nine. In both cases, I am convinced from frequent conversations that their adherence to a church represented an urge for some form of symbolic expression of the conviction of an orderly purpose in the harmonious operation of eternal laws. A subconscious streak of mysticism may also have played a part. In both cases, naked reason left them unsatisfied.

Darwin, in his letters, frankly declared himself an agnostic, for a reason that appears to me the strongest that can be advanced: "But there arises the doubt: Can the mind of man which has, as I fully believe, been developed from a mind as low as that possessed by the lowest animals, be trusted when it draws such grand conclusions?

"I cannot pretend to throw light on such abstruse problems. The mystery at the beginnings of all things is insoluble by us; and I, for one, must be content to remain an agnostic."

A similar point of view comes from Clerk Maxwell, speaking of the supposed Regulator of causes and effects: "If He is the Deity, I object to any argument founded on a supposed acquaintance with the conditions of divine foreknowledge."

Subsequent experiences have often made me wonder why theological schools do not include a rigid discipline in the fundamental sciences. To be sure, it might modify religion in some of its most tradition-cherished minor superstitions. To offset this, it would almost certainly strengthen the inevitable conviction of the unalterable harmony of the natural laws which govern the universe and all that moves and lives within it. And on this, the revelation of the marvelous orderliness, is based, after all, the final refutation of chance and purposelessness.

The questions of immortality of the soul and freedom of the will, though they have called forth libraries of controversial literature, continue to appear not only utterly beyond any possibility of satisfactory proof but, indeed, trivial in being so definitely personal, once the principle of an all-pervading and ordering force is accepted. And the conception of a God so constituted that we are, as individuals, of direct concern to Him appears both presumptuous — considering our individual insignificance in the scheme as a whole — and unnecessary for that feeling of helpless reverence in face of the universal order which is the essence of religious experience. Moreover, palaeontologically considered, one would have to assume that such a "personal" God existed long before the evolution of man. "Why did He wait so long to create man?" asked Diderot. Yet reward, punishment, immortality of the soul in the theological sense, could have no meaning whatever until there had developed creatures possessing a nervous organization capable of abstract thinking and of spiritual suffering. One cannot imagine such a God occupied through millions of years, up to the Pleistocene, with personal supervision, reward and punishment, of amoebae, clams, fish, dinosaurs, and sabre-toothed tigers; then, suddenly, adjusting His own systems and purposes to the capacities of the man-ape He had allowed to develop.

All this, of course, merely signifies that I have been utterly incapable of that "over-belief" which William James postulates as necessary to faith. Moreover, to give religious experience — as he does — a merely pragmatic value seems both to be begging the question and to be making light of a grave problem. We cannot believe purely because it seems to be necessary to our equanimity and strength of character to do so. To paraphrase Professor James, placing my own modifications in brackets, one may say: "Humbug is humbug, even though it bear the scientific [religious] name; and the total expression of human experience, as I view it objectively, urges me beyond the narrow scientific [theological] bounds."

Greater men and more devout than I have tried in vain to force their reason into beliefs that they so fervently wished to embrace, but could not. Luther said: *"Gott helfe mir, ich kann nicht anders."* And I think of poor old Galileo, after his abjuration, muttering into his beard: *"Eppur si muove."*

CHAPTER VII

R.S. and women: "Cras amet qui nunquam amavit,
quique amavit cras amet"

THE psychoanalytical method of writing biography has, in recent literature, been very much overdone. Yet it is unlikely that any revealing portrait of a human being has ever been written without a good deal of psychological insight. Even Plutarch draws his characters against the background of the events and mores of their periods and, in this sense, is quite modern. For, at all times, character has been shaped by the impact of society and events, personal and public relations, on the individual. There is possibly no modern biography which is more thoroughly infiltrated with psychological interpretation than Plutarch's account of the Antony-Cleopatra episode, though it is quite apparent that the psychological approach, in this case, is not a skillful one. And how could anyone deal intelligently with the life of Sappho — who adored her little hetaerae, but leaped to her death from the cliffs of Leucadia for love of Phaon, the fisherman — without Freudian insight?

However, in the older literature the subconscious and the sexual influences were either neglected or developed with crude ignorance of true motivations. To-day, as Fuller — a genial critic of philosophy — says, the Freudian ideas have worked a profound revolution. And "it may well be that the psychologist of the future will be as little able to ignore or to reject

them as the astronomer of to-day is able to pass by Galileo and
return to Ptolemy, or the contemporary biologist to flout the
doctrine of evolution," and so on. If, as he believes, the psy-
choanalytic psychology has come to stay, as heliocentric astron-
omy and Darwinism apparently have, "it has administered a
blow to human self-importance and pretensions [pride in one's
so-called individual personality, he implies] far more severe
than that dealt by man's loss of his central position in the
sidereal universe and his discovery of his animal ancestry."
Thus Fuller. And even if he is only partly right, it would be
a gross omission to attempt to paint a balanced portrait of R.S.
without some reference to his relationship to women and his
amorous constitution.

One need not, however, take upon oneself — as so many
biographers have attempted to do — any analytical interpretation of one's subject. This is a technical task for the professionally trained, who may consider the conscientiously recorded
facts and analyze them with the experienced judgment which
they alone possess.

In taking up this side of the character of R.S. I therefore abstain from any pretensions to psychological wisdom,
and set down without comment what I could find out about his
emotional life. The reader can draw any conclusions he may
be able or inclined to draw. Our friend may be "analyzable"
from these data, even as Hamlet and Lady Macbeth have been
analyzed — though with more difficulty, since, being a real
person and not the creature of a miraculous imagination, he
is far less consistent.

However, even this simple recording was not a simple matter, because of R.S.'s dread of psychoanalysis. In part, this
dread was due to his fundamental belief in the soundness of
Professor Freud's methods and the fear that, if applied to him,
the system might reveal a number of things which, all his life,

he had endeavored to conceal. More directly, his apprehension was rooted in a period of intimate association with one of the most accomplished psychiatrists of his time, the distinguished Dr. Trout.

As far as I could gather, the circumstances were somewhat as follows: —

On the transport, returning after nearly two years of foreign service in France, R.S., being one of the ranking medical officers on board, was assigned to share a stateroom with Dr. Trout, who had been an important psychiatrist of the A.E.F. When R.S. found his way to the cabin, he discovered that the naval surgeon in charge of assigning quarters, who was an old acquaintance, had exercised that peculiar sense of humor that is often the result of being too long at sea or herding sheep in the desert, and had lodged Dr. Trout and R.S. in the space reserved for the care of commissioned officers who were recognizably — that is, more than usually — deranged. As a natural complement to this distinguished joke, the naval surgeon had whispered into a number of ears that R.S. had been assigned to this cabin in Dr. Trout's charge because he had shown signs of mental eccentricity. Of course, the rumor spread from the mastheads, and it was said that R.S. had been deprived of his razor and that Dr. Trout was to devote most of his time to the supervision of our friend. The consequence was that throughout the voyage the officers of the New York Division, many of whom had been fellow troopers of R.S. in the New York Cavalry Squadron, treated him with a degree of consideration and gentle solicitude quite foreign to their ordinary robust habits of association and quite incomprehensible to R.S., who had no idea of the reasons for their unnatural behavior.

Dr. Trout was a tall, albino-blond gentleman, with watery blue eyes and a drooping moustache, who was generally dreaded throughout official circles because no one could ever be sure whether personal attentions from this otherwise agreeable companion, or even the most casual conversation, might not be — as they say in the Army — in line of duty. Indeed, it was said about the Colonel that he had once been invited to a dinner at Headquarters with instructions to make careful observation of a certain colonel who was to be placed next to him at the table, and to appraise him from a psychiatric point of view. Dr. Trout is said to have made a report to the effect that the colonel was a pronounced manic-depressive. But unfortunately, since Trout sat between two colonels, his report was made about the one on the left instead of the suspected one on his right. What was finally done about this I never heard.

Colonel Trout had himself the reputation of a well-developed sense of humor. It was he who told the story of a field clerk who, having copied a letter in which the word "psyche" was used, remarked: "Ain't that the hell of a way to spell fish!" When, at a later date, Colonel Trout accepted the Professorship of Psychiatry in a well-known medical school, before an organized psychiatric clinic was available, he said that this didn't bother him because he could occupy his time studying the faculty. Asked whether his constant association with the mentally deranged did not depress him dreadfully, he replied that he far preferred the company of the feeble-minded, because they were as a rule far more docile and honest than the so-called "normal" people he knew — and he meant it.

Like many others of his branch of the medical profession, Colonel Trout had acquired the habit of always being on the job. Thus you could never be sure when speaking with him whether you were being conversed with or led into the betrayal of some hidden abyss, some iniquitous collection of psychic evil that you had succeeded hitherto in concealing in the underbrush of the unconscious, and which the slow development of character was gradually managing to encapsulate just as fibrous connective tissue imprisons a tuberculous lesion. There were certain Freudian ground rules in this game with which only the psychiatrists were thoroughly familiar, but of which the victims were so ignorant that, even on their guard, they could never be sure that they might not be caught in some revealing offside play. Few were aware, in the innocence of their ignorant hearts, of the fact that an unguarded reference to a lead pencil, or a church steeple, a barn door, a pitchfork, or a doughnut might immediately strike the psychiatrist's nose and set him baying on the malodorous trail of a psychic stench.

At a period slightly later than that during which R.S. lived in close communion with Dr. Trout, the development of endocrinology expanded the study of mental characteristics from concentration upon a single set of glands to include at least several, and the guilty feeling which oppressed all nervous sufferers was to some extent relieved by the hope that one of the other glands might be at fault. The time of which we speak, however, still fell into the later years of what might be spoken of as the "uniglandular" psychiatry, and such expressions as "libido," "phallus," "Oedipus complex," "paternal fixation," and "inversion" had crept out of their hiding places in the medical dictionaries and had entered the drawing room. To dream at all in those days was a misfortune; to mention it, indecent; and to reveal the substance, reckless. One of my friends at this time became a veronal addict, because he could not overcome his taste for Welsh rarebits after the theatre; and a dear old lady on Beacon Street jumped into the Charles River Basin, because she repeatedly dreamt of the Bunker Hill Monument.

The joke about being confined with Dr. Trout in the cabin which had a grid over the door soon wore off; but night after night, R.S. lay in the upper berth in the evenings while the Doctor was receiving visits from officers of the New York Division, many of whom had been boyhood friends from the region in central New York which had been his home. None of them came for professional advice. All of them were very fond of Trout and he, obviously, of them. But all conversations, most innocently begun, gradually turned into a sort of analysis of the visitors. After the usual questions and answers concerning past experiences and relatives, Trout's professional instinct came to the surface — quite amiably and without evil intention, of course, but guided by spontaneous interest in the mental development of his visitor. Some such question would be asked as: "What became of the redheaded girl who lived over the post office?" or "Who was the man your aunt married after your uncle died?" etc., etc.; and within ten or fifteen minutes the visitor's character began to be revealed. Even R.S., entirely unskilled in this technique, would gradually feel that he knew a great deal about these people, and sometimes — when one of them left — he had the slight sensation of shame that comes with looking through a keyhole.

It was this that made R.S. permanently shy of psychiatrists and of anything that might involve the risk of revealing his sexual reactions. I was never able to get him to talk at all about any of the women who had really influenced his life, but I did succeed in stimulating him to reminiscences which, in their totality, — though none of them were of any serious significance, — may reveal to some extent the manner of man he was in his relations to the other sex. These I have recorded as nearly as possible in his own words and in a chronological sequence of my own arrangement, since they were gathered over the course of years, whenever I could guide the conversation into these channels.

1

The first girl I ever noticed in what, later, I recognized as a sentimental emotion was called Mamie. She was the daughter of a truck driver in my father's chemical factory. We used to play in the large factory yard, where hundreds of barrels of resin were stored on end, and it was great fun to jump from barrel top to barrel top. Mamie had a brother who became a bosom friend, and games of tag on the barrels were organized in which Mamie — being several years younger — was patronizingly allowed to participate. She and her brother were sweet children, amiable and gentle, and I loved them both very dearly. Their lives were hard. At twelve and ten, respectively, they were called upon for severe domestic service, and their poor mother, — a stout, red-faced woman, — kind enough when she was sober, was less so when drunk. Their happy moments were the ones they spent with me, playing on the barrels; but when I went back to my playroom to have my feet dried and to be fed my supper, they went back to a little frame house where dirt, noise, unmerited abuse, and frugal tolerance were their lot.

Mamie was blue-eyed and blonde, with a bright blondeness that shone through the dirt on her face and the squalor of her clothes. And how humbly grateful she was to be allowed to be "It," chasing us over the barrels. There must have been a faint dawning of the endocrines in me even then, baneful prophecy of a long life of struggle, for while I was sorry for Jimmy when I happened to think of being so, there was always a protective tenderness in my heart for Mamie.

One day — it was drizzling — the wet drove us from our playground into a little shed where carboys of sulphuric acid were stored. I dug a nickel out of my pocket and Jimmy was dispatched to the store on the corner to buy some barber-pole candy sticks. Mamie and I sat close together, for we were damp and a little chilly. She stuck up her wet face to be kissed, and I gazed down at her with the warm intention of kissing her. But when I looked into her face, I saw two little rivulets running from Mamie's nose to her pouted upper lip. I had never noticed them before, although I had often observed her sticking her tongue out and upward, whenever she sniffed. For ours was a catarrhal climate. Now I looked and saw. But I have always been proud in later days that, even at this early age, I mastered my repulsion and kissed Mamie on her salty lips. Dear Mamie! What has become of you since? You were a lovely child, in spite of the rivulets on your upper lip, and — no doubt — you deserved more consideration than the world has given you. What happened to me at that moment has never left me since and is perhaps the only achievement that may eventually entitle me to some measure of self-approbation — namely, the mastery of arrogance and disgust by tenderness and pity.

We played in the great court of my father's chemical factory and the atmosphere was redolent with odors of resin, sulphuric acid, and amyl acetate. I never pass a chemical factory or smell amyl acetate without thinking of Mamie and our games on the barrels. Yes, the sense of smell is the most nostalgic of our senses. I recall a charming lady from the West who stayed with us in New York, but left suddenly — long before she had intended to. She was in the recently cleaned bathroom one morning and, smelling the household ammonia, got so homesick for her twins that she couldn't stand it and had to go home.

2

It is strange that after all these years I should remember their names. They were called Galeoti, and came from Florence; and the name of the English governess was Miss Satterthwaite. For a month, in the late spring, we played together, the two little girls and I, in the garden of the hotel at Pegli, on the Italian Riviera. Everything was bursting into flower, and the garden had bushes blazing with white and red; there were gravel walks, and a fountain with a spout in the middle, and goldfish which were fed conscientiously every morning by the fat proprietress. We skipped and laughed in the garden, for the little Galeoti girls — one of them my age, the other two years younger, which would make her ten — were merry and great chatterboxes in a mixture of Italian and English that was frequently corrected by the governess. We took long walks together into the hills, and came home with great bunches of violets. Late in the afternoon, Miss Satterthwaite often read to us. Among other things, she read an English translation of De Amicis. She was only a child herself, about seventeen, I should judge, and pretty as blonde, high-colored British girls so often are at that age. To me, she seemed a young goddess. I sat very quiet when she read, and followed her about like a little dog. She was very lonely — probably it was the first time she had been away from home and isolated, as a young English governess would be in an Italian family. The parents Galeoti were away most of the time on excursions and at night played cards with my father and mother and other people in the hotel, drinking large quantities of *Asti spumante* and having very jolly times, as we children could hear after we had gone to bed.

I slept in a room that faced the garden, and the warm fragrance from many flowers and shrubs came into my window. I used to pretend that I was going to bed outside, among the bushes. One night, I remember I could not sleep because the moon was white in the window; and, feeling restless and adventurous, I tiptoed through the hall and crept out into the garden. There, on a bench, Miss Satterthwaite was sitting, and when I slipped up beside her, I saw that she was weeping. I was very sorry for her, but she took my hand between hers and told me that it was only the moonlight, that she had felt lonesome and was crying only because it was so terribly beautiful. And suddenly she said: "Hush!" and I heard my first nightingale. But it was a great disappointment. I was thinking of Miss Satterthwaite and the terrible grief I thought she was enduring when she led me to the door and told me to be a good boy and go to bed.

3

Of course I have been more or less in love all my life. But in the golden, adolescent days I fell in and out much faster than I did later. A look, a touch of the hand, a word, or — as in one case — only the sound of a snatch of song heard through a window on a summer night, and I was off on the new, sometimes before I was out of the old. Even this was not embarrassing, because the ladies in question had been fallen in love with, adored in half a dozen execrable sonnets, taken on honeymoons to Spanish castles that I kept always ready and fully equipped for such purposes, and dropped again for a new love before they themselves had become aware that they were participating in a romantic adventure. I used them, so to speak, as lay figures for my sentimental education. It did me a lot of good, and them no harm.

There was Marie-Louise, the New York society girl, ten years older than I, indeed approaching thirty, an accomplished musician with a magnificent, almost Wagnerian soprano, but a figure pathologically — that is, incapacitatingly — fat. She would have made four of me, and she thought I was "a nice boy but a little funny."

There was Maud, the harness maker's daughter, a young Diana, but always suspecting melodramatic perils to her virtue from the rich man's son.

There was the Smith girl, who really had no particular attractions except that she lived in a hotel across the lake and tempted my Hero and Leander complex by sitting out on the wharf with a lantern at night; knowing that I would swim across a half mile of cold, black, starlit water just because of the stage setting. I might have been drowned half a dozen times, and no one the wiser till the next day; and when I did arrive and sat dripping and cold on the dock, we had nothing to say to each other — she, because she was a stupid little doll, and I because I was blown. Yet even she served a purpose, and I used to swim home and climb up the hill through the woods, half-frozen but feeling elatedly heroic and devoted.

There was — but why catalogue them? They were all appropriate in their individual ways, and played passive, usually unconscious rôles in my development. Unlike François Villon, I know more or less what life made of them — poor things. Not one turned out to be a princess, and those I've seen within the last ten years had become just as one would have expected — quite commonplace, with no signs whatever of having lived

for a time in a cloud-swept castle somewhere between Barce-
lona and Bourg Madame.

In all this there was — I should say, in my own justification
— a minimum of the physical. In defense of romanticism,
which in so many of its aspects appears silly and affected, one
should not underestimate the service it does, at a certain age,
in sublimating into its lovely hocus-pocus what might otherwise, and, in its absence, often does, become a gross or careless attitude toward physical love. The romanticism which
had me in its grip at that age was associated with hard riding,
frugal living, — as far as food and drink were concerned, — and
intellectual intoxication, under George Woodberry's influence,
with the English romantic poets and their idealization of love.
The cult of physical hardness helped considerably in keeping
this state of mind from becoming, as it might so easily have
done, a morbid one; for by instinct I knew the wisdom of
Guarnerius's prescription for love-melancholy: "To go with
haircloth, etc., as monks do, but above all to fast."

Also, the ladies as a rule were far from sentimental themselves. One of them, now the mother of four and the still
attractive grandmother of two or three, — Ella, — how lovely,
but, withal, how sensible she was! She was the daughter of
the principal of a well-known boys' boarding school, and had
an apartment of her own, on the corner of the big barrack-
like school building, high above the road. I used to serenade
her at night, riding under her window on my big gray horse,
Harry, and singing softly to the twang of a lute — with many a
sour chord, for Harry was young and lively. The first time, Ella
came to the window for a moment in a lovely pink nightgown.
The second time, she didn't come to the window at all. She
pretended to be asleep, and didn't mention my visit the next

day. The third time, just as I was really finding my voice, the window just above her own was thrown open and a bucket of cold soapsuds came smack down on my horse's head. For a mile, I just hung on, trying not to drop the lute. I was halfway to Shruboak before I had the horse under control. Ella didn't mention this the next day, either. The boy who threw the water was, I believe, the one whom she married a few years later. I trust she had little comfort of him. He had a depraved sense of humor.

4

There was a chestnut girl, who lived over the grocery store in the village. In those days, I classified girls as chestnut, sorrel, or bay. Her father was quite a celebrity. He was very old, a carpenter by trade, and had fought in the Civil War. When my father once complimented him on his hale-and-hearty appearance, and asked him how he had managed to live to such a healthy old age, he made a remark which I then thought original with him: "Ye want to know why I've lived so long, mister? Well, it's because I had sense enough to run like hell at the second battle o' Bull Run." Pansy was the apple of his eye. She was pretty, in the slightly oversolid, bucolic manner, and was what was called "pert" in her conversation. On warm summer evenings, when the roads were fragrant with locust blossoms, I often rode down to the store to sit on the piazza with her and the old man, who would tell us stories of what was still known as "the War." He often told the same tale, but since he was a great liar and never told it the same way twice, it was never stale. Pansy was amorously inclined, and in this case, at least, any ideas I got into my head were initiated by her. She was something of a local belle, and had acquired the habit, in a gently bovine manner, of exercising, in male company, beguilements which were highly effective with the young farmer boys, grooms, and store clerks throughout the township. This is not to insinuate that she was not a thoroughly nice girl, and if I was flattered and inclined to dangerous plays of imagination in her regard, I was probably like the foolish one of the verse: —

> *Stultus quando videt*
> *Quod pulchra puellula ridet*
> *Tum fatuus credit*
> *Se quod amare velit* —

which is to say that when a fool sees a fair maid smile at him, he thinks it love when it's only flirtation. At any rate, Pansy in her way was a dear girl, and I might have made a fool of myself with her as with others had it not been for one of those fortunate flashes of common sense which have so often snatched me, by mere accident, from precipices of imbecility.

One evening we were sitting on the porch. The old man had talked himself to sleep, and began to snooze right in the middle of the Wilderness. Invention had tired him. Pansy and I were sitting closer together than the temperature warranted, and her arm was pressed caressingly against my shoulder. There was a crescent moon, and a gentle breeze enfolded us with the fragrance of the honeysuckle vine. If her head had followed her arm at that moment, God knows what might have happened. But Pansy, though — I still truly believe — a good girl, possibly intent on a bolder yet — I insist — entirely innocent (innocent in the conventional sense) attack upon my emotions, asked me suddenly whether I would like to see their new calf. It was so darling, she said, and had such lovely eyes and such a soft, wet nose. It was a temptation, for the calf of course was in the barn; and the barn was isolated and dark and full of hay. I fell, and said I'd love to see the calf. Merely for convention's sake, I think, Pansy lighted a stable lantern, so that we might at least fulfill the ostensible purpose of really looking at the calf. Oh, how sweet and aphrodisiacally caressing is the odor of a cowbarn at night, with its indescribable blending of clover, cow manure, sour milk, and animal! A gentle tremor ascended my spine as I stepped over the threshold, and I drew Pansy's soft form closer to my side as we stumbled over the rough boards by the dim and swinging light in her hand. I had lost all interest in the calf, and dear Pansy I believe had completely forgotten it. Yet we dared not *not* look at it — half craving, half dreading what might happen when we had seen it. But here Pallas Athene — ever my guardian goddess — intervened. Pansy walked into the stall, put her chubby arm about the calf's neck, and held the stable lantern at arm's length in front of her. And here they were — both confronting me, the dim rays of the lantern illuminating both their faces. Fascinated, I gazed upon them. They appeared like two sisters — helpless, bovine, kindly; infinite vacuity looked out at me from these two pairs of large, swimming eyes. The expression of Pansy's warm and moist lips was not more invitingly tender than the soft, velvety nozzle of the calf. There they stood, — poor innocents, — two calves together; and I gazed and gazed, hypnotically held in the light of the lamp, until I did not know which was Pansy and which calf. And I bent down and kissed the calf tenderly on the nose. Then I went out quietly, and untied my horse from the hitching post. Pansy followed me out. There were tears in her eyes when she said good-night, as I mounted and rode away — sadly, but not without a sense of relief.

CHAPTER VIII

R.S. continues his romantic reminiscences

1

FLOWERS blooming in the Luxembourg gardens and little bare-kneed children throwing colored balls to and fro. Under the trees on the terrace, old men playing very scientific croquet to an admiring gallery. Across the *allée*, a guignol, with Lilliputian chairs and benches for audiences that never tired of seeing the venerable but thrilling story of the *Brigands de Fontainebleau*. The paths full of comfortable strollers, some of them with moth-eaten beards, velvet trousers, and wide black hats; and, on the benches, happy couples that cared not at all whether they were seen kissing each other. Spring in the Luxembourg gardens; twenty-one, and the head full of Villon, Ronsard and Verlaine, Dumas and Victor Hugo! These were the gardens through which the little Anatole France had skipped to school "like a sparrow" — hands in his pockets, a pack of books on his back. And here, as a young man, he sat on a bench to marvel at the extremes of genius which the French spirit can produce, as he saw walk by, first, the austere mathematician, Henri Poincaré, stiff and formal in his black coat; and, a little later, Verlaine and his disreputable companions, after a night in a neighboring wine cellar. Here walked the shades of Henri Quatre, of Diderot, of Voltaire, of Danton, of Murger, and of countless others.

Now that I have come to know French thought and the French people through many years of close association, and am irritated by their faults as I am charmed by their virtues, Paris is to me only the most civilized city in the world. In those enchanted days, it was for me the city of romantic history, of revolutionary fervor, of political exiles, and of poets and painters. I walked the same pavements on which d'Artagnan and Cyrano had strutted, in a wide feathered hat, and with a rapier at my side; in every pretty shopgirl I saw a Louise or a Mimi, in every dilapidated, bewhiskered art student an Alfred de Musset or a young Rimbaud. Heine and George Sand and Chopin were my neighbors, and Balzac and Alfred de Vigny lived around the corner. On every street I saw the pageant of great events parade before my imagination, without taking sides, in that happy irresponsibility one feels for the past; and the aristocrats who jested in the conciergerie cellar were not less heroes to me than Desmoulins and Danton.

I had a room giving on a garden in a house behind the Trocadéro. Roses were in bloom, and a cherry tree; and there was a warm fragrance of box and gooseberry bushes. Every morning I had a French lesson from my landlady, a cultivated spinster of the terrifying age of forty. She had a pointed nose, a little moustache, and a mole with hair on the end of her chin. We had our lesson, with coffee and croissants, in the garden; and we read Fénelon's *Télémaque*, and odds and ends of Pascal's *Pensées*, for she was very pious. But she was an old romantic, too, for I shall never forget the emotion with which she read the opening lines of *Télémaque*, in which Calypso bewails her immortality because Ulysses is gone never to return. And we read *Cyrano* with fervor and compassion. I suspected a personal sorrow, but it was probably my own state of mind.

After the daily lesson, I would walk across the bridge, over to the Petit-Luxembourg, where the École Coloniale was giving courses in nineteenth-century French literature, in political history (here I heard the learned Thalamas), and in phonetics — a course in which we repeated for criticism such ingenious phrases as *"Paul et Pierre, appuyant le parapluie contre le parapet du pont, ne parlent presque pas,"* and so on.

In the afternoons I would saunter into the garden, or take a *mouche* up the river, or walk for exercise in the Bois until the mellow afternoon dusk faded into darkness and the cafés became brilliant with light.

The world is always as young and as happy, or as old and as unhappy, as we are. I was in a state of being constantly in love, not only with every pretty girl I saw, but with the city and the people and with the sensation of being in love. Indeed, like Heine, I even fell in love with the beautiful Milo and regretted her lack of arms. Much later, during the years after the war, when I saw hordes of underbred Americans drinking and chattering till all hours of the night in the cafés along Montparnasse, finding in Paris only the opportunities for playing at Bohème, and pretending to see genius in any artistic eccentricity that could be exploited without hard work, utterly untouched by the strong heartbeat of this country rising from its knees with wounds still bleeding, I was glad that I had been there as a youth. And I was glad, as I associated with French students, scientists, and teachers, that the real life of Paris, the life of the people and their intellectual leaders, was going on essentially uninfluenced by the barbarian invasion. Parts of the Left Bank were merely set aside as a

sort of ghetto for American Pernodians, where they could dis-
port themselves temporarily until the franc should rise and
the visitors be reclaimed by Greenwich Village, Kansas City,
and other points west. A few of these Americans, of course,
worked hard, were stimulated to productive labors by their
European experiences, and eventually came through. Very
few, however, either wished or had the opportunity to enter
into the intellectual or artistic life of France, but spent their
precious months utterly unconscious of the treasures that the
centuries had here accumulated for their taking. Most of my
compatriots reminded me of two engineer officers I had known
during the war, who for two months after the Armistice lived
in the basement of a ruined house in Thiaucourt, drinking
bad whiskey, without knowing until too late that under their
feet, accessible by a trapdoor, there was a cave filled with bottles of Chablis, Nuits-Saint-Georges, and old, old cognac.

2

That summer I saw the parade at Auteuil to celebrate the
return of Marchand from Fashoda. He marched with his
company of Senegalese, escorted by the garrison of Paris, and
was acclaimed the young Napoleon. There were riots in the
crowd about the Dreyfus business; blows and shouts of
"*Conspuez les juifs!*" and calm cleaning up by the unhur-
ried and silently effective *agents*. That night the streets
were lighted; cabs — each with a garlanded, coal-black Colonial soldier and two or three white girls — rambled through
the streets; and bands played on the corners. I danced on the
Place Voltaire with my good friend the fat wife of the *patron*
of a restaurant-bar opposite the Odéon. She was still alive
last year, and greeted me with a hug.

Although these were not the days of the artistic Bohème made famous by Murger, Paris was then — as always — full of students of all nationalities, most of them hard-up, who lived in little furnished rooms in the narrow streets near the Sorbonne, the Faculté de Médecine, and the Beaux-Arts. They were not tourists, and they had to be reasonably sober to do the hard work that was required to keep them in good standing. But they were gay and free and different from students anywhere else in the world. There was, and is even to-day, a residue of the spirit of the mediaeval student life in Paris. That they have not essentially changed I learned when, teaching a few years ago at the Faculté de Médecine, I renewed my youth many a merry evening, in the cafés and the *Salles de Garde* of the hospitals, with the postwar generation of medical students and their friends.

At the time of which I was speaking, there was an architectural student who lived with another American on a little street running into the rue de l'Université. His rooms were on the third floor, and under him the proprietress of the first-floor shop had on her window sill a goldfish tank in which she kept several fish and a very small turtle. These were the delights of her leisure moments, sharing her affections with her old husband and her cat. My friend, leaning out of his window on mellow evenings, smoking his pipe, could look down directly into the tank, and he often watched her as she broke bread crumbs for her pets, muttering terms of endearment. On such an evening he suddenly conceived a brilliant idea. The next day he went to the fish market and bought a series of six turtles, ranging in size from one like a five-franc silver piece to one about six inches across. At the same time he bought wire, a bit of cheesecloth, and a bamboo fishing pole, which he smuggled into his rooms after dark and from which he fashioned himself a very small scoop net. Each day after that, very early in the morning, he would lean out of his window, fish out the old lady's turtle, and put in a bigger one. The first exchange she didn't notice. When the second one went in, this time about three inches across, she looked surprised, but only said: *"Tiens! Tiens!"* When the third one appeared, she began to show signs of excitement. First she called her husband; then the neighbor's wife; gradually the other neighbors. There were animated discussions. The *facteur* offered advice; said she was feeding too heavily. The fourth turtle changed the place into a public sensation. The old lady began to tell people her system. The fifth one, about five inches across the top, started a riot — not without some tragedy, for this turtle began to chew the fish. The old man bought a separate small tank for the sole surviving goldfish. A reporter from the *Paris-Midi* came in and wrote a story. It was a headliner. Madame Perrier became famous. She was interviewed, and it was said that her husband would be decorated.

The architect never put in the sixth turtle — the tank wasn't quite large enough. But he had a still more brilliant idea. He now began to make the turtles small again. He skipped the fourth one — took it out and let it loose in the Seine. He put in the third, which diminished the animal to half-size in a single night. Now the excitement really began. An official from the Jardin des Plantes paid a visit. He pulled at his beard, wagged his head, and, being from Rouen, said: *"C'est vraiment cocasse."* The shop did an enormous business. All the children of the neighborhood came in for *sucres d'orge* and had a look without extra charge. My friend skipped to

the original beast and destroyed the evidence in his washbasin, putting the remaining turtles into his pocket and carrying them out to the Bois. When he came home that night,
he stopped in to see the turtle. Madame Perrier had become
a national heroine. She had given her magic turtle to the
man from the Jardin des Plantes for observation.

At the École Coloniale there was a very pretty Alsatian
girl called Eugénie. I don't give her last name because of what
follows. She sat directly in front of me, and we became good
friends. She was one of those Franco-German types that show
how little real racial difference there is between the border
people on either side of the Vosges. Of course I fell in love
with her, but since I was also in love with Roxane and the
Venus of Milo and the Gioconda and the lady at the Odéon
bar and the girl in Zola's *Rêve*, whose picture hangs in the
Louvre, the situation was not dangerous. At that age, indeed,
it is so much safer to suffer from multiple loves which spread
it out thin than from the sort of coeducational single infatu-
ation that leads to premature uxoriousness in our own country. Eugénie was not only handsome; she was even intelligent. She is now married to a chocolate manufacturer, and
is very well off. Eugénie was also well brought up, and would
never have lunch or dinner with me alone; but once she took
me home to meet her father and mother, with whom she lived
in a flat on the rue de Babylone. This was more of a step in
the serious direction than I then realized, and, in my inex-
perience of the French point of view, things might have gone
from one thing to another, as such things will, if it hadn't
been for an episode with her father that was not my fault.

I took an immediate liking to the old man, and he to me. He
was a wine merchant by profession, but also an amateur of

letters, and was delighted with my eager interest in all he could tell me. Indeed, I owe him a great debt, for he introduced me to the *Chanson de Roland*, the *Légende de Guillaume d'Orange*, to *Flamenca*, and other mediaeval legends and epics in which he was a specialist. In his early enthusiasm for our friendship, he presented me with a flea-bitten copy of Héloïse's letters which I still cherish. Gradually I became an *intime* of the family, and Lord knows what might have happened had it not been for the following incomprehensible occurrence.

I had been to dinner with Eugénie's family two or three times and had, in return, entertained father, mother, and daughter in a restaurant. The old man — he was short and stoutish, with a gray tassel on his chin, and very jolly — invited me out one night to meet some of his cronies. Unsuspected by me, he must have begun to regard me as a possible son-in-law, or he would not have extended this invitation. Of course I went. And it was a good evening. We met in a room over a *brasserie* not far from the Luxembourg. The dinner was excellent, the wine better, and his friends a jolly lot of middle-aged bourgeois who took in the young American with benevolent and familial intimacy. There were a *pharmacien*, a couple of *fonctionnaires* from the Ministère de Justice, a retired bookseller, and the proprietor of a restaurant on Montparnasse. The talk was good and, when it was not political, — which it often heatedly was, — not over my head. My host, in deference to my studies, turned the talk to literature, and of course I answered innumerable questions about America, of which they knew less than I thought it possible for adult white men to know. The wine flowed freely, and was followed by a series of *fines*. When it came time to go home, Eugénie's father was not exactly "lit," but considerably exalted. Indeed, he kissed me on the cheek and told me to stay a bit longer. As he went downstairs I noticed a certain amount of caution as he descended from step to step — but nothing more. I left a few minutes after he did, and strolled toward home. Across the street were the gardens, surrounded by a high iron picket fence. As I approached the corner of what is now the rue Guynemer in the deserted street, I noticed a figure hanging onto the pickets with both hands and pushing back and forth as though a foot were caught in the fence. As I got nearer, the figure looked familiar. I crossed the street and recognized my host. He was braced against the fence with his feet. He held tight to two pickets and tried to push away, but he could not seem to free himself. I was frightened. I thought the old man had gone off his head. He glared at me with terrified eyes. "*Ça ne bouge pas,*" he said. "*Je suis accroché comme un poisson. Mon Dieu, qu'est-ce qu'il faut faire?*"

"*Attendez,*" I said. I looked closely. It was quite simple. The old man had stopped, as Frenchmen will, to make himself more comfortable for walking, with the help of the grass on the other side of the fence. Then he had buttoned his breeches around a picket.

I released him. He called me his savior. He tried to embrace me. We sauntered to his house together, the best friends in the world. He was entirely clear in his head and very jolly. But what he told his family I don't know, even to-day. Eugénie cut me dead the next day, and I was never invited again. Thus did the fates watch over me.

About the episode of R.S. with Maud I heard from an old friend, George S. Hellman, one of that Woodberrian group who, with W.A. Bradley, Keppel, and a few others, contributed considerably and, I may say, beneficially to the development of the character and tastes of my friend during his premedical "storm and stress" period. Hellman, who has since then become a man of more than ordinary distinction as a critic and writer, was an amused though sympathetic witness of the episode which R.S. himself had apparently forgotten. Indeed, it came out in a conversation I had with Hellman shortly after R.S. had died and we were discussing what I should do with the disconnected piles of manuscript of which I had become executor.

Maud was a prostitute — a miraculous creature who, in spite of the dreadful vulgarities to which her calling subjected her, retained a certain youthful bloom and gentleness which, except when she was drunk, enveloped her personality with a superficially appealing charm. She had not yet progressed too far along the easy *descensus Averno* to lose all discrimination, possibly because she had specialized, as far as this was possible, in college students and cast her nets chiefly in those social shoals known as dance halls. Her particular fishing ground was a place called the Haymarket, tough by all implications of the term, but not without a certain atmosphere of gayety. In this place, R.S. and his friends occasionally — though rarely — spent an hour or so for a last drink before going home from late parties or dinners.

On one of these evenings the group of students with whom R.S. was sitting was joined by Maud and two of her companions. R.S., to whom this kind of experience was obviously quite new, attracted Maud's attention — possibly for that very reason — and she exerted herself to fascinate him in a manner that was probably crude but, under the circumstances, quite adequate. R.S. became sentimental about her. He had recently read De Quincey's *Opium-Eater* and remembered

with sympathetic emotion the tender little story of the noble
prostitute who had picked up the suffering De Quincey one
night on the steps of a London church, had taken him to her
room, and had fed him and tended him. R.S. felt waves of
pity and horror at the thought of the dreadful life this child
— hardly older than himself — was leading. She told him, of
course, the age-old stories of the manner in which she had
slipped into this life, how dreadfully she suffered from it, and
how lovely it was to meet nice boys who were "considerate and
refined." Though it may not have been her purpose, her conversation drove out of the mind of R.S. the lustful thoughts
which might have been financially profitable for her. Far
otherwise — it aroused in him a compassionate desire to save
her, if it were possible within his slender means, for at least
one night from the brutalities of her existence. Eventually he
asked her how much she expected to profit on her nightly
rounds and, assuming that he was making preliminary advances, she pitched her estimate to what she believed were
the reasonable limits of his purse, saying: "Oh, ten or fifteen
dollars." Upon this, R.S. pulled ten dollars from his pocket,
borrowed five from his friend Hellman, and said that he would
give her the entire sum if she would allow his companions and
himself to escort her to her room and leave her there. He
conceived this as quite a noble idea, but some of the others,
who had been listening, broke into raucous laughter, and even
Maud seemed at first to snicker. She mastered this impulse,
however, and quite solemnly accepted the offer. The money
was passed over and the entire company marched out of the
Haymarket, only Maud and R.S. and Hellman quite serious,
the others taking it as an extraordinary lark.

Maud lived in an apartment house in the Thirties, west of
Sixth Avenue. It was one of those walk-up buildings that have
an atmosphere of furtive evil even in the hallways. Maud lived

on the third-floor front. The whole party — girls and young
men — marched up together. The scene in front of Maud's
door was a touching one. R.S. was very serious; Maud put her
arms around his neck and kissed him; the others for the moment held their peace, perhaps impressed by the strange turn
their evening had taken. Maud unlocked her door, went in,
and shoved home the bolt. The others, now released from the
sobering solemnity of the scene, walked out to the street.
R.S. thought them objectionably hilarious.

The suggestion was made by one of the girls that, now that
they had disposed of Maud, the rest of them might go back
to the Haymarket and have a last drink. The implication was
probably that someone else might have the same idea, and
it seemed easy money.

At the Haymarket, however, when they sat at a table with
their whiskey and sodas, the early joyfulness of the evening
seemed lost. R.S. himself felt a little ridiculous, perhaps. At
any rate, he seemed to have dampened the festive spirits of
his company, and the conversation grew at first quite serious,
then a little quarrelsome, especially on the part of the girls,
who felt that they had fallen on a dull crowd. They sat for a
long time, until finally the girls left and the boys, getting sleepy
and some of them a little alcoholic, became resentful of what
they called R.S.'s childishness.

It was a little after midnight when they decided to leave,
and as they passed out of the door they came, face to face,
smack against Maud, accompanied by a gentleman in a high
hat, slightly drunk. Even the scoffers were sorry for R.S. In
him it left a sadness which it took him almost until the next
morning to get over.

CHAPTER IX

He begins to speak of medicine, but wanders

AFTER graduation from college, R.S. had considerable difficulty in choosing a career. Although his early ambitions had been in the direction of literature, he lost some of his self-confidence in this regard. As a consequence of his own recognition of the very low quality of a booklet of poems which, together with his friend W. A. Bradley, he had privately published, he questioned his talent for a writer's career, not without a permanently wistful desire in this direction, and turned to his second love, biology, in which he discovered — to his surprise — a romantic appeal hardly less potent than that which had at first attracted him to the arts. With Professor Bashford Dean, R.S. had his first introduction into research, and learned the incomparable satisfaction that lies in the exploration of the unknown, even when the problem is a small one, and the application of reasoning, controlled imagination, and precision of technique to the study of natural phenomena. On his trip to Texas, he had had a look-in on geology and palaeontology. And now the broad vision of Edmund B. Wilson, who was at that time engaged in those classical studies of chromosomes and cell division by which he paved the way to scientific genetics, aroused an enthusiasm in R.S. hardly second to that stimulated toward literature by Woodberry.

His teachers advised him to study medicine. He was twenty years old, and they believed that four years of rigid discipline in a medical school would mature him and lead him naturally into fields of medical biology for which they thought he was fitted.

As a matter of fact, R.S. always held that medical training has for certain types of people a ripening influence that no other field of education possesses. Aside from the habits of hard work that it demands, it embraces a broad survey of the biological field, enforces a considered correlation of the fundamental sciences, and, on the human side, brings the thoughtful student face to face with the emotional struggles, the misery, the courage and cowardice, of his fellow creatures — to say nothing of the familiarity it gives him with sociological conditions, vice, crime, and poverty. There is in it a balanced education of the mind and the spirit which, in those strong enough to take it, hardens the intellect and deepens the sympathy for human suffering and misfortune.

His medical-school days were like those of thousands of others. He did well enough, enjoyed himself, and managed to pass a competitive hospital examination which, in those days, was the climax of the medical student's career. Once in a good hospital, he was a doctor, and in full cry.

About his hospital days and early experience as a practitioner (he practised a while because he couldn't get a job in a laboratory) I managed to persuade him to talk freely, though I had to let him do it in his own way.

1

There is, in my early medical experience, nothing so extraordinary that, in one way or another, it might not have happened in the lives of any number of my professional contemporaries. But these more or less ordinary experiences contributed materially to my development. For similar events arouse widely varying reactions in the grotesquely tumbling kaleidoscopes of individual minds. One man's disillusion may be another's inspiration; the spirit of one may be permanently maimed by accidents of fate which spread the wings of another; and the same exposure to pain, misery, and sorrow which coarsens the mind and callouses the soul of one may give to another a power of compassionate understanding and humility without which mere achievement remains primitive.

A diploma and a state license under my arm, I took the competitive hospital examinations as a matter of course. Precedent, as well as the advice of teachers, indicated a thorough clinical training as essential to any further progress, whether toward practical medicine or a career of investigation. Although I had entered medicine only in order to devote myself to laboratory study, there seemed — at that time — no other approach than through the wards of a hospital. Of course, this was not strictly true, even then. Medicine needed — then as now — investigators trained primarily in the observation of the sick, coördinators prepared to bring the laboratory to the wards, and the wards to the laboratory. It had further need, however, of another group more deeply disciplined in the fundamental sciences, who could approach the problems of the diseased body with a precision of technique impossible to those trained primarily in medicine. I might have substituted organic and physical chemistry and mathematics for the hospital years, had I been so advised. I would have turned out differently. I often wished I had chosen this course. However, I would have missed much — including, perhaps, the unenvious admiration I have always had for some of my scientific collaborators. My later affectionate friendships with men distinguished in my own subject — Loeb, Landsteiner, Northrop, and others — were based to a great extent — I take pride in saying so — on the pleasure I took in accomplishments of which I myself was incapable, but which I could often translate into the more practical world of my own activities.

However that may be, the opportunity was missed for lack of foresight, not only on my own part, but on that of most of the medical profession of the period. The coöperative team-work of the clinician with the applied sciences, bacteriology and pathology, and with fundamental chemistry and physics, which are the heart and soul of medicine to-day, was still a dream of the future. It was, of course, written clearly on the horizon for all who had eyes to see, whither the direction of medical progress must lead; and, here and there, gifted and clear-headed individuals were beginning to follow along the paths mapped out by Claude Bernard, Pasteur, Ehrlich, Behring, and other pioneers. But before these things could become obvious to the profession as a whole, there was needed a great deal of exploration of the vast territory intervening between purely observational biology and those isolated and relatively simple systems which were amenable to the methods of the exact sciences. With the rest of biology, medicine was — as to a lesser degree it still is — far removed from being a true science by the definition with which Kant precedes Eddington and Dingle by a century or so, namely: "*Dass in jeder Naturlehre nur so viel eigentliche Wissenschaft anzutreffen ist als sie Mathematik enthält.*"

There has always been, in medical progress as possibly in that of other human activities, though I am not competent to say about the others, a curiously prolonged lag between the recognition of needs and the actual adoption of reforms. The examples most often cited are the well-known opposition of medical men to the revolutionary doctrines of Pasteur, a chemist, and the unwillingness of the Virchow school of pathology to accept Koch's demonstration of the tubercle bacillus. There are, however, numerous other examples. Martha Ornstein quotes Aubrey as hearing Harvey say that, after the publication of his discoveries on the circulation of blood, " 'twas believed by the vulgar that he was crackbrained and all physicians were against his opinions," and that his practice "fell mightily." However, the conservatism which delays but cannot inhibit progress may, on the other hand, be of inestimable value in impeding acceptance of the torrents of worthless and purely speculative half-science which accompany all periods of active advance. That academies and learned societies — commonly dominated by the older foofoos of any profession — are slow to react to new ideas is in the nature of things. For, as Bacon says, *scientia inflat*, and the dignitaries who hold high honors for past accomplishment do not usually like to see the current of progress rush too rapidly out of their reach. On the other hand, the conservatism of rigid criticism on the part of serious investigators is the only safeguard which stands between the public and charlatanry. Our task, as we grow older in a rapidly advancing science, is to retain the capacity of joy in discoveries which correct older ideas and theories and to learn from our pupils as we teach them. That is the only sound prophylaxis against the dodo-diseases of middle age.

To a moderate degree, then, conservatism is useful. But by far the more important causes of lag lie in the nature of the work which medicine is called upon to perform. The doctor's profession is, in part, an art — since it deals with matters that demand manual skill; in part, again, it is a branch of that vague middle ground between the physical and the psychological, in which emotional intelligence and great sanity of judgment are required; it is, like all biology, an application to an unlimited variety of problems of the reasoning and the techniques of all available science.

Although it was quite clear to the leaders of medical thought, during the early nineteen-hundreds, that the progress of medicine depended implicitly upon the correlation of chemistry, physics, and mathematics with biology, there was not available at that time the machinery by which this could be accomplished. The examples of a few brilliant discoverers had pointed the way, but the average medical practitioner was not competent by training or point of view to forge the new weapons of precision for which the fundamental sciences were furnishing the principles and the plan. For this it needed a new generation, prepared by disciplines which can rarely be superimposed upon the middle-aged intelligence. In science, the mind of the adult can build only as high as the foundations constructed in youth will support. A reorganization of the approaches to medicine was needed. And to one who has seen the transition, it is amazing, not that there was a lag, but rather that the adaptation was so rapidly and splendidly achieved.

2

Bacon, who knew all this long ago, says, "Neither is it possible to discover the more remote and deeper parts of any science, if you stand but upon the level of the same science, and ascend not to a higher science." The ascending to "a higher science" is the task with which medicine has been occupied in the twentieth century. But this ascending, which Dampier calls the "resolution" of physiology into biophysics and biochemistry, cannot be achieved without an immense preliminary labor of pure observation by which problems amenable to the methods of the exact sciences are isolated and simplified. As concerns medicine, the process implied both a complete reorganization of preliminary education and — before this could be undertaken — a revolutionary change in the points of view of the leaders of medical thought, who controlled the schools and the hospitals.

This resolution of the medical division of general biology from a meagrely scientific art into a true applied science had begun slowly, like a chemical reaction at low temperature, a hundred years before. It gathered velocity progressively until, at the time when I was ready to enter my hospital service, its forces and reactions were beginning to pervade all phases of medical activity from the premedical laboratories to the wards of hospitals and the offices and clinics of physicians and surgeons. It was a period of new enthusiasms by which even the most reactionary of the older school — fervently or reluctantly, according to temperament — were carried forward. If the stubborn insistence of a few die-hards upon the superiority of eyes, ears, and hands over the test tube and the retort was occasionally irritating and obstructive, it had — on the other hand — the beneficial effects of saving from complete neglect the traditions of the personal art and skill of mind and hand without which the most scientific medical training must remain imperfectly applied to the problems of the bedside.

About 1900, the young men who were finishing their school years were able to survey the forces of transformation, trace the sources from which they were flowing, and foresee the directions in which they were destined to go. It was an inspiring time and, intellectually, not less exciting to the young

and eager than analogous political and philosophic *Sturm und
Drang* periods had been a century before. A fresh breeze was
blowing across the horizons of scientific thought, revealing
ranges of new objectives and paths by which they could be,
if not immediately scaled, at least hopefully approached. It
was the dawn in which light from all the sciences was bringing never-suspected correlations; and a lovely orderliness was
emerging from the fog.

It was during these years, also, that medical research in
America began to blossom forth with the new vigor instilled
into it by the golden showers that were falling upon it in
benefactions unprecedented in the history of science. That is
not to say that there had been no individual American investigators of distinction in earlier years. There had been
groups, like those at Johns Hopkins, a few at Harvard, and
the school of Victor Vaughan in Michigan; and there had
been a few endowed research professorships here — as there
had been in Europe ever since Cosimo II appointed Galileo
to the Professorship of Mathematics in Pisa. But resources
had been limited, and laboratories few. Now, with the return
of a new type of trained investigators from the German universities, improvement in the teaching of the fundamental
sciences, and the appointment of young men, devoted to
inquiry, to the important chairs in newly endowed medical
schools, the spirit of investigation was carried into hospitals
and clinics. Research institutes, modeled on the Pasteur in
Paris, the Koch Institute in Berlin, the Lister Institute in
London, were founded in Philadelphia, Chicago, and New
York. The organization of the Rockefeller Institute in 1901
had an especially powerful influence, as it continues to have

to-day. Medicine seemed to capture the imagination of those who had accumulated great wealth, as religion inspired them in earlier centuries. As they built churches in former times, they now appeared to believe that they could make camels go through the eyes of needles by building institutions for the improvement of medicine. The deep religious fervor that is so often associated with worldly ruthlessness has often expressed itself in noble altruism when ambition is satiated and the blood pressure has passed one hundred and eighty. It is not fair to say that the desire to balance the books with eternity was the sole motive. Sincere benevolence surely played a part. At any rate, it brought the desired results. And almost too rapidly for a time. Opportunity was made available faster than the brains needed to take advantage of it could be mobilized. There was, at first, much mere rediscovery of what was already well known in Europe and, in many places, half-trained people in magnificent laboratories were sitting on sterile ideas like hens on boiled eggs. But there was much earnest effort, great velocity of improvement, and by the time of the World War, American medical schools and research institutes could hold up their heads with any in the world. It was a most astonishing demonstration of what could be done in a short time by the wise expenditure of money. But of course the time was ripe, and — wisely unlike many other countries — we were not nationalistically narrow-minded or arrogant. We admiringly borrowed what we needed of knowledge or example from wherever we could get it, sending our young men all over the world, and honoring achievement regardless of race or nation. And in this transitional period we had the good luck to have leaders like Welch, Simon Flexner, Christian Herter, and others, whose encouragement of talent and enthusiasm wherever they found it makes most of us of my generation deeply their debtors.

Of Welch, the greatest of these, much might be written. Without him, American medicine might have taken much longer to develop. It is amazing how many of the medical investigators alive to-day came under his beneficent influence. There are few scientific contributions that bear his own name. But if all the work that he stimulated and that was encouraged by him could be gathered together in one place, it would fill a small library. The thought of him warms my heart with affectionate reverence for that fusion of wisdom and courtesy which is as rare as genius. I made a pilgrimage to Baltimore to his bedside during his last illness. The hour I had with him a week before he died is one of my most treasured memories.

Of course the research world is not devoid of a certain amount of hocus-pocus. There has been, and is, a good deal of personal and institutional rivalry, growing as public interest increases; and this leads to premature publication and to the frequent ballyhoo of relatively unimportant stuff as the work of genius. Growing popular interest, unwisely exploited, has much to do with this. There is also burglary of ideas and consequent secretiveness. Positions are gained by volume of output, as much as by quality. And vanity plays a part rather more important than financial or worldly gain. Many a man whom you could trust with the keys of your safe-deposit box you would hate to leave alone at your desk with a sheaf of experimental notes.

Indeed, the pressure for premature publication has ruined a considerable number of good men, who might have built up sound and permanent reputations. From some of our greatest institutions for research, within half a generation, have come utterly erroneous publications announcing such major discoveries as the cultivation of poliomyelitis virus, of the syphilis organism, of a bacillus of epidemic influenza, of a yellow-fever leptospira — all of these widely publicized and applauded, few of them ever corrected from within. Mistaken assertions of causes and cures of Hodgkin's disease and of cancer are almost annual occurrences. Without competitive pressure, such errors would usually be discovered by the workers themselves; or the technical criticism of specialists would correct them before they escaped from professional circles; and disappointment, even occasional tragedy, would be avoided. For while it is, of course, impossible in a majority of biological investigations to measure, weigh, and check accuracy by mathematical computation, it is nevertheless possible for men who know their business and have mastered the art of "control" experiment to differentiate between the surely false, the probable, and the demonstrable truth. But such judgment is not possible for the untrained. For this reason, the publicizing of a biological discovery before the matter has been fought out in expert conclave is not only stupid, but in many cases is cruel by reason of the false hopes it arouses, and the vain expenditures of money and effort it imposes on those who may be misled. To be just to the scientists themselves, it may be said that the most serious delinquencies of this kind committed in our country in the last decade or so must be laid at the doors of administrators and directors impelled by desire for institutional advertising.

We have probably passed through the worst of this. It was one of the growing pains of medical research. In some ways, the newspapers are doing as much to improve the situation as the laboratories themselves. Reporters are beginning to be specialized, and make praiseworthy efforts to confirm their information before publication. But the evil effects of publicity on the minds of younger workers still remain. Science has acquired news value, and the livelihoods and careers of many talented youngsters often depend on attracting attention. Also, unwise pressure is often exerted from above. When pressure for production and notoriety gives way to conscientious appraisal of talent and integrity, irrespective of poundage of publication, the situation will improve. As a matter of fact, it is not really bad now. The traditional spirit of the fundamental sciences is gradually penetrating medicine, and the majority of those engaged in medical research are in it because they love it and are frugally devoted. They are also fiercely alert to tear to pieces spurious work. Sometimes errors get by for a little while; and an occasionally successful bit of burglary doesn't do any lasting harm. Often this arouses more amusement than wrath. But those once found guilty run the risk of having all their subsequent work regarded with suspicion, as in the case of the wives of some of the Caesars. Taking it by and large, medical research in this country is in a pretty healthy condition, and growing more so every year.

However, all this has little to do with my hospital days, which is what you wanted me to talk about.

CHAPTER X

The background of modern medicine in America. Largely constructed from notes left me by R.S. and, of course, owing to his habit of digression, much abbreviated

YOUNG Americans who entered medicine at the time that R.S. did were more fortunate than they knew, for they were destined to participate in a professional evolution that has few parallels. The development of modern medicine in our country is a thrilling chapter in its intellectual history, and illustrates, more than is generally recognized, the magnificent self-corrective vitality of this profession. At the present time, there is a strong popular movement for the socialization of medical practice, and an effort, essentially praiseworthy, to bring the benefits of discovery and of improved care within the reach of the population as a whole, irrespective of ability to pay. This is as it should be, and there is little question of the fact that the old system of charity clinics and hospitals no longer meets modern requirements. Moreover, it is morally sound to postulate that all discovered means of alleviating suffering and sorrow, maintaining health and preventing death, should be freely available to all that need them — without reference to social, racial, or economic condition. This will demand a complete reorganization of practice, in which the medical profession must, and should, play the leading rôle; and undoubtedly it will — though there has been a tendency on the part of reformers, sociologists, government agencies, and professors of the teachers'-union type to assume that reluctance to accept any and all proposals indicates a conservatism of self-preservation based on purely venal motives. Let it not be forgotten that the situation as it now exists is entirely the consequence of the progress made in medical discovery by the profession itself; that the enhanced power for good which is now claimed as the latest of the inalienable rights of man is the result of the labors of medical investigators and practitioners, and that public-health organization, social service, group practice, and all other advances which have revolutionized the relationship of medical knowledge to the population — even housing, nutrition, and the sociological conditions that influence health, such as wage scales, public parks, industrial hygiene, etc., etc. — were given their basis of factual observation and their early organization for practical application by the insight of medical men.

There is in the practice of medicine a unique quality that is a source both of inspiration and of terror to the conscientious young physician. Dealing as it does with matters of life and death, any lack of knowledge or of skill becomes a positive fault of omission and even guilt. If a patient dies or is incapacitated — with all the heartbreak and suffering that this implies — because the attending practitioner was ignorant of measures that are available and that might have brought another outcome in more skillful hands, he is as responsible as though he had committed a willful injury. This is true not only of surgical procedures, but equally — perhaps more frequently so — in infectious diseases, where speed and precision of diagnosis by well-known methods and vigorous intelligent treatment may decide the issue within a few hours, one way or the other. It is this consideration, more than any other, which — with the growing accumulation of knowledge that no one man can hope to master completely — has automatically led to the organization of group medicine, the increasing coöperation of city and state health departments, and the more generalized utilization of hospital facilities. And since it is essential that all effective knowledge must be applied to rich and poor alike, unless our profession is to lose the fine, ancient traditions of its history, a considerable readjustment of its activities is inevitable. These simple considerations are at the bottom of all the agitation for the so-called "socialization" of medicine on which great volumes of reports have already been issued. It should not be forgotten, however, by the ardent lay reformers that evolution in these directions has long been going on within the profession itself, and, within a single span of professional life, enormous progress — almost entirely originated by public-spirited doctors — has been achieved. Controversies have turned not at all on the objectives to be attained, but rather upon the manner in which the reorganization is to be carried out.

Now it is always relatively easy to conceive an ideal scheme of organization which shall represent the perfect mechanism for social reform. But such conceptions are likely to neglect certain imponderable human values without which the machinery of service cannot run smoothly. In medicine, the problem is to find a solution which shall meet the requirements of effective scientific care of all those who require it, and retain at the same time that sense of personal responsibility, compassion, and judgment without which the physician becomes a mere technician. It is this consideration which has given the impression of exaggerated conservatism in many actually progressive physicians. We realize — more acutely than most of the lay reformers — the obligations of greater precision of practice and wider and cheaper application of the benefits of progress. But we are reluctant to lose our "horse and buggy" doctors, or to deprive the suffering patient of that solace and support which only the close personal relationship with a wise and compassionate physician can give.

During little more than the space of the professional lives of R.S.'s generation, American medicine developed from a relatively primitive dependence upon European thought to its present magnificent vigor. How this came about is a unique illustration of coöperative effort, wise benevolence, and healthy self-criticism. To understand it wholly, we must sketch the dependence of modern medical development upon that of the basic sciences, its emergence — in Europe — from mediaevalism, and the manner in which these influences were transported to the new continent.

Since the Renaissance there have been no complete breaks in the continuity of the sciences comparable to those sterile periods which have, from time to time, interrupted the progress of the arts. There has been an alternation of slowing down and acceleration, but the progress has been a reasonably steady one, the intervals between great advances being occupied with the organization of strong points within the conquered territory. The preparatory accumulation of minor discoveries and of accurately observed details by conscientious drones is, in scientific pursuits, almost as important for the mobilization of great forward drives as the periodic correlation of these disconnected observations into principles and laws by the vision of genius. In this, the lesser men of science are happier than the minor poets or painters. Thus the roots of modern medicine trace back deeply into the seventeenth and eighteenth centuries.

The earliest of the great Baconians, Harvey, not only clarified the facts concerning the circulation of man, but carried his observations into the animal world and, in his *De Genera-*

tione Animalium, into the field of exact study of embryological development. If any single individual can be named as the first to introduce, into medical thought, exact methods of observation and experiment for the correlation of structure and function, this credit belongs to William Harvey. Moreover, it is probably not unreasonable to appraise him as the most important individual force in the transition from mediaeval into modern medicine, in the sense that there could be no rational physiology until Harvey had refuted the old doctrine of Galen that there were two kinds of blood — the venous and the arterial — serving different functions respectively.

The period in which Harvey lived was the most momentous in the history of science. Harvey was born in 1578. Between 1564 and 1596 were born Galileo, Kepler, and Descartes. Pascal was born in 1623, and Newton nineteen years later. Between 1623 and 1630, when Kepler died, all these men except Newton were alive. Even when compared with the flowering period of biology which laid the foundations of modern medicine in the nineteenth century, this golden age of physics and mathematics represents the most powerful forward surge of the human intellect, equaled in the history of art only by the miracles of Homer, or Leonardo, of Shakespeare, of Bach and a very few others. And it is quite clear that in the logical continuity of scientific evolution, this development of physics must have preceded any possible advances in chemistry and biology and — therefore — in medicine.

Apart from Malpighi, the first great histologist, and Mayow, who anticipated — within the limitations of available chemistry — Lavoisier's discoveries on the physiology of breathing, Harvey had no contemporary peers. The nature of medical practice was, in that age, discouraging to scientific inquiry.

In Bacon's words, "the physician . . . hath no particular acts demonstrative of his ability . . . for who can tell if a patient die or recover . . . whether it be art or accident? And, therefore, many times the impostor is prized and the man of virtue taxed. Nay, we see the weakness and credulity of men is such, as they will often prefer a mountebank [Montabank] or witch before a learned physician. And, therefore, the poets were clear-sighted in discerning this extreme folly, when they made Aesculapius and Circe brother and sister, both children of the Sun. . . . And what followeth? Even this, that physicians say to themselves, as Solomon expresseth it upon a higher occasion: If it befall me as it befalleth to the fool, why should I labour to be more wise?"

That a competition of physicians with superstition and gullibility, if not with witchcraft, still persists is attested by the power of Christian Science, osteopathy, chiropractice, and the mass of purely meretricious advertising. There have lately also been lapses into a sort of rationalized mysticism on the part of individuals — sometimes eminent scientists — which are dangerous only when they are combined with skill in popular exposition, as in the case of Dr. Carrel, to whom we shall refer presently. That the fight is practically won, however, is apparent from the fact that, except among the lowest classes of intelligence, "cults" such as those mentioned are themselves attempting to find justification in scientific reasoning, and are slipping into legitimate medicine by the back door.

From Harvey's time on, there was a consistent effort on the part of leading physicians to emancipate the profession from superstition and tradition, and to evolve a science of medicine. Anatomy — and with it the beginnings of physiology — was considerably enriched by Meckel, Morgagni, Boerhaave, Haller, and their followers. In clinical medicine, Sydenham,

John Hunter, Auenbrugger, — the inventor of percussion, — Benjamin Bell, and a host of others were applying principles of exact observation to case studies, and thinking in terms of the primitive physiology at their disposal; progressive schools of surgery appeared in England and on the Continent.

Early eighteenth-century medicine made its chief advances in practical directions. Physics and mathematics were not ready for any kind of immediate influence upon medical theory or methodology; the intermediary — that is, chemistry — was still too primitive in technique and conception to bring the two together. It was the century of philosophy, and the reaction of all human thought against theological domination had a considerable indirect influence upon medicine as well. Helvetius, Maupertuis, and above all Voltaire, — who, with the aid of the *éducation de l'oreiller* from the learned Marquise du Châtelet, brought the Newtonian physics to France, — these, with Diderot, d'Alembert, and others, revolutionized the attitude of all educated men toward the observation of nature. La Mettrie, who anticipated Schopenhauer in his postulation of egoism as the basis of morals, was a military surgeon. Cabanis was a medical man. Buffon had timid suspicions of the common origin of animals. Linnaeus classified men with the apes. The Abbé Spallanzani was leading up to Pasteur's refutation of the spontaneous generation of life. Stahl, to be sure, put a handful of sand into the scientific gears with his conceptions of "Vitalism"; but Boerhaave of Leyden and his pupil Haller were beginning to teach medicine on the basis of what was known of physiology and of microscopic anatomy, and trained some of the most eminent physicians of the next generation. It was a period of preparation for the true beginning of sound medical theory, which started gradually toward the end of the century with the chemistry of Priestley, Boyle, and above all Lavoisier.

American medicine, quite naturally, was during this century under the influence of the British school, and the most eminent physicians of Revolutionary times were pupils of such great clinicians as John Fothergill, Huxham, John Hunter, and others. Progress, however, was largely along purely empirical, clinical directions. Surgery advanced remarkably, considering the lack of anaesthetics. But, though there were men of unusual wisdom and skill, no fundamental advances were made — except in the discovery of Jennerian vaccination, which, against considerable opposition, was established in America, with the aid of Thomas Jefferson, by Dr. Waterhouse of Boston. The history of these times would reveal an interesting collection of strong personalities, wise and alert, but would be found, with a few exceptions like that of Jenner, to be largely a period of groping, without any notable advances in the discovery of fundamental fact. It was a time of theorizing and of "systems." John Brown of Edinburgh founded a school which explained all disease as fluctuations in the "irritability" of the nervous system to external and internal stimuli. It is not worth while to detail his views, since it is all clever nonsense; but "Brownianism" developed a considerable vogue in other European countries. Then there was "Vitalism," founded by Sauvages, Bordeu, and Barthez, at Montpellier. As in the "Animism" of Stahl, the "life principle" or "soul" was, for the Vitalists, the seat of all morbid processes; and the vital principle resided in the central nervous system, in which all disturbances from the normal originated. It was a primitive neurology, based on speculation without structural investigation, and it became curiously involved with the observations, by Galvani, of the stimulation of muscle contractions by electrical currents. Galvani observed, too, that a muscle contracted when it and its nerve were placed in contact with two dissimilar metals. He postulated the existence of "animal electricity," and thus it was a short cry from Vitalism to elaborate theories of electrical "fluids" as governors of all life processes. And even the soul acquired a galvanometrically measurable quality.

An interesting offshoot of this was "Mesmerism," a movement which had much similarity to the sort of thing that survives in the best modern medical circles. The first thought that comes to one on reading Dr. Carrel's book is that there is nothing new under the sun. The same sort of thing that seems to be happening to our distinguished friend happened to many medical men in the days during and following the cult of Mesmerism.

Friedrich Anton Mesmer studied medicine in Vienna, where — thanks to a rich wife — he became a successful general practitioner. There he developed theories of therapeutics dependent on the influence of magnetism upon the human nervous system. Out of this there rapidly grew a school of treatment in which a sort of "chiropractic" massage at the hands of a strongly "psychic" physician (as he would now be called) claimed a considerable number of extraordinary cures. The medical profession, skeptical then as now, was not at first persuaded; but Mesmer appeared before various academies and found enthusiastic disciples in Paris, in spite of the unfavorable report of a commission — one of whose members was Lavoisier. By Parisian followers, the theory of "Animal Magnetism" was then expanded into what was called "Magnetic Somnambulism" and, by the influence of the Marquis de Puységur, it became a theory of clairvoyance. Thus Mesmer said that "living creatures, which are in contact (by magnetic waves) with all of nature, are capable of feeling (or perceiving) other distant living bodies and events. From this, it is easy to understand that the will of one person can be communicated — by an inner sense — to the will of another."

The thing spread far and wide, as this sort of business does to-day, was taken up by imaginative writers like the physician-poet Justinus Kerner, who projected the mesmeric communication into the spirit world, into ghosts and creatures like "Margery's" brother, the brakeman. Finally, in 1815, in the hands of German professors, the movement developed into a "Christian Science," and Ennemoser, Windisschman, and others declared that all disease originated in sin, and what was needed was a *Christliche Heilkunde*. The French shook it off at this point, but in England a great physician of St. Thomas's Hospital and the physiologist Herbert Mayo swallowed it hook, bait, and sinker, until — as in some more recent cases — it was discovered that these learned gentlemen had had their legs pulled. It is almost a modern story.

It is not to be supposed that medicine stood still or receded during these years of speculation. Much practical progress was made. There were notable advances in obstetrical and surgical technique; there was sound progress in the botany of drugs; and, above all, the development of general anatomy was clearing the ground for pathology and physiology. Much exact anatomical observation had resulted from the studies of the Vitalists of Montpellier. A great deal had been added by others, notably by Galvani and the Italian school. Chemistry began to assume physiological significance through Lavoisier. Buffon and Linné had developed logical systems of nature.

Strangely enough, it was Bichat, pupil of Montpellier and convinced Vitalist, who was so far able to separate his theoretical prejudices from his observational precision that he became the actual founder of the modern conceptions of structure as the basis of function and thus, in his *Anatomie Générale*, made possible the immediate development of rational pathology and physiology. Bichat may be regarded as the most powerful single influence in the rise of the French school of clinicians which, by the middle of the nineteenth century, had become the most effective and intelligent medical group in the world.

From the second half of the nineteenth century on, young Americans of talent had been getting into the habit of spending a few years either in the clinics of Paris or in the laboratories of German universities.

In Paris, Corvisart, who had translated Auenbrugger's forgotten book on percussion, developed this art into a powerful diagnostic instrument. His most brilliant contemporary was Laënnec, himself a pathologist of accomplishment, classicist, flute player, and horseman, who added to percussion the invention of the cedarwood stethoscope, a device which was suggested to him — as he told his friend Kergaradec — by children playing in the gardens of the Louvre. He noticed little boys putting sticks into their ears and scratching the ends of these with pins. The story reminds one of that told by the late Professor Pupin, who claimed that his first clue to the physical principles of long-distance telephone transmission came to him from the trick of the Serbian cowherds, who signaled to each other by thrusting their knives into the ground and tapping the handles with sticks. At any rate, Laënnec, when he came back to the clinic after his walk, rolled a piece of paper into a tube, set one end against the chest of a patient, and held his ear against the other.

His treatise *De l'Auscultation Médiate*, and so forth, published in 1819, brought this new method to almost modern perfection. But in judging the amazing effects on medical diagnosis of these extraordinarily simple devices one must not forget that they were applied and developed by a group of men who had been brought up under the influence of Bichat, the father of pathological anatomy, to whom may be credited the emancipation of practical medicine from the vagueness of "natural philosophy," theories of "irritation," "dynamism," "animal magnetism," and so on. With this group began the effort to correlate observations at the bedside with the revelations of the autopsy table and the microscope. Bichat's prediction that medicine "*aura droit d'être associée [aux sciences exactes], au moins pour le diagnostic des maladies, quand on aura partout uni la rigoureuse observation*" was carried closer to realization by Corvisart, Laënnec, and their associates, Bayle, Broussais, and others, who were both skilled clinicians and experienced pathologists. With them began what is often spoken of as the Golden Age of French medicine. When our young Americans (of whom a good account has been recently written by Dr. Riesman of Philadelphia) came to Paris, they found a school of clinical medicine which could not be equaled anywhere else at that time and which, apart from its intrinsic value, was to render medicine receptive to the influence of the chemical and physical sciences which were shortly to develop with such amazing velocity. Among the great teachers of Paris were Chomel, Bretonneau, Andral, and Cruveilhier. The greatest of them all, however, was Pierre Louis. Louis, who was noted chiefly for the classical study in which he defined typhoid fever as a clinical entity, taught both in the wards and at the autopsy table. He is said to have performed five thousand autopsies with his own hands. A simple man, with much personal charm and an incisive, analytical mind, he seems to have represented, for his own time, the ideal physician — much as Dr. Osler did, at a later date, in our country. Indeed, these two great teachers must have approached medicine by essentially similar methods, for Osler, though aided in precision by laboratory developments not available to Louis, was yet, like the former, preëminently the trained pathologist and clinical observer, without much —

if any — personal interest in experimental methods. Out of
the school of Louis, there came — for the incalculable enrichment of American medicine — James Jackson, Oliver Wen-
dell Holmes, Pennock, Gerhardt, and George C. Shattuck —
to mention only a few of the more gifted. And these men
were the teachers of a great majority of the physicians and
surgeons who were active in American medical schools during the latter decades of the nineteenth century.

The influence of Claude Bernard and of Pasteur, though
both of them were at the height of their powers at the time
of this first American invasion of Paris, was not directly felt
in America until later, when it reached us circuitously by
way of the German universities toward which the stream of
our students was directed in the years immediately following.
This may have been owing to the fact that Claude Bernard
was lecturing chiefly at the Collège de France, and Pasteur
was too deeply occupied with research to have time for foreign
medical students.

Yet our young American wanderers could not have lived in
the Paris of the eighteen-sixties and seventies without falling
under the spell of the hopeful spirit which flowed into medicine from these two superbly great men — one of them, Bernard, originally a mediocre medical student who wrote tragedies and poetry; the other no doctor at all, who painted pastels
and water colors in his spare time. Entirely apart from the discoveries which made these men immortal and in which not
many of their medical contemporaries were quite ready to
follow them, they demonstrated the possibilities of the experimental method in biology; they brought the study of the
phenomena of life into the same category as that of the
study of physical and chemical systems.

Bernard particularly — though, as Paul Bert tells us, always
skeptical about physicians, speaking of them "with the thought

of Sganarelle always in the back of his mind" — taught that medicine could be a science. "We must," he said, "have recourse to the analytical study of the phenomena of life and must make use of the same experimental method which chemists and physicists employ in analyzing the phenomena of inorganic bodies. The difficulties which result from the complexity of the phenomena of living bodies arise solely in applying experimentation; for, fundamentally, the object and principles of the method are always exactly the same." And in another part of his *Introduction to the Study of Experimental Medicine:* "I propose to show, therefore, that the science of vital phenomena must have the same foundations as the science of the phenomena of inorganic bodies, and that there is, in this respect, no difference between the principles of biological science and those of physico-chemical science."

The great clinicians of whom we have spoken performed a revolutionary service when they based diagnosis and therapy on exact observations at the bedside and in the mortuary. Bernard and Pasteur carried observation further, into the realm of experiment.

Medicine, Bernard remarked, cannot afford to remain merely a science of observation. It cannot be carried forward, however, without experimentation.

"A fact is noted; apropos of this fact, an idea is born; in the light of this idea, an experiment is devised, its material conditions imagined and brought to pass; from this experiment, new phenomena result which must be observed, and so on and so forth."

There was a profound difference in outlook, as Lawrence Henderson has pointed out, between Bernard and Pasteur; the latter, more the intensely preoccupied specialist, lacking the reflective intellect of the former. But, together, they founded experimental medicine in recognizing, in their own work and in their teaching, that the approach to biological knowledge is the same as that to physical and chemical comprehension; and that biological observation must eventually be carried into the biochemical and biophysical analysis of the manifestations of life, where — except for infinitely greater complexity — the fundamental laws of reaction will be found the same.

While it cannot be claimed that they were the originator of this idea, it was still their influence which brought this view to bear on medicine and guided it into the paths on which it has been progressively embarked ever since their time.

In yet another quality these great men were alike — in one which could profitably be emulated by some of our own contemporaries. While both of these masters of experiment believed that the forces of what is called "life" rested upon physicochemical reactions, they did not, in any sense, believe that that was the whole story. They piously — if one may use the word in this connection — believed that these forces were guided by a preëxisting design, the purposes of which were beyond the powers of scientific analysis. When obscure or inexplicable phenomena presented themselves they accepted them, each according to his nature — Pasteur unspeculatively, Bernard hopefully, as something which some day might yield to eventual explanation. They did not turn over the whole show to the clairvoyant or the parish priest and bring comfort thereby to the charlatan and the bigot.

During these years of French hegemony, German medical science was lagging behind — largely, perhaps, because the universities, preëminent in philology and philosophy, were still deeply under the influence of the *Naturphilosophie* of Hegel, Schelling, and their followers. As has been noted, in France and England science was fostered largely by academies and societies — the Collège de France, the Royal Society, and similar bodies. In Germany, progress depended on the emancipation of the universities themselves from tradition. Medical faculties had been established as early as 1384 at Vienna, 1386 at Heidelberg, and between that time and 1607 in a dozen other places. At first, all medical teachers were required to be clergymen. But after the middle of the sixteenth century, lay teachers were permitted. After the Reformation, all German universities became state institutions, but in spite of this — with a wisdom astonishing to the observer of modern Germany — they were given, from the beginning, *Lehrfreiheit* (academic freedom of faculties) to teach and investigate as they pleased; and still more surprising, since it is not a recognized privilege even in our own universities to-day, *Lernfreiheit* (the right of the student to choose his courses and his teachers on his own responsibility) — the only limitations on this being the examinations which, in each field, must eventually be passed. These traditional principles, to-day destroyed, with such incredible stupidity, gave the German university an extraordinary adaptability and liberty of action. They were in every way ready to react vigorously, therefore, to the fresh wind of scientific enthusiasm which blew across to them from the French border. Even the deep preoccupation of some of their best scholars with the mystifications of the "Nature philosophers" was, in a reverse sense, a preparation, since it must have convinced serious students of nature of the desperate need for more facts and less metaphysics.

Between 1830 and 1840, the medical schools of Germany began to feel the impact of the amazing velocity of biological discovery. The cell theory was founded by the botanist Schleiden. Baer founded the science of embryology. Schwann carried Schleiden's discoveries to the cellular structures of animals. Liebig, a pupil of Gay-Lussac, and indirectly therefore of Berzelius and Lavoisier, set up a laboratory of biochemistry at Giessen. It is a long and wonderful story, the Golden Age of the German universities, which then began and which lasted uninterruptedly until common sense became counter-revolution in 1933. It has often been told. What interests us here is that, by the close coördination of the medical schools with universities, there was — from the beginning — a powerful reaction of the basic sciences upon medical training, and a true spirit of research pervaded medical laboratories and clinics. The German professor gained his position by research. He was far more than a teacher — rather, the leader of a school of investigation and thought, whose authority was derived from his contributions to knowledge and his ability to guide his pupils into channels of productive observation. The training of students became one of preliminary mastery of natural history, anatomy, pathology, and chemistry, and by the end of the eighteen-sixties the German medical schools were unequaled centres of creative energy. It was at this time that American students began to be diverted from France to Germany.

It is perhaps one of our most praiseworthy traits as a nation — which I pray may persist — that we have never been reluctant to admire and emulate the intellectual achievements of other nations. At the time that R.S. began his medical studies, there were few eminent American teachers of the fundamental sciences who had not spent a few graduate years in Europe, chiefly in German seats of learning, and could not proudly call themselves pupils of Virchow, Koch, Cohnheim, Dohrn, Weismann, Helmholtz, Ludwig, and countless others of the masters, to say nothing of the great clinicians and surgeons whose wards were intimately related to and influenced by adjacent institutes of pathology, physiology, bacteriology, and chemistry. Gradually, Americans returning from these training grounds began to shape the course of American medicine. Preëminent — the most potent individual force — was William Welch. But there were also Abel and Howell, Christian Herter, Victor Vaughan, Prudden, Huntington, Mall, Minot — to name only a few. The leaders were assembling, but the opportunities for leadership of the right sort had yet to be organized.

America had before this time many medical schools. But with few exceptions they were "proprietary" ones — that is, privately founded corporations of groups of physicians and surgeons who organized courses without a well-conceived educational plan, often without hospital facilities. In a few places, this was being corrected by intelligent faculties who voluntarily placed themselves under university control, or allied themselves with well-run hospitals. But taken as a whole the situation was a deplorable one, lacking any uniformity in educational standards, care in the choice of teachers, laboratory or clinical facilities. In a few places, owing largely to financial support, university influence was gaining power, and in Philadelphia, Boston, Ann Arbor, and New York, schools of increasing strength developed. An especially strong pressure for improvement was exerted by President Eliot, at the Harvard school. The situation was distinctly improving before 1880 and probably was on its way to better things, largely under the influence of the young men returning from Europe. But, at best, this would have been slow and might have taken many wrong turnings had it not been for the opening, in 1893, of the Johns Hopkins Medical School. Whether we attribute it to good fortune or to extraordinary wisdom, the group eventually assembled at Hopkins — Osler, Welch, Halsted, Mall, Howell, and Abel — became the model for American schools, and it was not long before men trained by them became the leaven that raised the general level of all other progressive institutions.

But Johns Hopkins had an endowment and a hospital of its own. It was equipped with laboratories and backed by a university. Few other places could, even with the best will, meet the new requirements. By 1900, great improvement had taken place. But the country was still full of second-rate proprietary schools and university schools that were limping along in penury. Then came Abraham Flexner's report to the Carnegie Foundation.

Oh, Abraham Flexner! We have fought with you on minor points, have alternately admired and disliked you, have applauded you for wisdom and detested you for opinionatedness. But in just retrospect — layman as you are — we hail you as the father — or, better, the uncle — of modern medical education in America. You did, on occasion, hit below the belt, yet in the spirit in which the Christian knights slashed off the infidels' heads while shouting "Kyrie Eleison!" It was your report — uncompromising, cruelly objective, courageous and incisive — which opened the eyes of the medical profession to the state of their training schools, aroused public opinion to the need of better education of the guardians of health, and set the floodgates of the golden streams of philanthropy in medical directions.

For a decade, Abraham Flexner — backed by the huge resources of the Rockefeller Foundation and, indirectly, by similar funds; and advised by such wise men as Welch, Mall, Edsall, Pierce, and less wise ones who, like R.S., gave unsolicited advice which he did not follow — dominated the educational situation in medicine. Meanwhile, laboratories were founded in the schools; young men of spirit, training, and ambition enlisted; professorships were bestowed for promise and accomplishments; and research institutes began to step up the pace of creative production.

One reads the increasing mass of literature on the origins

of the great American fortunes of the nineteenth century, and one takes bicarbonate of soda. But however one feels about that, one must acknowledge that the preëminent position of American medicine to-day would have been impossible without a certain amount of rich malefaction in the eighties and nineties.

Thus, modern American medicine is, in a way, a phoenix arising from the ill-smelling ashes of a big business that is forever gone.

CHAPTER XI

1

RIDING an ambulance is, for a boy in his early twenties, an experience that teaches him little medicine but introduces him to phases of human life which he can see in no other way. It is both shocking and maturing, but if the heart is right it does him no harm and gives him an unforgettable insight into the manner of life of the poor and the miserable. There is probably not anywhere in America to-day such abject poverty as there was in the worst tenement quarters of New York in the first decade of the 1900's. We found people frozen on the street; we saw families dispossessed in winter, with their furniture on the sidewalk, and utterly destitute. Private and public charity, as far as they could help, were miserably inadequate.

I accumulated a considerable respect for the activities of the Catholic Church at this time. The Paulist Fathers, who had their headquarters beside the hospital on 59th Street, were constantly circulating through these districts and were intimately acquainted with the Irish families in most of the tenement houses. Father Cafferty, a redheaded priest with whom I formed a firm friendship, was often present at the place of need before the police or the ambulance arrived.

Often, too, I found him, when I came to pick up a mother with pneumonia or a laborer with some serious disease, at all hours of the night, standing by, heating milk on the stove, doing all kinds of little services, and — most important — taking the responsibility for the family when one or the other parent was taken to the hospital. Furthermore, when drunkenness or physical brutality threatened completely to ruin one of these small groups, a word to Father Cafferty or one of his colleagues was followed by visits and conferences during which he would put the fear of Hell into the guilty, so that the situation was often relieved. I gained, then, a lasting impression of the pragmatic usefulness of Hell. The trouble with the modern world, I am convinced, is not so much the weakening of faith in salvation as the loss of the fear of Hell.

Emergency childbirth was one of the chief problems. I have spoken of some of these cases in another place, but hardly a week went by without some odd obstetrical occurrence — the sudden birth of a baby in a streetcar, or in other circumstances under which the best obstetrics are not easily done.

Some of the suicides were extremely ingenious; others were unbelievably maladroit. There seemed to be a sort of fashion in the technique of suicide. For a time, they were almost all illuminating gas. Then, in succession, it was carbolic acid or lysol, bichloride of mercury, hanging, shooting, and throat-cutting with amazingly inefficient utensils — jackknives, or even slivers of glass. The most sensible ones, I thought, were the illuminating-gas people. Many of them, however, made too little allowance for the fact that the odor of the gas would attract rescue. Only one man I found had taken precautions against this. He had done so by sticking an ordinary tin kitchen funnel into the gas hose and tying it over his face with a string above the ears. These people became unconscious rapidly, and if they were rescued before they died, some of them continued to live for five or six days in coma.

The carbolic-acid cases could often be rescued if the ambulance got there soon enough. All that was necessary was to get a stomach tube into them and wash them out with dilute alcohol or, if that was not available, with whiskey. Sometimes, however, it was difficult to get the stomach tube into them, since they had spasms of the diaphragm where the oesophagus enters the stomach. Then, occasionally, the stomach tube slipped into the larynx. In a case of this kind in which I had eventually reached the stomach in time to wash it out and save the patient, I had first slipped my tube into the larynx, and had pumped whiskey into the lung. This unfortunate, though he got over the carbolic acid, developed a pneumonia from which I am glad to say he recovered. While demonstrating the case to a class in my presence, Dr. James humiliated me deeply by saying that it was the only true alcoholic pneumonia he had ever encountered.

Another carbolic candidate, ignorant of course of the fact that alcohol is the antidote, walked into a saloon near the hospital one night, asked the barkeeper for a double whiskey, then pulled out a little bottle from his pocket and, saying to the bartender, "Well, Bill, this is the last drink I will ever take," swallowed the contents of the bottle and followed it with a large dose of bad whiskey. He then sank to the floor — purely because that seemed to be the proper thing to do. When I got there a few minutes later, and washed out his stomach, he was considerably annoyed because I made so little fuss about him.

It has always seemed ridiculous to me that the poor people

who try to commit suicide should be regarded as criminals
before the law and placed under arrest. Since the tenets of
Christianity — either Catholic or Protestant — do not seriously influence our politics or our business practices, it is
strange that ecclesiastical tradition should so rigidly determine
our official attitude toward suicide and birth control. It is
still a punishable offense to make an unsuccessful attempt on
one's own life. Yet philosophers through history have justified
the lawfulness of "self-violence" under special circumstances.
Robert Burton has half a chapter on it and cites Socrates,
Plotinus, Epictetus, and Seneca in its favor. "I pity thee not,"
said Diogenes to the sick Speusippus, who moaned complaints, *"qui cum talis vivere sustines"* — since, being thus,
you continue to live. Diogenes himself is said to have acted
on this sentiment, though it is hard to credit the report that
he committed the act by voluntarily stopping to breathe. I
have seen too many sincere and enthusiastic suicides repent
after the deed and try to save themselves to believe that anyone could voluntarily refrain from breathing at the moment
when the medullary centre is beginning to react to lack of
oxygen. Schopenhauer thought suicide the only logical result
of an intelligent assessment of human life, and Nietzsche said:
"The thought of suicide is a great comfort and helps one over
many a bad night." He did not, however, try it. Few people
are ever sufficiently miserable and hopeless to do more than
think of suicide and comfort themselves with the "back door"
from time to time. Usually, they are deterred by the consideration which Stendhal expressed, when he said: *"Souvent je
m'aurais tué, si je n'avais pas eu peur de me faire mal."* I have
seen a number of attempted suicides where the execution
became pitifully inadequate as soon as the knife or the sliver

of glass began to burn into the neck, or the rope began to shut off the windpipe. Yet whenever misery was so great that the attempt was made in all seriousness, and rescue resented, I have felt sorry that it was an automatic medical obligation to defeat the poor devil's purpose by all possible efforts. To rescue them against their wishes was bad enough; but, in addition, to place them under arrest appeared excessively stupid.

Related to this problem is that of the physician's duty of keeping patients alive for short periods of uncontrollable suffering, when all hope of even temporary improvement is gone. This question of "euthanasia" is one that is arousing a good deal of discussion among intelligent people. To put hopeless sufferers deliberately out of their agonies with lethal drugs may often be desirable, but to admit even a consideration of this implies the exercise of judgment that will inevitably be fallible in a small percentage of cases. It might be worked out under reliable boards in a limited number of conditions. But it would open the doors for dreadful possibilities. One can easily imagine these, if one considers the manner in which psychiatric experts — even in groups — can be induced to testify on both sides of cases where insanity is an issue, or the ease with which lawyers can find doctors to testify in accident insurance cases and in matters of veterans' compensation. The average integrity of the medical profession is perhaps a little higher than that of the population as a whole, but not high enough for euthanasia.

It is quite another question, however, whether a doctor should continue to keep a hopeless case alive for a few weeks or months, when judicious inactivity would bring rest to the patient and peaceful resignation to his family and friends.

This is a problem which has troubled me on a number of occasions. And always I have come to the conclusion that the safest principle — except in a few special instances, such as the last stages of cancer or of leukemia or of Hodgkin's disease — is to continue to work with all means at one's disposal as long as the pulse keeps going and the breathing continues. I remember the experiences of two of my young colleagues who purposely gave up — one, the case of his own father — with the compassionate thought of not prolonging a tragic situation. In both instances, I am sure their judgments were right. In both cases, however, they never entirely got over reproaching themselves. On the other hand, I have graven in my memory a typhus patient in a Serbian hospital, whom we had given up for dead. It was my job to do autopsies on such cases as soon after death as possible, in order to take material for culture before secondary post-mortem infections of the tissues could take place and before the responsible — then uncertain — virus could begin to die out. For in some infections — such, for instance, as syphilis — the infecting organisms die quite promptly when the body dies and the cells cease to respire. This patient was hardly breathing, and his pulse could be detected only with a stethoscope. He was in that state of final exhaustion which I have seen to a similar degree only in this disease and in typhoid fever. I postponed a short walk into the hills because I thought that this boy would be carried into my autopsy barrack at any minute. But my friend George Shattuck, who was the physician on the ward, kept working at him. His persistence fascinated me. He gave saline infusions; he stimulated him with camphor and strychnin; he covered him with hot blankets. Shattuck omitted nothing that might feed the little flame that still flickered. He was hopeless, as I was, but he kept on. We expected death by noon. At two o'clock the patient was unchanged, but still going. By four, we could begin to feel the pulse. By six, there was distinct hope. Six weeks later, the young warrior was lying in the sun near my autopsy barracks, drinking a glass of thin milk, and beginning to feel blood-thirsty again — hoping soon to kill an Austrian.

A girl with typhoid fever at the Roosevelt Hospital came back from the inner gates in just the same way. I was young enough then to ask her later whether she had had any sense of death, or any visions. She said she had no memories what-ever. A year later, I went to her wedding, when she married a policeman. Were we wise in saving her, after all? At any rate, he was not a traffic officer.

One of the questions that troubled me a great deal in those early hospital days — as, indeed, it still does to-day — is that concerning the extent to which the physician should tell his patients the truth in regard to their own illnesses. Usually, in acute conditions in which the patient is too sick to care, and in the less dangerous ailments, the problem does not arise. But there are so many prolonged, inevitably fatal diseases in which the patient's state of mind is an important factor to his own comfort and to that of his family that the doctor's judg-ment in this matter may determine whether the last months or years are to be reasonably tranquil or a *supplice*. And a physician's duty extends beyond the mere direct care of the body, as we are increasingly learning. The power of the mind over physical welfare is not a discovery of Mrs. Eddy. Changes of the pulse, as Struthius, the Polonian, knew, may betray the passions of the mind: "*Si noscere vis an homines suspecti tales sint, tangite eorum arterias.*" (If you wish to know whether the men suspected are these, palpate their arteries.) Avicenna knew it, as did Galen, and the Church has acted upon this knowledge for centuries.

So often, in the history of medicine, scientific discovery has merely served to clarify and subject to purposeful control facts that had long been empirically observed and practically utilized. The principles of contagion were clearly outlined and invisible microorganisms postulated by Fracastorius over a hundred years before the most primitive microscopes were invented, and the pre-Pasteurian century is rich with clinical observations that now seem a sort of gestation period leading to the birth of a new science. In the same way modern psychiatry is striving to organize on a basis of scientific precision the vague, but observationally significant gropings of centuries of half-charlatanry, faith-healing, Christian Science movements, Carrelism, and miraculism — endeavoring to segregate the truth from the fantastic, determining limitations, and directing therapeutic possibilities.

In their crude ways, practising physicians have long appreciated the importance of the mental approach in physical illness. And great physicians of all times have combined with medical erudition that intelligence of the heart which is the essence of a distinguished personality.

To return to the matter of frankness with a patient about his own illness, no rules can be set down. Those who have tried to do this have dismally failed. A well-known American physician who was at the same time — to my mind — a canting moralist held on occasion that absolute, uncompromising truthfulness is the only justifiable position, however cruel. That principle may lead to the sort of situation that once occurred in the practice of one of his colleagues who adopted his views. An old lady had what is known as an "epithelioma" of the lip, a growth occurring in the aged which has all the structural earmarks of a cancer, but represents a variety that never extends to other organs and usually yields to appropriate treatment. To tell this poor soul, for the sake of one's distorted conscience, that she was suffering from "cancer," planting this spectre in her sensitive old mind, was — however well meant — inhumanly stupid.

This and other examples of uncompromising truth-telling remind me of a story told me by the great Norwegian oceanographer, Hjört. Hjört was on a fishing smack off the Norway coast, engaged in studies of fish migration. Somewhat of an experienced sailor himself, he was disturbed by noticing that the old captain of the smack was inexcusably careless about writing the daily log. On some days he neglected making any notations at all, composing a partially fictitious two- or three-days' entry whenever it suited him. Hjört reproached him for this; appealed to him on the basis of tradition, professional ethics, the honor of the seamen's calling. It made no impression. The old captain remained obdurate; said it was unimportant; insisted he didn't care a damn — nobody ever read a fisherman's log anyway, etc, etc. Hjört kept on. Finally, the ancient became irritated. "You are a professor," he said. "I am a captain. I have lived a long time, and I have seen many things. And I tell you, Professor, — and you can remember it, — the truth can be exaggerated, Professor."

The old mariner was quite right. The truth *can* be exaggerated when the doctor talks to a hopeless patient. There are no two cases alike. Judgment, tact, and compassion can be the only guides; and external circumstances must be taken into account. In some cases, the cold truth may bring panic and serve no useful end whatever. In other cases — those in which the patient accepts tranquilly the philosophy of Seneca, "*Stultum est timere quod vitari non protest*" — the certainty of impending death may clear the mind for the resigned tendernesses of the precious remaining days which lend dignity and gentleness to death itself.

I learned something of this as a young interne in long midnight conversations in a hospital ward with a poor old Irishwoman, who knew she was dying and taught me much of the nobility of quiet resignation. And a gallant young officer in the Argonne, struggling in agony with a machine-gun bullet in his spine, became calm and serene when told he had only four hours to live; dictated a letter to his wife; asked to have the Lord's Prayer read to him; and, saying, "That's great stuff, doctor," composed himself to die.

One must pick one's situations and one's cases, and adjust the truth to the judgment of wise kindness. But one must not "exaggerate" the truth without purpose.

2

An interne who doesn't sooner or later fall in love with a nurse is usually a depraved fellow. And if he doesn't marry one of them before he's House Surgeon, it does him no particular harm. But at first they are only terrifying. "Doctors," my Onkel Fritz used to say, "may be roughly divided into physicians who know a lot but can't do anything, and surgeons who can do a great deal but don't know very much." Of course, this has changed a good deal. But the poor interne, when he first enters on his service, feels as though he didn't know a great deal and could do nothing whatever. He approaches patients with fear that they may see through his lack of confidence, and as for the nurses — he knows that they do.

Later, he finds out that they are quite as ignorant as they should be to be good nurses. But, at first, how he marvels at the way they roll a patient over from one side to the other, while making a bed; how they sling a baby across their laps by its legs; put on binders and dressings; and bustle around among the bottles and hypodermics with placid efficiency. If he's a wise interne, he approaches them modestly, and learns from them. They soon find out whether he knows his business or not. And the coöperation of able young doctors and competent nurses in the care of the sick in hospital wards is possibly one of the most satisfying associations between men and women that exist. It brings out the best in both of them, and a wholesome mutual respect. One soon gets over the "ministering angel, thou!" attitude toward them. The element of grimness in the nature of their occupations diminishes the proclivities toward sentimentality. And they help you out of many a hole.

One of my first jobs in the hospital was to be left alone on a Sunday afternoon in charge of a patient dying of tetanus. Except for hydrophobia, there is no form of death more frightful to witness. I did all I could, but when it was all over, I broke down. The nurse, no older than I was, closed the door of the little private room, wiped my face, patted my back, and stood guard until I had myself in hand. I was able to return the favor some time later, when — by an accident that was not her fault, but for which she would have been made miserable by the supervisor (Incidentally, most supervisors of nurses get to be little female Caligulas. They must have been nice girls once) — she broke off a glass catheter in the bladder of a fat lady. I spent the night picking it out, and nothing was said.

There was another — a very pretty and well-educated girl

of French extraction. She eventually married one of my colleagues, and later they moved to San Francisco. It was she who once amusingly parodied Mistral. We had a sick Eskimo in the wards. They all get tuberculosis when they come down here. He was telling us, when we made evening rounds together, that up in Greenland he had eight children. Miss Dubois smiled at me and quoted: —

"Comme les poissons dans la mer,
Malgré le froid, ils font l'amour."

So you see I owe nurses a great deal — and not only medical education. To one, I actually owe my life. She nursed me when I had typhus, and kept me from jumping out of a fourth-story window. I had, and retain, a soft spot in my heart for the whole profession, and I do hope they stay as they are — instead of trying to become half-baked doctors.

At midnight rounds, I always got to know the nurses best, for — in the half-lighted wards, with most of the patients asleep and no bustle and disturbance — we could concentrate on the really sick patients. At night, one's graver and humane qualities seem to expand.

Romance, of course, was not wholly lacking in these relationships, and a number of my friends married into the training school — the courtships carried on under considerable difficulties, since the supervisors, like the wasps they were, had eyes that could look backward. In one case, the entire love story took place on a fire escape in the winter evenings, and the actual engagement, my friend told me, occurred over a sawed-off leg that had been laid there to freeze until a dissection could be made. All through the declaration her eyes were fixed on the leg. In another case, the binding words were spoken in a hot delivery room, while the doctor was holding back the baby's head and the nurse was wiping his face with a towel. Poor things, they've had no baby of their own. On the other hand, I really don't know whether they wanted one after that.

3

Far be it from me to make fun of the Law. I am too much afraid of it. Lawyers, except when met at dinner, give me the same feeling that I have had on an operating table, just before I "went under" and could still see the distorted image of the hooded nurse carrying a clinking basket of knives to the little table next to my ear. When I go to court after driving through a traffic light or having hit someone in the leg or running into another man's car from behind, — for I am apt to be a little absent-minded when driving, — I go with more terror than I have ever felt on truly perilous occasions. Quite recently I was "up" on one of these charges, with the opposing lawyer a little old man who wore a Prince Albert and a high hat, in which he kept papers, like Lincoln. Fortunately, the case was settled in the corridor outside the courtroom. For just looking at him and into his steely, accusing eyes took any capacity for logical thinking clean out of me. Felix Frankfurter and other philosophers of the law don't scare me. It is the practising ones, the ones who get me on what is called "the stand," ask impossible, unanswerable questions, and then turn to the jury — while one is stuttering either in confusion or in indignation — with a sort of "Well, gentlemen, look at this criminal imbecile" kind of expression. My only consolation on such occasions — a sterile one, I confess — is to think: "Would that he could get smallpox or pneumonia and I could see him in consultation." As soon as I am out of the courtroom, with my tail between my legs, I usually think of some clever rejoinders that would have made the jury laugh at *him*. But I have rarely been able to think of the right thing until a little too late under any circumstances. I never get away with this sort of thing with lawyers because I am always too much rattled. And it is not sordid cowardice. I have been in too many tight places to believe that. It is owing to the early experiences I had with law courts while I was a young doctor, was summoned as witness and made a fool of for no fault of my own but for naïvely thinking that all I had to do was to tell the truth. But I soon gave up the expert business. I was not built for it. I either simply told the truth and was made to look like a well-meaning imbecile, or I lost my temper and was made to appear a malicious liar.

In the ordinary ambulance case, the procedure may be illustrated as follows: I had had a two-in-the-morning call to a tenement house on the second floor of which I found a man who had been shot in the chest. He was lying diagonally across a small room lighted by a single gas burner. He was bleeding heavily into his clothes. He also had a scalp wound which bled profusely. My business was to get him to the hospital as fast as possible, after a hasty dressing and stimulation. I got him there alive, and he was immediately taken care of — but he died. The question of murder arose. My cross-examination by the defense followed these lines: —

"How long have you been a doctor? Do you feel competent to handle cases of this kind? How many windows were there in the room? How many people were there? Do you recognize the two persons sitting on the bench as present in the room that night? How far was the deceased's head away from the corner of the bureau? Could his head have hit the bureau and caused the wound in the scalp?" Etc., etc.

Of course, having concentrated on the job in hand, I had no idea of any of these things. The jury thought I was a poor stick. The lawyer said so.

On another occasion — I was already concentrating on problems of immunity — I was sent a piece of cloth from the trousers of a man accused of murder. There was blood on it, and the problem was to determine whether or not it was human blood. The prisoner said he had been duck shooting and that it was duck's blood. Now, this examination is relatively easy. It depends upon the theoretically mysterious, but practically simple principle that if one serially injects human or other kinds of blood serum into rabbits, or other animals, the blood of the injected animal eventually acquires the property of causing visible precipitations of material containing blood from the species used for treatment of the rabbits. In this way, the protein of any species of plant or animal can be determined and detected in enormous dilutions and, if appropriate control experiments are made, with complete accuracy. I did such tests on the blood soaked out of the cloth, and the answer was that the prisoner — against whom there was also plenty of other evidence — had lied. It was beyond any shadow of doubt human blood. There was, however, an irregularity in the test, not significant as far as the species of blood was concerned, but extremely interesting to me because, at that time, I was much occupied with the analogy of such serum reactions to so-called "colloidal" precipitations — that is, the mutual precipitation of substances containing extremely small particles in suspension. If I went into this matter — on which I worked for some time — it would make my story needlessly tedious. At any rate, the trousers from which the cloth was taken were an old pair of those stiff, striped pantaloons that had seen better days in the company of a Prince Albert and a top hat. They were stiffened, as such leg coverings are, with some kind of gum that holds the crease. This gum dissolved with the blood and acted as a "protective" colloid, considerably slowing down my reactions. I was delighted, because it put me on a new trail. But foolishly, when I wrote my report — partly from enthusiasm, partly to be precise — I described my irregularity and wrote a scientific dissertation on probable causes — of course asserting the utter lack of bearing on the accuracy of the determination of human blood.

This was good luck for our criminal. (The jury were mostly prune ranchers from the Santa Clara Valley.) After the district attorney got through with me the defense took me in hand.

"You consider yourself an expert? . . . Gentlemen of the jury, look at this young man closely. He is an expert. Did you carry out this reaction, by which you help in condemning this fellow man, by the methods usual in such cases? Were there any differences in these tests from those ordinarily seen?"

I stuttered out a short lecture on colloidal chemistry to the prune ranchers.

"Well, Mr. Expert, have you ever seen exactly the same kind of irregularities in similar tests? No? Have you ever seen exactly this kind of result — in all particulars, mind you — in carrying out such experiments? No? Gentlemen of the jury, I ask you to listen closely: This 'expert,' gentlemen, is willing to imperil the life of a fellow man on the basis of a test which, by his own evidence, is different from anything he has ever seen before!"

Even the prisoner grinned. He had reason to. He was ac-
quitted largely on my evidence.

I met the lawyer not long afterward at a dinner party. He
gave me a friendly smile. And why not?

In the long run, I suppose the methods of the law make
for the highest average of justice. At least, I am generous
enough to believe so. But queer things will happen.

4

There was a man by the name of König who ran away with
a butcher's wife. One couldn't be very severe on her for running away from a butcher. But her choice of a substitute was
unwise. König, a blond and stocky ruffian, didn't love the
butcher's wife very long, and when he got tired of her —
perhaps she wasn't a very nice woman anyway; she looked as
though she might not have been — he strangled her to death
with a piece of wash line. He must have done it more absent-
mindedly than in anger, because he immediately regretted it
and stabbed himself in the abdomen in two places with a big
bread knife, which I found on the floor beside him.

It didn't take long to make sure that the butcher's wife was
beyond resurrection. I declared her dead and turned her over
to the police. König, however, a tough individual, though
bleeding internally, was conscious and still had a strong pulse.
There was nothing I could do but stop superficial hemorrhage,
put a tight binder on him to discourage abdominal hemorrhage, and rush him to the hospital. It was about six o'clock
in the morning and, fortunately, one of the greatest surgeons
in New York — Dr. Joseph Blake — happened to be in, looking after a private patient. We got König into the operating
room and Blake, with his entire team of expert assistants,

aroused for this extraordinary case, did the kind of job for half of which, in private practice, he would have received several thousand dollars. König had cut off a slice from one of his kidneys; he had severed his small intestine in two places; and he had penetrated the peritoneum just under the pancreas. Dr. Blake took out a piece of intestine and joined the ends. He stopped the bleeding in the kidney, and sewed up the peritoneum. He cleaned up thoroughly, left in drains, gave the patient a large saline infusion, and König was established in one of the small private rooms off the male ward.

We didn't any of us expect him to live, but he did, and convalesced in the hospital for about three months, during which he was constantly guarded by bored policemen, who sat in the hall — costing the City of New York at the rate of twelve hundred dollars a year. After three months, König was fit as a fiddle, and from the quality of his mind I judged ready to murder another butcher's wife. But he was taken to prison, where — for another long period — he was fed and tended by the government. About six months after his discharge from the hospital, he was tried, — also at some expense, — declared guilty, and some months later was electrocuted. I had no sympathy for König, but I remember thinking how dreadful to have wasted all that extraordinary surgery. It was an education in criminal sociology that made a deep impression.

5

Our ambulance district extended from 14th to 86th Street, along the North River, and as far east as Seventh Avenue. It included the old Hell's Kitchen quarter, perhaps one of the most sordid tenement-house districts in the city and, in addition, two separate negro districts, one known as "Buck-Cat Alley," the blocks where the Pennsylvania Station and railroad terminals are now situated; the other, "San Juan Hill," north of 58th Street on the slopes leading down to the Hudson River. In both places, negroes lived piled up on each other — sometimes six or eight in a single, small flat. There were holes through the back fences and between the cellar walls of the houses, so that a negro wishing to escape from the police could go into one house and come out of another a block away.

It is not a fairy tale that the negroes were fond of using razors. These were transformed into weapons by folding them over backwards and holding them blade outward in the palm of the hand. With this, they stroked each other's heads, and the wounds we sewed up sometimes started at the back of the neck and went clean over the top of the head, through the forehead.

They also shot. I once brought a huge, buck negro out of a poolroom, where he had been shot from across the table with a .45 army revolver. He was lying on the floor when I found him, but was in perfectly good condition. He had apparently fallen down either from the shock or because, when one is shot, it is a conventional thing to do. The bullet, by one of those fantastic accidents that happen to bullets, had entered the front of his throat, next to the larynx, and had skidded around under the fascia of the neck. I took it out easily from just under the skin of the back of his head.

The defenses of the neck in this respect are extraordinary, if things don't hit it squarely or with sufficient force. I once had a fencing *épée* enter my own neck in the same way, skid around on the fascia, bounce off the sternomastoid muscle, and come out again, without doing any damage to the large vessels.

Sometimes shooting was done with the old-fashioned pocket pistols of small calibre in such a way that the consequences were more amusing than tragic. A little man in one of the Irish tenement houses one evening shot his excessively fat and belligerent wife with a small .22 pistol. He managed to get in five shots before she fetched him a clap with something — I've forgotten whether it was a skillet or some other household weapon. By the time I got there, the little Irishman was completely laid out with a scalp wound. His wife said she had been shot twice, in both breasts. There were little holes in her enormous bosom, from which fat-globules oozed. I easily located the bullets, quite close under the skin, but when I had managed to remove these and clean out the wounds in the hospital emergency ward, she said she also had a pain in the place where she sat. Apparently, she had stooped over to pick up the weapon with which she laid out her peevish husband, and during that time he had taken another shot. She thought he had kicked her, but here, too, she was well defended and had almost forgotten the episode. She could hardly believe it when I managed to get another bullet out of the padding. It took a lot more trouble to bring her husband back to life.

It was during this time that I also learned that criminals do not like to turn over their personal grudges to the police. There was a saloon on the corner of 45th Street and Broadway which, at that time, was a well-known resort of sporting people — gamblers, race-track followers, and such. Kelly, a policeman whom I knew well, was walking his beat near the saloon one morning at about 4 A.M. when he heard a shot, apparently from the inside of the supposedly closed saloon. He battered at the door of the barroom, was let in by a frightened-looking barkeeper who emerged from the little restaurant next to the barroom, and there found two men and two women, sitting at a table. He thought that he smelled revolver smoke, and as he entered the room he asked: —

"Did anyone shoot a pistol here?"

They all looked at him, innocently. Then, just as he was about to leave, one of the men collapsed, and Kelly telephoned for the ambulance. I brought the man to the hospital. He had been shot, apparently, from under the table, in the lower part of his abdomen, and although promptly operated on, he developed peritonitis. There was very little that could be done for him. His name was Comstock, and he was a wrestler by profession. He had an extraordinary amount of nerve, and since he was under my care, I got to know him well. The other people at the table with him had been arrested, and a revolver was found under the table. There was no question whatever that the man opposite him had shot him, but when the police and a man from the district attorney's office brought his assailant to the hospital and asked Comstock to identify him, Comstock looked at him earnestly and said that he had never seen him before. He insisted on this, and never weakened. He told me afterwards that if he got well he wanted to get this man himself, and if he didn't, his friends would do so for him.

CHAPTER XII

R.S. learns that it takes more than professional knowledge to make a good doctor

R.S., finding that there was no competitive demand for his talents in any of the medical laboratories, established himself, for a time, as a practitioner in New York. He was not a success, though the experience did a great deal to develop his judgment. Yet his heart was never in practice. From the very beginning, he retained a place for work in the laboratories of the College of Physicians and Surgeons, where he was usually to be found when some patient asked for him. When he was telephoned for and conscientiously rushed to his office, he was so obviously annoyed by the interruption that few tried him more than once. That sort of thing doesn't help.

1

For the young physician, there is no more painful experience than the sudden transition from the proud dignity of House Physician or House Surgeon to the desolate situation of young doctor without a practice. Yesterday, he was absolute ruler over two hundred patients. Assistants reported to him, laboratory workers carried out his orders, nurses rose when he entered a ward. There were, in my time, no residents between the Senior Interne and the Consulting Staff, and when the latter had made their daily rounds, the House Physician was the responsible head of an active service. The two happy years over, his last midnight rounds made on the last day of June or December, he woke up the following morning a man without a job.

In my case, I had entered medicine only with the eventual hope of becoming an investigator of infectious disease. But the fascination of practical medicine is a powerful one. Once in a hospital, the feeling of power, the contact with patients, the opportunities to console, to comfort, and — not infrequently — actually to help, make a deep appeal to all that is best in youngsters of that age. Moreover, in those days, laboratory opportunities were rare. The scientific departments of medical schools and hospitals were small, and budgets at a minimum. There was room for a very few only; and even if one obtained entrée to a well-equipped laboratory, the wages for a beginner ranged somewhat lower than those of a scullery maid — from two hundred and fifty to four hundred dollars a year.

True to my early determination, I applied for one of these positions in the Bacteriological Department of my old Medical School, which was presided over by two dignified, but stern gentlemen known to the students — because of their superior aloofness — as "The Jesi." The Jesi received me kindly, and after much questioning and careful scrutiny of my record gave me a job representing a good deal of work but no pay. It included, however, a working place, the use of apparatus, and a free hand to do as I pleased in my spare time. Together with this, I picked up another job, which yielded $400 a year in real money, as Bacteriologist to a hospital where I obtained, in addition, the title of Assistant Pathologist, unlimited pathological material, and the instruction of a man who was unusually erudite and a born teacher. These two jobs might easily have filled my time, but I was ambitious — I think quite properly — of contributing more adequately to my own support. For this reason, as well as because of a growing reluctance to lose all contact with practical medicine, I opened an office in West 80th Street, together with a classmate, K.

K. was a born doctor. He was somewhat older than I was, and appeared much older. He had the not unimportant asset of a blond moustache that looked as though it belonged to his face naturally, and not like the red and downy stage whiskers that were the best my face could bring forth on one or two vacations during which I had abjured the razor, hoping that I might look more like a doctor. K. was the kind of man to whom patients were drawn in admiring and confiding awe. He has amply proved all this since then, in his large practice in a New England city. Thanks to him, our office started with considerable éclat. Older physicians, knowing K.'s qualities, began to send him patients. What little I had to do, at first, was in the form of laboratory examinations. But every now and then, even I picked up a neighborhood emergency or some case that no one else wanted — chronic leg ulcers, delirium tremens, old people without money, and such.

It was dull, keeping office hours. When the doorbell did interrupt my one-handed chess game (I didn't dare to play the piano), it was more often than not a book agent, or someone visiting my wife, or the grocer delivering vegetables. At first, this was exciting. On the sound of the bell, I would put on my coat, straighten my necktie, and seat myself behind my desk with a serious expression. When it really was a patient, I didn't believe it until I had him safely sitting in my office, with the door closed and myself between him and the door.

My great fault, apart from my youthful appearance, was

my excessive thoroughness. Most patients in those days wanted immediate directions and a prescription, after a bit of conversation. A physical examination they didn't mind if they felt very sick. But I never let it go at that.

The great Dr. J. had once said to me, after rounds on the private corridor: "My boy, you seem to know your stuff; but you'll never make a good doctor unless you pay a little more attention to the psychology of your patients. Now, that last woman is a damn fool. There's nothing much the matter with her, but she wants to be taken seriously. All patients, especially women, expect the doctor to act as though they were really sick — but bearing up bravely. Never act as though you took them lightly, and never seem in a hurry. Whatever else you may not do, never fail to sit down in the sick room as though all your time were for this particular case. Pat the hand, and say 'Brave little woman,' or something like that. Act thoughtful; and if you don't know what to say, say nothing; but say nothing deliberately and slowly, with an air of withholding a great deal. Then give them a good overhauling, with a lot of laboratory examinations."

This might have worked with the Fifth Avenue practice that crowded Dr. J.'s office. It is also possible that I overdid it. Anyway, I lost the few good patients that were referred to me, by just this technique.

First, I sat them down and looked at them penetratingly. Then, pad in hand, I began to ask them questions. The patient might be bursting to tell me about a pain in his foot. "Just a minute, just a minute! We'll get to that presently," I'd say. Then, still fixing him with an accusing eye, I'd begin to ask questions. "Taking the history," we called it.

"How old are you? What is your occupation? Were your parents healthy? Is there any tuberculosis in your family?

What did your father die of? And your mother? How old were they when they died? Have you any brothers or sisters? Are they healthy? Have you had any children? Are they healthy? Have you ever had any venereal disease? What! Are you sure? Do you drink? How much? Do you sleep well? How is your appetite? Do you sweat at night?"

By this time, many of them showed signs of fatigue or indignation. Some of them asked for a drink of water. But I gazed at them with disapproving severity, and began on their childhood.

"What diseases did you have as a child? Were you precocious? Did you ever notice any swollen glands in the neck? Were you premature? Did you ever have a rash on your skin? Do your bowels move regularly? Do you have to take medicine for it? What do you take? Do you suffer from colds? Do you cough in the morning? Do you bring up anything when you cough? Do you have to get up at night?"

All the time, I was taking notes. If any of the answers were unfavorable, I would appear to prick up my ears — the patient could see it in my face. Some began to look anxious. One got up and left at this point, the best prospect I had — she had driven up in a victoria. Old Dr. "Monkey" Jackson had told her I was a very thorough youngster. She believed it, but didn't like it in practice.

Those that lasted that long I would then proceed to examine. First, down the throat with a light and a hand mirror. The tongue was pushed down. "Say Eeeeh!" [1] They gagged. Then into the ears with a speculum. Then up the nose, ditto.

---

[1] The force of habit is powerful. A friend of mine, a throat specialist, was called upon to make a rectal examination in a case of lues of the larynx. He exclaimed, "Say Eeeeh!" while gazing at the wrong aperture, and lost a wealthy patient who thought him flippant.

And the ophthalmoscope! I was proud of that. It had cost twenty-five dollars, and I could see the eye grounds with it. It might disclose bad kidneys, or diabetes. Then, "Will you undress, please?" The heart — thump, thump! I outlined it with a blue pencil. The stethoscope. No murmurs. The lungs. "Say one, two, three. Again! Whisper ninety-nine, ninety-nine. Well, fine! That's all right."

"But, doctor — "

"Lie on this couch, please. Pull up your knees." I percussed the liver. I pushed for the spleen. I palpated the gall bladder, and McBurney's point, and the ovaries. "Does that hurt?"

"You push so hard, doctor."

"You can dress now. But first, step behind that screen and let me have a specimen of the urine."

Meanwhile, I'd be getting my things ready to take blood. A drop from the ear, for cell counts and a differential. A syringe, for the vein. I had just learned to do the Wassermann reaction. It was great fun, and I was proud of it. Every case must have a Wassermann done. No one tells the truth about such things.

Few lasted through. Those few got their money's worth — largely, perhaps, because they never paid my modest bills. Most of them walked out at one stage or another, because we didn't get down to the sore foot. Some even slammed the door as they walked out.

This was unquestionably the wrong technique, certainly for a young practitioner. K. was wiser. He allowed the patient to unburden himself, asked a few pertinent questions, examined as far as necessary, and prescribed.

Some years later, in a very busy office in a provincial town, a colleague showed me a large bottle into which all the left-over remains of dispensed mixtures were spilled together. In that town, twenty years ago, the doctors still dispensed their own medicines. The big bottle was marked "Bill Kelly," after a patient who was an insatiable medicine tippler. When anyone who had nothing obvious the matter with him, but had a lot of symptoms to show for it, came in, he was given a four-ounce bottle filled from "Bill Kelly," to take a teaspoonful three times a day, after meals. It tasted atrociously and, of course, was different every day. But it cured a lot of cases.

Apropos of medicine tippling, the elevator boy in my apartment, who also cleaned out the wastepaper baskets, used to take all the medicine that came to me from drug houses as samples. I found on one occasion that he had swallowed a quart of a preparation that was recommended for irregular menstrual periods. He said it made him feel fine.

We "fired" a negro cook at this time who left behind such a dirty kitchen that, being still young and helpful, I decided to clean it out myself. In a closet I found a whole case of empty bottles labeled: "Stimulates the reproductive organs and prevents tumors." I never found out for which of these effects she was dosing herself. It smelled like bad whiskey. Thus have some of our largest American fortunes been acquired.

The old practitioner adapts his method to the situation, with psychological insight. Dr. J., who gave me all that advice about making a big fuss over every patient, did not follow this out with all of them by any means. His assistant, who occasionally sent me a case, told me of an old lady who had come to Dr. J. faithfully, twice a year, for twenty years or more. When admitted to the inner sanctum, she never gave the doctor a chance to say even "How do you do?" She burst into the room with a "Now, doctor — don't move. I don't want you to examine me. Don't ask me any questions. Just write me a prescription for that brown tonic you gave me last year." She always got it, paid her money, and went out satisfied. Another, a younger woman who adored Dr. J., — as most of them did, — he dismissed one day, after a short conversation and a look at her tongue, saying: "Don't worry, my dear. You'll be all right. Just keep your bowels open and always wear mauve."

I might, of course, have learned this sort of thing if I had stuck at it long enough. But in the two years that I was a private practitioner I never got over the fear that if I didn't go into every possibility I might be overlooking some hidden danger that hung over my patient's unsuspecting head. And often the patient, who may have come in for the simplest kind of advice, sensed my own nervousness and rushed off to another physician for just the kind of overhauling I was about to give him.

Nevertheless, my method was professionally correct — if I had only been more adroit about it. It certainly saved me from the kind of thing that happened to a friend of mine who leaned rather too much toward "snap diagnosis." A middle-aged man, a coachman, came to see him one day, complaining of a stiffness and soreness in the throat. My friend looked into his mouth, saw a little redness, and prescribed a gargle. The next day, the man was back. His throat was still sore, and much more stiff on swallowing. Again the look in, a painting of the throat with iodine in glycerine, and a reassuring pat on the back. Two days went by, and back came the coachman. This time, he said he had difficulty in opening his mouth for examination. "You know, doctor," he said, "if you didn't say I was all right, I'd think I might have lockjaw." "Good God, man!" cried my friend in consternation. "Why didn't you tell me that in the first place?"

2

I had had, as I have elsewhere recorded, a not inconsiderable experience in acting as master of ceremonies at the "coming-out parties," one may call them, of unfortunate infants into a world that had little to offer them except squalor, hardship, and defeat. Of course I thought occasionally of Benjamin Franklin's often quoted remark when he answered: "What good is a newborn baby?" to a Philistine who questioned the value of an apparently useless scientific observation. But I thought progressively less of the wisdom of this rejoinder as I learned to forecast the futures of these babies by increasing familiarity with their elders, born under the same handicaps of heredity and environment. It started me on my way to becoming a confirmed advocate of birth control. And I never hear of the birth of a child among my acquaintances that I don't wonder, in each case, whether the parents have performed a useful service or committed an act of criminal negligence. When one reads Malthus — whom far too few read — one learns that unobstructed nature attempts automatically to regulate the numbers of its living creatures in various ways. And when man takes charge of the breeding of domestic animals, he proceeds, if not always scientifically, at least with the planned wisdom of the husbandman, adjusting numbers and improving breeds for specified purposes. Only for his own species he leaves the most important biological responsibility, over which he might have control, to blind instinct and accident. I have often been struck by this contrast between man's wisdom with animals and lack of it with his own species at hunt meets, where one sees underbred people sitting on the noblest horses. Sensible attention to these matters in their own families is rare. One of the few cases I can recall is that cited by Malthus, who says that "the ancient family of Bickerstaff . . . are said to have been very successful in whitening the skins and increasing the height of their race by prudent marriages, particularly by that very judicious cross with Maud, the milk-maid. . . ." It would be interesting to suggest to sociologists and anthropologists, who are always looking about for some fulcrum on which to brace their statistical crowbars, that they investigate this matter. It is fair betting that they would find the highest physical and possibly intellectual averages among families that could show a relatively recent bastard or two in the family tree.

There is really no valid argument against birth control. The encouragement of mass propagation in dictator countries is too admittedly based on the most barbaric and militaristic motives. The objections of the Church, though often laid to abhorrence of "unnaturalness," are really on a much higher moral plane, but so illogical for the modern world that even the Catholic Church is beginning to weaken by acceptance of adjustments of intercourse to the oestrogenic cycle and the "safe" period between menstruations. Some of the best work on this problem is, as a consequence, being done by Catholic physicians. As to the purely "moral" arguments, no intelligent person, nowadays, advances them without his tongue in his cheek. There is no historical evidence that, after two thousand years of Christianity, the fornication index of populations has materially declined under that of ancient Greece. And when Martin Luther laid down the rule, "*Zweimal die*

Woche macht Hundert und vier," he was encouraging human frailty in a manner that surely defeats in principle the only completely moral form of birth control which the Church is said to sanction.

As far as comparative morality is concerned, what can be more immoral than to put children into the world that are unwanted, that cannot be properly nourished, cared for, educated, and otherwise inducted into life with a reasonable expectation of happiness and usefulness? What can be more immoral than to give a woman the grim choice of being physically destroyed and deprived of strength and leisure for anything but the animal functions she shares with the cow and the cat, or living an asexual life that either produces the bitter, frustrated spinster or sends her well-to-do sisters to a psychiatrist?

Not even the argument that the free dissemination of birth-control information would tend to lower the selective propagation of the better genetic material in favor of the worst has any scientific justification. The human race is so "crossbred" that eugenic experiment is bound to fail. In animal breeding, we can ruthlessly eliminate all but the perfect sires and dams and can breed for particular characteristics — such as long ears in dogs, speed in horses, or milk production in cattle. In man, with his forty-eight chromosomes, each with its mosaic of genes, the problem is far too complex for practical application, unless we could keep a selected group of couples in corrals and inbreed them, during a century or so, for some special characteristic like tallness, long-nosiness, cupidity, or bad temper. Those who advocate eugenics have limited themselves, quite wisely, to the negative idea of elimination by breeding away objectionable or abnormal characteristics. Mohr, who is very learned in these matters, refutes even this prospect (the hope of the sterilizers, one of whom — Lenz — he quotes as making even *ausgesprochene Hässlichkeit* a cause for gelding) by quoting an example based on the calculations of Hogben. Albinism, lack of pigmentation of the skin, is a recessive anomaly that has an incidence of less than 0.01 per cent. In this case, the heterozygous offspring carry the characteristics. By this is meant that even those who appear normal may contain the latent albinic "recessive gene" and transmit it. Thus, as Hogben figures, if all the obvious albinos were sterilized "in every generation, it would require a period about equivalent to the Christian era to reduce its incidence to one half the present dimensions." And that holds good for all recessive characteristics. The best we can do is to continue the study of human genetics, and discourage the marriage of individuals with recognized dominant defects as these are revealed as "dominant" by statistical study of observed cases.

The dominant nature of defects in man can be determined only by the observed results of accidental matings. Among these, Mohr has studied cases in which the woolly, crinkly hair type was dominant over the soft, straight hair. In one Nordic strain, he observed this through five generations. In one of these a heterozygous woolly and short-haired woman, mated with a soft-haired husband, gave birth to three woolly and three soft-haired children. Another instance of a dominant human characteristic, cited by him, is a family afflicted with hereditary short-fingeredness, traced back six generations to a Norwegian woman whose "every second child had — like herself — a shortened or curved forefinger, with one joint only." Genetics may eventually give a rational basis for mating. But even then it will meet the ancient obstacle, — long encountered by the proponents of reason in mating, — the heavenly madness, love.

The natural checks of population, to the study of which Malthus devotes his first two books, "result principally," he concludes, "from an insufficiency of subsistence." The age of chemical and physical discovery which developed industry and agriculture to a degree unpredictable in the eighteenth century has neutralized these natural "checks" so that for a century they have given a negligible slope to the rapidly rising curve of production. In consequence, as Professor East — among others — has shown, the population of the world has increased, during these hundred years, by an increment never before attained. Now again a point has been reached at which the two forces are more equal and the curve flattens. And such flattening, if maintained, seems our only hope for the eventual subsidence of international rivalry, nationalism, and war. It is interesting to contemplate whether we may now hope to pass into an era in which biological discovery may take a hand in the situation and correctively modify the purely material and industrial civilization of the last generations. Let us consider the stupendous consequences which might result for world economy if we could precisely establish a non-fertile period in the monthly cycles of women, a principle of birth control now accepted as permissible by the Catholic Church and at the disposal, without expense or appliances, to all women. My experience of women, even the poor things in the slums, is such that I do not question for a moment that such knowledge would automatically limit a large percentage of families to the number of children that could be properly taken care of — even if dictators ranted and the men in general cared nothing about it. The spirit of Lysistrata is more alive to-day than most men suspect.

3

However, all this has led us far afield from my own practice. I had, as I said, done my reluctant duty as an accoucheur with a considerable number of ambulance and hospital babies, and felt that I had mastered at least the first principle, the Fabian strategy of "watch and wait," with reasonable skill in the rudiments of manipulation. There is quite a difference, psychologically at any rate, — which the institutionalized doctor will never understand, — between that sort of thing and handling one's first private case.

Obstetrics is not the pleasantest of medical occupations, although it pays well and is one of the things that the young physician with any kind of practice can count on as a financial backlog. Yet it takes a great deal of time and means a lot of night work. While the statement may not be statistically correct, it does seem to the medical man as though the large majority of all babies were born at night. An observant medical student in my class once asked one of our instructors about this. "Dr. V., why is it that most children are born at night?" Dr. V., who was something of a wag, replied: "Well, my boy, that's simple. It takes just nine months."

Helping babies into the world was becoming more and more of a specialty at the time that I started to practise, and most physicians, after they had attained the financial security in which they could begin to pick and choose, referred their obstetrical cases either to a specialist or, if among the poorer classes, to a young colleague who needed the money. Some of them gave up obstetrics purely for reasons of convenience. Old

Dr. T., famous as one of the last physicians in New York, who made his reputation largely by giving his patients the most extraordinary doses of assorted drugs, once told me why he gave up obstetrics as a young practitioner.

"When I was a young man," he said, "I took everything that came along, just as you will, and I got quite a reputation, among other things, for my skill as an accoucheur; but I gave it up because it didn't pay. Let me tell you about my last case. I was up all night with a primipara, and things went very slowly. The baby finally came along about nine o'clock the next morning, and when I got things tidied up I went home. I had just had my place redecorated, because I was going to get married: new plaster, wallpaper, and a complete set of furniture downstairs. All this had cost me my savings. I went upstairs to run a bath, and when I had turned on the water I stretched out on the sofa until the tub should fill up. The next thing I knew was a crash. The bath water had run over. The water leaked through the ceiling, the ceiling came down, water splashed the walls — and the place was a mess. It cost me ten times as much as I collected. From that moment, I never took another obstetric case, and if I ever get any referred to me — which is now unlikely — I will send them to you."

My own first obstetrical case, however, did not come through Dr. T. It was sent me by a humbler colleague who was still himself taking all the obstetrics that came to him with money. Those who had little or nothing and wouldn't go to a hospital, he referred "for experience," as he called it, to beginners like myself. This one lived in a two-family frame house in East 173rd Street. My office was in 80th Street on the West Side. There were no automobiles — and if there had been, I

could not have afforded one. To make my visits, I had to take
the streetcar from 80th Street to 59th Street, another one
across to the Third Avenue Elevated Railroad and proceed
on this to 166th Street, whence I walked north and west fifteen minutes up a steep hill. I mention these details because
the case, a "first delivery," was very nervous, although not
more so than I was myself. In consequence, there were a
great many false alarms during the two weeks preceding the
actual event. Every time there was the slightest twinge, the
grandfather was sent out to the neighboring drugstore to
call me on the telephone. His usual formula was, "I don't think
it's anything, but maybe you'd better come up." I made three
round trips within twenty-four hours a week before the child
was born. The unusual thing about the case was that both
father and mother were deaf and dumb. They spoke to each
other with their hands, making weird sea-lion noises, and it
was only from the expressions on their faces that I could
gather that I seemed far too young, that they didn't think
much of me anyway, but that they couldn't afford anything
better. When there was finally no doubt that things were
beginning to happen, they were very much frightened; and the
gesticulations and the noises of animal panic added to my
tension. During the last forty-eight hours, I canceled all other
engagements and lived there, snatching an occasional nap on
a horsehair sofa that seemed stuffed with steel wire and had
leaked. In the early stages, when pains were not too frequent,
I soothed my disturbed nerves by walking around the block,
accompanied by the grandfather. He — good man — was much
sorrier for me than he was for his daughter, and consoled me
by saying: "Now, doctor, don't worry. Everything's going to
come out all right. There've been lots of babies in our family,

and nothing ever happened." Towards the end, I felt that the final stage was lasting much too long. I prepared a forceps by boiling it on the kitchen stove, and then went out to telephone to K. to come up and help me. He was out. It took five or six telephone calls in various directions to locate him. When I finally got back to the house, I was met in the hall by the beaming grandfather, who said: "Hurrah, doctor! It's a fine big boy! He was born about five minutes after you left."

When I made up my books, such as they were, I found that I had averaged about twenty-three cents a call on this case. Each trip back and forth cost me thirty cents in carfare.

At about this time I was making periodical visits to a well-known hospital for the mentally diseased in order to pick up what I might about advances in psychiatric practice. It seemed to me that were I destined, by lack of opportunity in my chosen field, to continue for some years in private practice, it was essential that I learn more about the manifestations of mental derangement in my fellow beings. For though I had not yet met Dr. Thomas Salmon, who later called attention to the importance of the study of the so-called "border-line" cases, I was already impressed by the large number of people in my personal and professional acquaintance who appeared to me — at least — quite unable either to think clearly or to hold their emotional impulses within the pendulum swings of average excursions. At the hospital, under the guidance of my friend the director, I saw a great many instructive cases, but was particularly interested in those who differed only in degree — and then only moderately — from a number of people whom I prized as friends, largely, perhaps, because of the deviations from the norm which they represented. Most especially was I impressed by a few of those patients whose insanities took the forms of ambitions and desires which in our society are regarded as highly praiseworthy if based on factual circumstances instead of imagined ones. There was one group who have stuck in my mind, since between them they enacted a satire on the civilization of our times which could not have been more effectively staged by Swift or Voltaire.

There happened to be in the hospital, admitted within a few months of each other, three patients of well-to-do families who, before admission, had been engaged respectively in the law, in the wholesale fruit business, and in shipping. The lawyer had delusions of persecution, which, however, had not affected his professional memory or technical knowledge. The merchant had the delusion that he owned all the dried apples in the world. The shipper thought, quite without justification in fact, that he had cornered all the world's steamship lines and was in practical control of the globe's entire merchant marine.

A clever young interne had considered these cases and, since there seemed no hope of permanent cure for any of the three, concluded that the poor fellows should be at least made as happy as possible. Accordingly, since all three of his patients were well off and their families quite willing to spare no expense, he brought the three together, furnished an office for them, and encouraged them to do business. A highly satisfactory arrangement resulted.

The fruit man kept books on enormous stocks, shipments, and sales of dried apples. The shipper agreed to carry these apples to all corners of the earth on his fleets; and the lawyer was kept busy drawing up contracts between them and attending to disputes that naturally arose in the course of this gigantic commerce. I found them, on numerous visits, exceedingly busy with accumulating files of transactions and records of great profits which made them all happy and complacent. They always received me with the ill-concealed impatience of men too busy with important affairs to have much time for idle conversation, but were never unwilling to explain the world-wide expansion of the dried-apple business, especially when I consulted them about the possibility of opening some new market for this commodity in territories like Abyssinia or French Indo-China.

Soon after one of these visits to the hospital I attended a dinner at which there were present several bankers, a very wealthy manufacturer of buttons, and a corporation lawyer. They made the usual kind of speeches and when the button manufacturer, who came last, was almost at the end of his discourse, I had the misfortune to think of my three crazy men and was taken with such an uncontrollable impulse to explode into laughter that — to save my dignity — I had to make a quick exit. These men were spending this one short life vouchsafed them by Providence in exactly the same way as my three friends in the asylum. The only difference between them and my patients was that the latter seemed to enjoy their occupations, while these princes of finance were worried and anxious.

4

One of the most beloved and distinguished figures in the New York medical profession at this time was Abraham Jacobi. He was one of the first great children's specialists in this country, and was honored by the German-American community of the city not only for this but because of his record as a courageous revolutionist who was said to have had a hand in the escape of Carl Schurz from a Prussian prison. He was a very small man with an enormous bearded head and was sometimes spoken of as "The Jewish Jupiter." Even in the later days of his practice, when all the medical honors at the disposal of his colleagues had been heaped upon him, he maintained free office hours for the poor. In our family he was regarded as a sort of benign deity who took care of the children and remained their friend as they grew up. I owed him not only early physical care but many acts of kindness, especially during the time when he was visiting physician to the children's service in a large hospital in which I was the interne in charge of his ward. One of his most engaging qualities was a quaint sense of humor. He was so kind that people often imposed on him, stopped him on the street and asked him for advice. Naturally he got tired of this, and in this connection the following story is told of him: —

On one occasion a man whom he knew only slightly accosted him on the street and said: "Dr. Jacobi, I know you are busy, but I, too, am a very busy man. I've a little sore throat this morning, and wonder whether you would take a quick look at it to see if there is anything I ought to do about it. Maybe you will look at me right here on the street." Dr. Jacobi smiled at him and said: "All right. Come over and lean against this lamppost. Now stoop, open your mouth, close your eyes, and stick out your tongue." Then he walked away, and when he reached home said: "I guess the damn fool is standing there yet."

5

Early in my medical career I developed a deep and lasting admiration for the old-fashioned, self-reliant country practitioner, the "horse and buggy doctor" so sympathetically de-scribed in the recent book by Dr. Hertzler. While a medical student in New York, I was accustomed to recuperate from strenuous days and nights under a lamp by spending occa-sional week ends on my father's farm in Westchester County. I slept in a cold house, with a wood stove in my bedroom, stoked till the lid glowed red, with my collie dog keeping my feet warm. All day and into the night I would ride the horses — each one in turn — across country over the snow-covered hills. Those were unforgettably lovely vacations. The utter loneliness of the big house (the farmer lived at the other end of a beech wood), the nights silent except for the cracking of the frozen branches of the big trees in the wind, the brittleness of the air and the incandescent brilliance of the stars! And the rides! Physical fitness that could spend itself on three successive unexercised horses, and the spiritual peace that only a good horse or a small boat at sea can give — the white landscape, woods and fields crisp, cold, and lifeless except for the silent testimony of tracks in the snow, an occasional squir-rel and, once in a while, a flock of crows angrily clamoring away from a leafless perch. I knew all the paths and openings and the hidden spots in the birch woods where, in the sum-mers, I hunted birds; where the foxes went to earth; and where, among the big rocks on Piano Mountain, one could get a glimpse of the Hudson. I still remember those rides as among the happiest gifts of a Providence that has been munificent. Often, galloping through the fields and across the hills be-tween snowbound villages, I would see far off on the valley roads the familiar "cutter" sleighs of our local doctors — Jenkins and Hart — answering calls that often meant hours of driving and small fees, irrespective of roads or weather, with an unfailing and expected fidelity not demanded of the rural delivery. Sometimes I would meet one of them, whiskers frosted, nose red and dripping, with not much more showing than these between the fur cap and the muffler. Always they stopped for a chat, to tell me about the case and exchange medical gossip — for they treated me as a professional equal who was getting things they wished they had time to catch up with. For their difficulties made them modest; whereas I, with the arrogance of a young and silly student (arrogance, being a state of mind, I have noticed is always intensified by sitting a horse), was just a trace patronizing. I lost all that as a matter of course when I tried to practise by myself. But a good deal of it was jarred out of me by the episode of Dr. Kerr.

Dr. Kerr is now dead. He is probably forgotten by all but a few old farmers' wives. He had neither fame nor more than a frugal living. He was probably unhappy, while he lived, not for the reasons mentioned, but because he never could do for his people as much as he wanted to do. He practised in St. Lawrence County, near Chippewa Bay. His office was a little surgery extension of a small village house. He was tall, thin, and very dark, with hairy wrists, a big nose, a bushy moustache, and kind, tired brown eyes. I was camping on my island in the bay and was known to the grocer in the village as a young doctor from New York. One day at about 4 A.M. a motorboat approaching my island aroused me and the grocer's son shouted through the fog and drizzle that Dr. Kerr needed my help in a difficult case. He landed while I dressed, and we were off four miles to the village. There Dr. Kerr was waiting for me with his buggy. I had never seen him before and he impressed me, in my young self-confidence, as probably a poor country bonesetter whom I would have to show how a case should be handled. This, however, lasted only until we were bumping along a muddy country lane and he had begun to tell me about the patient.

It was a woman, a farm hand's wife, who was having her first baby. She had developed eclampsia seven months along, and the child had died. She was having convulsions. The problem was to deliver the dead baby from a uterus with an undistended cervix, and the mother dangerously toxic. At this point, I was thoroughly scared. I had had training at the Sloane Maternity, but this was a "high forceps" under difficulties, a case for Professor Cragin in a well-equipped operating room, with an assistant and two or three nurses.

We drove about four miles into the river flats. I could see the little unpainted cottage next to a haystack a mile away. I offered no suggestion while I was trying to recover my old ambulance courage. He didn't ask me any questions.

The place was a picture of abject poverty. The husband, a pathetic little bandy-legged, redheaded fellow in torn overalls, was waiting at the door, anxious and silent. The kitchen was a mess from his efforts at housekeeping. In the next room the woman, half-conscious, her bloated face twitching, lay on a dirty double bed, on a mattress without sheets under an old quilt half kicked off, leaving her almost naked.

While I stood looking at her with frightened sympathy, Dr. Kerr unpacked his bag. Without asking me to do anything, he filled a wash boiler with hot water from a kettle, added a little lysol, and put on his forceps to boil. Then he took off his coat, rolled up his sleeves, filled a basin, and began to soap and lysol his hands. Not until he was doing this did he speak.

Then he began to give me directions. In a few minutes I

was cleaning up the patient, spreading clean towels under her, preparing a chloroform cone and jumping at his words as though in Dr. Cragin's clinic. With no essential help from me, he performed as neat a cervix dilation and forceps delivery as I had ever seen. When, after the long and arduous task, with everything complete as possible, he began to clean up, he didn't even thank me. He took it for granted that, being a doctor and being in the neighborhood, I was on call. It was his only compliment, except for a friendly smile.

He asked me to stay there the rest of the day while he made his rounds, gave me a few directions, and left a sedative. Then he went out, patted the husband on the back, and drove away. The woman recovered. Dr. Kerr, I heard later, spent the first two nights after this on a rocking chair, drinking cider with the husband, and napping when he could. His fee, I also heard, accepted to please the husband, was a peck of potatoes.

Some time later, I had occasion to ask him to open a boil on my neck. He sat me down in a chair, wiped my neck with alcohol, took a knife out of a little leather case, wiped that with alcohol, and let me have it. I made no suggestion whatever. I saw him often after that, and I sincerely hope — even now — that he liked me.

One of Dr. Kerr's colleagues from up near Ogdensburg, whom I had met at this time, did a most extraordinary thing. I met him on the river one day when we were both fishing off the head of Watch Island. Just as I came in sight of him as I rounded the point, he pulled out a magnificent pickerel.

"Good for you, doctor!" I shouted to him.

"What d'ye think, young feller?" he called back. "I caught that fish with a nice fat appendix I took out this mornin'."

6

Speaking of Dr. T. reminds me of a case in which I was credited with saving a life under peculiar circumstances. While still House Physician at the hospital, during Dr. T.'s visiting period, we had a poor fellow on the male ward who appeared to suffer from advanced nephritis. Dr. T., as I have remarked, was a virtuoso at compounding drugs. During his short annual reign of three months, the order sheets of every patient were covered with the red ink in which medication orders were entered. They got something or other "t.i.d." (three times a day), other things with meals, something else on waking up, another before the lights went out, and a few odd pills or injections "p.r.n." (pro re nata). Many of them had to be waked out of sound sleep to get one of his "black draughts" or "blue pills" or "brown decoctions" — all of them proudly originated by the Chief himself, and most of them quite complicated, with strong medicaments. The particular old boy of whom I write was getting a formidable sequence of daily doses and was slipping out of our hands — taking it patiently, with good humor and courage. We all liked him, and during his month on the ward he became a favorite. One night, when he was pretty low, I was making my midnight rounds with the ward nurse. We stopped at his bed and held a whispered conversation. He was in bad condition, the nurse said, and she didn't think he'd last long. She hated to force all that medicine down his throat. It bothered him and didn't seem to be doing him any good.

"All right," I said. "He's going to die soon anyway, and we'll stop all medication. Just leave the orders on the chart, and we'll steer the old boy around him as well as we can. Give him anything he wants to eat, within reason, and a shot of my Scotch when you come on at night. I'll bring you a bottle. He might as well die happy."

From that moment, our friend began to improve. Pretty soon, by respectful and adroit suggestion, I arranged to have official sanction for the omission of one pill and "draught" after another. In two weeks our patient began to sit up in bed for extraordinarily hearty meals. In three weeks he was up — his old self, he said. In four, he was out and I forgot about him.

The sequel came one Sunday afternoon during the following winter, when I was sitting in my office. The doorbell rang, and in walked a short, fat, ruddy man of about sixty, behind him a shorter, fatter, and ruddier boy of twenty or so. Neither of them did I recognize. Yet the older man stuck out his ham of a hand and said: "God bless you, doctor, how are you?" Then I suddenly remembered him. "I hope you're not sick again," I said.

"Oh, no, doctor! I'm fine. I just brought in my son" (who, apparently in the horse business, was embarrassedly rolling a flat-topped derby in one hand while he kept adjusting a white piqué tie with a horseshoe pin) "to show him the man who saved my life. You remember, doctor, that night in the hospital when I was nigh dead? You came around about midnight with the nurse. I was feelin' awful low, an' everybody thought I was goin' to die. I was thinkin' so my own self. You thought I was sleepin', but I wasn't. I was just pretendin'. You had a long talk with the nurse in front of my bed an' then you give her some orders. From that minute, I begun to mend.

"This is the man, my boy, as pulled your Pa out of the claws of the Reaper," he said poetically.

7

I was at that time beginning to become deeply interested in that disease which is called by a venerable French writer "*une punition divinement envoyée aux hommes et aux femmes pour leur paillardises et incontinences désordonnées*"; by Sytz of Pforzheim, on the other hand, "*die bösen Franzosen*"; and by Goethe, with his prophetic vision, — considering the worm-like appearance of the *Treponema pallidum*, — "*der Wurm in der Liebe.*" I was to spend a number of subsequent years on this malady, in an effort to gain insight into the properties of the strange microorganism which the great Schaudinn had discovered. For the time being, I was engaged in introducing the so-called "Wassermann reaction" into the laboratory practice of St. Luke's Hospital. This reaction, in its original form, was based on a principle too technical for these pages, established by the Belgian bacteriologist, Bordet, and taught to me, out of the kindness of his heart, by my friend Noguchi, in whose room at the Rockefeller Institute I sat for hours to pick up what I could. According to the old technique, one of the reagents required for this reaction was tissue from heavily infected syphilitic organs. And the most heavily infected organs known to medicine are those of stillborn, syphilitic babies.

Accordingly, I had a standing order at the Sloane Maternity Hospital that syphilitic babies were to be kept for me. And whenever one of these coveted treasures appeared, it was put into a large paper bag on which my name was written, and I was notified by telephone. I would then stop at the hospital on my afternoon journey to St. Luke's, tuck my prize under my arm, and proceed.

On the occasion of which I write, I received the happy news that "one of your babies," as the facetious head nurse called them, was ready for me. I was just about to leave my laboratory for a luncheon meeting of the newly formed Society for Cancer Research, which was to take place at a downtown hotel. It was only natural, therefore, since I was due at the hospital after this meeting, that I should stop to pick up my baby and take it to the meeting with me.

The society was not a large one. At the hotel, therefore, a convenient bedroom had been assigned for hats and coats. Arriving late, I shoved my paper bag under the bed, laid hat and coat on top of the bed, and went to my place at the table. It was not a very thrilling meeting. There were hardly any ideas, and those there were were neither new nor very intelligent. But I was very young, and proud of being present; and I listened to every word spoken by my elders with hopeful attention. One or two of the speeches were needlessly long. And when the meeting broke up I found that I was at least an hour behind my usual schedule. I rushed to the improvised cloakroom, picked up my hat and coat, and ran out to the subway. I had an incubatorful of work waiting for me, an autopsy to perform, and cultures to examine. Toward the end of the afternoon, an interesting case turned up on one of the wards, and I was asked to make several examinations, including a blood culture. It was not until 8 P.M. that I got home to a late supper, and not until 8.15 that suddenly, gazing into my soup, I exclaimed, "Good God — the baby!" When I remembered that my name was plainly written on the bag, I began to sweat. My appetite left me. It was not easy to decide what to do. I still remember to this day the number of the room. It was 217. I couldn't very well call up the clerk and say:

"Look here — I forgot a dead baby under the bed of 217. Take care of it for me." If I went down there, what could I say? On the other hand, I couldn't very well leave the baby where it was, if only for aesthetic reasons. Yet if my name — good God! — had not been on the bag, this is what — in the state I was in — I might have done. It would have made a first-rate police mystery, and in the end, with sufficient publicity, might even have proved amusing. However, my name was on the bag. By this time it was 8.30.

I got into a cab and went down to the hotel. It needed all the little courage I had left to address the room clerk. I tried to be what is called nonchalant.

"I wonder whether you could let me go up to room 217," I said to the young man at the desk. "I was at the cancer meeting to-day, and I left something behind when I took my hat and coat out of that room."

The clerk, I thought, didn't seem to like my looks. Perhaps it was just my nervousness. He said that if anything had been left behind, it would have been reported by the chambermaid who had cleaned up. What was it I'd forgotten, anyway? "A package," I called it.

"Hey, Miss White," he called over his shoulder. "Was a package reported left in 217 this afternoon?"

Miss White, who sat behind a glass partition, fumbled about in a pigeonhole, read three or four paper slips, and said: "No. Nothing reported to me."

Could I see the chambermaid? It was a very important package.

"She went off duty at seven. Back in the morning."

Could I go up and have a look around the room?

"The room's been taken."

Could I ask the people now in it to let me look around?

He guessed "they went out to the theatre. Young couple from Milwaukee."

I had not stopped sweating, but now I sweated harder. The clerk looked at me suspiciously, I thought. "May I ask who you are?"

I told him. I looked pretty young for a doctor. Obviously, he didn't believe me.

"Do you mind if I call up the room and see if they're in?" Reluctantly, he consented. Their name was Richards.

"Hello, is this Mr. Richards?" I asked.

"What do you want?" answered an excited voice.

Here I made another mistake. I should have explained what I wanted; but all I could think of was to get into that room.

"May I come up to see you a minute?"

I heard a whispered conversation, — "Ask him who it is," — then: —

"Who are you?"

"You don't know me." I said the wrong thing again. "I just want to see you a minute." He hung up abruptly.

"He told me to come up," I reported to the clerk, and went right up. I didn't bother about the elevator, and I went three steps at a time. I knocked at the door of 217.

"Who's there?"

"It's the man who called you on the telephone."

"What do you want?"

The door was opened a crack and I saw the pale face of a frightened man with a chin beard. I shoved my foot against the crack. He pushed, but couldn't close the door.

"Better let him in, Frank. We can prove we're innocent," I heard in a woman's voice.

We stared at each other through the crack. "Stop pushing," said the man. "Don't resist him, Frank" — the woman's voice. Frank weakened. The door opened, and I slipped in.

On the bed sat a stout woman in a kimono. She was quite handsome, I noticed later, but now there were signs of recent tears and her hair was in disorder. She stared at me. At her feet on the floor was my bag. She looked at it and shuddered.

I turned and closed the door. The bellboy had followed me up. I could hear him in the hall. As I turned around, the husband confronted me. He was in his shirt sleeves, suspenders hanging. His chin whiskers stood out like the hair on the back of a frightened cat.

"Look here," he said, "we can explain all this, though you may not believe it."

"Good Lord, man, there's nothing for you to explain."

They hadn't seen the name on the bag.

"Do you mind if I sit down?" — my knees were shaky. I told them my story. As I told it, I could see them gradually relax. Then, as I finished, Mrs. Richards began to laugh. First she laughed silently, with her face only. Then she began to make a noise, and the laughter spread down to her shoulders and chest. Then her whole body began to laugh, and she shrieked. She fell backward on the bed, writhing and shaking as though in a convulsion, stuffing the pillow into her mouth. Then her husband began to laugh. He leaned against the door, and his big shoulders made it rattle. At first, I didn't know whether to laugh or to cry. Then I laughed. We tried to speak, but we couldn't. There were tears in our eyes, and every time one of us stopped laughing, the sight of the others started it over again. Finally, we recovered, and Mr. Richards ordered a round of highballs. When I left, we were old friends; but every time they looked at me, they started to chuckle.

As I walked out of the hotel with my "package" under my arm, I felt the clerk's eyes boring into my back. But now I didn't care. I took the subway to the hospital, clutching my baby, and — once there — I put it into the ice box.

I heard from the Richardses a year later. They had a real baby of their own. I still hear from them from time to time. They are among my most grateful patients.

My private practice did not grow. At the end of the first year my collections had amounted to about eleven hundred dollars, my uncollected bills to almost the same sum. My expenses had been about six thousand. Probably I would never have made a successful practitioner. My heart was in the laboratory. And when I was offered a full-time position in the Bacteriological Department of the University, I jumped at the chance, and felt that my true career had begun.

CHAPTER XIII

Thoughts on the new humanism, with preliminary remarks on university presidents

FROM almost the beginning of his adult life R.S. was connected with universities. He spent short periods as a student in Vienna and Berlin, and taught successively at Columbia, Stanford, Harvard, Paris, and Peking. Although his subject was a highly specialized branch of medicine, — or, perhaps, for this very reason, — he became much concerned with the premedical academic training of his pupils. From this it was only a step to a general preoccupation with education as a whole. He was opposed to premature specialization, and felt that barring an occasional single-track genius, true distinction of any kind could be achieved only with a thorough, basic liberal education. He spent much time discussing the modern conception of a "liberal education" and, being by nature a busybody, he even wrote a good deal about this subject with his habitual, often ill-advised cocksureness. Some of his ideas on what he called the "new humanism" represented, I thought, an interesting reaction of the specialist to general educational problems. In leading up to these matters, however, he became garrulous on the subject of American university organization and, particularly, college presidents — whom he considered a peculiarly American contribution to academic organization.

1

My acquaintance with the American college president began early and inconspicuously when I was summoned for purposes of reprimand before the Honorable Seth Low, enthroned magnificently in his office in the New Library at Columbia. I had attracted unfavorable notice in various ways, the most recent of which had been the liberation of a goat in the lecture room of Professor Hyslop, the psychologist of Mrs. Piper fame, who was at that moment describing the technique of afterimages. I had been caught playing poker and drinking beer in the basement of Hamilton Hall. My scholarship record was deplorable. It was not a proud accounting, and Mr. Low told me so quite justly, and as one gentleman to another who might not turn out to be one — though a trifle pontifically and not without a soupçon of contempt. I came out of his office feeling less than nobody, but got over it presently, believing, with sudden amazement, that I had met the first human being in my experience — and he the unquestionable founder of the new Columbia — who possessed absolutely no vestige of a sense of humor. It was a great pity, for I must have been extremely silly, and a little good-natured ridicule might have clarified my self-appraisal into wholesome channels.

It was a long time before I met another college president. Indeed, it was not until I had been a member of the teaching staff of the Columbia Medical School for several years. For if President Butler — who in my opinion, some others to the contrary, has many virtues — possesses one outstanding talent, it is the quality of letting an institution run itself. It was my experience at Columbia that one could serve a good many years in positions of varied responsibility without ever being conscious of the fact that there was a president, except when one needed help — a remark which I consider and intend as high praise.

The next president after Mr. Butler whom I met face to face was David Starr Jordan. I found him sitting on the edge of a bed in a small and modest room in the old Hoffman House in New York — the famous hostelry on Broadway which I had known before this only because of its magnificent barroom. Dr. Jordan had sent word to have me come to his room, although he was in the act of dressing. This was half accomplished when I entered. He was sitting, as I said, on the edge of his bed, doubled up, with a shoe in his hand — or, rather, in both hands, for he was just about to pull on one of those boots with elastic sides then known as "congress gaiters." It was an unbelievably immense shoe, but the white-socked foot for which it was destined seemed too large to get into it. I had never seen such a big foot, and I stared at it with a speechless fascination which was hardly the most favorable introduction to an interview in which I was to be appraised for a job. The spell was broken by the pleasant greeting which came in a booming voice that sounded as though it issued from the bottom of a barrel. It reminded me of the voice of Fafner singing out of the papier-mâché dragon in *Siegfried*. But the words were friendly and accompanied by a smile.

David Starr Jordan was a big man in more than his feet. I noticed this even during that first interview, while we were discussing the vacant post at Stanford and my fitness for it. To be sure, our conversation was a little syncopated, because the old gentleman was making heavy weather of dressing while we talked. He wore one of the old-fashioned, stiff-fronted shirts with holes in the dicky for screwing in studs; and when he dived into it from the bottom, groping for the armholes, he stuck with his head and stopped to rest. He was telling me, through the shirt, about the beauties of the Stanford campus. And there we stood: I against the wall, to make room for the struggle; he with his head buried in the shirt, and his trousers — as trousers will in such a situation — sagging with hanging suspenders. There was an appeal to my affections in his awkward naturalness, and I think I won his heart by tugging down on the shirttail, meanwhile holding up the trousers. It may well be that I owed my first professorship to the holding up of a president's pants more than to my scientific achievements — which, if not too dignified a manner of getting a job, is still far less ignominious than many things that have been done in similar regions of presidential anatomy for worse positions. When he finally got into his shirt and was tucking it in, with his back to me, the rear of him looked pathetically like an elephant's hind legs, and stirred a warmth of filial friendliness in my heart. And this was undoubtedly showing in my face when he finally turned around to shake my hand.

I remember this moment — and I have always wondered what it is about the seats of people's trousers which has always stirred affection, sympathy, or distaste in my heart. I am quite sure that there is nothing Freudian about it — though of course one can never tell. But I recall how occasionally on snowy days I have been impelled to put my arm over the shoulder of a vagabond or bum and urge him to accept a quarter, merely because I had been walking behind him and had been touched by the shiny, threadbare pathos of his trouser seat. Had I met him from in front, I should probably have turned away with distaste and suspicion.

In the same way, the appealingly droopy lines of the posteriors of old men who, from in front, were dreadful old bores have softened my heart with a gush of affectionate pity for the sadness of old age. Conversely, on the other hand, I remember often riding behind a lady — quite charming from in front — the seat of whose well-stretched "amazone" rising and thumping like a pile driver on the flat saddle ruined me for any appreciation of her irrefutably splendid character when dismounted, or of the courage she displayed in repeatedly risking her neck in order to introduce into the hunting set a daughter who rode beside her with the same terrified thumping of a less mature but promising "sit-upon."

However, this is carrying us far from the subject of college presidents. In writing of them I am not indulging in the current biographical spirit of boasting of my intimate relations with the great. I have known university presidents only, as it were, *ex inferiore loco*, my view a sort of worm's-eye one. I have served under them remotely, as I did under General Pershing during the war, and cannot speak of them as, for instance, our newspaper boys could speak of the American General Staff, whom they guided in strategy while I quite obscurely, in the outlying army areas, was worrying about the spread of diarrhea. Indeed, the only time I ever saw General Pershing during almost two years in France was on an occasion when I had barely time to jump to attention in a ditch beside the road and get a splash of muddy water in my face as the C. in C.'s car flashed by. Of course my relations with the crowned heads of the universities were somewhat more dignified than this, and I was never splashed with muddy water from their triumphal chariots — though doubtless I often deserved to be. However, my immunity to wrath may have been due to the nature of my subject, since whatever one may discover or believe about bacteria, virus agents, or epidemics has little or no relationship to those worldly affairs in which a professor can be a veritable primary sore to a president just on the point of leading another blushing million to the academic altar.

To return to President Jordan, I was warned against him — among others — by the man whom above most others of his contemporaries I admired — Jacques Loeb. Here was a man; undoubtedly almost a genius in modern biology, and fundamentally one of the kindest and most idealistic of men; gentle in personal relations with intimates, and generous with advice to youngsters in whose eyes he saw the admiration which he deserved. But, withal, a harsh critic of the second-raters, and a wretched judge of character. Jordan, just before this time, had sailed through several severe academic tempests, in one of which — the so-called "Ross affair" — he had brought his young ship with its untried crew safely to harbor only by appeasing Mrs. Poseidon's wrath by making the sincere but impractical Ross walk the plank. There was a good deal to be said on both sides, as I found out later, but for the time being Jordan was regarded by the academic world as having horns and a tail. Loeb, like most intellectual individualists, also by race and by nineteenth-century German tradition, was radical. Jordan, in his eyes, was *ein Schurke*. I well remember the sorrowful evening when my idol, the great Loeb, came to look at our house, which he was thinking of taking off our hands. We had accepted the job in Palo Alto, we were packed to go, and we sat on trunks in the front room, while the baby was asleep in a picnic hamper.

"A man of your temperament" (how proud that made me feel, coming from him!), said Loeb, "will stand it about six months. Then you will come to me to help you get another job. But if you wish to be a success at Stanford, work on fish. Jordan himself, when he works at all, works on fish. He counts the scales on their behinds (*am Hintern*). J., the physiologist, he knows a little physiology — but he works on fish. S., the biochemist — he isn't much of a chemist, but he works on fish. G. and H., in the Zoölogical Department, they work on fish. The geologists, the palaeontologists, the botanists, the English Department, the Romance Languages, even the philosophers — they all work on fish. Go there, my boy, be happy, and work on fish — or, at least, if you are too honest for straight fish, work on the bacteria you can find in fish. But if you love your family, don't get very far away from fish."

We sat there on two trunks after he had left, looking at each other with the despondent expression one sees in the eyes of dead fish. But the contract was signed, our belongings packed — in fact, there seemed no way out. In the end we laughed, for we knew our Loeb and loved him, partly because of his extravagances.

We found Palo Alto and Jordan quite otherwise. Golden days at Stanford! Adequate equipment, small classes composed largely of men who had worked their own ways to an education, complete independence of teaching and research. Most of the faculty, indeed, a little stodgy as usual, but among them a few brilliant spirits like Stewart Young, the physical chemist; the truly great organic chemist, Ned Franklin; Angell; Branner; Stillman; Marx; and Wilbur, the future president, shrewd, kindly, able, and humorous in the Abe Lincoln tradition.

Jordan himself we grew to love. He was actually far from a tyrant; rather a dreamer, bullied by a turbulent and largely radical faculty. While, at academic meetings, he gazed through the windows at the blue California skies, lost in reveries of the future glories of free education for the boys and girls of the ranches of paradise, the faculty outvoted — often fortunately for his dreams — his dearest projects.

Jordan was a strict teetotaler. I offered to inoculate his acidophilus milk for him, if he'd send his Japanese boy to fetch it every morning. I added sugar and a high alcohol-producing yeast to these daily bottles, and in consequence the old gentleman was drinking a species of beer all winter, loved it and thrived on it — in fact, got well on it. All the faculty knew about this except good old Dr. Jordan, who, I am happy to believe, had affection for me as I did for him.

Stanford has left many other memories which have little academic bearing. To me, it was a paradise of cheap horses of that attractive California type in which the toughness of the broncho has been preserved in mixtures with the nobler breeds, some of them, in my time, stemming from the magnificently large thoroughbreds of the Ormonde family. Since I have never been for very long without a horse, I did a lot of horse trading in the Santa Clara Valley. Among others, I had one half-bred broncho-Arab that was a chronic runaway and had a habit of lying down in the shafts when tied to a hitching post. For this reason I got him cheap — and found him satisfactory after I devised the method of carrying a sawbuck on the back of the buggy and shoving it under his belly whenever I stopped for any length of time. He was better under the saddle. Here at Stanford, as at home in Westchester County and, later, in Massachusetts and elsewhere, horse traders were always among my most intimate friends.

We left Stanford for Columbia with regret. Happy Stanford! The lovely Santa Clara Valley, indescribably peaceful in its golden sunshine; the fragrance of blossoms from its orchards; and the evening fog streaming from the big redwoods silhouetted on the crest of the coast range. Freedom for work, freedom from urban interruptions, few — but good — students, and cheap horses. And Jordan — not all-wise or completely tolerant, but a sort of educational Moses, part poet, part legislator, patient and moderate — except, of course, in his enthusiasm for fish.

2

The original American college president was usually an ex-member of the faculty or a well-known divine who, except for individual force of personality, was as little in the public eye as most of his colleagues. Indeed, in the pre-expansion days, professors of extraordinary achievement were often far more widely known than the administrative officers who oiled the academic machinery.

In the European universities there is no one corresponding in power and permanence of tenure to our president. There no one cares who the president is. Who, for instance, has any idea who was Recteur of Paris when Claude Bernard or Pasteur or Poincaré was there? Or who was head of the Berlin University when Helmholtz and Kirchhoff were professors? But, no doubt, without government organization and under the circumstances of expansion which prevailed in the United States, a temporary leadership of this kind was necessary. As standards mature and the tempo slows down, we too may eventually work out a more democratic system.

But during the era of mushroom growth of our universities, administrative problems became correspondingly more pressing. It is fortunate that men were available as leaders who possessed, together with a considerable culture and high purposes, the executive ability to carry the burden. To this generation belong Low, Butler, Jordan, Lowell, Angell, and — probably the greatest of them — Eliot.

Mr. Eliot I met only twice, long after he had retired from the presidency of Harvard. He was, I believe, eighty-eight or eighty-nine years old, and at that time was complaining — I was told — that he felt old age overtaking him because he found it difficult to stand on one leg while putting on his socks. He seemed to me like Nestor, who, "having ruled over three generations of men, was still renowned for wisdom, justice and a knowledge of war." The only conversation I ever had with Mr. Eliot was a one-sided one. I was the only guest at a luncheon club of which he was the presiding member, and with the courtesy which was a part of him, he seated me by his side, and concentrated on me with a degree of inquisitiveness which — coming from him to me — was flattering, whereas it might have been unpleasantly embarrassing from almost anyone else. I answered, in turn, the following questions: —

"How old are you? Where were you educated? How long have your ancestors been in America? Where were you born? Are you married? How many children have you? How long were you at Columbia? Why did you leave there? What was your salary at that time? What is it now? Did you take a smaller salary here because you have money of your own?

Why did you leave medical practice to become a bacteriologist?"

These were not the idle questions of an old man's curiosity. His gentle civility was such that, to my own amazement, I was more flattered than irritated. He was sincerely interested. There was a Jove-likeness about him which seemed to give him the right to appraise his younger fellow men — kindly, impersonally, but minutely. I was reminded of the remark of a philosophical Chinese student of mine who, looking through a microscope one night, said to me: "Do you suppose that the sun may be the lens of a microscope through which God is looking at us as I gaze upon these bacteria?" I was a slightly aberrant specimen of the species "professor," a subdivision of the *genus homo* which Mr. Eliot had been studying for years, as President Jordan studied fish. But I also had the impression that the interest was of a similar nature, and I was glad that my appointment fell under Mr. Lowell's urbane and very human administration. Mr. Eliot seemed to me, not only from this interview but from all I had heard and read of him, a man of unquestionable distinction but of no less unquestionable conviction of his own infallibility. I had also been told — by Mr. Owen Wister — a story which gave me certain ideas about him, and which I repeat with some hesitation, since both the gentlemen concerned have since died. But my memory of it is accurate, and Mr. Wister was not in the habit of imagining such things.

Sometime during the war, Mr. Wister told me, Mr. Eliot had written or said that the Germans had never produced any man of the first intellectual rank. It was probably one of those careless remarks that, rare with Mr. Eliot, were made in profusion by the rest of us at that time. Mr. Wister, seeing the opening, wrote to Mr. Eliot: "How about Goethe?" The reply he received stated that Goethe could not be accepted as of first rank because "his relations with women had been irregular." I've often wondered whether Emerson might have said the same thing — but I doubt it.

Of Mr. Lowell, though I knew him far better, it is not easy to write, since I cannot see him objectively. He is one of the great gentlemen of a generation in which this species is growing rare. In relations with his faculty, he seemed to me to attain, by his manner and his manners, a tone which, under the most controversial circumstances, completely eliminated any suggestion of the employer-employee relationship that is in danger of growing in these up-and-coming days of university efficiency, together with the loss of scholarly dignity fostered by such things as "teachers' unions."

My experience of university presidents would not be complete were I not to include my affectionate reminiscences of a president of the University of Paris. One chilly April day a few years ago, I sat in the "best" room of a village house in Touraine, drinking local wine with a peasant and his wife, their grown son, and with the two companions who had introduced me to this lowly home — one my good friend Debré, the Professor of Bacteriology at the University of Paris, the other the Recteur (or President) of this ancient university, the learned and beloved Dr. Charlety. We spoke of this and that, largely of the quality of last year's vintage, the different methods of *collage*, and the political opinions of the French peasantry. Dr. Charlety chatted with our host with that utterly unpatronizing urbanity which characterizes the relations of the so-called upper and lower classes only in France, and which is one of the charming qualities which make that country so dear to me. The French seem to remember subconsciously that Pasteur was the grandson of a serf, that Pascal, Voltaire, La Fontaine, Molière, Diderot, Claude Bernard, and countless others of their greatest men were of middle-class or of peasant origin. There was a deep respect in the manner in which Professor Charlety conversed with the gray-bearded wine grower, and there was a responsive, entirely unservile courtesy in the farmer's reaction to the great savant who directed the most influential educational organization of France. They were Frenchmen together, appreciating and respecting each other as necessary and honorable collaborators in the life of their nation. I wondered whether this and other manifestations of a similar spontaneous democracy — familiar to me through many years of travel and study in France — might not be explained as a remote but lasting imprint indelibly stamped on the national character by the Revolution.

I asked the old peasant, among other things, my stock question of those days: "How do the farmers feel about the Blum government? Are they communistically inclined like the industrial workers or, being small landholders, are they leaning toward fascism?"

Our farmer winked both his eyes (the French have not learned to wink one eye only) at Charlety.

"My friend," he said, "we have no communists and no fascists in France. We are all either anti-communists or anti-fascists."

Charlety continued to chuckle at this on our way home, during which he told me much about the manner in which he thought France had been kept spiritually and intellectually rejuvenated through the centuries by the continual replacement of the weakening stock of the urban populations by talent and character from the farms and the small towns. He explained how the system of selection in their educational institutions, beginning in the rural schools and continued through the *Lycée* to the *École Normale* and the University, though not perfect, *did* tend to carry to the highest development only those who were worth the trouble; and this at the state's expense with a minimum of discrimination (always inevitable) due to social or economic rank. "This peasant's son," he said, "if diligent and talented, might be almost anything he chose to be, provided he were willing to submit to the discipline and were successful in his *concours*. For a very poor boy, of course, a greater manifest talent is necessary at a given age, while, with the rich, late development can be taken care of by private instruction. But in other respects the chances are equal."

He told me many other things that were probably exaggerated by his enthusiasm for what he believed to be the most effective and democratic system of education that had ever been devised; and while I was quite convinced that to a large extent he was right, it was not this that seemed most remarkable to me in the conversation of this simple, sagacious, and kindly old gentleman. I compared him in my mind with the American college presidents I had known. Not a word did I hear him say about "administration," or "pedagogy," or "methods of appointment." His interest and enthusiasm were purely for the opportunities, the content and sequence, by which the selected best could be developed into broadly cultivated men and women. And I remembered, as I talked to him, that he was not telling me about new theories or recent developments. For, recalling such accounts of French education as one finds — for instance — in the autobiography of Arago, the first Permanent Secretary of the Académie des

Sciences, I realized that even then, just before Napoleon I became Emperor, in the course of a revolution that shook every other institution of France out of its grooves, the educational system of the country was soundly following paths of which the present ones are logical extensions. Arago, as a matter of fact, was able in the first decades of 1800 to find an education which compares favorably with anything an American college has to offer to-day. There was less dessert and savory, but, with the same foundation in mathematics and the basic humanities that Arago had at seventeen, a modern student could easily enter the junior year at Harvard or Yale.

3

Considering in retrospect the American university presidents under whom I have served and some others with whom I have had unofficial acquaintance, I feel that it is impossible to overestimate the services they rendered in transforming some of our colleges from mediocre high schools into great institutions of learning. For the performance of this gigantic task centralization of power was necessary, and it is not surprising that often administrative functions and the publicity incident to the provision of endowments have taken precedence over preoccupation with what Lasserre has called the *importances philosophiques*. The administrative tail had often to wag the educational dog.

But the work of these great pioneers is done. Many of our universities have already outgrown in magnitude the needs of the numerically small percentage of truly educatable material in a stabilizing population. Serious educators are beginning to realize that the country might be better served by an improved high-school and a Lycée-like junior-college system leaving the universities to pursue their true functions with a minimum of rah-rah boys and sorority sisters. The period before us will be one of intensification and scholarly reorientation. But, in the transition, a crushing task lies on the shoulders of the poor college president, for the corporations and trustees from whom he receives his portfolio — largely composed of bankers, merchants, and local Poo-Bahs — have rarely sensed the change in the educational atmosphere, and expect of him the combined talents of the director of a biscuit factory and those of a great intellectual leader.

Let us examine his predicament. The lay college of cardinals endows its new pope with omnipotence, without being able to grant him at the same time infallibility. Then what do they expect of him? He must supervise the wise distribution of an income of anywhere from two hundred and fifty thousand dollars to a million, or more. He must preside over the deliberations of faculties, discussing educational problems, economics, history, literature, languages, classics, mathematics, physics, chemistry, biology, medicine, law, engineering, theology, philosophy, and so on. He has riveted to his legs the academic balls and chains of business schools, schools of education (to teach teachers to teach teachers teaching), schools of journalism, advertising academies, and similar vocational callings foisted upon universities by well-meaning philanthropists. To these may be added, with the rising dignity of labor, graduate schools of taxidermy, plumbing, embalming, salesmanship, and chiropody. These he must so fit into the academic picture that they may do the least harm without breaking the deed of gift. He is chairman of all committees and administrative boards, which he must appoint with sagacity. He is court of last resort on all disciplinary measures of student body or faculty, and must get rid of old wood and take responsibility for new appointments, becoming thereby involved with the American Federation of Labor. He must preside at commencements, alumni dinners, educational conventions, conclaves of a dozen varieties of visiting firemen, and make at least one speech a week, with new stories and profound and original educational theory; unless the occasion demands criticism — or prophecy — of domestic politics, European turpitude, or the future of democracy. He must be ready at any time to don his academic robes and by *his litteris* . . . *unanimi consensu et hoco poco academico* perform mediaeval rites.

Alone to make the speeches would drive most ordinary beings to schizophrenia, even if they did have willing members of a widely learned body to furnish apt citations from de Tocqueville, Voltaire, Diderot, Goethe, Condorcet, Kant, Schelling, Benjamin Franklin, Rousseau, or P. T. Barnum, as the occasion demanded. Thank God for the dictaphone! I know of one college president who has a dictaphone even in that last ditch of privacy where we all have some of our best ideas — incidentally, an interesting phenomenon.

By such things are many of our ablest presidents diverted from the questions that really matter — namely, the problems of readjustment, on the one hand, to the increasing mass of available knowledge, and, on the other, to the background of the civilization which it serves. The encouraging feature in the situation is the fact that, in spite of these handicaps, there are a number of strong personalities among our younger college heads who are primarily scholars, are alive to the changing trend, and may succeed, by working from within, in minimizing the emphasis on material expansion in favor of intellectual values.

Professional education and specialistic education present few problems. They have been taking care of themselves quite adequately for some time. The crux of the problem lies in the modern definition of a "liberal" education. And here there remains a considerable difference of opinion.

Mr. Hutchins, for instance, dissatisfied with what he calls the "confusion of higher learning," would eliminate from our universities the very things which make them indispensable to modern civilization — namely, the spirit of research and the guardianship of sound professional training. Even Abélard, whom we may call the first university president, knew better than this when, almost a thousand years ago, he urged doubt and inquiry as the essence of scholarship. No greater misfortune could happen to American universities than if Mr. Hutchins's views were to be adopted and research were relegated to a minor position. Man, unlike other animals, from the beginning of time has been driven by the "how" and the "why," yearning to achieve greater moral, aesthetic, and scientific clarity. From this uncomfortable impulse, the most painful penalty for the theft of the apple, has sprung intellectual progress. The teacher of almost any important branch of learning who is not interested in the exploration of new ideas or understanding is as out of place in a university as a prohibitionist in a wine cellar.

One may agree with Mr. Hutchins, however, that fundamental to research or all other university functions is the major obligation of providing what is spoken of as a "liberal education." For the ideal of any educational system, probably never quite attainable but always to be pursued, should be to find that formula for training which shall make men capable of appraising what Huxley has termed "that immense capitalized experience of the human race which we call knowledge of various kinds." Specialization can take off soundly only from such a foundation.

But it is not easy to define "liberal education" and to determine for every period what should be its content. The conception of a liberal education must be recognized whenever the pressure of knowledge accumulates a sufficient charge to spark across vacuums of past ignorance. Preceding these periods there are always long preparatory stages before the necessity for intellectual reorganization becomes obvious, during which the various fields of learning seem to grow farther and farther apart. Up to a point, established organization holds them together sufficiently for working purposes. Eventually, however, the tension becomes too high for the old machinery.

This is the present situation which has given Mr. Hutchins the impression of "confusion," but the fundamental fallacy of such a diagnosis is the failure to realize that sound generalization can follow only after the determination of precise facts. "Data collecting" is the indispensable means to synthesis. Indeed, the most exciting and encouraging feature to-day is the reversal of scientific separatism by the discovery of common fundamental laws. As the little mosaics of fact fall into patterns, the apparent confusion gives way to simplifying order. The important achievement of modern science is the revelation of an orderliness both in physical and in organic nature which, to the scholar, is a sort of religious experience and which — and this is its significance for liberal education — must profoundly influence the philosophy, theology, and even the art of the future. The supposed intellectual isolation of the specialized investigator is becoming the exception. Biologists depend on chemists and physicists. Chemists and physicists are, by different but interdependent methods, engaged in studying the same phenomena. Mathematics pervades them all. The astronomer, observing things infinitely large, has interests in common with the student of things infinitely small. The application of scientific principles and methods to practical life is beginning to influence sociology, economics, and government. And through these, science is not without effect upon the historian and the classicist, and may even eventually fertilize the imagination of the poet and the "criticism of life through literature." Thus the study of science would seem to have earned the right to be included, by original definition, in what we may term a New Humanism.

What Pater says of the Renaissance appears to be happening again at the present time: "The various forms of intellectual activity which together make up the culture of an age, move for the most part from different starting points, and by unconnected roads. As products of the same generation, they partake indeed of a common character, and unconsciously illustrate each other; but of the producers themselves, each group is solitary, gaining what advantages or disadvantages there may be in intellectual isolation. . . . There come, however, from time to time, eras of more favourable conditions, in which the thoughts of men draw more together than is their wont, and the many interests of the intellectual world combine in one complete type of general culture."

There is much reason to believe that we are to-day again on the threshold of such an era of intellectual integration, a Renaissance in which the philosophical implications of modern fundamental science will exert a revolutionary effect analogous to that exerted by the ideas of Copernicus, Kepler, Vesalius, and Galileo in the sixteenth and seventeenth centuries. And with this idea in the minds of those who are occupied with the formulation of the new "liberal education," it is not impossible that this Renaissance will strike much more deeply into the lives of populations than any that has gone before; especially in this country, where — laugh as we like at the crudities and academic antics of some of the fresh-water and prairie colleges — the conception is sound and there is going on a mass experiment in education the success of which is the only hope of a shivering world. Not everyone will be educated, but few will be totally neglected, and talent will rarely miss its opportunity. The mathematical chances for a Dante or a Leonardo will increase a hundredfold; a thousand will read Whitehead where one read Giordano Bruno. We might even eventually develop a not too ignorant critic. At any rate, a constantly increasing percentage of the population will reach the age of fourteen by the Binet scale, instead of twelve as at present. And that, if not much, is *déjà quelque chose.*

CHAPTER XIV

Serbia — first experience of mass misery

1

You know, said R.S., I can write with the greatest enjoyment about Rickettsiae, leprosy, allergy, syphilis, the foibles of the ladies who have contributed to my education, the seats of the trousers of college presidents, and my religious convictions. But when it comes to writing about truly dramatic episodes like war, epidemics, revolutions and riots, bombs bursting in air, etc., etc., I become pen-tied, and what I write reads like a railway travel folder. I envy that recently developed type of foreign newspaper correspondent whose acquaintance I first made during the war, — the "Touring Club de France," we called them, — who flitted in and out of combat areas, measured out for themselves, like stiff shots of cognac, stimulating but safe doses of excitement, and then drove back to the Continental or the Meurice to take hot baths and write their thrilling dispatches. Of course they must have served a useful purpose; otherwise they could not have borne the strain of making copy of wholesale murder. Somebody has to do it — like many other things one wouldn't care to do oneself. If I resented them at all, when on rare occasions I ran into them, it was largely from envy for their comfortable transportation, which contrasted with the superannuated Fords, sidecars, mules, and — most often — wet boots on which we others pursued our humbler duties. And in any event I have long forgiven them, since out of their stock sprang such men as Vincent Sheean and Gunther. But, apart from sheer literary ineptitude, my inability to write vividly of dramatic happenings is partly attributable to the fact that I have rarely been in the position of observer, and in the most exciting situations I have had detailed tasks to perform which limited both my vision and my sensibilities. Thus, while the most historically decisive events were going on about me, I was occupied with what that splendid officer, Colonel Grissinger, called the "toilette of the battlefield," with water supplies, with diarrhea and diphtheria in active zones, or with delousing and similar this-and-thats as directed.

I find, therefore, that my reminiscences of the Serbian typhus epidemic of 1915, as terrifying and tragic an episode as has occurred since the Middle Ages, are on the whole rather prosaic and completely — try as I may — unconvincing of that heroism which the Arrowsmith type has made so familiar in prose and cinema, and which, despite de Kruif and others, I have never — thank God! — observed in any of my numerous professional colleagues in action. I was working in my laboratory in New York, chiefly on theoretical problems of immunity, when war was declared, and into the winter of 1914–1915 I was growing increasingly restless — partly from temperament, partly because, as a German-American, the war seemed to me to offer the prospect that a defeated Germany might, at last, be transformed into the free republican state for which so many of our stock had hoped. I felt I ought to get into the war in some capacity, and my chance came in March, when Richard P. Strong organized the Red Cross Typhus Commission for Serbia.

This epidemic had started with the cold weather among the troops on the Belgrade front. The disease is always endemically lurking in that part of the world, and the conditions prevailing during that unhappy winter gave it an opening it had not had for a century. It spread from the army to the villagers, and, when the Austrians had been pushed back beyond Belgrade in a heroic and ferocious counterattack, infection traveled rapidly southward with the peasants and townspeople who streamed out of the zones of combat. The southern areas became crowded; there was shortage of shelter, clothing, food, and fuel. Large numbers of Austrian prisoners aggravated the situation. About 35,000 of these died of the disease. By February and early March, there were easily 150,000 cases, with a mortality of between 60 and 70 per cent. The Serbs lost 126 of their total of 350 doctors. British and a few American medical units came to help. Our own group started late, arriving in early April, but the epidemic was still going strong, and there was plenty to do. Yet the work accomplished was largely in the way of salvage. One cannot "arrest" epidemics of this sort when they are in full cry. Epidemics can be prevented, when energetic, well-organized counterattacks are made at the very beginning under reasonably normal conditions and with more information than — at that time — we possessed about typhus fever. With things as they were in Serbia, one could reduce suffering and improve the care of the sick, but actually stopping the epidemic at that point, or even modifying its natural course, was like trying to put out a fire with a nose spray. Our director, Dr. Strong, made vigorous efforts to delouse entire villages, and if courage and energy alone could have done it, he would have succeeded. But to delouse the Serbs, at that time, was as hopeless as exterminating the ticks on Cape Cod — which, incidentally, may become a real problem in itself before long, since during the last two years we have isolated spotted-fever virus from that region. So the epidemic followed its sinister course until the hot weather stopped it. Nevertheless, in conformity with our national character, there was much beating of drums and congratulatory heroics about the "saviors of Serbia" when we got back. It made me feel a little shoddy.

2

We crossed from Brindisi to Santi Quaranti and thence sailed down the coast, passing Corfu, where Nausicaa tried unsuccessfully to vamp Ulysses, through the Gulf of Corinth, and then to Athens. Without even seeing the Parthenon, or going to a night club, we passed on up the east coast to Salonica.

Except for the lower end of the Cannebière and the streets surrounding the old harbor in Marseilles, Salonica in 1915 was the toughest waterfront I had ever seen. It was the true melting pot of the West and the Near East. Along the quays were tied up the painted ships, reminiscent — with their colored sails — of the thousand that went to Troy. Size, build, and rigging have probably changed little through the centuries. On the streets were Greek mountaineers in native costumes; Bulgarians; Serbs; Turks; heavily veiled women, some of them with coal-black hands; and Jews still wearing the long talars and the headdresses they wore in the fifteenth century, when large numbers of them fled from Spain to find safety from that early Inquisition that is losing so much of its impressiveness now that we are having bigger and better ones. On the hill behind the town, below the ancient walls, was the native

Turkish quarter, with narrow, crooked streets — indescribably mysterious at night — and lovely with glimpses through Moorish arches, toward the harbor. Far to the south, Mt. Olympus towered high, its snow-capped peaks crested with clouds. The life in the waterfront city was one of holiday and drinking, with women of all colors, races, and varieties of chastity. There appear to be recognized degrees of this virtue in the Near East. If I am rightly informed, an exalted American lady who nursed the Turkish wounded was decorated by the Sultan with the "Order of Chastity of the Second Class."

Greece had not yet entered the war, the opinions of the population were said to be divided, and it was even rumored that there was serious internal dissension in the royal family, since the Queen was the Kaiser's sister and the King was inclined to worry about the British battleships concentrated at Malta. Salonica, still a neutral port in a strategic position on the very edge of the whirlpool, was full of military agents, propagandists, and observers of all the combatant nations, and was beginning to develop that irresponsible and reckless gayety that characterized noncombatant areas throughout the war and which, extending over the world after the armistice of Versailles, contributed materially to the earth-encircling hangover.

The town of Salonica itself was relatively free of disease. While epidemics of typhus and relapsing fever were devastating Serbia, not so many miles north, the Greek sanitarian Dr. Kopanaris — German-trained, a pupil of Loeffler — had established an extraordinarily efficient supervision of all border communications. It was through the kindness of this wise and able colleague that I obtained a few cages full of guinea pigs from Athens, most of my own animals having died on the trip over. Kopanaris showed me a small concentration camp near Salonica, where I saw my first cases of bubonic plague.

It was an exciting town to me, whose ideas of the Balkans had hitherto been either of the *Chocolate Soldier* type or those gathered on various occasions from Austrians who regarded this peninsula more or less as we used to think of the Central American republics. As a matter of fact, the Balkan States — Greece excepted — were just emerging from Turkish domination, and what culture they possessed, in the intellectual and professional sense, stemmed almost entirely from Vienna, with a less important French influence in the upper classes and diplomatic circles. The *Chocolate Soldier* conception, as I noticed later, was not so far wrong, and seeing the Balkans as they were in 1915, I formed opinions of the "self-determination of smaller nations" that later helped to classify me as the reactionary which I am not, when radical let-the-chips-fall-where-they-may emotionalism became fashionable among my more radical friends. The Balkan nations were not then — nor were they in 1918 — ready to hold their own in the European cockpit. The human stock was magnificent, but its development had been held back by centuries of Turkish domination. The Serbs were only then beginning to emerge slowly from the half-savage peasant-clan stage of development. They had practically no first-class modern cultural resources of their own and were borrowing technical and professional training from Vienna, Paris, or Russia. There was neither sense of organization nor were there feasible national policies. Every Balkan state had historical traditions which entitled it to the whole peninsula and was fired accordingly by a sense of national mission to reconquer the old empire, backed by patriotism so fierce and arrogant that it appeared childish.

The only organization in the Balkans that seemed to me to be running with smooth efficiency was the Standard Oil Company. If only Mr. Wilson and the Bonzes of Versailles had had the wisdom to make the entire peninsula a Socony protectorate for ten years or so! Some of the profits might have gone back into the country, a magnificent orderliness would have been established, and if it had led to a dynasty — after all, a Rockefeller is as good any day as a Battenberg or a Hohenzollern-Sigmaringen.

The money of Salonica was largely in Jewish hands. The bankers were Jews, and most of the important business was under their control. From what I saw of the Greeks, I have no doubt that by this time the Jews are lucky if they haven't lost their shirts.

The train that took our unit north crossed the border into Serbia at Gevgeli, and there I had my first glimpses of war. The bridge across the river had been destroyed within the week. In the town were the fresh graves of two hundred people who had been killed in a Bulgarian raid. Others had been wounded and mutilated — cutting off the ears was a favorite witticism. Bulgaria was not at war with Serbia at that time, but the situation had Balkan traditions behind it. The *comitadji* system is as old as the Turkish Conquest. In all these Balkan states there were organized bands of raiders, safe in the mountain fastnesses, well armed, — probably with the connivance of their own governments, — who made a habit, even in times of official peace, of crossing borders, attacking villages, killing and robbing peasants, burning houses, and then slipping back into the mountains when reënforcements arrived. Their own governments took no responsibility, since they were theoretically outlaws. It was not a Bulgarian specialty, however. Later, in a little border town in Montenegro, an affable old fellow of sixty, who drank with me in the local *han*, boasted that he had been the leader of a *comitadji* band for thirty years and, having sustained innumerable wounds, was now an honored veteran, living on a Serbian pension.

3

The hospital at Uskub, now known as Skoplje, was established in a former military barracks in the river valley, about three miles from town.

There is no country more lovely in all the world than the valley of the Vardar in the Macedonian mountains. Surrounded by broad fields, white in the spring with opium poppies, the town — with its mixture of Turkish and Western architecture — stretched along the turbulent stream. Snowcapped mountains hedged in the valley on all horizons. Here I first heard the melodious chanting, at dawn and evening prayer, of the *Hoji* from the minaret tower, and in an outlying village a Serb tobacco smuggler hid me behind some pillars in a mosque to witness a Mohammedan service. He said it was very dangerous, as we picked our way over the congregation's shoes in the courtyard. This gave it the necessary kick, but I found out later that I'd had my leg pulled. The thing was done all the time.

We were lodged for a few days in an elegant mansion facing the Vardar, the most palatial residence in the main street, said to have been the pride of the town and its most elegant bawdyhouse — the requisitioning of which, an act of extreme patriotism, indicated how desperately the Serbs were sacrificing all for resistance.

After a short period our group was broken up, three of us being assigned to the typhus hospital known as the "6th Reserve" and run by a British unit founded by Lady Paget. The roads around the buildings, reaching down to the river, were ruts of mud; and on slight rises to the east there were at least twenty acres of little wooden crosses over the graves of the typhus dead of the last few months. As many as eighty cases a day were still arriving. It was pitiful to see them carried in, stumbling between supporting relatives, or lying on straw in oxcarts, then laid out on the hospital grounds for preliminary cleaning and delousing before disposal in the wards.

My first concern was to establish a laboratory and autopsy room, which I did by reconstructing a barrack shed that had been used for the storage of odds and ends. Fortunately, for this work I had the assistance of Austrian prisoners. There was a prisoners' camp behind the hospital which held some five to six hundred, most of them typhus convalescents. The hospital and the camp were under British supervision, and in consequence these prisoners were well treated and given a great deal of liberty, escape across the mountains being quite impossible. These Austrians were now out of the war — and therefore relatively happy. At night they sang, and played on improvised fiddles and guitars. I often sat with them, because their parties were much more amusing than the solemn conversations at the British mess table. Among them, two good masons, a carpenter, and a plumber soon converted my shed into an autopsy room and a serviceable laboratory. Two of the prisoners — Otto, an ex-clerk from Vienna, and Wilhelm, a former bank cashier — I trained as laboratory technicians.

I noticed at the "6th Reserve" what I confirmed by later

observations in France: the British have, more than any other nation with which I have worked, the sporting spirit toward a defeated enemy. Their kindness to these prisoners and their lack of any dislike or hatred were a natural reaction. They are brutal only in their propaganda and when money is involved. Austrians became trusted orderlies, and all of them felt that — in British hands — they were completely protected from reprisal and abuse. I have often been irritated by the English, and I have often laughed at their insular conceits. But I'd rather be captured by them in war than by any other nation.

Life in the "6th Reserve" was at first difficult. We Americans were accepted as members of the Staff, assigned decent quarters, and taken into the mess; but the word "welcome" as we understand it did not apply. I at first took great pains to be polite; to say "Good morning" and "How do you do" at the proper times, and never to take my place at the table without bowing to the Commanding Officer. These overtures were met with cold stares. Courtesy marked me as a "blighter." After the first few days, I was fed up, became silent, looked the other way when I met someone in the corridor, and sat down to meals without a word. This broke the ice. A few days of nasty manners proved that I belonged to the better classes. In the end, they treated us more cordially than they did their own Colonials, and I developed a warm friendship for many of these courageous and kindly colleagues. An American, once accepted by the British, is made as much at home as a New Yorker is in Boston. But a Canadian, New Zealander, or Australian can get as far as — and no farther than — a Bostonian born in Roxbury.

My work at this hospital led to little immediate discovery.

I gathered a great deal of information about the clinical aspects of the disease, did a great many autopsies, and learned the things that one can learn about typhus by living in an epidemic region. But scientific studies were hampered, not by any lack of opportunity or equipment, but rather by the fact that in typhus investigations at that time there was much underbrush to be cleared away. Before the true causes of the disease were uncovered, almost every known microorganism had, at some time or other, been implicated. An American bacteriologist, ballyhooed by an important hospital in New York, had, a short time before, described a "bacillus" of typhus fever which had been much advertised. It required much of my time in Serbia to eliminate this error, and since the methods demanded by such work were quite at variance with any of the approaches later found to be significant, it was a lesson in the incalculable waste of time and money that can result from false observations backed by institutional propaganda. Nevertheless, this time was not entirely lost, since it set me definitely on the right path and convinced me, once and for all, that the solution lay in another direction. I drew on my Serbian experience and the thorough knowledge of the disease it had given me when, some years later, I resumed my typhus studies. I was then able to work with a sound knowledge of pathology and clinical manifestations which I should not have had without the Serbian observations.

The work was trying on the nerves, since often, while I was doing an autopsy on a case still warm (it was desirable to perform these operations before secondary post-mortem invasion of bacteria had occurred), I could hear the families of other recent dead keening over the bodies on the farther side of a thin partition. Also, some of the burials were harassing. I remember one dark, rainy day when we buried a Russian doctor. A ragged band of Serbian reservists stood in the mud and played the Russian and Serbian anthems out of tune. The horses on the truck slipped as it was being loaded, and the coffin fell off. When the chanting procession finally disappeared over the hill, I was glad that the rain on my face obscured the tears that I could not hold back. I felt in my heart, then, that I never could or would be an observer, and that, whatever Fate had in store for me, I would always wish to be in the ranks, however humbly or obscurely; and it came upon me suddenly that I was profoundly happy in my profession, in which I would never aspire to administrative power or prominence so long as I could remain close, heart and hands, to the problems of disease.

4

As August approached and the epidemic relaxed, the work at the hospital became less strenuous, and I decided that I should like to see for myself what the conditions were in the outlying districts. I took as an excuse the wish to look after a younger colleague, Grinnell, who had been assigned to sanitary "cleaning up" of an area in and around the village of Ipek across the Montenegrin border, and from whom we had had little news. To reach his station it was necessary to take a one-track spur railway to its terminal at Mitrovitza, where I arrived late one afternoon.

As the train came to a halt, I opened the window and got a sudden unpleasant whiff of something compounded of man mixed with garlic. I saw no one on the platform, and as I stepped off the train I looked about me carefully. At this moment, a Serb appeared from between two cars, about forty paces away — indeed, I paced him off. I had smelled that isolated peasant for all of thirty yards on an almost windless day.

I put up at the little hotel — a flimsy, two-story wooden building, surrounding a court. On the lower floor, facing the street, was a café in which peasants, a few soldiers and gendarmes, and the picturesque old brigand to whom I have previously referred, were drinking. In the courtyard were filthy barrels, mud, and a few pigs. A balcony ran completely around the second story, above the court. The plumbing arrangements consisted of holes in the balcony floor — the "openest" plumbing in the world. The ordures fell prey to the pigs in the yard, who thus fulfilled a sort of Board of Health function. The bedrooms opened off the balcony and were reached by steep wooden staircases leading up from the four corners of the court.

I made inquiries about getting to Ipek, and established communications with the local woiwode, an affable sergeant who fortunately spoke a little German. He said the only way to get to this place was on foot or on horseback; that it was some forty kilometres away, and that the entire distance would have to be covered by daylight, because the Albanian mountaineers were playful at night. After much argument, he consented to my going on the following day, promising to send two mounted gendarmes with me.

Returning to the hotel, I took a room and — luckily, as will appear later — was given one of which the door was opposite and only a few feet away from the top of one of the staircases. I then proceeded to clean up.

The technique of traveling in epidemic countries — especially when the prevailing epidemics are carried by lice, bedbugs, and fleas — is a special one. I never slept in a bed on such journeys, however tempting. I carried a Red Cross blanket, an extra suit of underwear, a beer bottle full of kerosene, and another of chloroform. Also, a cake of soap. Upon arriving in places of this sort, the first thing to do was to strip to the skin. Outer clothes were hung on a hook or laid over a chair, away from the washing area. The discarded underwear was loosely packed into my boots, a tablespoonful of chloroform poured into each one, and a string tightly tied around the tops. This executed any vermin that happened to be in the underwear, and made the clothing safe for use the following day. Then came a thorough wash — especially of the hairy parts of the body — with soap and water. After this, I could put on the clean underwear. Before wrapping myself in the blanket for sleep on the floor, I would sprinkle it with kerosene. I used my stuffed boots as a pillow, and usually managed a fair night's rest.

My routine in this hostelry was rendered difficult by the fact that, according to local custom, in addition to being a wayside inn the place was also a temple of Venus. The landlady herself was a buxom Serbian woman full of loud laughter, who joked with the soldiers, especially with a young and pomaded Serbian field clerk. Her humor, I could guess without understanding a word, was not of the most delicate. There were also some handsome maidens of not more than eighteen or twenty — of the same type, but more timid. Following the hospitable traditions of the house, one of them — and she was really a very nice girl — attached herself to me, followed me into my room, sat on my bed, and proceeded to watch my preparations with interested anticipation. We could not speak to each other, and I tried in vain to intimate by gesture that

I was about to take a bath. I ostentatiously opened the door. She would gently close it as often and return to sit on the bed, smiling at me. I decided that if I stripped to the waist and started to wash, she would eventually get tired and leave of her own accord, but my ablutions intrigued her enormously. Such exaggerated cleanliness appeared fantastic. When I had finished with this part of the exercises, I had to take her by the arm and lead her out. She accepted this in good part, however — indeed, patted me on the back affectionately, assuming the hour had not yet arrived. If the incident did not end as did an analogous one in the *Sentimental Journey*, it was perhaps as much due to my acute sanitary sense as to innate virtue. I say this because in biographical records of this type the imaginative reader is apt to suspect a certain degree of reticence. However, this is the way it was.

I finished my ablutions, had a meagre meal of boiled eggs, the inside of half a loaf of bread, tea, and an ample dose of Slibovitz, in which not even the toughest germ could survive. To this I set up the crowd, thus establishing merry approval. Then, looking forward to an early start, I retired to my room.

I was wakened by a dreadful row just outside my door. A struggle was going on; someone was evidently hanging on to my doorknob, and someone else trying to pull him or her away. If the door had looked less frail, my judgment would have been to sit tight; but it seemed that the couple were about to crash into my room at any moment. I arose and put my hands on the most obvious weapon, a chair. The kerosene bottle would no doubt have been better, but I couldn't see it in the obscurity. The door seemed to be giving, and I wondered how soon it would fly open. Though I had not yet heard of Marshal Foch, I concluded that counterattack would be the best defense. I silently drew the bolt and — since the door opened outward — pushed it with all the vigor I possessed. The effect was fortunate. It seemed that my girl friend had been intending to come into the room, and an enamored drunken soldier was trying forcibly to dissuade her. She must have been close to the door, and was merely pushed aside when it flew open; but he, standing just a little behind, with his head forward, received the full impact on his nose. His drunkenness was a great help — that, and the element of surprise. Whether he was actually laid out or not, I don't know; but he lost his balance, stumbled backwards, missed his footing, and described a curve into the mud of the court. Naturally, I was anxious. I looked about, but the girl had vanished. I peered over the balcony to see the soldier getting unsteadily to his feet, and I rebolted my door.

Before dawn the next morning I made my way to the woiwode's office. My gendarmes were waiting for me. They seemed glad of the trip, and were very friendly. One of them had a black eye, but he was none the less amiable. He had probably been too drunk to remember. There were two horses for the three of us, which meant a walking pace, but they were generous in changing off, so that none of us walked more than a third of the way.

The road toward Montenegro, after five or six miles of cart track, degenerated into something more like a brook bed. It was hot going, but we maintained a fair pace, since it had been made quite clear that we must reach the town of Ipek before dark. In a little valley we came upon an isolated *han*, a little oblong building, the typical wayside rest. The interior consisted of a central passage, on either side of which ran raised platforms. The solitary old Turk proprietor boiled us some eggs and served us with thick, sweet coffee. My gendarmes, who were less fastidious than I and who had probably had every disease that the neighborhood afforded, filled up with bowls of pilaff, a confection of rice, butter, sugar, and bits of meat, which under safer circumstances I have learned to appreciate as far and away the least painful method of eating rice.

While we were eating we heard the sound of approaching horses. My companions ran out with me and we saw, riding down from the hills, a picturesque troop of a dozen horsemen. I half expected them to burst into song, for they looked like an *opéra bouffe* company. The horses were small and shaggy; the bridles gay with color; and the men themselves dressed in the tight white breeches of the Albanian highlander, with short embroidered white jackets bordered with black braid. In their broad sashes were stuck pistols and knives. Most of them carried rifles of various makes and periods. There was one Mauser. These were the first hill men I had seen, and I was struck by the fact that their physical type was similar to my own. Their complexions, build, and hair were those of Anglo-Saxons. I tried later to learn about the ethnology of the Albanians, but nothing much is known of them. They are called Pelasgians or Illyrians. It seemed quite likely to me that they might be descendants of the Greek gods who, one gathers from Swinburne, fled across the Gulf of Corinth when Christianity moved too close to Olympus. Menelaos, one remembers, was ξανθός, light-haired. This idea recurred to me when, on my return to Mitravitza, I had an interpreted chat in the town jail with an Albanian girl imprisoned for knifing a Serb who had tried to rape her. She looked exactly like the

Venus of Milo — only, of course, she had capable arms. In the same jail, that day, I saw a German aviator — a charming young lad who had been on his way to Bulgaria and had had a *panne* on Serbian territory, where armed peasants gathered him in. I managed to get a good meal to him, and we drank a bottle of wine together. It was terribly bad wine.

I watched the approach of these mountain sportsmen with some apprehension, but, to judge from this crowd, their ferocity had been exaggerated. Here in broad daylight they were a friendly lot. They dismounted and gathered about us, examined me closely — and grinned. I held out my hand to the central figure, a redheaded, bearded patriarch who might have been Vulcan. He grasped it and seemed to know what I meant when I said, "Delaware and Lackawanna!" He had a huge revolver — a muzzle loader — which, I was amused to find, had been made in the United States in 1859. We all went inside to have coffee together; after which we departed without interference.

From here on, the trail mounted rapidly toward an imposing, jagged range. The scenery became wilder, the hills began to enfold our path, and soon we entered the pass leading to Cetinje. Shortly after dark, we arrived at Ipek and made our way to the walled, fortified enclosure where lived the Bishop of Montenegro, in charge of the cathedral in which the great Czar Doujan lies buried. Through the heavy gate in the high wall, we were let into the court by an armed, Montenegrin guard.

My friend Grinnell, I found, had been down with dysentery, which, together with relapsing fever, malaria, and a growing enteric incidence, was increasing as typhus diminished. He was recovering when I arrived and later showed me his district. He had done a splendid job, and demonstrated how much could be accomplished for these miserable villagers with common sense, hard work, and the simplest equipment. If we had had a few thousand like Grinnell scattered through the country, we might have made more of an impression — possibly lasting — on the general conditions. He had trained squads of the garrison to carry on his work, and he promised to follow me out as soon as he was strong enough to travel.

The Bishop was a hospitable soul. I suspected, also, that he was overjoyed to have a little party. He had been sitting in this isolated spot for God knows how long, with a retinue of black-robed monks and some hundred or so Montenegrin militiamen — the former recruited, like most of our own run-of-the-mill clergymen, from the less intelligent and less interesting of the lower middle class; the soldiers were half-savage peasant lads. The Bishop was thoroughly fed up with the whole show, for he was a cultivated man of the world and bored.

He was a fine-looking person — tall, black-bearded, his impressiveness increased by his long black robes and the high black headdress. He welcomed me in excellent French, and sent me to a clean, whitewashed room with a bed with real sheets, a washstand, and clean towels.

He had dined. But his monks served me an excellent meal while he sat in attendance and plied me with a not too terrible red wine. Then he took me to his study, where there were a bottle of marvelous cognac and a box of his own particular cigarette tobacco.

His chief interest at this time, war or no war, and unmindful of epidemics, Albanians, or Austrian invasion, was the problem of the possible union of the Greek Orthodox Church with the High Church of England. His apparent utter indifference to the war and the epidemics was not unlike the attitude of the masters and dons of a Cambridge college at whose high table I dined while waiting for orders in England during the darkest months of the conflict. The conversation dealt almost exclusively with references to gardening in Roman literature. In the case of these scholars, however, every one of whom had close relatives at the front, the motive was that high trait of British courtesy — the unwillingness to distress a guest with their own heartaches.

I might have learned a great deal from the Bishop had I not gone to sleep on him several times. In compassion, he led me to my quarters and wished me a pleasant night. I had no doubt of this. Luxuriously, I undressed completely, with happy confidence in the safety of the whitewashed walls. It wasn't a bad night, as a matter of fact — except that toward morning I felt a bite on my neck, scratched a while, swung my boot at a bedbug crawling up the immaculate wall, and disfigured it with a red splotch of my own blood. I was too sleepy to worry, and became comatose again. When I finally awoke the sun was shining into my window and I was conscious of the fact that I had been waked by a rifle shot. I thought the place was being attacked, and went to the window to look out. There in the garden the Bishop was sitting at a little iron table, with coffee, cigarettes, and cognac before him, and a Mauser across his lap. Just after I caught sight of him he raised the rifle to his cheek and fired upward into the mountains.

"Good morning!" I shouted.

"Come down," he said, "and have some coffee. I amuse myself shooting at an old rabbit that feeds on the slope — but

I won't let you shoot. You might hit him, and then my morning *plaisir* would be spoiled."

I hated to leave him. But I had work to do at the hospital and started back across the hills with my guards.

5

In the hospital at Uskub there was an Austrian Serb, Sirovitch we will call him, who acted as liaison officer with the British. He was in charge of stores and supplies, represented the Serbian Government in non-professional matters, and was in command of the prisoners' camp. He was a tall, handsome person, about forty years old, slender and dapper in his blue uniform and black boots, with a little waxed moustache and attractive manners. I came to know him well. He was good company, always had a store of Scotch whiskey, and enjoyed talking of America. Born in that part of Serbia that had been ceded to Austria some years earlier, he had emigrated to the United States. There he had taken out first citizenship papers, and had worked for one of the oil companies. They probably employed him because of his knowledge of Balkan languages, for early in 1914 he was sent to negotiate business in the Rumanian oil fields. When the Sarajevo murder occurred, Sirovitch was in Bucharest, but promptly went south and enlisted in the Serbian Army. When, in 1915, the British units arrived, his knowledge of English — rare among the Serbs — led to his appointment to his present post. Among other things, he was a lady-killer of skill and concentration — the sort of man who never passed a good-looking woman without adjusting his necktie or twirling the end of his moustache. In this respect he reminded me of an Italian officer I once knew in Paris who, standing before the Venus of Milo, said to me: "Poor woman! How she must regret her lack of arms when she looks at me!"

It is always amusing to hear of our own country from immigrants, who describe an America quite different from anything familiar to the native. Sirovitch's American adventures turned largely about a boarding house in Brooklyn, New York, and the niece of his landlady, who — by his own account — was heartbroken when he left. As a matter of fact, as I found out afterwards, this was actually the case, and she had followed him as far as Athens, where I later saw the poor thing.

Sirovitch, whose off-duty interests were concentrated almost exclusively upon the pursuit of ladies, was very much taken with an extraordinarily beautiful head nurse. This nurse was not an Englishwoman. What she was, I don't know. She spoke with that exaggerated correctness of diction that indicates the cultivated foreigner. I guessed that she was from one of the Scandinavian countries. She was both amazingly efficient and impressive. Living so near Olympus, one thought of Juno. She was large, with a crown of blonde hair, a pink and white complexion, and the wide forehead and clear eyes of a commanding personality. To the surprise of everyone in the hospital, including myself, she seemed very much attracted to Sirovitch. Our astonishment came partly from the fact that she often talked about her prewar engagement to an enemy officer; indeed, the freedom with which she spoke of this aroused wonder that, under the circumstances, she should have enlisted in a British unit. She was not regarded as entirely safe. Yet she was one of the best nurses in the hospital, and in full charge of one of the larger wards. Her friendship with Sirovitch gave rise to gossip, and there seemed good reason for it. Often on Sunday afternoons, when walking in the hills, a group of us would come upon her and Sirovitch picnicking on a slope with a view, obviously making a point of going off by themselves.

The night before I left Uskub for home I had a parting drink with Sirovitch, and he gave me some letters which he asked me to mail in France. Fortunately for me, I mailed them in Athens when I was delayed there. Within three days after my departure, Sirovitch was arrested for espionage, and shot. Later, I was told that our head nurse was the one who "got" him. In addition to her splendid efficiency in the wards, she was in the Secret Service. She caught him by that perilous sixth sense which Norman Douglas says is so much more highly developed in man than in woman that it makes man — despite frequent superiority in the other five — always the weaker sex.

The little coastal steamer on which I left Salonica was delayed, and I missed connections with the direct boat for home, but my forced stop in Greece was fortunate for me. I saw the Parthenon, Corinth, and the lovely Achaian hills on which the daphne — Apollo's beloved — was in flower. I crossed to Patras in the vain hope of catching another steamer, and saw the shores of the Corinthian Gulf.

In a bookstore I picked up secondhand texts with translations of the *Odyssey* and of Thucydides. And with their help I renewed some of the adventures of my youth — remembering the resounding voice of the great schoolmaster, Julius Sachs, rolling forth the mighty vowels of Homeric periods with impressive wagging of his Olympian beard. And I felt glad that I had been a dishonest little boy. For while many of the good boys were conscientiously learning which verbs governed the dative or the ablative, and were detecting examples of synecdoche, anacoluthon, and pleonasm, I — in a back seat — was following the great classicist with a well-concealed "trot," getting a romantic kick out of the wanderings of Odysseus and of Xenophon, and, incidentally, passing better examinations. And I pondered on the stupidity of most classical teaching, which smothers what might be the most thrilling intellectual adventure of youth under rubbish heaps of syntax and grammar. Why not read all these things with a good trot, for those who have a talent and a taste for it to pick up a reading knowledge, if they will; but for all who have any slumbering seeds of imagination to sit for a while on Olympus with the henpecked Zeus, the shrew Hera, and the emancipated Pallas Athene; to be tossed on the seas with Odysseus; to be turned into a pig by Circe; sweat inside the Trojan horse; fight with the Nazi-Spartans or the Parisian Athenians — in short, to be subjected for an impressionable time to the magnificent pageant of Greek mythology and history which leaves an indelible imprint for which no Montessori, sex education, teachers' college psychology, or self-expression pedagogy can ever substitute. All this I thought as I gazed upon the Parthenon at night, and, thinking it, I completely forgot to take a good look at those remaining relics of sculpture which Lord Elgin — though quite justly realizing that Phidias should have been an Englishman — generously left behind.

6

On the sands of the Phaleron I met an unfortunate young lady who proved to me that some things still *do* happen as the penny thrillers describe them. She was sitting with a couple that in themselves were something to remember. The man was small and fat, with a pince-nez and a little Hitler moustache. His wife was enormous, redheaded, deep-bosomed, and forbidding in spite of a labored smile. Her reddish moustache was bigger than his. Imagine Charlie Chaplin married to Brunhilde. These people were Jews from Smyrna and were very rich, as her jeweled hands and ears bore witness. The young woman with them was slight and timid. She and I left for Athens together on the tramcars, and her story was almost a perfect plot of old-fashioned melodrama. She was a minister's daughter from the North of England who had come to Athens as governess in a rich Greek family. She had been "several times betrayed," and now she was almost penniless and spots were coming out on her skin. The spots — which she insisted on showing me after she had begged me for medical advice — persuaded me that, however much of a cliché her story, she needed help. And she was truly a well-educated and charming young girl. Fortunately I had by this time plenty of extra money. Through a Greek doctor with whom I had had professional correspondence I managed to have her admitted to a good hospital for the treatment she needed. She was utterly unwilling to go back to England, though I did my best to persuade her. I've often wondered what became of the poor thing eventually — cultivated, gently reared, penniless, luetic, and afraid to go home.

It was not easy to get home from Greece in those days. I used to row about in the harbor of the Piraeus trying to find some tramp or freighter that would take me at least as far as Italy. Finally a small French Messageries steamer came in, and one of the engineers told me that they took a few passengers but that they were under government control and could not guarantee where they would go after they got to Malta. However, they took me as far as that, and from Malta

I made my way to Marseilles; thence to Bordeaux, and home on the old *Touraine*. I had to sneak aboard the ship with the help of one of the officers, because I had not the necessary military permits to leave the country and no time to get them. The purser of this ship — Le Dantec was his name — was a poet of some repute. It turned out one of the jolliest voyages of my experience, except that the ship's doctor and I had to listen each evening to the good *commissaire's* daily harvest of dreadful imitations of Lamartine.

The next few years crowded me with other problems, and I did not get back to typhus until eight years later.

CHAPTER XV

An effort to avoid speaking of the war without leaving it out entirely. Some reflections on democracy and a consideration of whether anything good at all came out of the war. Stimulation of preventive medicine by the war

AFTER his return from the Serbian epidemic, R.S. said he felt as though he were already enlisted for service in the war. To be sure, he went back to his academic duties, but his mind and heart were in Europe, and he could not shake off the feeling that he ought to be at least sharing in the general danger and misery, instead of leading the peaceful life of an academic investigator while the foundations of the old civilization were trembling. Later, he admitted to me that this kind of restlessness was a weakness, and expressed the highest admiration for those of his friends who "had the courage to stay at home" and carry on, keeping life behind the fronts as normal as, under the circumstances, it could be kept. And, indeed, in this he was right, for there were countless brave men whose urge for adventure and excitement was quite as strong as his own, who made the harder choice of sticking to their necessary jobs. He worked through the winter, then, in a state of constant excitement, and as it became more and more apparent that America would eventually be involved in the general cataclysm, he joined the Army Reserve. His desire for actual service was somewhat assuaged during the following summer, when militia regiments returning from the Mexican border were sent to Camp Whitman in New York, suffering from perhaps the most concentrated paratyphoid "A" epidemic that has ever been studied, and R.S. and his friend Derby — both under the command of Colonel Henry Page of the Regular Army — were sent to investigate and take charge. This kept him busy and contented for a few months. In itself, this study was of extraordinary interest, for this group of paratyphoid organisms, first cousins — as the name implies — of the bacillus of typhoid fever, can cause a manifold variety of maladies in man, ranging from mild, dysentery-like diarrheas to typical typhoid fever or an acute form of gastro-enteritis, a so-called "food poisoning." These infections were puzzles to medical practice until bacteriologically analyzed; and since many members of this bacterial group are prevalent among animals, — mice, rats, hogs, cattle, and so on, — their definition represents a pretty chapter in bacteriology. A para-A epidemic of such extent and uncomplicated purity as this one among the troops was a rare and absorbing opportunity for observation. But when this job was over, R.S. began to worry more and more about what he considered the peculiar responsibilities of German-Americans during the now unquestionably imminent conflict.

There were few Americans of English stock who could appreciate the feelings of people who, having become during two generations enthusiastic Americans, still cherished a reverent fondness for the German traditions of pre-1870, who had sung German children's songs, read the fairy tales, and had later learned to love German literature and music and to admire German science. To be sure, there were many "hyphenates" of more recent immigration whose hearts were with the new imperialistic Fatherland. But to men of R.S.'s stock, nourished on traditions of an anti-Prussian Germany, whose heroes in America were men like Carl Schurz, Jacobi, and Kudlich; whose fathers had worn the black-red-gold ribbons of the democratic *Burschenschaft* under their waistcoats, this war seemed a call to arms. They felt that they might continue the work of their ancestors toward a German Republic. This, they thought, was their '76, their coming of age as American families. For R.S., as he pondered on these questions, wondering whether, with the German name of which he was proud, he would ever see foreign service, the only comfort came from Theodore Roosevelt and from a revered Boston physician, Fred Shattuck. These men had read one of R.S.'s speeches, one for which he was anonymously reviled by resident Germans, and they understood and sympathized.

At any rate, these were in part the sentiments which drove R.S. into the army as early as he could get himself accepted. There was another feeling, however, which played a strong rôle in his wanting orders for foreign service. This was a purely emotional reaction to general conscription when it came. He first became conscious of this sentiment one day in Washington when, looking out of a window of the Surgeon General's offices, he watched a regiment march down Pennsylvania Avenue. War had been declared, and these were among the first troops to go over. Colonel Goodwin, the British liaison officer, was standing behind R.S., and when they turned from the window the Colonel looked at him sadly and said: "Poor fellows! Poor fellows!" There came over R.S. at that moment a heavy wave of pity — an emotion of brotherhood with these poor devils so proudly marching in ranks, none of whom knew what it was all about, none of whom had any conception of the pain and misery ahead of them. He visualized the scenes he had witnessed in Serbia, the state of France as he had passed through it on his way home, the hospitals and the training camps. And he knew that there could be for him no peace and no pride unless he could be with these young, helpless, and courageous pawns in the dreadful game — to live with them, to be cold and uncomfortable, lousy and frightened, and to share in his own person whatever fate held in store for them.

In this connection, R.S. was much puzzled by the attitude of many of his more radical friends. He was not himself inclined either by training or by environment to take a rigidly conservative view of society. He had seen misery and destitution in the slums of New York and in European cities. And one of the most difficult episodes of his late adolescence had been when, still in the New York Cavalry after the Spanish War, his squadron had been ordered with other troops to help suppress the strike on the Croton aqueduct. His sympathies passionately with the strikers, he spent days and nights patrolling roads and helping to make arrests. It was his first experience of being caught helplessly between the millstones of conscience and of a social machinery whose purposes confused him. Around the campfire at night he made himself obnoxious — and was unhappy. He had also been much attracted to the group of younger radicals who were at that time associated with or interested in the old *Masses*. One or two of them were his intimate friends, and John Reed, whom he had met, and Max Eastman, whom he knew casually, he admired sincerely for their earnestness and intelligence. Yet in none of these people — men or women — did he find any of the same kind of emotion that had him in its grip. Most illogically, they seemed actually pro-German — a sort of overcompensation for their disapproval of the Allied governments. But, with few exceptions, none of them appeared to be impelled by a desire to share the misery and dirt and danger of the "American masses" that were helplessly washed into the maelstrom. R.S.

noticed this same, possibly philosophical impersonalness in the attitude of settlement workers with whom he was associated for a time. They worked among the poor, but again, with a few exceptions, without any impulse to share sorrow and suffering at first hand. And R.S. found himself many nights and through several hot summers in the tenement houses of the back alleys, sitting up with sick babies, when the "settlement workers" were either giving parties and dances or were away at the shore on long vacations. For a time he was exasperated at this, but later he recognized that the defect lay in him. These other people were less emotional and took the longer view. They knew well enough that the solution lay not in sentimental impulse, but in attack on fundamental causes.

Now R.S., an instinctive Girondin, was at first confused and inclined to swallow much that his radical friends — so learned in revolutionary catchwords — told him. It was not until many years after the war that his mind achieved a certain degree of clarity about these issues. Comparisons of the conditions prevailing in foreign countries with those he observed at home eventually convinced him that none of the revolutionary states, fascist or communist, had succeeded in even temporary alleviation of the desperate economic emergencies which had made them possible. In Russia, certainly, they created more actual misery than they alleviated. R.S. was quite ready to agree that the "democratic" states — his own country, France, and England — had not succeeded in abolishing poverty or oppression of the dispossessed classes. But he did observe that, even so, the lot of the poorest in these countries was far superior in material circumstances, but particularly in dignity, to that of the terrorized masses under the dictatorships; and the private exploitation of labor — reprehensible though it was — seemed more amenable to possible correction than a state exploitation against which there was no redress short of bloody revolution.

From early confusion he finally became more firm than before in his conviction that only education and slow evolution under perfected democratic constitutions could eventually solve the economic problems of the world. He saw in his own country, and he witnessed in France, an awakening of social conscience, a free, forensic struggle, impossible in Russia, Italy, or Germany, for better economic adjustment, a desire for raising the general level of popular responsibility and evolving, in the masses, that increased capacity for self-government which alone can lead to permanent improvement. In dictator states — he knew by observation — stability could exist only so long as the people were kept in ignorance, silenced by fear, and regimented by force and propaganda. It appeared unthinkable that régimes of force, even when idealistically conceived, could last much longer than the emergencies that had fathered them. For the instinct for personal liberty and power, within reason, over one's own fate appears a natural attribute of the human mind, like the capacity for thought and the desire for knowledge. The Girondin attitude, therefore, which recognizes the need for social justice but believes it can be attained by education and persuasion, seemed worth fighting for. The democracies, he strongly felt, at least offered a remote hope of achieving a society in which, ultimately, adequate plenty could be combined with a dignified degree of personal liberty. Democratic organization was temporarily out of joint and had not caught up with the industrial age, for it had been conceived in simpler times. With change in the sources of wealth from land to industry and trade and the almost cancerous growth of riches, democracy had developed diseases which, indeed, called for surgery, but did not appear incurable. Most of all, he thought they needed the development of a new aristocracy that could develop from the masses by force of the only legitimate propaganda — education; not only in the scholastic sense, but in that as well of the moral responsibility which should gain force with the dignity of unhampered freedom of belief, speech, press, and equality before the law. Socialism gone berserk, whether in the form of communism or of fascism, he could see only as "quasi-criminal" and conspiratorial. He did not question the nobility of motive of the various leaders of socialistic theory of his time, nor did he share H. G. Wells's idea that many of them were consciously exploiting the hopes of the oppressed. But he could see no prospect of ever achieving the objectives of legitimate socialistic leveling of human happiness except by changes which might grow — however slowly — out of the humane intelligence of the people as a whole; and not by the harnessing of the brute horse power of mass hatreds to a Juggernaut's car driven by fanatics. He gradually, by his own observations, while admitting inexpertness, lost his authority worship for those who, as supposed social scholars, sneered at opinions which saw some good in the achievements of the late eighteenth and early nineteenth centuries.

It was not, as I have said, until later that he reasoned this out with himself. But the fundamental trust in democracy as an objective was there, both by training in the faith of his fathers and by virtue of his belief in the soundness of the so-called "common" people. For he had been intimate with the poor in a manner shared by few of his radical friends. He had played with the children of his father's factory hands, he had served in a tough militia company and in the A.E.F., had traveled with cowmen and sheepherders, worked with farmers and grooms, sailed to the Banks with Maine fishermen, and consorted with the miserable and wretched of several nations — to say nothing of his service in the tenement districts of large cities. Few of the "experts" had anything like his direct laboratory experience of the dispossessed. And he believed that, in America and France at least, these "lower orders" were the stuff from which the girders of democracy are forged. Thus, in retrospect, he justified his desire to go to war by the feeling that he wanted to serve democracy. But while he never lost the conviction that a corrected democracy was worth fighting for, and fervently believed that most of his companions in the ranks were animated by the same motives, he became equally certain, as far as this particular war was concerned, that they had all had rings put into their noses. And for this he did not blame the leaders collectively symbolized by the word "government." For they had rings in their noses too. Indeed, it seemed as though all mankind had rings in their noses, and the great problem was to find out what puts them there. For in all history there appeared to be only a very few rulers — like Solomon, Solon, Pericles, Washington, and Lincoln — who did not seem to have their noses ringed by the same delusions with which they similarly decorated their followers. And he wasn't sure of Pericles, who was essentially a superlative New Dealer who climbed to political heights on rungs of idealism and then kicked the ladder away. Can democracy ever be so organized that wise and incorruptible men will be those selected for responsible power?

R.S. didn't know the answer. In 1917, indeed, he gave it little thought, for, after all, the chief impulse that took him into the army was an emotional one. He wanted to be with these conscripted boys. They were his people, whether native Americans, hyphenated Germans, Poles, Jews, Irish, etc., etc. He belonged with them — to wallow in dirt and vermin, to share and, if possible, to alleviate the bestiality and suffering of their helplessness. Yet his two years in the army gave him the rudiments of an answer to his question.

Of his military service, nineteen months were spent in France. Into these nineteen months were crowded the most stirring events of his life and his most intense emotions — elation, terror, compassion, admiration, disgust, and pride. But he utterly refused to discuss any of his experiences. On the way home, while Sanitary Inspector of a ship carrying twelve hundred sick and wounded, he came down with pneumonia and was taken to the New York Military Hospital in an ambulance.

In the depression which followed his reinduction into civilian life he was ashamed that he had not been killed. He had seen so many better men torn to pieces on battlefields or dying of mutilation on hospital cots that he could not get himself to make boastful anecdotes of his own small part in the great tragedy. Only men in the line and aviators really had a right to speak of the war. There was something obscene to him in the books and articles by which correspondents, observers, and others in relatively safe positions made copy of agony and terror. For some of these, war had been a stimulating spectacle, enjoyed with poorly masked sadism and exploited with crude boastfulness. An all-time low of this war literature was a book by a female volunteer worker which will ever stick in his mind as the climax of masked vulgarity and cynical bad taste. He had been too close to it not to know how the men who really fought the war must feel about that sort of thing.

When people began to speak of the war and reminiscences were exchanged, R.S. remained silent or went away — not from the inverted boastfulness that often motivates such reticence, but because it made him think that there were few privates in the U. S. infantry (at least two hundred thousand of them) who had not suffered more or had not had occasion for heroism far exceeding his own. And his own hardships and exposures seemed little things and pale in comparison.

He did bring back a profound faith in these infantrymen, and often wondered why some peace-time formula could not be found to bring out the magnificent latent traits of courage, patience, and coöperative enthusiasm which the circumstances of war and danger appear to call forth in individuals who, in times of peace, are second-rate, or worse. What a nation they would make, what a triumphant democracy, if this secret could be discovered!

He also brought back a deep respect for the men of the Regular Army and Navy services, who, with astonishingly few exceptions, rose nobly to immensely expanded responsibilities. Here were groups of expertly trained administrators, artillery officers, engineers, sanitarians, doctors, navigators, applied physicists, and the like, who carried on in the government employ for small pay, while their equals in civil life were selling their services to the highest bidder. It seemed to R.S. that if something of the spirit of the government technical services could be instilled into the politicians, the professions, and even into business, democracy might be cured of some of its ills. It convinced him that the money motive is not essential for high standards of performance. The answer seemed to be professional tradition and pride of service. The medical profession has some of it. It might be developed for other callings. Even bankers and brokers, manufacturers, grocers, and merchants in general might eventually regard their work as necessary specialized functions in a well-ordered world of sane capitalism, and might approach their tasks — as doctors, lawyers, engineers, and men in the learned professions approach their own — not perfectly, of course, and not without exception, but in general with a sense of responsibility and a tradition to restrain the greed of the unadulterated profit motive. It is not a new idea. Juvenal expresses it in the passage (*Satire XIV*) beginning "*Sponte tamen iuvenes imitantur cetera, solam inviti quoque avaritiam exercere iubentur,*" and so on. (All vices but one the young imitate spontaneously; avarice alone is enjoined upon them unwillingly. For that vice has a deceptive mien and resembles virtue, gloomy in face and apparel. The miser is praised as a thrifty one — etc., etc.)

Marcus Aurelius says: "Pursuit of the impossible is idiocy." And the hope that men, in the competitive struggle for power and wealth, should develop this sense of social responsibility may be that kind of idiocy. But R.S. had seen just that spirit operative among the groups he had known most intimately — academic associates and physicians, and especially the technical personnel of the Army, Navy, and Public Health services; and he believed that in an expansion of such points of view and pride of calling lay the hope of humane democracy.

From these considerations he was inclined to expostulate on the influence which educational systems might have on the realization of this miracle, and then he usually went on to the governing class of Plato.

But not a word could I get out of him about his service in France.

It seemed incredible that mankind had failed to learn its lesson. When it started again, just before he died, he realized that the new generations would have to learn all over again — and so on, hopelessly through the future as in the past. Peace had lasted just long enough to allow a new crop of youth to mature for the scythe, like a long season between wheat and wheat.

1

The question is often asked whether anything came out of this war that — by any stretch of the imagination — can be called "good." It is quite possible, of course, that the pressure of military and naval necessity may have stimulated and speeded up improvements in applied physics, in radio communication, sound detection, and such, and in the constructive engineering of aeroplanes, submarines, and other forms of mechanical production. These things might, however, have been equally developed under the influence of commercial, peace-time competition. There can be little question of the fact that the circumstances of war — the camps of mobilization and the management of large masses of men in limited areas — provided tragic, yet highly instructive and permanently valuable occasions for the study of epidemics. And although many of these episodes were handled in a manner that fell far short of perfection, it may be stated with some pride in our profession that, after the first confusions incident to speed and magnitude, the army sanitary organizations functioned about as well as could reasonably have been expected. In our own country, cantonment construction was ably supervised by the Engineering Corps, and the medical organization — apart from hospital personnel — was centralized in the Surgeon General's Office under Colonel F. F. Russell, the best selection General Gorgas could have made. For Russell, a seasoned army doctor and a distinguished bacteriologist in his own name, was able — as no one else at that time could have succeeded in doing — to enlist the best talents of the civilian profession for his service. The standards he set were carried to France with the divisions and were there adjusted to expeditionary and combat conditions by a group of regular officers, headed by General Ireland and including men like Colonels Siler, Charles Reynolds, Grissinger, and others, who were keenly alive to the importance of their tasks and displayed extraordinary capacities for administrative wisdom. There were incompetents, of course, in the regular service, as there were —

in much larger proportions — among the reserve. But, throughout the war, in the medical service it was rare that an incapable officer either achieved or, if he did, continued to hold a position of power.

The most striking results were those accomplished, from the very beginning, in the prevention of enteric diseases. This was to be expected (in spite of the disastrous experiences of preceding wars — our own Spanish War one of the worst) as a result of civilian developments of typhoid prevention and of the excellent records of military prevention achieved by the Japanese in their war against Russia. The necessity of water control, fly-proofing, sewage and garbage disposal, was well recognized. And anti-typhoid vaccination, started but imperfectly applied by the Germans in their slaughter of the Herreros and by the British in the "civilizing" of South Africa, had been brought to practical success by Russell in our own army. The consequences of all these measures rigidly applied — even against considerably localized opposition on the part of occasional fundamentalist groups — resulted in almost eliminating typhoid and paratyphoid fevers. Indeed, in the camps, the soldiers were statistically forty-five times less liable to these infections than the same young men would have been in their civilian surroundings. Of course, under the circumstances of the July (1918) advance in the heavily polluted triangle of Rheims–Soissons–Château-Thierry, such protection partially broke down. But even so, with an immense gastro-intestinal sick rate, there was relatively little serious disease and, no doubt thanks to vaccination, what might have become a major calamity remained merely a difficult situation.

With many of the so-called "respiratory" diseases — that is, those conveyed with the secretions of the respiratory tract —

prevention was, for obvious reasons, next to impossible. Yet lessons of immense value were learned in regard to transmission, principles of prevention, early diagnosis, and specific treatment.

One of the gravest problems was that of epidemic cerebrospinal meningitis. This is a disease which, more than most others, illustrates the benefits which coördinated bacteriological and clinical efforts may achieve in the face of conditions which at first appear hopeless. We know relatively little of the remote history of meningitis, because specific diagnosis was impossible until 1887, when the good old Hofrath Weichselbaum first cultivated the meningococcus from spinal fluid. Since many other bacteria can, on occasion, cause acute meningitis, and since the general symptoms of the disease may have much similarity with forms of acute virus encephalitis, it is quite impossible to be certain whether descriptions antedating the bacteriological age refer to our "meningitis epidemica cerebrospinalis" or to superficially similar conditions. When accounts of cases are joined with epidemiological data, we can sometimes make a fair guess. There is nothing pertinent in Hippocrates' *Epidemics*. There are passages in the *Causes and Indications of Acute and Chronic Diseases* of Aretaeus (second half of the second century) which might be taken to refer to this disease. Haeser cites a passage from the Alexandrine physician Paulus Aeginatus (seventeenth century), describing an acute epidemic disease in Italy and the provinces which, in manner of distribution, acuteness of seizures, high mortality, and paralyses, strongly suggests meningitis. A disease that accompanied an influenza outbreak in France in 1483 (Mézeray) was very probably meningitis. It was a "*maladie épidémique toute extraordinaire qui attaquait aussi bien les* grands et les petits. C'était une fièvre continuelle et violente qui mettait le feu à la tête, dont la plupart tombaient en frénésie et mouraient comme enragés."

There is, as a matter of fact, no reason why meningitis — caused by the Weichselbaum diplococcus — should not have existed for many centuries, in the same sporadic form in which it prevails with us in interepidemic periods. Such cases would not be easy to recognize in purely clinical descriptions, partly for the reason that they are very often much more mild than the same disease in epidemic outbreaks. It is true of many infections, and of typhus and meningitis in particular, that severity and mortality step up as an epidemic progresses and that, with the decline of mass infection, the individual cases grow less severe. And after epidemics are over, the cases which trickle along for months and years are, as a rule, of a relatively mild character. In ancient times, epidemics developed only in crowded centres and at times of distress. And since, at such times, the same circumstances are favorable for a number of different maladies, few epidemics consist purely of one disease, and diagnostic descriptions are often confusing. Moreover, except in times of mass wanderings or troop movements, travel in ancient days was relatively slight and slow. Diseases, consequently, were apt to be more localized or, if widely spread, more likely to remain endemic in widely separated regions. All this has changed to-day. The world is constantly on the move and infections travel de luxe on railroads, steamboats, and aeroplanes. If, nevertheless, we keep down epidemics to a greater extent, this is due to improved knowledge and skill. Yet modern conditions have tended to scatter potential foci much more widely than they were in ancient times. And since the world to-day is far more crowded, the embers of epidemics

— that is, the endemic, sporadic cases and the immune carriers of virulent infectious agents — are kept smoldering in many thousand different places, from any one of which new epidemics may originate.

2

During the war, meningitis was one of the chief problems in the cantonments. At Camp Jackson, the incidence and mortality of this disease were probably higher than they had ever been in an accurately observed epidemic. A close second was the outbreak among the Canadian troops on Salisbury Plain, near London. The experience gained during these epidemics taught us much concerning the conditions which favor extension, about the existence and discovery of carriers, the importance of early diagnosis and methods of treatment. And if a similar situation should ever face us again, we are far more ready to cope with it than we were in 1917 and 1918.

What the war experience did for our knowledge of meningitis it did to even a greater extent for that of the pneumonias. A new era in the understanding of the acute pulmonary infection caused by the pneumococcus had begun in 1902, when — as a result of the discovery of Neufeld, confirmed and extended by American bacteriologists — the multiplicity of pneumococcus types became established and rational efforts at serum therapy were thereby made possible. Until the war, however, such methods and their clinical appraisal had been limited to the better hospitals in large cities. The army organized both personnel and materials for the typing of pneumonias and for serum treatment; and in consequence a volume of experience was accumulated without which the considerable progress which has been made in a difficult problem might have been indefinitely delayed. And after the war large numbers of physicians were discharged from the service into civilian life with a training in the management both of meningitis and of pneumonia which they would never have obtained without their army experience.

The particular epidemic disease which was directly and indirectly responsible for the greatest loss of life during these years was influenza. During the two decades that followed the armistice, this infection has been definitely recognized as caused by a filtrable virus agent. Susceptible animals (ferrets and mice) have been made available, and the virus has been cultivated by a variety of tissue-culture methods. It has at last become possible to study this ancient scourge as a biological entity and to carry out, with scientific precision, those fundamental observations which may lead eventually to partial or complete control — although it should always be borne in mind that even complete knowledge of methods of transmission, properties of a virus, and mechanism of resistance does not necessarily mean that anything can be done about it. Yet these facts are the *sine qua non* of conquest, and the influenza problem — once a quite hopeless one — has begun to yield to systematic study. It is doubtful, however, whether without the world-wide epidemiological studies made during the war the extraordinary subsequent progress would have been possible. The army observations once for all accurately defined a disease which had before that been again and again confused with entirely unrelated respiratory infections. The past clinical confusion is, in a way, surprising, since epidemics and pandemics have been quite accurately described since the sixteenth century (Galenus, 1579; Jacques Pons of Lyons, 1596; Sydenham, 1675), and after that time outbreaks recurred with periodic disastrousness at least two or three times in every hundred years. Moreover, some of the available descriptions were so concise that they might easily have prevented later uncertainties. Thus Huxham of Plymouth (1743) writes: "About this time a disease invaded these parts which was the most completely epidemic of any I remember to have met with; not a house was free from it. . . . Scarce a person escaping either in town or country; old and young, strong and infirm shared the same fate." He described the symptoms almost exactly as we ourselves observed them at Chaumont and Baccarat in France in March and April of 1918 — the sudden onset, fever, chilliness, pains, and rapid defervescence in about four days.

Arbuthnot (1732) and Thompson (1852) published equally accurate and more clinically recognizable accounts of the disease. Yet in spite of this, when the influenza pandemic of 1889 first appeared in Russia it was regarded by Heyfelder as a peculiar form of malaria and later as, possibly, dengue fever. And again when, during the last war, the first cases developed at Camp Oglethorpe, Georgia, in March 1918, the precise nature of the cases was long undetermined, though their similarity to influenza was acknowledged. Vaughan and Palmer, writing of this outbreak, say: "The identity of the disease has not been positively determined after nearly a month of observation." They speak of it as "a disease with a strong resemblance to influenza." In Italy, Sampietro suggested sandfly fever, a thought which seems to have occurred to a number of British writers, and which led us, as well, to make a brief study of prevailing insects upon our first contact with the epidemic at Chaumont. Wherever the disease was first seen during the spring and summer of 1918, it was characterized by explosive suddenness of onset and an enormous morbidity in individual groups within a few days; but it was mild in nature, with little or no mortality, rare complications, and so few of the catarrhal symptoms usually associated with clinical conceptions of influenza that those that did occur were not always regarded as characteristic manifestations of the "new disease."

Fortunately placed observers, however, could follow with considerable clearness the gradual transformation of the clinical types encountered in successive outbreaks, from the mild "three-day fever" of early spring to the grave, respiratory illness of autumn. But there was still in the minds of a considerable number of people some question as to the basic identity of the early mild cases and the severe epidemic bronchopneumonias of October and November.

The result of all this work was eventual clarity that recognized true influenza as a virus infection which, when it first appears in uncomplicated form, is sharply characterized, enormously and rapidly disseminated, but relatively mild, with a low mortality and of short duration. But — and this is both the source of early confusion and the reason for the seriousness of these outbreaks — the basic influenzal infection predisposes to such a degree to secondary invasions by more serious infectious agents — pneumococci and streptococci — that the first waves of pure influenza invariably become transformed into epidemics of particularly vicious types of pneumonia. It was this epidemiological definition of the disease which rendered possible the subsequent successful isolation of the influenza virus in ferrets, mice, and tissue culture, and these laboratory achievements have now put us in the position of facing a well-reconnoitred enemy instead of a hidden, mysterious terror.

It would be possible to write at considerably greater length about the medical lessons taught by the World War. Measles, diphtheria, and mumps became military and camp diseases. Lethargic encephalitis appeared for the first time — at least, was first defined — and the now important chapter of the epidemic forms of encephalitis was started. Never before, moreover, was there such an enormous scope for the testing out of diagnostic, preventive, and therapeutic methods and for the training of young physicians in modern practice. Of surgery, I am not competent to speak, yet I know from discussion with surgical colleagues that — apart from the actual work accomplished in the service — the training given to thousands of young doctors who later went back to civilian practice had an incalculable effect upon the general quality of American surgery. Moreover, the physical and mental condition of recruits from certain impoverished rural areas in our country furnished a survey — often so shocking that it led to energetic public and private health campaigns — that should have been started fifty years sooner. Among other things, the World War awakened the public conscience to the problem of venereal disease. But that will have to be a separate chapter.

CHAPTER XVI

Continuation of preceding chapter. R.S. was long occupied with syphilis, both in the laboratory and in campaigns of prevention. He cites this disease as an example of the lag between information and its preventive application

1

IN other connections, it has already been pointed out that there has often been an inexplicable lag between the determination of the facts necessary for preventive measures against a disease and their sensible application. Of no infection has this been more inexcusably true than it is of syphilis. And it seems likely that the present long-delayed energetic campaign against syphilis owes much of its *vis a tergo* to the shock to the public conscience resulting from the examination of recruits inducted, at the beginning of the war, into the army and navy. The war opened the eyes of those good people who had insisted upon regarding venereal diseases as problems for purely moral approach instead of as serious sanitary situations. Even the necessarily superficial examinations of the first million youngsters showed 43,000 cases of gonorrhea, over 10,000 of syphilis, and about 1500 chancroids. That these figures were far below the actual incidence was a foregone conclusion, since in gonorrhea and, especially, in syphilis the stages of easy diagnosis are relatively short, and therefore only the most recent and obvious cases could be picked up in such preliminary examinations. When more delicate methods were later applied and serological tests were carried out, — as, for instance, at the Fort Riley camp, — it was found that 18 per cent of the whites and 24 per cent of the negroes showed signs of infection, present or past, but uncured.

These conditions led to the organization of a separate military machinery for the control of the venereal sick rate, initiated under the energetic direction of Dr. William F. Snow, which was later perpetuated as the American Social Hygiene Association and became, to a large degree, responsible for preparing the public mind and clearing the ground for the antivenereal campaign now carried on by the United States Public Health Service.

If syphilis had been a disease acquired by inhalation or with a can of spoiled beans, instead of being what it is, we should have made infinitely more progress and might almost be rid of it by now. We need only consider, in substantiation of this statement, the enormous progress made since 1900 in the much more difficult sanitary, but morally uncomplicated problem of tuberculosis. The contagiousness of syphilis was recognized immediately after its appearance in the late fifteenth century, in spite of the fact that the primary genital lesions are often negligible as compared with the widespread and manifest affections of the skin, throat, and mucous membranes of the secondary stages, or the destructive ones of the tertiary period, which attract attention long after the sexual source of infection may have been lost sight of. Fracastorius, in his *De Contagione*, was the earliest influential advocate of its contagiousness. The disease spread rapidly in his time and was widely prevalent in its most repulsive general manifestations. Children were frequently infected by contact with their parents, and suckling infants transmitted it to their mothers. In 1577, Jordanus of Basel observed that people who, over a certain period, frequented a particular barber-surgeon, Adam, for the purpose of bloodletting and cupping, suffered from abscesses and ulcers which developed into the well-known "French Evil." The literature of syphilis during this period became enormous and the disease spread in a manner comparable only to some of our modern epidemics. The chief contributory cause for rapid distribution seems to have been the failure of all moral restraint fostered by wars and disbanding armies and by an apparently complete abdication of the moral influence of the church. Modification of the infection in the direction of greater mildness, within the first century of its acknowledged prevalence, is attested by many authorities, of which the most important, again, is Fracastorius.

In view of the present belated agitation for a sensible and energetic attack on this scourge, it is appropriate to remember that active anti-syphilis campaigns were waged hundreds of years ago, and that if the public conscience had kept pace with discovery during the lavender-and-old-lace periods of modern times, we might now be much further along than we are.

There was an Italian regulation formulated in 1497, reported by Mittarelli, which recommended the public branding of prostitutes who continued to ply their trade after they had contracted the "French disease." About 1500, in Nürnberg, barber-surgeons were forbidden to admit syphilitics into their establishments or to use lancets employed in the treatment of such persons on other people; and in Würzburg, according to Reuss, at about the same time, the hospitalization of syphilitics — a matter not yet accomplished in our modern organizations — was established by setting aside an old plague hospital for the afflicted poor. The same thing happened later in Prague, where cases were so plentiful that they lay about in the streets and became a public nuisance. At first they were excluded from the city and formed a shanty town outside the gates. Finally, a small hospital was established for them.

In Switzerland, syphilitics were quarantined in isolated huts. Even the lepers refused to associate with them. They were excluded from the Canton of Baden and from Zurich, and when any were discovered, laundresses were forced to separate the clothing of such people from that of others. In Berne, in 1570, syphilitics were made to isolate themselves during the first three months of treatment with mercury.

In Paris, as early as 1497, there were regulations which at the present day could not be enforced under a democracy — though perhaps they might be possible in Germany, Russia, or Italy. Chereau describes an edict of the sixth of March of 1497 — approximately two years after the disease became noticeably prevalent — by which foreigners afflicted with syphilis were constrained to leave the city within twenty-four hours. Those who had no resources of their own were given small stipends for travel. Parisians, if well-to-do, were not permitted to leave their houses until cured; if poor, they were isolated in a building in St.-Germain-des-Près. Disobedience of the order carried a penalty of death.

Most interesting, because identical with a futile type of modern efforts, are the suggestions of Torelli, who believed that the disease could be exterminated if public prostitutes were systematically examined by an appointed group of "honourable women."

Fracastorius believed that syphilis might die out of itself because it was so rapidly growing milder. Fernel, however, erring on the other extreme, characterized syphilis as the "*Comes humani generis immortalis.*"

It is probably the increasing mildness and chronicity through the centuries which are partly responsible for the long-continued indifference of the public and a partial acceptance of this fatalistic view of Fernel — that the disease is just one of those inevitable trials which came to mankind with expulsion from the Garden of Eden, inflicted upon men from on high, "*pour leurs paillardises.*" The greatest obstacle to prevention in our time, however, has been the prudery which was so long offended by frank discussion. There was long a strong feeling that to abandon reticence in these problems might serve to undermine a public morality which, to those of us who read statistics, could not easily have been worse. The war opened the eyes of some of our moralists who had been inclined to believe that diminution of the fear of venereal infection by sanitary safeguards might weaken sexual restraint. In the face of the records, however, a little increase of immorality becomes obviously of vanishing significance. Moreover, it is problematical whether, even if methods of relative safety could be guaranteed, the number of those whom Venus irresistibly lures would be materially increased over the present statistically indeterminable number. At any rate, the sentiment is changing. The American Social Hygiene Association, cautiously steering its narrow channel between the Scylla of moral turpitude and the Charybdis of women's clubs and the clergy, has done much to prepare the way. The popularization of psychoanalysis and the vogue for indecent literature have some credit in this to balance their sins. People have begun to discuss freely — indeed, like to discuss, go out of their ways to discuss — matters that were formerly whispered in the woodshed. In some respects this may be deplorable, but as regards syphilis it has made possible the present energetic campaign.

No one engaged in these campaigns, the world over, wishes to diminish the efforts of aesthetic and religious influences that are no doubt of immense assistance. On the other hand, there are certain aspects of the struggle, perhaps our strongest weapons of defense, which have had to be delayed because they still appear to many well-meaning people in direct conflict with standards of public morality. These are the questions of prophylaxis.[1] It is not a pleasant subject, but — for that matter — neither is the examination of stools for typhoid bacilli, or the examination of sputum for tubercle bacilli. It has, perhaps, even a peculiarly unpleasant individual quality. But, at its worst, it is far less unpleasant than the disease it may prevent. The facts of the matter are more or less as follows: —

In 1903, Metchnikoff and Roux of the Pasteur Institute in Paris successfully inoculated a female chimpanzee with material from a syphilitic sore. Subsequent work by others demonstrated that, in addition to chimpanzees, many of the lower monkeys, as well as rabbits, can be infected, and that mice

---

[1] This matter of venereal prophylaxis brings to my mind a recent literary observation which I mention only as a clue for the more learned. I have not been able to determine with certainty whether the M. de Condom repeatedly mentioned by Mme. de Sévigné and a friend of M. de la Rochefoucauld is actually the same great Condom whose beneficent invention has "prevented" so many unwanted human beings and so much dreadful affliction. I believe it is the same man, however, and — if so — a passage in one of the famous letters, *"Je ne savois pas que M. de Condom eût rendu son évêché,"* indicates that the great inventor was once a bishop — a discovery for which I beg to claim priority, if correct.

injected with syphilis — though showing no symptoms — may harbor and keep alive the organisms for periods of months. As a consequence, syphilis became amenable to planned and purposeful laboratory study.

Metchnikoff then turned to experiments on prevention. Quite naturally, he chose for first attention mercury and its compounds, the time-honored specifics ever since the time of Fracastorius. Indeed, the word "syphilis" is derived from the name of the shepherd who, in Fracastorius's poem, bathed in the river of mercury. The most effective substance for what is now known as "prophylaxis" was found to be a 35 per cent calomel ointment put up in a mixture of lanoline and lard. In inoculated apes, the local application of the calomel ointment, when practised within two hours after infection, prevented the development of the disease in all his animals.

Having proved his point on animals, Metchnikoff proceeded to an experiment on a heroic young medical student by the name of Maisonneuve, who allowed himself to be inoculated and then treated with calomel, and who ought to have a statue which I should like to design. The experiment succeeded.

The Metchnikoff system was introduced into the United States Army just before we entered the war, and was carried out on a large scale in the American Expeditionary Forces. Thirty-five per cent calomel ointment was used for inunction of the exposed parts. Prophylactic stations were established to which the soldier could go as soon as possible after exposure. In the British and the French Armies, the matter was left to the judgment of the individual soldier by the distribution of packages containing the necessary materials.

Stokes, who has consolidated the observations made on the expeditionary forces in France, states that of 242,000 treatments, there were only 1.3 per cent failures, and Moore, who was working in the Paris area, — where, as in other noncombatant zones, syphilitic infection was apt to be high, — stated that in men prophylactically treated there was only one case in 247 exposures, whereas without prophylaxis there was one case for every 37.

Such figures, and these are only a small part of those available, speak for themselves. Is it more moral or less moral to keep such information from being as widely disseminated as possible?

2

One of the most astonishing and — if one is inclined to look at it that way — tragic examples of the manner in which the conventional attitude toward syphilis has obstructed clear thinking, even in the medical profession, came to my attention while I was still teaching in New York. A lady in a New England city whom I knew quite well wrote me about a friend — a wealthy, unmarried woman of fifty — who had been ill for two years or more with vague complaints of headache, anaemia, pains in joints, and a number of other things that are irrelevant, but none of them sharply characteristic of any well-defined condition. She had seen a number of excellent doctors, any one of them the equal of the best men in New York. All kinds of things had been tried without relief.

My friend wanted to know whether I could recommend some good New York diagnostician. She felt that the local men were beginning to regard the patient as a pronounced neurotic whose symptoms might disappear if she lost her money and social position and could get a little healthy scrubbing to do. They were recommending Austen Riggs, and, indeed, in her city social position was not completely attained at this time without at least one nervous breakdown at Stockbridge. I told her to send her friend along and referred her to an able young practitioner whose thoroughness I trusted. Within two weeks a diagnosis of syphilis had been made and the patient was well on her way to cure.

Her own doctors, who had seen her in their offices, just didn't allow themselves to think of the — if not obvious, at least possible diagnosis. All of them could have done the same thing that my friend accomplished, and would have if the patient had been unknown to them or had been poor and admitted to the wards of one of their hospitals.

Entirely apart from this aspect of the case, I have often thought of the tragic human struggle and suffering of the spirit that formed its never-to-be-disclosed background.

There are among the well-to-do, lonely women of our upper classes, especially in provincial towns, many tragedies of a similar kind which, unfortunately, have been treated in our native literature — as, for instance, in the *Spoon River Anthology* — in a manner that brings out only the sordid and neglects the often Greek starkness of their dismal causes. Usually, in the few I have seen in my connections with medical practice and with asylums for the mentally sick, the roots of such situations extend deeply into a soil of frustration and renunciation for which the spirit lacked the necessary strength.

In the practice of one of my friends, in a small up-state town of New York, there were two old ladies, a mother of over eighty and a maiden daughter of sixty, who had allowed life to flow away from her in order to care for her mother. For forty years she had stood on the banks of the stream and had watched in resignation as, one after another, her contemporaries and even their children sailed away on the voyage of discovery which is normal life. Year after year she had sat in the big house with the heirlooms and the portraits and the aging servants, taking physical care of the increasingly exacting old lady, gradually giving up one thing after another. Friends drifted away; relatives died or forgot her; mental resources — slim to begin with — atrophied completely; and the daily round of meals, taking the Pomeranian to his favorite trees and hydrants, reading aloud and going to bed with the *Saturday Evening Post*, succeeded each other in deadly, automatic routine. A ring on the doorbell was an exciting event, and somewhat terrifying. The blinds were drawn in the front rooms, and the hall was dark. I met this poor thing — small, gray, and wrinkled like a November apple — one day as she was leaving the doctor's office. He told me the story. "Those two old ladies," he said, "live like affluent hermits for six months at a time. About twice a year they go on a terrible binge. They send the servants away and buy up, at various places, to avoid comment, a considerable supply of gin, Scotch, and ginger ale. Then they proceed to get tight. And they stay tight, and more so, day and night for two weeks. At the end of that time, the old lady is completely knocked out and the younger one has hallucinations. Then they call me in and I straighten them out. They tell me the daughter was once a considerable belle. There was no unrequited love affair or any other romantic episode which would at least give her something to remember. She was the oldest, and when all of the few eligibles had been scared away and she was supposed to be on the shelf, it was up to her to settle down and take care of her cantankerous mother. I don't try to cure them. I wouldn't deprive them of their semiannual bender for anything in the world."

CHAPTER XVII

Russia. R.S. learns that true communism can probably exist only in heaven and that the modern communist can thrive happily only in a democracy
where he can be properly protected in his beliefs

"Il y a trois sortes de gouvernements: le républicain, le monar-
chique et le despotique. . . . Quant aux principes des trois gouvernements, celui de la démocratie est l'amour de la république, c'est
à dire, de l'égalité. Dans les monarchies . . . le principe est l'honneur, c'est à dire l'ambition et l'amour de l'estime. Sous le despo-
tisme, enfin, c'est la crainte." (Preface to an edition of Montesquieu
published in the Fourth Year of the French Republic)

WHEN, in March 1917, Kerensky established his provisional
government in Russia, R.S. was thrilled with enthusiasm. A
great representative democracy was about to take its place by
the side of America, England, and France. The calamity of
the war appeared to have achieved at least one magnificent result. Democracy, accepted so clearly at that time as the ultimate goal of political evolution, seemed at last to have begun
its march eastward — perhaps into Asia. It was indeed a brave
and noble episode while it lasted. How fine it was the historians
— except for isolated voices like that of Seton-Watson and a
very few others — seem now to have forgotten. A Russian
friend, who was in Kerensky's cabinet for a time, described
to me how his chief, on a dramatic occasion, vowing that this
was to be "the one bloodless revolution of history," harangued

a turbulent Duma, declaring that the Czar would be executed only if they killed him (Kerensky) first. He told me too that, on the night when the extreme Left took control in Petrograd, Kerensky was within striking distance with two loyal regiments, but held his hand because he could not bring himself to give the signal for Russians to fire on Russians. It was a sad day for the world — indeed, for Germany herself, as she has since discovered — when she passed Lenin and Trotsky across the Russian borders and helped, in other ways, to smother the young democracy.

Of course, it is a platitude to say to-day that the Treaty of Versailles was as stupid as the war it ended. Yet, whenever one reads indignant German condemnations of this treaty, one cannot help remembering the terms of the earlier Treaty of Brest-Litovsk, dictated to Russia by the German General Staff, and not officially communicated to the Reichstag until accepted by Russia. By it, Russia lost 34 per cent of her population, 32 per cent of her agricultural land, 85 per cent of her beet-sugar land, 54 per cent of her industries, and 89 per cent of her coal mines.[1]

It was characteristic of R.S. that he wanted to express his enthusiasm by naming his newborn son "Kerensky." The common sense of his family prevented this, fortunately. What a calamity it would have been for the boy had he been condemned to go through life in an Anglo-Saxon country with the given name of Kerensky! That, at least, was saved from the shambles.

A German name during the war was a source, if not of humiliation, at least of considerable annoyance to so-called "hyphenated" Americans with family pride. Curiously enough, this situation was more difficult in the United States than in

[1] Wheeler-Bennett, *The Forgotten Peace*, William Morrow & Co., New York, 1939, page 269.

other Allied countries. A few there were who understood the feelings of people like R.S. and myself. But these were exceptions, and by most of the "old" Americans their fellows of German stock were regarded as a sort of parthenogenetic breed who reproduced without ancestors until they learned mitosis in America. It was only toward the end of the war, when troops — especially from Wisconsin and from other regions of German settlement — had reëstablished records comparable to those of the hundred thousand odd Germans who fought in the Civil War, that this offensive superciliousness of the Anglo-Saxon element partially subsided.

However, R.S. told me that as soon as he had left this country with orders to report in London on the way to France, all discrimination or even unpleasantness due to a German name ceased completely. There were two episodes which, far from annoying him, furnished evidence that both the British and the French were less provincial in these matters than the Americans.

The first of these experiences he described to me as follows: —

It was at a luncheon given at the British Army Medical College, to which he had been invited by Sir Robert Bruce. During a lull in the conversation, his neighbor, who had asked him his name, said in a loud voice: "Major, tell me, just how German are you by blood?" It was a dreadful question to ask at that time, and at a military mess. Fortunately, R.S. had one of those rare inspirations that usually come to one on the way home, or the next day. This time, it flashed out at the right moment, and while a tense table of officers gazed at him in the silent apology of gentlemen not knowing how to protect a guest, he replied: "I believe, sir, that I am just about as German as the King of England." The roar of relieved laughter that followed made him feel not only happy, but — as I could see by the way he told the story — inordinately smart.

The second episode was a year or so later, in a dugout near Rougemont, on the Belfort front, whither he had been sent to look into an outbreak of diphtheria in the 32nd (Wisconsin) Division, which was holding this line. He had wandered in when the Colonel in command was having a "canned" luncheon with his French liaison officer. R.S. had been roaming through the woods from company to company all morning, and was grateful when the Colonel asked him to join them. In the course of the conversation, this hearty officer said, with some pride: "You know, these boys of mine are quite wonderful. Never have I seen a regiment that showed more enthusiasm, discipline, and guts. And yet they are fighting Germans, and the roster of my regiment might be that of a Saxon guard unit."

R.S. was a little puzzled, wondering — hypersensitively — whether, perhaps, the Colonel were feeling him out. But to bring things to a head, he pretended to assume that the Colonel hadn't heard his name.

"That doesn't surprise me, sir," he said. "My own first name is Rudolf."

He had apparently guessed right. The Colonel looked at him with an expression of kindly embarrassment, for their relations had been businesslike and cordial for a week or more. But the Frenchman was an unknown quantity. He was the typical middle-aged, still snappy French reservist — a captain, — with the ribbons of the Croix de Guerre and the Légion d'Honneur on his field-worn tunic, and he had probably served a strenuous year or two in the lines before he joined our forces. He gazed at R.S. thoughtfully and seriously. R.S. hadn't any idea what was coming, and was fully prepared to resent the probably offensive remark or the equally offensive silence. Gradually, a thin smile spread over the Frenchman's tired face. Then his hand came across the board table and closed over that of R.S. with a gentle friendliness.

"You have nothing on me," he said, in pure New Yorkese. "My name is Gustav Ehrman."

Some years later, after the turning back of the Russians from Warsaw by Weygand, when Lenin's Marxian empire had become diplomatically isolated from the rest of the Western World, Russia became for R.S. an object of particular interest because it seemed to be passing through a sanitary period not unlike that prevailing in Europe during and after the Thirty Years' War. Three million deaths from typhus (thirty million cases) is the estimate of Tarassevitch from 1917 to 1923. Cholera began in 1920. In the train of these two diseases came relapsing fever, tuberculosis, the enteric fevers, malaria, syphilis, and odds and ends — to say nothing of a famine, the greatest and most devastating since the Middle Ages.

And when R.S. was invited by the League of Nations to go to Russia as a Sanitary Commissioner, to report on the situation and to coöperate with the Russian Government in problems of vaccination and border protection, he jumped at the chance. The following notes on his journey I give as closely as I can in his own words.

1

In Warsaw I saw the prettiest girls I have ever seen. Of course I have also said this of New York, Paris, Vienna, Rouen, Tunis, Salonica, Peking, Tokyo, and Shruboak, New York. I must not omit one — the very prettiest, I believe — who was in a stagecoach that ran from near Rock Creek, Texas, to the railroad at Amarillo. She was so pretty that I have never forgotten her; but I had been in the desert for several months, had a very ragged, reddish beard, my hair was long, and I wore

blue overalls, boots, and an old coat. She went forward to sit
with the driver, and after that first look I saw nothing but
the back of her pink neck for the rest of the day. Also, to be
just, I shouldn't forget the harness maker's daughter, who
lived at a crossroads in Putnam County and stuck her head
out of the window whenever I rode by. *She* was really the
prettiest of all. Anyway, I did not say it of London or Boston,
and the Warsaw ones are so vividly in my mind that they
merit a few words.

The Warsawettes are something to remember — especially
the blonde ones. A blonde Polonese, with that complete
blondeness of hair which graces the best Slavic type — and the
pink cheeks! They have blonde complexions with brunette
temperaments. Nothing of the washed-out sentimentality of
the German blonde. The Polish blonde is like a sunny day
with a heavy wind blowing — fair, but not calm; or like a fine,
red apple that looks as though it could bounce like a rubber
ball. There was one, the cousin of a friend — Wrobczinsky,
the Professor. I saw her only a short time, at lunch, for she
worked in a bank, but I have never quite forgotten her perfection of looks and manner. *"Polen ist noch nicht verloren,"*
I said to myself, when I saw her.

And there were others. A wonderful people, the Poles. I
did not like the men so much, but then, I never do. Moreover,
the women — in the upper classes at least — are the most
cultivated, taking them as a whole, that I have encountered
in any nation. The wife of almost every professional man I
met was either a doctoress or a lawyerette or a musician or a
government functionary, and that without any of that loss
of charm, or the flat heels, flowerpot hats, and wild hair that
one generally associates with the bluestocking. I liked, also,

the red beet soup and the *Starka*. The latter is a sort of distillate of the beauty of the ladies, and a thimbleful — trickled down the back of the tongue — warms the body with a comforting courage from the neck down. It is the concentrate of Polish patriotism, and an army fed on *Starka* should be invincible. Yet, much as I admired the intelligence of the upper classes and the splendid energy and vigor of the young government, especially in those matters which I could judge, — educational and public-health efforts, — I could not help feeling that Poland had a long way to go before she could take any significant place in European civilization. The spirit was feudal, the poor in villages and cities indescribably miserable and abject, the peasants serfs in every actual sense, docilely subservient to an immensely wealthy and arrogant class of land-owners. Nothing had changed in regard to these matters in three hundred years, and to count Poland among the democratic states — whatever the form of government — was as absurd as to regard Russia as a haven of liberty. I began, at this time, to realize with amazement the unlimited capacity of men for self-deception — or, rather, for the ignoring of facts — in formulating the political or sociological conditions for which they are willing to let other people die. Later I learned that I had still underestimated it.

I left Warsaw with a heavy heart, especially since an English officer recently back from Odessa, who came to see me off, said, with the type of humor I associate with *Punch*, "Well, good-bye, old man. I hope you get back. Remember that it's Friday, the thirteenth."

The trains left for Moscow in those days on schedule, like ships, twice a week — Tuesdays and Fridays. Everyone on them had the holiday air of a convict train starting up the Hudson for Sing Sing. Gloom pervaded the bushy countenances of my entirely male fellow travelers. The train had hardly started when an anxious-looking Pole addressed me in poor French and begged me to change berths with him, because the second man in my compartment was a friend of his. I readily complied, because his roommate didn't look any hairier than mine. But when I had changed my baggage over, I found that I had been tricked — because now I found myself in berth number 13. So I traveled into Russia during that summer, when Lenin's illness was putting extra vigor into the bourgeois-hating, in berth number 13, on Friday the thirteenth. I am not superstitious, and always make a point of walking under ladders, insist on being the third to light a cigarette from the same match, and so on. But I confess I was annoyed at that Pole.

Crossing the border was depressing. One had the feeling of stepping behind a curtain which shut off the rest of the world and deprived one of that protection by law the sense of which — except in actual battle — the civilized man carries about with him. It was a strange feeling to be without it. And the lack of it was almost immediately brought home by the utter absence of any kind of courtesy — indeed, a sort of active contempt — with which the shabby train crew treated the passengers. Everyone aboard had some specific mission that made the journey necessary. Under ordinary circumstances, there would have been a lively interchange of purposes and ideas. There was almost no conversation after we crossed the frontier, and there was an atmosphere of strain when the customs officers, accompanied by a squad of Red soldiers, bayonets fixed, came aboard and took all passports, to disappear with them for an hour. I had to get off the train to put several chests of cholera vaccine through the formalities. They were destined for the Red Army, and I was cynically pleased that this material gave disagreeable reactions. That was a small satisfaction, however. I was spared nothing in respect to explaining myself, in spite of the quadruple history of my life, military activities, political views, etc., etc., which I had had to write out for the Soviet Mission in Berlin. The Soviets at this time cared about as much for the League of Nations — which I represented — as the rest of the world does now.

In Moscow, I was received by a young Italian who was to act as my interpreter, and he led me to the officials with whom I was to deal. I had visions of getting to work promptly, but I had read *Oblomov* and was not wholly unprepared for what followed. Basically, the Revolution had not changed the Russian character. Procrastination and inefficiency remained. Only now it was devoid of any of the formality and good-natured courtesy which prevailed in other days. Also, the disorder and sloppiness which were everywhere obvious were being inexpertly disguised by a pretense of bustle and much talk.

It was difficult to get a place to sleep. My guide tried to install me in a former hotel now run by a shaven-headed ruffian and four or five frowsy women. But when I found that I should be likely to lose any clothing or other movables that I could not always carry on my body, I preferred to establish myself in a hallway in the house occupied by the Nansen Mission, having borrowed a military cot from the stores of the American Relief Association, which was just preparing to liquidate.

Incidentally, those who have forgotten everything about Mr. Hoover except that he was not smart politician enough to appeal to our sovereign people for a second term might profitably be reminded of what his American Relief did for the Russians. As far as I could judge, the Russians themselves had forgotten it before his organization had moved out. He was, of course, working against insuperable obstacles, for the governing mob cared little in those days about a hundred thousand lives more or less, starving children, suffering and sickness, if only they could attain the noble ideals of Marxian theory. But Hoover and his people *did* feed many thousands who would otherwise have starved, — and possibly did, later on, — vaccinated many millions against cholera and typhoid fever, and were, as far as I could ascertain, the only agency of mercy and compassion practically expressed in an empire where hatred and persecution were the official government policy. But the Hoover Commission was moving out at the time I entered Russia, having spent some $50,000,000 of American money for purely humane purposes, for which it was getting no local credit. Indeed, the Soviet Government was anxious to get rid of these Samaritans, since they were a disturbing factor, had been granted too many privileges, and, possibly, were feeding and vaccinating occasional people who were not entirely convinced that a world ruled in the name of the "workers" by fanatical Jacobin theorists was the Kingdom of Heaven. Also, they were in the position of contradicting from time to time the rosy accounts of the Socialist heaven which were being brought back by American radicals, gullible professors, and social workers. Even without Belgium, the Russian relief work alone should give Hoover a high place in our history. He invaded Russia with the weapons of pity and mercy, and, though Russia rejected him with small thanks, he *did*, for a time, in a world inconceivably brutalized and debased, make the name of our country synonymous with kindness and humanity in the hearts of countless desperate people. It is too bad that he became only a President later on.

After my first night in Moscow, I asked my Italian friend to take me to the Commissar of Health.

"Don't be in a hurry," he said. "I will make an appointment for you for Tuesday morning, and then you may see him on Thursday afternoon. He will mean to see you on Tuesday, but he will most probably spend the preceding night conversing with his friends about his soul or some fine point of Marxian theory, and they will not go to bed until the next day at about the time for your appointment.

"Ask a Russian," he said, "whether he is sitting down or standing up, and he will reply somewhat as follows: 'Do you mean physically, spiritually, or intellectually? Physically? Physically, I am sitting down. Spiritually, I may be standing up. For my father was a minor official in Samara. I was born in Omsk. My mother was the daughter of a nobleman in the province of Ekaterinoslav. She was partly Jewish, but her hair was blonde,' etc., etc. It takes a long time, my friend, in this country, to come down to what you Americans call 'brass tacks.' "

He was right. I finally got to see Dr. Siemashko, the Commissar of Health, on Friday. He was a pleasant, bearded gentleman, with the general allure of the country doctor which, I believe, he actually was before the Revolution. I asked for access to information concerning the prevalence of certain diseases, and a permit to go to regions where epidemics were prevailing or had gone on recently. He referred me to various subofficers. Everything looked fine, as described, but it took several other interviews before I found out that the health organization was, indeed, almost entirely on paper. There were still a few of the specialists and scientists of the old régime on hand — splendid and patriotic men like Tarassevitch, Barykin, Korschun, Zabolotny, and a few others. But the rank and file of the medical profession had been rooted out, being largely bourgeois, — as is the habit of our tribe, — and medical training had practically stopped. Personnel was lacking, the old, fine laboratories were empty of supplies and apparatus, and the most important administrative posts were occupied by ignorant incompetents whose sole qualification was party loyalty, and who treated the men I have mentioned like lackeys, summoning them, letting them wait in anterooms, reprimanding them, and keeping them on starvation rations.

I did manage to obtain considerable information — largely by conversations with these older colleagues — and never have I encountered finer examples of courage, devotion, and patriotism. Some of these men later went to prison, two committed suicide. But while I was there they carried on against unbelievable odds from sheer desire to help their own people. I obtained permission to go to the Black Sea, where the tail of a cholera epidemic was trailing along.

The existence of cholera in Russia has always been a matter of the greatest importance to epidemiologists, because practically all the great epidemics that have spread across Europe and occasionally traveled to America have swept across Russia from Asiatic origins.

2

At this point R.S. indulged in a rambling account of the history of cholera, its origin in India, its description by Susruta and Charaka, and the successive pandemics in which it swept northwestward across Russia into Europe. At first, he wanted me to include all this in our book. He was especially interested in the effects of the cholera outbreaks on the British conquest of India — the decimation of the army of Coates in 1779 and of General Hastings's troops in the 1818 epidemic. When I had all this material in publishable shape, he suddenly changed his mind. "All that stuff," he said, "has been written up. If we put it in here, we'll only be making another of these popular compilations of well-known things that are flooding the market and appeal to people who are too lazy to go to the sources."

Nothing I could say — though I thought his historical outline of great interest — made any impression on him. So finally I was forced to leave it out in order to avoid more argument. When I had consented to his view, he continued about his Russian experiences.

During the 1891 epidemic, he continued, there were over 800,000 cases of cholera in Russia alone. Eastern Europe, and particularly Russia, had now been thoroughly *durchseucht*, as the Germans say, and the general picture of the disease appears to have become modified to the extent that later outbreaks could no longer be so easily traced to slow invasion from Asiatic sources. There were repeated visitations of Russia in 1908, 1909, and 1910. Again, during the Balkan War of 1912, there were cases among Austrian troops in Galicia, and in Bulgaria, Greece, Turkey, and Mesopotamia.

The problem in which I was particularly interested was, therefore, the following: Had cholera now become established in Eastern Europe, where it remained smoldering in inter-epidemic foci and could blaze up in new epidemics without importation from India or intervening Asiatic sources?

For, as far as Russia was concerned, the disease had again become epidemically prevalent from 1920 on. The greatest incidence for these years occurred in 1921, but continued through 1922 into 1923, distributed over a wide region. Between January and June of 1922, something over 12,000 reported cases came from localities as widely separated as Siberia, Turkestan, Georgia, along the Black Sea to the Rumanian border, the Ukraine, and along the Polish border up to Lithuania.

The problem which confronts epidemiologists in regard to this disease is not unique, for in many epidemic maladies modern conditions of travel and rapidity of communication have modified epidemic movements. In influenza, for instance, where — formerly — a similar regular extension from east to west was assumed, it is now likely that the infection is permanently established, though latent, in many parts of the world; and Frost, who studied the conditions in the United States, thought it probable that, during the last influenza epidemic, the disease started gradually in the course of several years, from a large number of different points of origin. Of cholera, the same thing seems to be true. Though its original endemic centre lies in India, from which it has spread in successive waves, the infection has now become endemic, or permanently established, in a great many other parts of the world. For instance, it has been prevalent for a good many years, with variations of intensity, in Siam and Indo-China. With the exception of 1929, it has appeared annually in the Philippine Islands. In Shanghai, it occurs during the warm weather, without any certainty of importation from other cholera foci. And there are many other examples.

The problem is particularly important in Russia, because through Russia and Poland cholera has made its most important inroads into Europe. If foci exist, it means that the cholera spirillum in its virulent form, or at least with a capacity to reassume a virulent condition, survives in endemic regions within the bodies of convalescents or healthy carriers, or in nature. The consensus of opinion is that chronic carriers of virulent cholera spirilla are either extremely rare or do not exist. As a general thing, most investigators have found that the virulent organisms disappear from the stools of convalescents in at most from five to twenty-two days. The carrying over of cholera organisms through the winter in the bodies of carriers seems, on experimental evidence, extremely unlikely. In water and sewage, the organisms may survive for a time, yet as a rule such surviving spirilla "dissociate" into a form that is non-infectious.

It would take us too far into technical problems to discuss the fluctuations of virulence in bacteria. This question is particularly difficult with cholera because there is no laboratory animal available, except some of the higher monkeys, in which a cholera infection simulating that of man can be produced. The fundamental question even now, sixteen years after I was interested in it in Russia, is still unanswered. Yet I spent a good deal of my time there, with the full coöperation of Soviet health authorities, in making an extensive plan for the study of these matters along what may be called the "cholera frontiers" of Europe. This plan was submitted to the League of Nations, but the only possible source of money — from America — was blocked by the fact that the United States had no diplomatic relations with Russia at that time. The plan therefore sleeps peacefully — if it hasn't been thrown into the wastepaper basket — in the Geneva archives. It was really nobody's fault that it got no further than paper. In view of what I have said about the general inefficiency and confusion of the Russian health organization, it is only fair to state that sensible suggestions, even for large-scale investigations, appealed to the authorities and found enthusiastic reception on the part of the poor, harassed, and overworked bacteriologists who remained. But undertakings of this kind require money and a type of organization which no country torn by a revolution can command.

Nevertheless, the conception of this work was an inspiring experience. There is an epic appeal in the planning of a wide-flung campaign against a powerful and ancient scourge with the weapons that modern knowledge has placed in our hands. And it is in thinking of this problem, as well as the other times when I have been blessed with the chance of participating in anti-epidemic campaigns, that I feel that I can — like Montaigne — "*me féliciter d'avoir vécu d'étranges aventures.*" And the best of this experience was that even in the hearts and minds of the otherwise hostile and cynical Soviet chiefs with whom this planning was done there arose a fellow feeling and warmth of zeal that swept away, in these matters, all political differences.

In this connection, the European world, and especially Germany, owes an inestimable debt to Poland. If typhus and cholera did not sweep across the Russian borders into Western countries during these years, it is to a large degree owing to the splendid sanitary organization by which the Poles guarded their frontiers. The accomplishment of this task by a young state, within a few years after being overrun by hostile armies, with little help except that given by the League of Nations, represents a feat of intelligence and energy that has rarely been exceeded. It is gratifying to know that active in this work were a number of young Poles trained in American laboratories.

3

Russia was my first experience — even considering the worst phases of the war, or any epidemics I have seen — of living in an atmosphere of universal fear. It was as though the Kremlin were a great cave in the centre of the city from which a dragon might emerge at any moment to snatch people out of their houses or their beds. There is a picture by Boecklin in the Schack Gallery in Munich which symbolizes Russia of that time. It represents a mountain gorge through which, on a narrow road overhanging a precipice, a troop of tiny human beings are driving a pack horse. They are striving to hurry across a little bridge in the distance. High above them, a dragon is just emerging from his cave, and slowly uncoiling. And there is not the slightest chance of escape. Suppressed panic was the state of mind of all the Russians I met, except those in official positions, and most of these — though not all — were cynically arrogant. The condition in Russia was analogous to that which for a time existed in France when, as Lenôtre says, there was a "symphony of terror" affecting the hunters as well as the hunted. Those of whom the proscribed were most afraid were themselves so terrified that they dared not show mercy and concealed their own fears under an assumed brutality which they did not truly feel but which became a habit. The shaven-headed *seksot* or spy in the house in which I lived acted the sullen brute most of the time and was particularly harsh with a poor old gentlewoman — delicate and cultivated — who stood in daily terror of losing her job as charwoman. But in the evenings he often sat in the courtyard next door, singing sentimental ballads with the neighbor's children, and to me he spoke tearfully of his longing for the old happy days with his wife and children in his native village. This association of ferocity with sentimentality has not been uncommon in history. Souberbielle, the doctor of the Conciergerie and one of the jury that condemned the widow Capet to death, was a tender family man; and the frightful Sergeant Marceau, one of the most ferocious of the sans-culottes, lived a lifelong and gentle romance with Marie Desgraviers — an idyl that has been compared to that of Philemon and Baucis. The best-known paradox was Robespierre, who, while not exactly sentimental, was as much a Puritan as Jonathan Edwards.

Lenin was sick. Trotsky was in command. I saw him several times driving across the Red Square, a dreaded and sinister figure, now free to put uncompromising theory to test on human beings, as we use guinea pigs and mice. All means of communication and all military and police power were in his hands, and not even in whispers behind closed doors was anything significant said. No day passed without platoons of troops or police guards moving through the streets (grass growing between the cobbles) with some ragged wretch led away to no one knew what fate. And always, for popular effect, the soldiers marched with a totally unnecessary show of violence, drawn revolvers or lowered bayonets. Often at night, usually toward morning, the tramp of marching files would awake me. I would hear them stopping at some house and banging at the door with the butt of a gun. I could imagine the people trembling in their beds, wondering which one it was to be, knowing that there was neither justice nor succor. Six people in a room together after dark was "counter-revolution," and every second person was a spy.

There was a dance at the Nansen Mission to which Russian girls of the former upper classes came in their pathetically tinsel finery. Gorvin, the able and courageous British Agent, warned me not to say or ask anything in the slightest indiscreet, since there were sure to be among them employees of the Cheka. In every house there was a spy-concierge; all domiciles were assigned and government-controlled; and our own private ruffian had unlimited power over the inmates. He went through papers and baggage, kept note of whom one saw and where one went. The old lady of whom I have spoken was the scrubwoman in our house. She was sick. I found malaria in her blood, gave her quinine, and tried to befriend her. She begged me to pay no attention to her. It would mean persecution by our supervisor, and she wanted to die anyway. Her husband had been shot and her son had disappeared. X. and Y. (they are still alive), two gifted scientists of the old school, requested me not to call on them. Association with a foreigner would put them under suspicion. Another (he later killed himself), whom I asked why he didn't stay out of the country when on one of his missions to Geneva, said that if he did so his wife and son, who were held as hostages, would be arrested. A., an ex-professor of Kharkov, told me that an edict had been issued, some time before, announcing that children of bourgeois parents over seven years old were to be arrested and removed from their parents — to disappear, he said, because they were too old to be trained as good proletarians. His wife hid the children in a sub-cellar for a week, when the edict was modified and they were merely requisitioned for state training.

As for foreigners, the Russian Government "en-fiched"

itself of foreign passports and citizenship. H. was a Czechoslovak electrical engineer who had been invited into Russia to make a report on the state of power plants. He was given all facilities and submitted a survey with recommendations. But he had learned too much for his own good. They paid him his fee and put him on a train to Warsaw. At the border they took him off, appropriated his money and passport, brought him back to Moscow, and turned him loose on the streets. He was taken under the wing of a foreign mission and fed for a while. During this time I saw him often, and tried to work out some scheme to take him out of the country. Two nights before I left Moscow, at about 2 A.M., his Russian landlady, frightened and in tears, rushed into our house. H. had just been taken away by a squad of soldiers. As far as I know, he was *spurlos verschwunden*.

I was acquiring an education, here in Russia, which all my previous experience of death, misery, war, and mass disease had failed to give me. For the terror, cruelty, suppression of all principles of liberty of speech or action, and general perfidy of private and public policy, I was, of course, prepared. I did on entering Russia, however, cling to the hope that underneath these possibly transitional evils there might be a strong idealistic and eventually feasible humane purpose. I cherished this idea as long as I could. But I was not a tourist, and I had a chance to come into unsupervised contact with a large number of people, including ex-aristocrats, railway employees, minor Jewish bureaucrats, former professors, and a few experienced foreigners. And I had a necessarily thorough look-in on one of the government departments. After a month of this, I felt quite satisfied that there was no idealistic communism, either Marxian or Leninian, in Russia. Whatever may have been the high purposes of the founders, the present state of affairs was a savagely cynical and bloody autocracy maintained by espionage and brutality, utterly inefficient, and rapidly developing — in spite of its *internationales* — an extreme form of military nationalism. It seemed to me to be a sort of "state capitalism," with all the means of production in the hands of a ruling minority which controlled the army and the police, a "capitalism" with all the faults of our own, none of its efficiency, and no hope of modification and control by popular pressure, trade-unionism, or competition. Indeed, a railroad strike had just been suppressed with the killing of a thousand strikers.

This was my own reaction. I was so sure of its accuracy that I lost patience with many of my "intellectual" friends, professors, writers, and such, among whom "communism" had become a sort of snobbism, and who, comfortably uxorious and safe in the suburbs of New York, Chicago, or Boston, swallowed the rawest propaganda and condoned murder, perfidy, and the assassination of liberty because they innocently, or stupidly, thought there was really communism in Russia. As a matter of fact, a sincere communist in Russia in 1923 would have lasted just as long as necessary to get him into the nearest cellar.

Thinking these things, I walked one evening to the grave of John Reed, under the walls of the Kremlin, took off my hat, and considered affectionately that, after all, Shelley too had dreamed of the impossible. It is well, I thought, that they are both dead. If Reed had lived, he would have been "purged" by this time. Typhus killed him more mercifully and without slandering his memory.

4

The amiable Dr. Siemashko gave me his private car to ride to Rostov. There were two hundred soldiers scattered among the crowded coaches, for the Ukrainians had not yet been entirely "persuaded" that sovietization was the key to freedom. Bands of the beloved Makho's disorganized forces were still roaming the prairies, and their favorite game was to tear up a hundred feet of track, attack the trains, and take what they could in the form of clothes and food. A little while before they had successfully carried out such a surprise on a northward-bound train, and had sent the passengers, the crew, and a few high government officials into Kharkov as naked as God had made them. We were well-guarded, therefore. The car was shabby but comfortable, except that I have never seen so many bedbugs assembled in one space. They were in the sink and the toilet, under the beds, in the beds, in the chinks along the windows; they got into cups and glasses, and seemed to be peering at us from the ceiling. They tortured my two companions, but except for one or two occasions, bedbugs have never bothered me. I caught a dozen of them and we let them run races on the breakfast table. We passed through immense plains of rich prairie with hardly a house. Occasional villages stood out in the distance like passing ships at sea. I was impressed by the prodigious untapped riches of this country. Nebraska and Iowa must have been like this before 1860.

In Kharkov, the train stopped for several hours and my two interpreter companions, getting off to visit friends while I stayed to take a nap, were left behind. They caught up with me at Rostov. Meanwhile, however, I was left alone in my

car, trailing a series of coaches crowded with a noisy, unwashed, hairy, and unbelievably down-at-the-heel collection
of people. Unable to speak a word of Russian, I wandered
through the cars hoping that I might run into someone who
spoke one of the languages familiar to me. My conductor,
who, having received a dollar bill, was ready to risk his neck
for me (in spite of disdain for our bourgeois capitalism, a
dollar bill or a paper pound was more useful than a passport;
how the poor devils got rid of them for useful purposes, I
don't know), made inquiry in a loud voice, as we struggled
over legs, bundles, and boxes in the dirty aisles. Finally we
discovered a middle-aged Jew who spoke German. It was an
enlightening experience. As I first walked through the cars,
I felt an atmosphere of hatred and dislike. Hostile eyes
seemed to be boring through my back; disdainful laughter at
my expense, and other grumblings that perhaps it was just as
well I did not understand, followed my course. But now I sat
on a box next to my gray-bearded and kind-eyed Jew. His son
had just been banished to Siberia for asking an irrelevant
question at a party meeting. Others joined our group, while
my friend interpreted. More and more of the passengers became curious about me. They were all eager for information
about America. I was again and again astonished by the un-
concealed admiration which, in spite of political hatred, the
Russians expressed for the institutions of our capitalistic
country. While they pretended to detest us as the Hinden-
burg line of reaction, they appeared eager to build up an
industrial system imitative of our own — believing, poor
things, that in their hands avarice, greed, and exploitation
could be eliminated, a sort of celestial system of Standard
Oil Companies and steel trusts.

In half an hour of conversation, on this occasion, not talking politics, of course, I felt that I sat in a friendly crowd. An
amiable grin appeared here and there. Somebody at the end
of the car struck up one of those interminable, sorrowful Russian ballads — endless narrative repetition of verses in minor
tones, usually describing the life and career of some Cossack
Robin Hood. I caught the tune and began to sing. My group
was amused, and also joined in. My heart went out to these
frightened, ill-clad, and hungry people, so instinctively friendly
and good-natured, yet bullied and propagandized until their
poor minds were no more than confusions of uncomprehended slogans about "bourgeoisie," "capitalism," and other
catchwords. Made to work for wages over which they had no
control; deprived of the power to strike, of freedom of movement, domicile, speech, choice of occupation, and even juris-
diction over their own children; without chance of profiting
legitimately by superior qualities of character, physique, or
mind; terrorized into complete acquiescence — they believed
their slavery a new form of liberty. Truly, I reflected, the
Soviet chiefs have succeeded in the principle expressed by
Montaigne in another connection: *"Qu'il est besoing que le
peuple ignore beaucoup de choses vrayes, et en croye beaucoup de faulses."* And these smiling and cheerful Muscovites,
I knew, would not hesitate to denounce me or each other, and
hand us over to the slit-eyed officer who commanded the
escort, for a careless expression or a critical question. What
makes people behave like this, I wondered. Fear, misery, and
propaganda, which seem to be able to implant blind obedience
and hatred into the most kindly human hearts. Add to this
Russian formula the factor of nationalism, and you have the
situation of Germany. The slogans are a bit differently con-

ceived, but the only real difference is that instead of shooting dissenters behind the ear or hitting them on the head with a mallet, in Germany they stand them before a firing squad.

However, the Bolshevist's ferocity I had now discovered was, in the common people, skin deep. As far as I was concerned, a dig in the ribs and a smiling "Delaware and Lackawanna" usually brought a good-natured grin, even from the soldiers with the gold stars on their caps and the nasty-looking bayonets on their guns.

In Rostov, I saw some of the survivors of the famine. Hundreds of ragged souls — men, women, and children — camped around the railroad station, begging for food, cooking what they could get in tin kettles, their wretched belongings piled around them, exposed to sun and rain, waiting for a chance to steal rides on freight cars in the direction of possible food supplies. It was a new experience of human misery, and more dreadful to see than battlefields or death from disease. Two little boys to whom I gave a small loaf of bread made me ashamed of the breakfast I had eaten. Having done my job in Rostov, I came back to Moscow more shaken by this glimpse of hunger than I had been by anything else I had encountered. Truly, I reflected, five years after a so-called "liberating revolution" I have observed the unhappiest, most terrified, and least free people the world has seen since Ivan the Terrible.

The rest of my task in Russia was purely observational and advisory, and a few weeks longer gave me all the information that I could reasonably expect to obtain for transmission to Geneva. It took me two weeks to get permission to leave Russia, however, and that it took no longer than that was owing to the kind offices of Mischa Rosenbaum, a young New York

Jew who had once studied at Columbia and now held down a desk in the Foreign Office. It was necessary to get a permit to board a given train on a specified date at a certain place. They were wise to make it so difficult to get out; for I truly believe that if the border valve had been freely opened all the Russians, with the exception of the inner circles and possibly the eastern Tartars and Kirghizes, who knew no geography, would have streamed across to the at least unknown horrors of "bourgeois" countries. If the ordinary Russian could get a chance to leave, there would be a *Völkerwanderung* into the democratic countries which would dislocate the world more than when the Ostrogoths came down the Danube.

CHAPTER XVIII

*Academic interlude, with an irrelevant discussion
of life in Boston and the insects of the city*

AFTER his return from Russia, R.S. was content to settle down
in his laboratory. He now spent some of the happiest years of
his career reorganizing his teaching and picking up the threads
of his investigations. While the experiences in the field had
been sterile in the sense of scientific production, they had
taught him a great deal about the manifestations of "herd"
infections or epidemics and had stored his mind with unanswered questions that he was now eager to formulate in terms
of experiment. He worked hard and steadily, but, as I stated
at the beginning of this book, it was not easy to induce him
to discuss the technicalities of his scientific interests. He believed that these belonged in the professional journals in which
he published them, and that he could not tell about them in
a popular way without appearing either to exaggerate his own
professional importance or to make capital of the sensational
interest which medical details appear to arouse in the public.
I happen to know, however, that during these years he was
engaged in theoretical studies on antibodies on allergy in
tuberculosis, began his work on typhus, and felt about for
clues to the nature of the invisible virus agents. These were
relatively tranquil years, as tranquil as he could live them —
for his temperament was such that he never knew he was
happy until later, and the past always looked better to him

than the present. He loved his work, he enjoyed his students, he spent his spare time and money on horses, and he wrote a great deal about all kinds of things both in prose and in verse. But something was always irritating or exciting him. He was not a comfortable man to live with. He was either *himmelhoch jauchzend* or *zum Tode betrübt*. His state of mind depended a good deal on the success or failure of his experiments; and whenever, as often happened, a hopeful idea blew up in smoke and a lot of effort seemed to have been wasted, he became insufferable. At such times he drank a lot more than was good for him and spent his evenings writing sonnets — some of which were published and thought good by others, though never quite as good as he thought them himself. He always said that his poetry was best when he was able to attain just the right degree of intoxication. A sonnet usually cost him a quart of Scotch, and, since he favored the Shakespearean form, he never got the last two lines on the first quart. After he had worked himself to the second or third quatrain, he usually miscalculated, was too fuddled for the perfect ending, and put it off until the following evening. For prose, scientific or otherwise, as for riding horses, he believed one should be stark sober; when he was writing essays on educational subjects, he felt that a spot of beer put him into the solemn-ass mood and thus a little closer to the state of mind of the professional pedagogue.

He was really a very happy man during these years, and rather stupid in not realizing it. People were much better to him than he deserved, and those most intimately associated with him made allowances for his peculiarities and his failings. There were lucid intervals when he gratefully realized this. And as his life approached its end he often spoke to me with *Wehmuth* (there is no English word that exactly expresses it) of the chances he had missed of making others happy.

I have jotted down in his own language some of the things
he talked to me about in our many evenings together during
these middle years, when — for a time — he uninterruptedly
led the life of a university professor.

1

While war service and epidemiological work have their adventurous charms, there comes sooner or later to the investigator trained in laboratories a hunger for his accustomed
environment — a sort of nostalgia for the familiar smells of
ether, phenol, formalin, xylol, monkeys, and guinea pigs,
which are sweeter to the laboratory nose than attar of roses.
Moreover, ideas have accumulated, new techniques have been
devised, and the heart longs to get back to an occupation
which, once in the bones, is harder to shake off than a beloved
vice.

There is in this profession, especially as it concerns itself
with infectious diseases, a fascination which holds the spirit
with feelings that are not exaggerated by the word "passion";
indeed, like the happiest personal passions, it feeds on the
intimate daily association of long years and grows, like love,
with an increasing familiarity that never becomes complete
knowledge. For what can be more happily exciting than to
study a disease in all its natural manifestations, isolate its
cause, and subject this to precise scrutiny and analysis; to grow
it apart from its host, study its manner of multiplication, its
habits under artificial conditions, its changes, its possible toxic
products; then to carry it back to the animal body and follow
the processes by which it injures and kills; explore the details
of the animal defenses, and pursue it again into the epidemic;
examine its manner of conveyance from case to case, its rela-

tionship to water and food, animal carriers, insect vectors; its geographical, climatic, and seasonal distribution; the laws of its epidemic waves; and then, with all the weapons of the knowledge gained, to assist in its arrest and circumvention, even contribute to protection and possibly individual cure. For few diseases has all this been entirely done, and in those few in which all necessary knowledge is available — as, for instance, in diphtheria and smallpox — the conquered territory must be occupied by garrisons which one helps in training and disciplining. For it is a war without armistice, and continuous mobilization is the only guarantee of safety. Once one is thoroughly involved in this work, it gets into the blood and few either want to or can escape from its fascinations.

And the opportunity for living such lives is given to us bacteriologists by the universities. They supply our workshops and our equipment; they risk money in the venturous investment of our originality and ingenuity, and leave us free, with the wide ranges of the unknown, to wander and prospect whither the trails lead us. All they ask in return is a little teaching, to train others to take up where we fail; and for this they pay us besides. We are among the blessed ones who, in a perturbed world, are allowed to do the work we love best. We should be very happy people.

2

We medical men never really think of ourselves as professors because we look upon university connections as opportunities for doing our own work. As for our teaching obligations, as we grow wiser we learn that the relatively small fractions of our time which we spend with well-trained, intelligent young men are more of a privilege than an obligation. For these groups are highly selected, each year more thoroughly prepared, and they force the teacher continually to renew the fundamental premises of the sciences from which his speciality takes off. It keeps us as keen as we are individually able to be, for, in a rapidly moving subject, there is a *vis a tergo* that keeps pushing us up, and we profit from it most directly through the fresh young blood that is pumped into our brains each year by the eager youngsters who won't stand for pedantic nonsense.

So while we are, technically speaking, professors, we are actually older colleagues of our students, from whom we often learn as much as we teach them. This, and the sense of humility that is constantly forced upon honest investigators by the incompleteness of their own small victories over the secrets of nature, keep us from developing that sense of sacred superiority that is shared by some academicians only with the monkeys of Benares.

In America the professor never held the respected position occupied by his European colleagues. The title was too often shared in our country by cornet players, boxing instructors, and dog trainers. Also, the American professor suffered from the fact that in many smaller colleges the teacher was a sort of underpaid employee of a president and lay board of trustees, who regarded him as something more than the janitor and a little less than the football coach. This condition was never strongly prevalent in the better universities, yet it was not until quite recently that the public in general had any respect for men who worked for small pay on matters that seemed to have no obvious economic value. All this is rapidly changing, and the professor was figuring much less in the comic literature as the absent-minded imbecile who times his boiling watch while holding an egg in his hand, until he began again to lose some of his hard-earned prestige by the record of the recent professorial advisory boards in Washington.

By and large, however, professors have gained immensely, as they deserve, in the public esteem. Yet they remain, and always will remain, a peculiar group by reason of the very qualities that induce them to enter careers of scholarship. Moreover, the lives they lead, in concentration on highly specialized disciplines, are apt to bring out traits that differentiate them from their run-of-the-mill contemporaries. There are all kinds of professors: the inordinately vain type most common in literature (particularly "appreciation of poetry"); the Jehovah-complex type (philosophy); the very much man-of-the-world type (government, economics); the women's-lunch-club and general after-dinner type (education, psychology); the notoriety-hunter type (almost any department); the recluse type (classicists, English philology, Norse, Icelandic, and so forth); the we-are-the-really-important-ones type (almost any science), etc., etc. Of course I specify departments only as far as, in those named, I have met most of each variety. And then there are the mathematicians who, like the Dodo, belong in a class by themselves. But even so, the types named are, for each department, the exceptions. By and large, professors are a dignified, learned, and superior class of human beings, differentiated from the herd by hard, intellectual discipline; frugal, cultivated, and possessing the mental poise that comes with the sound mastery of some branch of important knowledge. I speak, of course, of professors in the central structures of universities, not including the bay windows that have been added in the form of schools of education, journalism, business, and the like. Yet, as a complement to the specified virtues, there are among professors more than the normal proportion of eccentrics. And as a class, it seems not unjust to say that the practical-common-sense index is relatively low.

I had a colleague once, a distinguished mathematician and a Scotchman, who had lived in America twenty years. At the end of this time he made a trip to Aberdeen, and on his return told us the following story: —

"You know," he said, "the jokes about Scotch thrift are quite correct. I'd lived here so long I'd forgotten about it. When I was home in Aberdeen, I went into a cigar store one evening and bought a cigar. I bit off the end and asked the man for a light. 'I canna gie ye na licht,' he replied, 'but I can sell ye a box of matches for a ha'penny.' 'In America,' I said, 'they give you a box of matches when you buy a cigar.' 'I'm sorry,' he answered, 'but this is na America.' You know, I had to walk half a mile back to my hotel to light my cigar."

There was a friend of mine, a physiologist. When he came home one night his wife reminded him that they were to dine with the president, and said that she'd laid out his dress shirt. He went up to dress, but got thinking of conditioned reflexes, and when he had his day clothes off he fell victim to one and went to bed. After she'd waited for half an hour, his wife went upstairs and found him asleep. She roused him, helped him with his shirt, and then — poor woman — went downstairs again. He resumed his ponderings on conditioned reflexes and again fell victim to one. This time, realizing that he was going out to dinner, he took off the shirt she had just put on him, put the studs into another one, put that one on, stopped to think again, took the second shirt off, looked for a third, and shouted down to his wife that there wasn't any dress shirt.

Another colleague, a classicist, was always reciting: —

> "Beatus ille qui procul negotiis,
> Ut prisca gens mortalium
> Paterna rura bobus exercet suis
> Solutus omni faenore . . ."

> (Happy the man who has no business cares,
> And, like the ancient fathers of his race,
> Ploughs his ancestral acres with his steers
> Free of the barter of the market place.[1])

and had bought himself a farm on which to retire. He was saving to equip it, and had ten thousand dollars laid by. One day, on an excursion to a neighboring town, a horse dealer stuck him with a carload of Percherons, and talked him into going into horse raising. When he got home, he didn't dare say anything about it. But the next day, while he was lecturing on his beloved Horace, his poor wife was called on the telephone and was told that there was a box car at the station with six Flemish mares and a stallion waiting delivery. I think the university lawyer got them out of this with moderate loss.

But stories about professors are endless. They were once a stock witticism, like mother-in-law jokes. There was even a time, in the Roosevelt-Wilson campaign, when the *New York Times* editorially reproached Mr. Roosevelt for having unfairly ridiculed Mr. Wilson in speaking of him publicly as a "professor." However, the times are changing, as academic scholars are emerging more into public life. Perhaps it is a

[1] Very free translation by R.S.

pity. For there was, in spite of the harmless ridicule, a great advantage in academic seclusion, and great scholars, like other productive talents, develop best in quasi-loneliness. To-day many a gifted youngster is lost to his true career by premature pressure toward the practical and the worldly. There should be an element of the devotional in the pursuit of scholarship, and this cannot survive the glare of publicity or the feeling that approval depends upon uninterrupted production.

The academic life should be and often is among the happiest lots of man. The unhappy ones are those who, in mid-career, discover that they have mistaken their talents and inclinations, lose interest in their work, and regard teaching as an onerous routine. Without gifts or training for other pursuits, they remain the permanent underpaid instructors and assistant professors. There are unfortunate individuals of this kind in every occupation, but they are particularly numerous in the academic world because young men, before they have mentally matured, often enter the university career on the impulse of an early but thin enthusiasm, or even because, after a graduate education, it seems the *locus minoris resistentiae*. They drift into it because, after ten or more years in the cloistered security of teaching institutions, they are afraid of the world. The situation cannot be entirely avoided. Teachers' unions will not cure it, for scholarship cannot be made democratic in that sense. It is already democratic in the truer significance — namely, that wealth, influence, and other extraneous circumstances actually play no appreciable rôle in academic advancement. I assert this on the basis of twenty-five years of observation. The provision of fellowships for the unusual student and the active search for talent by most enlightened institutions are constantly strengthening the democracy of scholarship. But, in another sense, by this same process scholarship develops in aristocracy of intellect uninfluenced by mass opinion or the pressure of an organized intellectual proletariat. If this sounds a paradox, I reply that I believe no democracy can maintain itself for any length of time without building up an aristocracy of ability and integrity to protect it from deterioration and eventual chaos. The responsibility of the university problem falls on the older scholars. It is their task to appraise and select, and not, out of laziness and the comfort of having their chores done by willing wheel horses, to permit men fundamentally unsuited to involve themselves until they are inextricably committed. This is not easy — but there is no other solution.

We have been living in an era of science. And it is not unnatural that our university administrators should have given the scientific departments a disproportionate degree of encouragement and support to the neglect of the humanities. Yet there are growing indications that the tide is turning; and men in leading positions are beginning to realize that the backbone of intellectual training lies in liberal education and in the adjustment of the content of the humanities to modern conditions. In this maturing of our hard-pressed democratic civilization the classicist, the historian, the philosopher, and all those other devoted disciples of the learning called useless in this era of national adolescence, will come into their own again. And when this happens, and the mass of high-school and college graduates go back into industrial and political life in ever-increasing numbers as educated people, there may be hope of the eventual triumph of humane civilization.

3

Boston is a much maligned town, said R.S. I've lived here for some eighteen years, off and on, and, being a rank outsider, have been let into secrets that hereditary members of the various clans take the greatest pains to hide from each other. No, Mr. O'Neill, though I hate to contradict a man to whose genius I do homage, I've not run into a single case of incest in all this time. And I cannot agree, my dear Benny DeVoto, whose gifted pen arouses unenvious admiration, that Beacon Hill is a rabbit warren. Upton Sinclair was too bitter to require refutation — his passion is its own answer. John Marquand, with consummate art, aroused in me a liking for George Apley — and of course he liked him himself. I wish the species were not dying out. And in *Wickford Point*, after all, he was painting portraits of his own friends — that is, special cases — so well done that, in spite of his restrained satire, everyone seemed to recognize them and, except for those related to his models, to be much amused. But his characters might have been from the Chicago lake front, or the banks of the Monongahela, had it been Mr. Marquand's misfortune to be born in Pittsburgh. Current rumor to the contrary, our lunatic asylums are not more crowded than those of other states, and unincarcerated morons are not more plentiful than elsewhere.

A common complaint against Boston is stodgy conservatism. To be sure, George Washington, ever riding toward Commonwealth Avenue on his pigeon-spotted horse to join the seated Garrison, who is eternally committed not to equivocate, has not yet raised his bronze arm in a Nazi salute or a Soviet fist. But neither has he in front of the subtreasury in

New York. Even our state and city politics have largely lost their alien Adamses and Bradfords and have become truly Americanized, with good native Reillys and Cohens. A brilliant magazine writer some years ago published a derisive article on the Boston "4 per centers." He meant, of course, that in Boston the well-to-do were safeguarding their offspring by establishing trust funds for them in expert hands, instead of buying them seats on the stock exchange, where they could make 6 or 8 per cent. I shouldn't wonder if he had changed his mind since. And if many of them do spend only the incomes of their incomes, that still is better than the prevalent habit of living on the interest of one's debts or the profit derived from not raising cotton, tobacco, or hogs.

I have often asked myself just what is the actual source of this persistent literary virulence against the town I live in. It is aimed, of course, not at the half million or so Irish-Americans, nor the sixty or seventy thousand Jews, nor the odds and ends of recent arrivals like myself, but at the survivors of the stock that made much of the early history of our country, and whose reservations or habitat, like those of the Ainus or the Ogallala Sioux, grow narrower and narrower in a strip stretching from the State House to Massachusetts Avenue, along the basin. Like the tribes mentioned, they are disappearing, but there the parallel ends. They are not disappearing for the same reasons. As a physical stock, they survive all over the nation and are multiplying numerically quite as fast as other sections of the population. Their fertility, once prodigious, has not diminished much below the old theological standards. But as a so-called Brahmin class they are going, because all but a few of the older ones are abandoning the time-honored tribal customs. The young men have followed the buffalo to New York and elsewhere, or are adopting the habits of the foreign palefaces who, on their part, are gradually infiltrating the remaining clans by intermarriage and business pressure.

For my part, I am glad I came here while there were still representative, unmiscegenated specimens left. They held out a little longer than their kind elsewhere, because more deeply rooted. They once were a patrician merchant class much like the Buddenbrooks of Lübeck, or of Bremen, Lyons, London, and so forth. And they have the defects and virtues almost of an aristocracy. A few of them linger in their traditions partly because their individual fortunes hold out, partly because some of them still draw a thin sap from the deep roots that once made New England flower. And they must disappear, because at this stage of the world's — and especially America's — history there is no survival value in the cult of manners or in the old-fashioned "reactionary" or "rightist" scruples against the minor and perfectly legal infringements of integrity, or in the prejudice of reserve against going out and "getting" things. So they will disappear, and when they are completely gone something irrecoverable will have gone out of American life — not the least the material they furnish for radical derision. They have been a great consolation and comfort to me. They are often rich, but carry their wealth with simplicity. It is possible to be relatively poor among them without the self-ostracism that one practises among parvenus. They are all related, of course, and are inclined to be a bit boring about this. They are a little like the English in that they are inclined to be nasty to each other but kindly to those strangers whom they accept as equals. The insides of their houses are often littered with terrible art objects, — large naked marble ladies sitting on tigers' backs, dreadful pictures, glass apples, and ivory elephants, — but these are mostly inherited from cruder days. There is a lot one can say about them in derision and criticism, but they are not in the true sense of the word snobs. Snobbery is usually a defense-reaction by which a consciously inferior individual takes refuge behind the accidental advantages of birth, money, or unearned position. There are snobs even among animals. At a dog show, you can see how the blue-ribboned useless Pomeranian has his nose turned up at the fox terrier; or consider the offensive snobbery of those purely ornamental Afghan hounds, as they call them, that look, with their tasseled ears, like homosexual English setters. Snobbery means usually some kind of decadence that needs to conceal itself under arrogance.

These Boston people are not snobs, nor are they decadent. The rushing world of America has grown away from their kind more rapidly than in other nations, and sometimes they overreact and appear amusing anachronisms. You will find their types in all old cities of the world, and if you come of a European family that belonged to the solider bourgeoisie, they will remind you of your own people. A good many of them are provincial, and too many of them live in the past. The rich ones have many of the weaknesses that are fostered by hereditary wealth. And, like all the "haves" in the world, they are conservative; the "haver," the more reactionary. Yet they still take a more vigorous part in the political, educational, and other public activities of their region than the well-to-do take in most other parts of the United States. They may not be artistic or aesthetically sensitive. But remember, they are of English stock. Yet even if they don't enjoy art and music themselves, they value it platonically, and support it;

and you can see more old ladies with ear trumpets at the Friday afternoon Symphony than anywhere else in the world. They may be funny on the surface, and some of them are funny all through. But in most of them there's a fine, solid core that makes me wish they could breed true. For I like them a lot better than I do their children and the relatives who have gone to other places and have become simonized till you can't tell them from the catalogue stock.

4

Boston is a well-sanitated city. This is entirely praiseworthy; but at times it made my own work a little difficult, particularly when I needed insects.

Now big-game hunting is a rich man's sport introduced by the English and practised, before the depression, by that type of American who rented a shooting box in Scotland and learned to speak of his morning ham and eggs as "tiffin." It is a complicated, though I understand quite comfortable occupation, in which one employs "express rifles" to shoot with, black boys or goats as bait, professional hunters to prevent accidents, and goes on "safaris."

Little-game hunting is much cheaper and may be quite as exciting. I am not referring to "microbe hunting," but to that closely related pastime concerned with insects. Insect collecting with butterfly nets and ether bottles was long confined to entomologists who grubbed in the earth, scraped the bottoms of rocks and logs, dug into anthills and assailed hives all over the world; putting their treasures into pickle jars, taking them home, counting their legs and wings and bristles, antennae, palpebrae, spiracles, halteria, ani, and stipes until they had upward of a million species; and a well-educated entomologist could take his little eyeglass, hold up a specimen by its pin, and tell you — just like that — whether you had one of the Diptera or Anoplura or Siphonaptera, or whether it was an *Echidnophaga gallinacea* or a *Pulex irritans*. They had a lot of fun. But it was as shooting clay pigeons is to potting grizzly bear with a bow and arrow to the real hunting that began when insects were found to carry malaria, plague, yellow fever, typhus, spotted fever, encephalitis, sleeping sickness, and so on; and when insect hunters began to stalk the ones that had a real come-back. For, unlike big game, this little game neither roars nor barks nor leaves tracks in soft mud. It may be right on top of you when you happen to be looking in another direction, and you can't sit up in the top of a tree or on the back of an elephant fifty yards away, eating sandwiches, until the game poses itself for a shot with a beater in its mouth. Also, unlike big game, — which is either being killed off or trained in preserves not to get ill-natured about being shot, — the little game increases whenever it gets half a chance, and every year new transmission possibilities of still another disease enlarge the scope of this grand sport.

My insect hunting has been concerned mainly with bedbugs, lice, ticks, and fleas, though lately also with mosquitoes. But the lice and fleas have furnished the most satisfaction. Bedbugs are a vulgar game. They are dull beasts and offer little play for skill or intelligence; are easily sneaked up on, and docile when caught. Fleas are the noblest game of all. They have speed and elusiveness, and, despite the evidence of flea circuses, are not easily domesticated. If they ever get loose, as a thousand or so once got loose in my laboratory, it is worse than escaped monkeys, and it's *sauve qui peut*. With fleas it is a matter of *toujours de l'audace*. They attack by the formula of Marshal Foch: "If you are driven back on the right flank, and repulsed on the left, attack in the centre." When they attack in number, nothing helps except wing shooting with a Flit pump.

The louse is not so active, but by far wilier. In a manner, it is the most thrilling game — especially if dangerously infected. It demands unflagging vigilance. One summer I was feeding Arab lice — three hundred of them — on monkeys. The idea was to find out whether one could keep a louse from a human being alive on monkey blood, because that would have facilitated a number of important experimental projects. I picked these lice originally out of the beards of Arabs, caged them, and now — day after hot day, in the Tunisian summer — I sat over equally uncomfortable fettered monkeys, picking up my lice with forceps, setting them, twenty or so at a time, on a monkey's belly, and, when they were red and swollen, counting them one by one back into the boxes. To lose one would have been a calamity. And how they can scram when they start for the underbrush! It takes steady nerves, and three or four of the men engaged in similar occupations in the course of ten years or so were caught off their guard and got typhus in consequence. In this case, my scheme did not work. My lice didn't do well on monkey blood, and the plan had to be abandoned.

But I don't want to be sensational about this. I wish merely to make the point that it has sporting advantages over the big-game business.

When one is hunting insects in epidemic zones, the circumstances are usually such that one has no difficulty whatever in finding the game. The problem is quite the opposite — that is, one tries to avoid running into it unexpectedly. One can pick it up almost anywhere in the luxuriant underbrush on the faces, heads, chests, or backs of patients, or in the fur of trapped animals. It often becomes necessary, however, to capture a stock of the responsible insects from regions in which no disease exists, so that one may establish colonies of uninfected specimens for experimental purposes. This may be quite another matter, particularly difficult in some of our highly "hygiened" American cities, where bathtubs and soap have become obsessions in the last fifty years. Michelet said, writing of Paris before the Revolution: "*Mille ans d'histoire et pas un seul bain.*" This was exaggerated, because there is reliable evidence that in the time of Louis XIV there were bathing places along the Seine. But with us in America, the thing has gone to the opposite extreme, and while the "cold bath in the morning" situation is probably to a large extent swank, the hot bath once a week or so has penetrated to the lowest orders of society. The result is that in Boston at least the catching of a louse requires a high degree of ingenuity — to say nothing of tact. Bedbugs one can always obtain locally by knowing where to go. Fleas one can have shipped from the South. For ticks of certain varieties, all one needs to do is to take a walk on Cape Cod and then pick them off one's pants. But lice — ! Well, Boston is, as I have said, being much maligned by novelists and Western academicians. Harvard and the New England states in general possess some subtle quality which gets under the skins of the rest of the country. But from one point of view, Boston is unimpeachable. Let me challenge Mr. Sinclair and Mr. Marquand to try to catch a louse in Boston. I'd like to see how far they would get. Of course, though cleanliness may be akin to godliness, it is not impossible that it is in inverse proportion to intellectual energy and artistic perception. The intellectually and artistically gifted people I have known in different parts of the world have often been the most unwashed. I once had a Southeastern European in my laboratory who was a gifted scholar and played Chopin as few can play him, yet who never learned to pull the string in the bathroom. Yet this is an impression, and it would be hard to establish a causal relationship between the two conditions.

But to come back to catching lice in Boston. I needed a supply of local lice in which all possibility of previous typhus infection could be excluded. I knew where I could get the little lads in New York — in a clinic in the Broom and Essex Street district, where, years before, I had picked them up often without wishing to. But the New York lice could not be regarded as reliably unimpeachable. I needed the Caesar's wife kind of lice, and Boston was the place — if any — to find them. I tried out bedbug preserves, lodginghouses, and so forth. No luck. I sent my scouts into those quarters of the city where the cover and exposure indicated possible pasturage. Not a spoor was uncovered. There are imaginable difficulties. One cannot accost likely groups of people, even in clinics, and say: "Do you mind if I examine your head, to see whether you are lousy?" There is a social implication in this which is resented. As a last resort, I sent out my most persistent and skillful associate, Dr. Maximiliano. He followed many a false trail. Finally, exhausted and without hope, he was almost ready to give up.

Maximiliano was standing on the corner of Washington and Summer Streets, trying to make up his mind what to do next. There was always a tragic air about him, for he was small and dark, with an intense look in his eyes — partly because he suffered from chronic gastritis, owing to putting chili sauce on all his food, even soup and oatmeal, and believed that he was incubating a cancer of the stomach. He stood in one place so long and looked so *désolé* that he attracted the attention of a policeman, who we found out later was Officer Clancy of the Joy Street Station. Just what he thought it is impossible to tell, but he approached Maximiliano and said: —

"Have ye lost yer way, young feller?"

Maximiliano, in his Latin despair, reacted with passion.

"In all Boston, Mr. Officer," he said, "I cannot discover a louse."

"A what?" asked Clancy.

"A louse," replied Maximiliano.

"Look here," thought Clancy, "this guy is nuts." But he was a conscientious soul. He asked, "An' what do ye want with a louse, me lad?"

Maximiliano explained. He said that he was a "scientific." He described the epic magnitude of the typhus problem. He told of the work upon which he was engaged at the Harvard Medical School. He expounded the need of normal lice; told how he would breed them on his leg; how he would lay them on little cakes of ice to anaesthetize them, and inject them into the rectum with typhus virus.

Clancy scratched his head. Maximiliano sounded crazy, but there was a convincing enthusiasm about him. Gently Clancy suggested that they go to the Station and consult the Captain. To the Captain the whole matter was recapitulated. "You mean to say you stick a glass tube up a louse's behind?" he asked. He had conveyed many sufferers of hallucinations to the Psychopathic, but this was a new one.

"If you will come to the Harvard Medical School, I should consider it a distinguished honor to demonstrate to you our procedure," declaimed Maximiliano.

The Captain was captivated by "the cause of science" to which Maximiliano recurred repeatedly. "Are there any lousy guys on your beat, Clancy?" he asked.

"Well, there's an old coon," said Clancy, "that sells pencils down near the South Station, who I think might fill the bill. We might give him the once-over."

With the Captain's blessing, Maximiliano and Clancy wandered the streets leading to the South Station. On Essex Street they came upon the pencil vendor. He looked promising, but Maximiliano could not get close enough. Mr. Collins was shy of policemen. Clancy engaged him in conversation. Maximiliano edged closer. Eureka! There were nits in the crinkly hair. Maximiliano got excited. He took out his little pillbox and a small scissors. Mr. Collins backed away.

"I ain't done nothin'," he exclaimed. "What you-all tryin' to do?"

"You ain't done nothin'," said Clancy, "but you'd better come to the Station. The Captain wants to talk to you."

Mr. Collins was frightened. But Clancy was determined. Together they all three made their way to the Station. By the time they got there, Mr. Collins was in a state of resentful jitters.

"Now, Collins," said the Captain, "there ain't no charge against you. But we've got to look at your head in the cause o' science."

"I ain't done nothin'," repeated Collins. "I'm an American citizen and I got my rights. I dunno what youse all talkin' 'bout de cause o' science."

"Collins," replied the Captain, "be a sport and let this Spanish professor look at your head."

"You tell dat man to keep off o' me with them scissors."

"Collins!" The Captain was now stern. "I place you under arrest in the cause o' science."

As he was being led away to a cell, Collins weakened. Maximiliano took him to the window and got his nits. Collins was discharged, and Maximiliano came back in triumph. He and Clancy became fast friends. The Captain had called up the college and I tried to assure him that Maximiliano was quite sane, but I don't know whether he believed me. I will pit the kindly intelligence of the Boston police force — always excepting traffic officers — against any in the world.

CHAPTER XIX

Tunis — Nicolle; portrait of a great scientist and scholar. With the usual digressions

1

How fervently I have often wished that my parents had been pious Christians and that, in the plastic years of childhood, before I had learned to think, my mind had been molded in the comfortable belief in a life after death! How pleasant it must be to look placidly forward to rejoining, in heavenly surroundings of one's own imaginative preference, those who have made our lives on earth richer and happier. The thought of death would be considerably mitigated for me by the expectation of seeing again — among others — Charles Nicolle, and renewing for a piece of eternity those summer evenings at Sidi-bu-Saïd where, as the cooling breeze came up from the sea, we walked together chatting of relapsing fever, trachoma, dysentery, brucellosis, Carthaginian archaeology, Roman mosaics, mediaeval legends, French encyclopaedists, and many other things dear to our hearts. And heaven might do worse than appear like Sidi-bu-Saïd, with the evening sun golden on the quiet waters of the Gulf of Bizerte and a cloudless sky darkening over the high shore where Carthage once stood. And if, together, we could have a small celestial laboratory and discover a few avian diseases like psittacosis, roup, or fowl pox among the angels, paradise were paradise indeed. Except for the infected angels, we had all these things, more or less, in Tunis for a little while.

I went to Tunis entirely on Nicolle's account. For years we had been in correspondence. In 1915, we had a rendezvous for work together in the Balkans, but the French Government needed him at that time and our meeting was postponed. Already, even then, he was beginning to stand out as one of the great living bacteriologists — with no contemporary peers, in my judgment, except Bordet, Landsteiner, and Theobald Smith. The World War and the intervening period of concentration on theoretical problems had, for ten years, carried me away from the fields of work in which he had gained distinction. But in 1928, again returning to problems of typhus fever, I wanted to see him. Differences of opinion had arisen, new methods had been devised, and correspondence was unsatisfactory.

It was the beginning of a friendship that started in our heads and soon extended to our hearts. North Africa is an Eldorado for the student of infectious diseases. There are Malta fever, fièvre boutonneuse, relapsing fever, typhus, kala-azar, leprosy, malaria, and odds and ends of tropical infection that come up from the oases in the south. There were many things to learn and much to discuss, and I was especially interested in trying to overcome some experimental difficulties by transmitting typhus to monkeys with human lice. Nicolle received me with open arms. He gave me a laboratory, a technician, and all the materials I needed — even to a supply of bearded Arabs, who furnished the insects. Best of all, he gave me his friendship.

Nicolle was one of those men who achieve their successes

by long preliminary thought, before an experiment is formulated, rather than by the frantic and often ill-conceived experimental activities that keep lesser men in ant-like agitation.

Indeed, I have often thought of ants in observing the quantity output of "what-of-it" literature from many laboratories. I once watched a swarm of ants, on a lazy summer afternoon, and wondered why they had acquired the reputation for sagacity attributed to them by sentimental entomologists. One ant, I observed, was carrying a weighty bit of straw from one place to another, obviously making heavy weather of it. Instead of going around grass-blades and sticks, he laboriously climbed over the tops of them, then painfully fell off and trudged onward — passing on the way, and even finding at his destination, bits of straw quite equal in beauty, size, and conformation to the one he had packed so strenuously over obstacles. My impression was that this ant was making a fool of himself. Yet there are bacteriologists and, for that matter, many people in other callings just like my ant.

Nicolle did relatively few and simple experiments. But every time he did one, it was the result of long hours of intellectual incubation during which all possible variants had been considered and were allowed for in the final tests. Then he went straight to the point, without wasted motion. That was the method of Pasteur, as it has been of all the really great men of our calling, whose simple, conclusive experiments are a joy to those able to appreciate them. For there is an "art" of experimentation which is as elusive of definition as the art of color, sound, or letters. Indeed, there is a Pegasus for science as there is for the arts; and he, like his mate, spreads his wings only when he feels on his flanks the thighs of one whom the gods have appointed to ride him.

In the case of the louse discovery, Nicolle had carried out no more than a half-dozen decisive experiments after years of observation of the disease and its epidemiology. In this instance, the experiments were easily confirmed. In some other matters his reputation was rather damaged than otherwise by this habit of doing just enough work to convince himself and not carrying through far enough to convince others. He was one of the first, if not the first, to assert — on the basis of a meagre experimental material — that epidemic influenza was a virus disease, and it was so described in French textbooks some ten years before the cultivation of the virus proved him right. Like other superb experimenters — Pasteur among them — he was always precise in his observations, but less interested in the theories based upon them. Practically all the work he did was of an intensely practical nature, suggested by the problems he encountered in the field and at the bedside. Next to his typhus discoveries, his greatest service was the determination of *infections inapparentes*, the fact that animals may contract many diseases and transmit them without showing any — or only very slight — symptoms.

Apart from his scientific distinction, however, Nicolle was of the stuff of which the French Encyclopaedists were made. I have seen his cultural scope approached only by a few Frenchmen and an occasional German of the old school — a type of learning that cannot be acquired by study alone, but represents the ripening of gifted minds that are attracted by everything about them worthy of interest.

Nicolle was novelist, philosopher, and historian. His day began at five A.M., when he sat down to write until seven-thirty. These were the hours that produced his essays and his prize novel. Then a frugal breakfast, and work in the laboratory until eleven. The heat then sent us to our rooms until three, a period of the day when the entire town of Tunis went to sleep; even the camels lay in the shade of the hedges, and the wandering bands of Arabs rested near the wells, sleepily scratching themselves. Although, as far as the camels were concerned, the above is not strictly accurate. They are strange and — to a horseman — mysterious beasts. I have seen some of them in the suffocating heat of an African summer noon lie in the sun, not ten feet from the shade of a green hedge, eating a stick of wood with all signs of sybaritic enjoyment.

After three, we all worked again until seven, and in the evening we wandered out to Sidi-bu-Saïd or Carthage for dinner near the shore, with good food, passable Tunisian wine, and amiable conversation.

Those evenings linger in my mind as among the most happily peaceful I have spent. Either Nicolle chose his men with unusual sagacity, or it just happened that he attracted kindred spirits. Burnet, now his successor, distinguished for studies on leprosy and Malta fever, was the author of a highly intelligent book of literary criticism. The entomologist was a poet; and one of the assistants a classicist who in his leisure hours was studying Roman archaeology. The conversation covered wide ranges from French literature to Arab architecture and Roman art. It is this wide scope of cultural interests in many people quite as competent as our own in their special fields which started me thinking about the superiority of the French and the former German secondary education over our own. I have met men, old and young, of these nations all over the world, and have often been impressed by the fact that, unlike most of our own compatriots of high specialistic learning, they showed signs of a richly cultivated intellectual subsoil. At the officers' mess on a French auxiliary steamship, I once took part in a conversation which started with Diderot and Lamartine and then, through Bergson, passed on to William James, the second engineer and the purser locking horns on *Science v. Metaphysics*. A discussion of this kind would be unthinkable under similar circumstances among American or English seadogs, perhaps for the good of our naval services. However that may be, as conditions are now, I believe it is wise for an American specialist to conceal his extraneous interests until eventually they die of inanition, lest he be regarded as eccentric and incompetent.

Subsequently I saw Nicolle almost every year. We spent hours with his friend the Père Delattre, head of the White Fathers and most learned on Carthaginian excavation. This old gentleman and his order again aroused in me that deep admiration for certain activities of the Catholic Church, to which I have been so often reluctantly constrained in spite of my utter lack of philosophical sympathy with its tenets. The White Fathers, so-called from the Arab burnous which is their costume, are trained in the Carthage monastery and then sent to Equatoria, whence only a fraction of them ever return. Like their colleagues of the various orders I later met in China, they are keenly alive to medical problems and carry physical as well as spiritual comfort to the interior. Delattre himself was an urbane, learned, and kindly gentleman whose friendship alone was worth the journey.

In subsequent years Nicolle and I explored the historical corners of Paris and of Rouen together, and when separated we wrote to each other once every month. In Rouen he showed me the house of Corneille, the residence of Flaubert's father, surgeon to the Hôtel Dieu, and a bawdyhouse that was installed in an ancient nunnery, which amused him greatly. We saw the old Abbey where part of *Manon Lescaut* was written, and the garden pavilion on the Seine where *Madame Bovary* was created, a page or so a day. He introduced me to an old man who had known the Bovary's first husband, the apothecary, the one whose feet were always cold in bed; and to another who had had a speaking acquaintance with Boule de suif; for it appears that, to the town's consternation, both Flaubert and de Maupassant took many of their characters from their neighbors in Rouen. There was another friend who had spent his lifetime determining precisely where Jeanne d'Arc was burned — about ten metres away from where it was supposed to have been. For this correction he has his bust of bronze in the public square.

I was with Nicolle and his family for a week at Nice a short time before he died. With him died one of the last great figures of the French school that took off from Pasteur, Roux, Chamberland, and Metchnikoff. Bordet is the only survivor of this breed of giants. For me, Nicolle's death was the end of something that I knew was irrecoverable. It was of the same order of sorrow as had been the death of my father.

There was much to be learned in Tunis besides typhus. Burnet, then Nicolle's Sous-Directeur, was studying Malta fever, a disease which, though conveyed in goat's milk, may possibly spread by a variety of indirect ways, such as in blowing dust, a manner of transmission which may also explain — though it has not been demonstrated — the mass infections with dysentery of troops marching in desert countries. The organism of Malta fever possesses a curious and still unexplained excessive degree of infectiousness. Laboratory workers who handle it almost invariably become infected sooner or later, though — with similar technique — they may work with cultures of typhoid or dysentery indefinitely without accident. The same thing is true of another bacillary disease common in America — tularaemia. In neither case are the principles determining this extraordinary tendency to infect quite clear. I was particularly interested in Burnet's work because the bacillus of Malta fever had been shown by Alice Evans to be almost indistinguishably related to the bacillus of Bang, which causes abortion in cattle and, conveyed by cow's milk, produces a form of undulant fever which is increasingly common on the European continent and in the United States. There is a third member of this unpleasant family, which passes to man from hogs. Between them, they have presented bacteriological and epidemiological situations which are being slowly unraveled, but still offer fascinating problems. It was conversations with Burnet, moreover, that aroused my interest in the epidemiology of leprosy, to which I was later to devote a certain amount of time.

I learned much from him about the leprosy situation in the Near East and was confirmed in a conviction that I had long held in regard to epidemiological work in general, and which I later applied with some success in typhus studies. In leprosy we still lack certain fundamental data concerning conditions of transmission and factors of susceptibility. And since, in this disease as in tuberculosis, no reliable prophylactic methods are in immediate (or even remote) prospect, any reasonable efforts of control must be based on elucidation of transmission. There is little hope of gaining such knowledge by going, as many investigators have done, to centres where large numbers of cases exist and where, in consequence, the paths from case to case are obscured by tangles of interwoven and confusing trails. The ideal setup for such investigations is a region in which there is chronic prevalence with relatively few cases, and where, as a result, it is possible to trace the contacts of early cases with some accuracy, possibly even into the preceding generation. It was as a direct consequence of these conversations with Burnet that, when later I became interested in the Leonard Wood Memorial for the Study of Leprosy, I decided to spend some time at Carville, Louisiana, with the able leprosy students of the United States Public Health Service, Drs. Hasseltine and Johansen, who gave me access to records which showed that the ideal situation for the study of leprosy existed right here in certain regions of the United States. While on the Southern borders and the Florida coast there is leprosy which undoubtedly has come to us from Mexico and Central America, there are areas and villages in the Cypress swamp regions among the Cajuns where the disease — brought with the people from Acadia in 1755 — is chronically prevalent in sparse concentration, ideal for precise epidemiological scrutiny.

2

Flaubert once came to Tunis for local color when he was writing *Salammbô*. As a result, he put American cactus hedges into ancient Carthage. As a matter of fact, these were not brought to North Africa until the time of Maximilian's adventure in Mexico. Now the cactus borders all the roads, and the wandering Bedouins live on cactus pears when they can't get anything else.

These roaming bands aroused my curiosity to penetrate south, for North Africa soon casts a spell over one that grips the imagination. But don't be afraid that I am going Robert Hichens on you! There were no romantic adventures, except that I spent a few bibulous evenings with a young Russian engineer and his two lady friends, exploring the walled Arab quarters, and with them was received in the home of a wealthy Arabian date planter. But Arab houses have been described ad *nauseam*. I did not get into any harems. The Russian, one of the poor expatriated upper class, glad to escape with their lives and to find frugal livings in the four corners of the world, was employed in a phosphate mine between the southern oases of Gabes and Tozeur. It has been a mystery to me, in my wanderings after the World War, why there has been so relatively little feeling for the exiled White Russians. There has been a laudable and entirely justified sympathy for Jewish expatriates, Spanish communists, and for the Chinese, with organized relief and humane propaganda. But of all the unfortunate exiles whom the dreadful brutalities of the modern world have victimized, I have seen none more miserable nor, on the whole, so appealing as these abandoned people. I have run into them in all corners of the world, — in Africa, in France, in China, Manchuria, and Japan, — utterly demoralized by suffering, only a few capable by intelligence and training to remake their lives on the old standards. My young Russian engineer was one of these. He invited me to visit him, and I traveled along the coast through Sousse and Sfax, the Hadrumetum and Taparura of Roman founding, later strongholds of the piratical lords of the Mediterranean. Wherever I went, I was impressed with the wisdom of French colonial policy. In every town, the old walled Arab quarters were surrounded by developing French settlements — the Arabs living and doing business as they pleased, the French establishing schools, developing agriculture, and in no way dispossessing the native populations. Many young Arabs go to French schools, learn the language, and, absorbing French customs, become Frenchmen. With the older ones, customs and religion limit social intercourse. But there is none of the White God attitude of the British, and much less of the business exploitation with which Americans go among foreign populations. The native Jews are referred to as "Israelites," and that alone gives them a dignity that they rarely enjoy among other nations. It appeared to me that the French gave the natives in their colonies a sense of being an important part of the empire and not a mere helotry. In the oases, the fertile, cultivable land was left to the Arabs, who were — at Tozeur at least — the rich proprietors. At Gabes, on the coast, there was a strong garrison of Spahis and native infantry, for it is on the border of the Italian possessions, and even then Mussolini was casting covetous eyes on Tunisia. The Russian and I went swimming at Gabes in a surf warmer than our bodies, rolling across white sand. With us at the time, bathing by military order, were a company of coal-black native troops driving camels and donkeys into the waves ahead of them. I rode a borrowed camel and got seasick.

One of the sanitary problems which the French manage very badly is that of venereal diseases. In France itself conditions in these matters are bad enough, but here in the colonies the situation was heart-rendingly dreadful. In the Arab quarters there are narrow streets set apart for prostitution. On either side there are open doors leading to small rooms containing bed, washbasin, and a chair or two. At the doors sit women — black and white and all colors between, native and European, drab, dreadfully pitiful, unspeakably pathetic. Coal-black native soldiers and all kinds of nondescript "white" sportsmen enter these rooms. The doors close and one turns away with nausea. My feelings as a sanitarian were engaged primarily with the physical effects of this traffic in gonorrhea, syphilis, and Nicolas-Favre disease. But I half rejoiced in these penalties for the gorillas — a sort of revenge for the desperate degradation of the poor women.

At Gabes I met the leader of a caravan that had come in from the south. He was a fine-looking old cutthroat — tall, bearded and dignified, swathed in cloth which seemed to me far too hot for the climate. They told me it kept out the sand and the "heat." It did not keep in the smell. Yet in spite of all these superficial differences I was again reminded of the essential brotherhood of man by the fact that this fellow was the spitting image of a distinguished professor of pathology in Boston, except that his aroma was not one of formalin and xylol. He spoke some French, and we talked horses. He showed me some of his, and almost dared me to ride a fascinating little white *barbe*, because I had "talked big" — as I often do when it comes to horseflesh. The little thing — it was only about fifteen hands — promptly ran away with me, out of the oasis into the desert, heading in the general direction of the French Soudan. When I got almost out of sight of the palm trees, I managed to turn him around and steer him where the sand was softest, and finally he got tired. We came back to the camel enclosure at a walk. The old man wanted to give me the horse for a thousand francs. But what I wanted to bring home was a camel — only the American consul stopped that, when I suggested it, because of a camel disease which was under quarantine. How I should have enjoyed showing up in full regalia at the Groton Hunt on a camel!

I should like to have seen more of my new friend, but I had to get back to Tunis to finish my work, via Kairouan, the sacred city where the "mosque of a thousand pillars" is built with marble columns stolen from the Roman villas on the site of

Carthage. On the way, I passed through El Djem, where the stone coliseum surrounded by desert, easily large enough to hold two or three thousand people, is impressive of the enterprise of Roman penetration and suggests that Roman Africa must have been fertile enough to nourish much larger populations than it can accommodate to-day. Much might be written about Roman Africa, where, under the vigilant valor of the Third Legion, a civilization was developed that gave Rome great soldiers, administrators, and scholars — among them Fronto, the rhetorician and tutor of Marcus Aurelius. This knowledge induced me to buy in a Tunis bookshop and re-read the great Emperor's *Meditations*, which had deeply impressed me in my youth. This time, though he still impressed me, he also gave me the feeling that he must have been a trying prig.

The thought which puzzled me, after seeing these monuments of past glory and realizing that Rome and the Vandals had been displaced by a vigorous Arab civilization, was the suddenness with which Mohammedan culture had been arrested after the twelfth century. For several hundred years these conquerors had represented the flower of human thought in medicine, philosophy, mathematics, and even in tolerance. Yet suddenly all this stopped. It remains a problem for the historian. Nicolle thought the answer was polygamy. "How can a man with four wives do any constructive thinking?" It is not as simple as this, and remains a mystery, especially since the Moslems under Mansur, in the eighth century, were familiar by translations with Aristotle, Euclid, Plato, Hippocrates, long before Greek thought had been rediscovered in Europe. They just didn't go on to a Renaissance. It is one of those problems that make endless opportunity for pleasant discussion, but it is just as insoluble as the mystery of the origin of syphilis.

I flew back across the Mediterranean, stopping at Ajaccio for gas. It was like a ride on the magic carpet. At eight A.M., in an African city — camels, Arabs, and the Atlas Mountains on the horizon. At seven in the evening, in a dinner jacket in the restaurant of a gay hotel at Antibes.

3

On the voyage home from Marseilles, I traveled on one of those small steamers that make regular round-the-world trips from West to East, stopping at many ports along the route at which freight or passengers can be picked up. Since she sailed under the American flag, during prohibition, it became necessary to take aboard a large case of assorted bottles. This fact, and the accident that my cabin was forward, quite close to that of the ship's doctor, contributed to a rapidly progressive friendliness between myself and this odd specimen of the medical profession, who, like a good many navigating doctors I have met in various parts of the world, was a brilliant man who might have been successful in almost any branch of the profession had he not been utterly incapable by temperament and habit of settling down in one place for longer than a few months. His considerable talents were not only wasted, but gradually deteriorated under the routine of relatively unimportant occupations, very little professional stimulation, and too much drinking with people like me.

The crew on this boat were Chinese; the officers American youngsters, the oldest apparently not over thirty years; and the captain a typical old Norwegian sailor, with squat figure and sea-battered face. Since the officers could speak no Chinese, the crew was presided over by a Number One Boy, who attended to hiring and firing and, on deck, transmitted the English orders to the crew. There was a curious and unusual life below decks, therefore, which led to all kinds of odd occurrences. One of the things that needed constant watching was "dope" smuggling by the Chinese sailors. On a preceding trip, the doctor told me, a Chinaman had been murdered. The smuggling of opium into American ports was a tempting source of easy money, and before every landing it was the duty of the doctor to go through the forecastle and detect, if possible, odd caches of what might be opium. On the trip of which he was telling me, there had been a violent quarrel in one of the watches, during which a young Chinaman was badly beaten by a boatswain. When the ship arrived at Boston and the customs officers came aboard, they undertook as usual a thorough search of the crew quarters, and questioned a number of Chinese boys, with the help of the Number One. This procedure rarely led to results. On this occasion, however, the boy who had been beaten in some way attracted the attention of the chief customs officer, who took him into a stateroom, apparently for search. Shortly afterwards the inspector came out, summoned one of his officers and a policeman, and proceeded to the pantry, where he lifted two of the floor boards in the corner and dug out a large consignment of opium.

The ship left for New York at midnight, and at about four o'clock in the morning, off Point Judith, the doctor was called from his bed and found the young Chinese boy lying on the forward steerage deck with his throat cut from ear to ear. It was useless to try to find out who had done it. Such investigations among the Chinese never lead to anything.

They buried the boy at sea, after leaving New York on the way to Panama. The doctor said they sewed him up in canvas and weighted his feet with scrap iron. The captain read the usual service, and they threw him overboard. But they had made the bag too big. The little Chinaman slipped down toward the iron weights and a large air space formed in the upper part of the sack. "As long as I could see him," the doctor said, "the poor damn Chinaman was standing on the waves upright, as though he were trying to run after us." It frightened the Chinese crew into a condition of jitters that lasted for the rest of the voyage. It was at dusk that the burial took place, and the walking corpse was still visible as darkness closed in. For days they seemed to believe that the ship was being followed, and at the first Eastern port the Number One Boy, the quartermaster, and half the crew deserted.

4

During the winter following my first visit to Nicolle, my collaborator, Castaneda, and I made considerable progress in demonstrating that the little rods seen in infected guinea pigs by Mooser were actually Rickettsiae — that is, the causative agents of typhus. The demonstration depended, among other things, upon a method of preparation which was not very easily repeated. The French had failed in confirming us and Nicolle, with whom friendship played no rôle when it came to scientific opinion, had written a paper casting doubt on our findings. Correspondence was unsatisfactory, and the matter fundamental. So I took passage on the *Île de France*, packed the instruments I needed for inoculation en route, and carried a hamper of a dozen guinea pigs (disguised as an ordinary handbag) into the ship. My purpose was to keep the virus going in the animals and to demonstrate our results to Nicolle, who was at that time in Paris, and to other colleagues at the

Pasteur Institute. This was easily arranged by cable. But to carry typhus-infected virus on a passenger steamer was another matter and, once installed in my cabin, I was considerably worried. My plan was to keep the guinea pigs under my bed, bribe the room steward to bring me *salade* and vegetable scraps, and when it became necessary to pass blood from the diseased to the healthy animals, to do this on the edge of the washbasin and then throw the dead guinea pigs and the infected instruments out of the porthole. This plan was feasible, but depended on a number of unforeseeable circumstances such as the steward's coöperation and silence, and the hazards of possible official room inspections. I decided, therefore, that when the ship had passed Sandy Hook and there was no longer any chance of putting me off, I would wander out to the office of the *Medécin Chef*, look him over, and — if he appeared a sensible sort of fellow — make a clean breast of the whole business and enlist his assistance.

I proceeded to do this. The surgeon's door happened to be open and, behind the desk, I saw a familiar figure. He looked at me, jumped out of his chair, and kissed me on both cheeks, shouting "*Ah! Mon cher ami!*" It was Bohec, the jolly Breton, my old *copain* of the *Touraine*, with whom I had crossed during the war and with whom, in the ensuing years, I had spent merry evenings both in New York and in Le Havre. He had just been transferred and this was his first voyage on the *Île*. The rest was easy. Unlike most ship's surgeons, Bohec is a keen student of laboratory medicine. He gave me a private room in the sick bay for my animals and assigned an orderly to their care. I made my transfers on his operating table and, later, he helped me through the customs. Nicolle was easily convinced, and generous in saying so. In such matters I found the French rather more ready to acknowledge an error than other nations. It is a part of their inbred passion for logical thought rather than a higher sense of morality.

CHAPTER XX

*R.S. catches rats in Mexico and is in turn captivated
by the Mexicans*

THE life of a student of any science is a constant series of frustrations. From his own observations and those of others, a trellis of theory is built up beyond the solid stakes of fact. The investigator tests these, perched on scaffoldings of experiment which break down again and again and are, as often, reconstructed with the weak points reënforced. Eventually, as soon as he has tied down an elusive shoot, he loses interest and is lured by the ones a little higher up. There is never an end, and never a complete satisfaction — as there may be in the arts, when a perfect sonnet or a good statue is, in itself, final and forever.

The scientist's temporary relief from constant dissatisfaction with his own accomplishment comes with those interludes in which he projects his technical and theoretical training into a problem of practical application. R.S. consciously used his opportunities for field work and hospital consultation for such purposes of intellectual consolation and reinvigoration. His work in Serbia, in Russia, and in the army had, moreover, given him a taste of periodical excursions into the practical. Possibly if he had concentrated his interests within narrower fields, he would have approached more closely to his own conception of the true scientist. But he was temperamentally so constructed that he could not help trying to run a three-ringed circus. He usually had two or three theoretical problems on his hands, was engaged — such was his nature — in a series of acrimonious controversies, was lecturing to students, directing assistants, and scribbling sonnets on the backs of envelopes and unpaid bills, besides eternally revising his books. When he suddenly, usually at a week's notice, ran away to some remote region on what he called a "job," I knew that it was as much a question of restlessness as of purely scientific purpose.

The Mexican journey was largely the result of correspondence between him and his friend Mooser, who had sent him a strain of typhus with which he and his assistants, Batchelder and Castaneda, had done much preliminary work, disproving the filtrability of the virus, confirming the causative rôle of the little rods that Mooser had seen in guinea-pig infections, correlating these with the European Rickettsia bodies, passing them through lice, etc., etc. When Maxcy's observations — of which he tells below — came to his notice, R.S. felt that proof of the Maxcy hypothesis could be brought only during an epidemic in a large city. Besides, he wanted to go to Mexico.

As usual, he had to get up steam by indulging in a little rambling.

1

It is an erroneous impression, fostered by sensational popular biography, that scientific discovery is often made by inspiration — a sort of *coup de foudre* — from on high. This is rarely the case. Even Archimedes' sudden inspiration in the bathtub; Newton's experience in the apple orchard; Descartes's geometrical discoveries in his bed; Darwin's flash of lucidity on reading a passage in Malthus; Kekulé's vision of the closed carbon ring which came to him on top of a London bus; and

Einstein's brilliant solution of the Michelson puzzle in the patent office in Berne, were not messages out of the blue. They were the final coördinations, by minds of genius, of innumerable accumulated facts and impressions which lesser men could grasp only in their uncorrelated isolation, but which — by them — were seen in entirety and integrated into general principles. The scientist takes off from the manifold observations of predecessors, and shows his intelligence, if any, by his ability to discriminate between the important and the negligible, by selecting here and there the significant steppingstones that will lead across the difficulties to new understanding. The one who places the last stone and steps across to the terra firma of accomplished discovery gets all the credit. Only the initiated know and honor those whose patient integrity and devotion to exact observation have made the last step possible.

All this is apropos of why I went to Mexico.

It was generally accepted, after 1912, that the bite of an infected louse was the only manner in which typhus could be acquired by man. In 1926, however, a young surgeon in the United States Public Health Service, Kenneth Maxcy, studied the sporadic cases of typhus fever which, for a good many years, had been occurring throughout the Southeastern United States. After a detailed investigation of the distribution of such cases, their seasonal and local occurrence, and the circumstances surrounding a large number of individual infections, Maxcy concluded that this Southeastern American disease was not, in these instances, louse-transmitted. He suggested some other insect vector, and the possibility of a virus reservoir in animals associated with man — possibly rats, or mice. His logic was as precise as his epidemiological survey, and constituted the basis from which his fellow officer Dyer, and our own group were able eventually to establish the truth of both conjectures — namely, that this variety of typhus has its interepidemic reservoir in domestic rats, is kept going among these animals, by lice and fleas, and is occasionally transmitted to man by rat fleas. I mention these technical details, however, only to establish the reasons why I went to Mexico in 1931.

The disease which Maxcy studied is in every respect identical with the typhus fever which occurs with regular periodicity in the highlands of Mexico City. There my friend the courageous and devoted Herman Mooser had long studied it, and from there had sent me not only material and information, but — best of all — his greatest gift to me, my faithful collaborator, Maximiliano Ruiz Castaneda. When Maxcy's papers came out, we were engaged together in a number of other jobs that had to be finished before we could turn to the rat question. But finally, in 1931, we were free of preliminaries, and when Mooser telegraphed in late March that an epidemic, probably starting from the old Belèm Prison, was going on, and offered laboratory space, I took passage on the old Ward liner *Orizaba* for the faithful Ruiz and myself.

In order to do the work projected for Mexico, it was necessary for us to take with us a strain of the typhus virus with which we had been working, the peculiarities of which were thoroughly familiar to us. We wanted this strain to compare with any similar ones we could pick up in Mexican rats. At that time, though we have improved all this now, the only known method by which a typhus virus could be maintained was by continual animal passage, either in rats or in guinea pigs. In consequence, it was necessary to take with us five or six infected rats and a similar number of normal ones, so that we could make transfers from rat to rat en route. It was essential that our infected animals should not be inoculated until the very last moment, in order that they might last without transfer at least until we arrived at Vera Cruz. For this reason, three rats were inoculated in our laboratory in Boston on the day before departure for New York, and another lot were inoculated on the sink of a friendly doctor's office in New York about an hour before the ship sailed.

On the night before leaving New York, I went to a literary cocktail party of the type that was in vogue among the young aesthetes in New York at that time, and at which the cocktails were composed of 50 per cent alcohol, with glycerine and a little flavoring of orange juice. At this party I met a short, stocky, and powerfully built young man, with a friendly, heavy face under a ferocious pompadour, who was slightly tight when I arrived and who impressed me, in spite of his uncouth appearance, by his excellent choice of English. As usual at such parties, I did not catch his name, but next morning I saw him again on the ship, and found that it was Hart Crane.

Hart Crane's tragic career has been described with rare understanding and gentleness by Horton. At the time that I met him, he was on his way to Mexico on a Guggenheim Fellowship, in order to saturate himself in the Mexican atmosphere while writing an epic poem on the Conquest, planned along lines which Archibald MacLeish somewhat later carried to such splendid fulfillment. Crane attached himself to Castaneda, to whom he took a strong liking; and in his poetic imagination — largely and incessantly stimulated by beer and highballs — the work in which Castaneda was engaged assumed heroic and fantastic proportions. Crane had much charm. When — obviously drunk — he walked along the deck with a glass in one hand, a bottle of beer in the other, and smilingly addressed other passengers, he gave no offense. He was rarely entirely sober, but even so his conversation was not only reasonable, but often impressively intelligent; and his literary discrimination and generous taste did not seem to suffer under his alcoholism. The books he had with him consisted almost entirely of critical essays and collections of poetry. He seemed to read immensely and — essentially self-educated — his breadth of literary information was extraordinary. He spent a great deal of time in Castaneda's cabin, solemnly contemplating the rats, which held a terrifying fascination for him. Unfortunately, he had spent most of his first quarterly Fellowship installment before he left New York, dining his friends, and long before we approached Havana he was in danger of running dry. By that time we had developed a sympathetic friendship for him, since he was a generous, warmhearted person, obviously drinking hard because of intense unhappiness. His unhappiness took root in certain freely acknowledged abnormalities against which he seemed to have ceased struggling and which had made life in the United States intolerable.

In Havana, there was a famous café — the Diane — where the meals were excellent and the wine was more so. We tied up to the wharf around five o'clock in the afternoon, and the three of us, — Hart Crane, Castaneda, and I, — after driving about the city for an hour, went to the Diane for supper. We ate and drank well, Hart Crane doing nobly with an extra bottle of Chablis. After supper, he borrowed some money with which he bought a couple of quarts of Bacardi. We were back on board at about nine-thirty in the evening. Crane retired to his cabin with the Bacardi, and Castaneda and I went to take a look at our rats. The infected animals had been worrying us because during the last day or two they had appeared listless and developed diarrhea, and three of them were near collapse. We were afraid that these had developed a paratyphoid infection and that the remaining animals might suffer similarly and die before we arrived at Vera Cruz, where we expected to be able to transfer virus. Two of our rats were lying on their sides, hardly breathing and obviously in their last moments. We decided to throw them overboard and clean out the cages so that we might have some reasonable chance of keeping the others alive. We wrapped the sick ones in paper and carried them to the top deck, hoping that no one would see us. The presence of the rats on board was of course unknown to anyone except to ourselves, Hart Crane, and the well-bribed room steward.

The ship was tied up to the wharf and freight handling was still going on. Lighters were alongside with strong searchlights playing on them. Nevertheless, we threw the rats in, landed them in the sea between two barges but — unfortunately — directly in a strong streak of light. Contact with the cold water revived the animals and we could see their glistening bodies swimming hard against the current, trying to get to one of the outboard ropes that were holding a lighter. It was an anxious moment, because the rats were typhus-infected and, although dangerous consequences were remote, we did not think with easy minds of the possibility of introducing infected animals into the hold of a harbor craft. However, the current won, and to our great relief the weakening animals were carried away and passed out of sight.

While we were concentrated on this spectacle, rather more

anxious than the circumstances warranted, Hart Crane had left his cabin and we found him standing beside us, gazing into the water, looking down with horrified eyes — seeing the rats, indeed, long after they had actually disappeared.

A year or two earlier, in Paris, Crane had had some trouble in a café, had been arrested and held for a night in an *arrondissement* police station. In the French jail he claimed he had seen a rat which he described as large and hairy and as big as a poodle. In that case, the rat was magnified by Pernod, as in this case by Bacardi. And now, considerably excited, he saw rats in every silvery wave that, in the glare of the searchlight, lapped against the sides of the lighter. He began to recite in his deep, loud voice, as though he were scanning lines from his *Bridge* poem: —

"The Doctor has thrown rats into the harbor of Havana.
The Doctor has thrown typhus rats into the water.
There will be typhus in Havana.
The Doctor has thrown rats into the harbor," and so on.

We tried to pull him away, but he was a powerful person, and while we were struggling we heard steps approaching and saw gold lace on a cap; whereupon both Castaneda and I thought it wise to disappear behind a lifeboat. The approaching person was, fortunately, the stolid Scandinavian First Officer, Mr. Jensen. We listened to the following conversation: —

CRANE. "The Doctor has thrown rats into the harbor of Havana. One rat is as big as a poodle."

JENSEN. "What's this about rats? You're soused, man."

CRANE. "No. Look, look! See that rat climbing up the side of the lighter! His eyes shine. He has typhus. The Doctor has thrown typhus rats into the harbor."

JENSEN. "Come, come, man — get to bed," pulling at his arm. Jensen, to our great relief, was taking it for granted that this was part of an alcoholic fantasy. But the situation became still more complicated. Out of the shadows stepped a dusky little officer in police uniform, the Cuban Port Officer. In very bad English he asked: —

"What's this about throwing rats into the harbor of Havana? Who's talking about typhus?"

CRANE. "The Doctor has thrown typhus rats into the harbor. See them swimming about. One is as big as a poodle."

JENSEN. "Don't mind him, Mister. He's just one of them drunken Americans."

Castaneda and I slid along the dark deck, found a gangway, and sat in my cabin uncomfortably waiting developments.

After another ten minutes, we heard a group of struggling men clatter along the corridor, and Hart Crane's booming voice: —

"I'm telling the truth! There are rats all over the harbor, and the rats have typhus."

Then we heard him shoved into his cabin, the slam of a door, and the turn of a key. We breathed more easily.

By morning, we were on our way. Crane came out of his cabin, walked the deck as usual with his bottle of beer, and ran slap into the Captain. The Captain was a Bluenose, of the fine-looking fisherman type, whose name — improbable as it may sound — was Blackadder. He had received a report from Officer Jensen and was roaming about with the intention of sizing up the alcoholic passenger. They met face to face, and the Captain engaged Crane in conversation. Fortunately, the rats had been completely forgotten for the moment, and

Crane — who could be very charming in his sober intervals — chatted with the Captain about the excellence of the ship and how pleasant the voyage had been.

"And what are you in private life, sir?" — the Captain.

Crane threw back his shoulders and proudly said: "I am a poet, sir!"

The Captain looked at Crane, shook his head, turned on his heel, and walked away.

I saw a lot of Crane in Mexico City and in a suburb where an American woman writer had given him a room. He used to drop into the Mansera Hotel when I was out and introduce himself to the barkeeper, who had orders to give him what he asked for. I had tried to cut down Crane's alcohol, but sobriety never lasted, and made him unhappy. The barkeeper always told me with pride: "Your friend the great poet was here and had three Bacardis."

The Mexicans are often charming and childlike. Crane was arrested two or three times, but when the police discovered that he was a poet they kept him only long enough to make sure he could safely go home, and then released him. Crane had an appealing and lovable nature, and was unquestionably a man of great gifts which might have flowered into coherent beauty had he been more stable. On the way home, some months later, again on the *Orizaba*, he leaped into the sea, one morning off the coast of Yucatán. On the trip following, Castaneda, inquiring about where this had occurred, strewed the sea with great handfuls of flowers.

We arrived at Vera Cruz and were met at the boat by the local Mexican Health Officer, who arranged the admission of our animals to the Republic of Mexico, immediately took us to the little Public Health Laboratory, where we were able to transfer blood from the infected to the normal rats, and then conducted us about to show us the town.

2

The Mexicans must be getting very tired of the gush of literature about them that has flowed from the pens of American travelers, artists, and correspondents during the last few years. They don't enjoy being patronized, nor do they like to be written about as though they were a sort of tragicomic theatrical anachronism on our continent. To understand them one must have intimate Mexican friends and develop some understanding for a civilization that, utterly unlike our own, yet has values which, in our intensely commercial and practical development, have been neglected and may never be recaptured. If they have no middle class, their greatest obstacle to the achievement of the national power to which their resources entitle them, it is largely because they have had an enormous Indian population to amalgamate into national solidarity; and if they seem to have exploited this Indian population in the past, they have not, at least, ruthlessly destroyed it — as we have our own — and are making slow but decisive progress in molding their Indians into an agricultural, self-supporting population from which, eventually, will spring the middle class they require. As a matter of fact, the Indian population is Mexico, and that is the main reason why we do not understand the Mexicans. Their developing civilization starts from a base line quite different from our Anglo-Saxon, fundamentally commercial one. They do not want to be exploited by our industrialists by the methods by which these "empire builders" have exploited our own natural resources. They may be right or wrong about this — for all I know. But they are right in being afraid of us. They also think that we are extremely funny. There is quite a lore of Mexican witticisms about Americans.

There was a beggar in Cuernavaca who used to rob the old graveyard of skeletons and sell them as souvenirs to American tourists, saying: "This is the skeleton of the great deliverer, Juárez." He sold one of these for ten dollars to a gentleman from Chicago. The next day the same customer was still in town, but the beggar didn't recognize him and again offered him a skeleton. This time, however, since he was running short of graves, the bones were those of a child.

"But you sold me Juárez's skeleton yesterday," said the American.

"Oh, yes," replied the beggar, "but this is his skeleton when he was a baby. This you may also have for ten dollars."

The American bargained him down to five dollars, and bought the baby.

Then there was the American diplomat who was in Mexico many years during the Díaz régime, and never learned Spanish. When he returned to the States he was asked whether the Mexicans were intelligent people. "Oh, so-so," he replied. "You know, I was in Mexico fifteen years and the Mexicans didn't learn English."

The difference in the points of view of the two nations is illustrated by the experience of an American lady whom I know who saw, in a shop in Mexico City, a wicker chair which she thought had exceptionally beautiful lines. She asked the price, which was ten pesos. "How much would you charge to make me a dozen like that?" she asked. "Two hundred and fifty pesos," said the carpenter. "What!" she exclaimed. "Ten pesos for one and two hundred and fifty for twelve?" "Yes," replied the Mexican. "It would bore me so much to make twelve, one just like the other."

Yet Americans used to be more like that before the business disease struck us. Up in Vermont there are some left, like the old storekeeper in Morgan Center who said, when children wanted to buy picture postcards: "I don't keep 'em any longer. There was too much demand for 'em." There are a lot more who would like to be like this. But they must overcome their wistful desires for tranquil frugality or be swept down the drains of competitive trade.

The Mexicans think that we are a sort of commercial Nazis who conquer with dollars and salesmen. Also, they believe that our tourists and artists, and the journalists who write sentimental, half-baked books about them, are extremely funny. For occasional Americans like Mrs. Nuttall, the learned and charming student of Mexican archaeology who lived for many years in the palace of Alvarado near Mexico City, — a woman whom I count myself fortunate to have known for some years before she died, — they have a reverence and admiration that similar unpractical and unadvertised accomplishment rarely achieves in our own country. Their treatment of Hart Crane is another case in point.

They resent the rôle that has been assigned to the Mexican in our "Western" fiction and the movies. They play up our racketeers in their newspapers in revenge. They think we have as bad manners with duskier nations as we actually have. They have been injured and hurt by us in large and little things until, toward an American, they carry their pride on their sleeves. Yet they are intelligent and friendly when they are approached with dignity and kindness. I know, for I've had a considerable number of them in my laboratory, among them some of my best friends.

In Vera Cruz extraordinary flocks of birds covered the trees in the plaza thick as plums, and awakened me with the happiest din of a thousand skylarks. I remember, too, the vultures; the slaughterhouse on the beach, where the gore, carried out to sea in long conduits, rolled back, a surf of blood, with pink foam flying in the breeze. And the meal to which Dr. Iturbe invited me: terrapin soup, a large fish with sweet potatoes, chicken smothered in rice and a thick sauce, frijoles, meat balls with chile sauce, a great dish of vegetables and little sea crabs, pancakes rolled in jelly — and all this washed down with "tres-eckes," Montezuma beer, and topped off with coffee and tequila. I was just able to get on the train, and the mere memory of that meal makes me incapable of writing a single word about the imposing scenery of the eight-thousand-foot climb along the path of the conquistadores to Mexico City.

3

Purged of all scientific jargon, our work in Mexico consisted of mapping the typhus foci in the city, selecting houses in which cases were occurring, and then setting to work catching as many rats as possible; also collecting resident bedbugs. When the rats were trapped, they were carefully gone over for fleas and rat lice. The rat brains (where typhus virus would be found if the animals were infected) were injected into guinea pigs; likewise the well-ground bodies of bedbugs, fleas, and so forth. For this part of the work, my Mexican associate, Castaneda, and I were given space in the American Hospital (largely served by German and Swiss doctors) in the laboratory of Herman Mooser. This lively, kindhearted Swiss was, and is, one of the best scientific observers with whom it has ever been my good luck to coöperate. Without him, we should probably have failed. He is a little, sturdy bombshell of energy whose brutal honesty has made him many enemies among all but equally honest people. He is now professor at the University of Zurich, every inch of his five feet four a man and a scientist; with a mind like a bell and the temperament of a Gatling gun. It was worth the trip to Mexico to know him. The laboratory where we worked together was on a part of the hospital lawn where, in a tent, one of our most brilliant American bacteriologists — Ricketts — died of typhus in 1910.

The rat catching would not have been possible without the coöperation of the Mexican Surgeon General, Dr. Raphael Silva. Silva was a type of the Mexican upper class which will probably disappear as an expensive sacrifice to socialism. Wealthy, highly cultivated and polished, almost a professional musician, a pupil of d'Albert, in his own name a composer of considerable accomplishment, Silva entertained me a whole evening in his palace playing his own compositions. At the same time, he was a good doctor and an administrator who developed as effective a health service as the conditions of the country permitted. He furnished us with traps, transportation, epidemic information, and a professional rat catcher.

Do not sneer at rat catchers unless you have tried to catch rats alive. Poisoning them is mere amateur stuff. And, besides, when you get dead rats, all their precious vermin are lost, since these little creatures have the wisdom, as soon as their host grows cold, to leave him and seek other pastures. But to catch rats alive is an art, and our Gustavo was an artist. He knew rats — he looked like one. He understood their psychology, the routes they were likely to take, and the places where food would not look suspicious.

Now when I first set my eyes on Gustavo, I did not expect much of him. He was about five feet high, dusky of face, distinctly *Indio* of type, dressed in blue jumpers and a red shirt, a wide-brimmed and very greasy hat perched on his thick mop of straight black hair. He looked dangerous, yet in spite of his dilapidated appearance there was that air of pride about him that characterizes the lowliest Mexican when confronted with a gringo.

"Can he really catch rats?" I asked, knowing that rat catching was not everybody's business.

"Can he catch rats!" was the answer. "*El hijo de un pez puede nadar*. (The son of a fish can swim.) His father was the best rat catcher in Mexico. His grandfather before him. It is in the blood. Be reassured. Place your faith in Gustavo, and you will have rats as you wish, when you wish, and from where you wish — old rats, young rats, mothers and babies. Leave it to Gustavo."

At this high praise, Gustavo drew himself up to his full one hundred and fifty-two centimeters and stuck out his chest.

Gustavo knew that a rat's most effective defense is his sense of smell. Now of course it did not require the acuteness of a rat's nose to become aware of Gustavo. Even with a cold, I knew where he stood without looking about. But he made up for this by his technique. He never touched a trap with his hands. The cages were flamed between usings; they were handled, baited, and set with long forceps. They were put in just the right places. And so, thanks to Gustavo, rats began to come into Mooser's laboratory with happy rapidity. The eighty-sixth rat from the Belèm Prison showed typhus. We established, together with Dyer's flea experiments, the rat reservoir of Mexican typhus. We got the credit. It was Gustavo who deserved it.

The University of Mexico is the student's paradise. Students have a voice in the University government. If a professor flunks too many pupils, out he goes on his ear. Not even the Deans are safe. It is as though Harvard were governed by the Editorial Board of the *Lampoon*. It may yet be so with us in a slightly different manner, if the young men from the teachers' union succeed in their present propaganda. We might have a sort of educational New Deal, with learning appraised somewhat as Granville Hicks appraises literature — if it isn't good, honest, revolutionary stuff, it's not good art or science; and Petrarch, Keats, Goethe, and the like, couldn't get to first base.

I should like to have stayed longer in Mexico. In few places have I felt so happily comfortable as among these simple and essentially courteous and docile people. Also, they have a lot of fascinating diseases up in the back country. But there was work waiting for me at home, and the job for which I had come was done. I left with the feeling that this country will contribute immensely and correctively to our Northern civilization when we learn to approach its people without the arrogance and avarice that have characterized most of our past relations with them. Of course they have had a lot of revolutions. But these are due less to political ineptitude than to a national indigestion engendered by their greasy flapjacks, their chile sauce, and their pulque and their fleas. Dyspepsia and insects have more to do with political upheaval than is generally admitted. For large masses of people with only two hands to scratch six places, and epigastric pain at the same time, are incited to riot by the most trivial irritations. Give the Mexicans a good home diet, cheaper beer, and tons of soap and flea powder, and we shall have a great, tranquil, and friendly neighbor.

CHAPTER XXI

> *Political incompetence of professional people. Can a citizen have political intelligence and mind his own business at the same time? No! France la Doulce. Some reasons why R.S. loved France. He visits the only political oasis left in Europe. French students* vs. *American students. Pasteur's testament*

BACON divided man's duty into two parts — "the common duty of every man as a man or member of a state, and the respective or special duty of every man in his profession, vocation and place." R.S. — though we have seen that he went through life with his eyes open and thought that he was learning as he went along — did not realize until 1929, when the economic skies began to darken at home, that he had, with countless others of his kind, totally neglected the former of these obligations. Though we have repeatedly heard him boast of his sympathetic observation of human wretchedness in all parts of the world, he had always, in such situations, been intent on those physical consequences of misery with which he was professionally competent to cope. The comfortable privileges of inherited economic independence he had accepted, without giving the matter more than parenthetic thought, as a fortunate but quite natural accident of a perfectly just and permanent system. He soothed his conscience, if it ever did twinge him, by the reflection that in working hard without thought of money he was living up to the principle which Goethe expressed (probably, like R.S., for his own mental comfort): —

> *Was du ererbt von deinen Vätern hast,*
> *Erwirb es um es zu besitzen.*[1]

When, in 1930, a drunken era of tinsel prosperity suddenly sobered into the dreadful hang-over of economic despair and hardship, he was at first inclined to throw all the blame on those who, he thought, should have foreseen and forestalled. On further consideration, however, he concluded that the responsibility was a far wider one, falling upon himself and many like him who had been satisfied all their lives to devote themselves to their own narrow activities, taking it for granted that economic and political problems, under the shibboleth of so-called democratic principles, would continue automatically to take care of themselves. The realization that the majority of educated and professional people had been progressively disenfranchising themselves troubled and confused him. He felt guilty for himself and his class — but, at the same time, he could see no remedy. For as knowledge accumulated and life became more complicated, it appeared that no one engaged in serious technical or intellectual service to the community could hope to participate effectively in the solution of political or economic problems. Indeed, preoccupation with one seemed to render a man unfit for the other. And now, in the desperate crisis of their country, the intellectuals stood staring, helplessly puzzled, like cows gazing at a new barn door. They had spent their trained efforts on studying the laws that governed organic and inorganic nature, had even scrutinized with meticulous care the past history of human thought and political evolution; but the volcanic tremors in

---

[1] "The possessions which you have inherited from your ancestors — *earn* them in order truly to own them."

the comfortable social order which they had passively accepted as permanently established and automatically continuous made little impression on them until the walls of their own houses began to show cracks. If they had given any thought to the matter at all they had assumed that someone, somewhere, somehow, was looking after it, and went back complacently to their bookstacks or laboratories. The sky was overcast, to be sure, but it had often been so before and sooner or later the sun would come out again.

The record of every mind, even of such a relatively unimportant one as that of R.S., becomes inevitably the history of an education, not only the education of the individual, but that of a class. R.S. had been exposed to Karl Marx, Henry George, Bebel, Bellamy, Veblen, and many of the minor prophets, and had read voluminously in the literature called "radical" during his settlement-house days. This had all passed through his mind as interesting, descriptive criticism of human society, but as remote practically from that comfortable world he lived in as the possible but equally remote consequences of the continuous expansion of the universe. Temporarily and sympathetically stirred from time to time, he still remained, politically speaking, like Henry Adams, but with far less excuse, in the early nineteenth century. Like millions of his contemporaries, he had closed his eyes and ears to the growing confusion, trusting — childlike — that Mother Democracy would somehow make it well again. In spite of his knowledge that in nature all systems come to a new equilibrium for every change of environment or content, of democracy alone his conception remained a static instead of, as it should have been, a dynamic one. Now he was suddenly nose to nose with the problem and, for the first time in his life, he took a serious look at Mother Democracy's face, and found that she appeared quite as disturbed and confused as he himself felt. Yet, though he had no illusions about the essential political impotence of men of his class, he could at least, as a result of his observations in other countries, think about democracy more clearly than many others. He was complacently astonished that his own early recognition of the inevitable dictatorial evolution of communistic experiments turned out to be accurate. And he lived long enough to see this confirmed when convinced American communists, — as, for instance, Gitlow, — after years of treacherous and stupid efforts to shape American institutions to the Russian pattern, confessed their error and admitted that only the democratic pattern of protected liberties could offer hope of eventual improvement. Fascism seemed hardly worth philosophical consideration as too obviously a mass phenomenon of economic despair.

Thus the faith of R.S. and his friends in the essential soundness of democratic theory and principles grew stronger as they surveyed the turmoil. But — as far as R.S. himself was concerned — he now, for the first time, began seriously to scrutinize the state of democracy and the diseases from which it had obviously begun to suffer. Quite naturally, he was led to compare Great Britain, France, and his own country. He had always believed England the most efficiently governed country of the world. But he had little faith in her ability to withstand the strain of the world tempest without profound change. Her liberalism was, as Heine had recognized long ago, an historical-intellectual one, built, like sustaining beams, into an old feudal structure. It possessed, to be sure, all the humane safeguards of justice and fair play, but retained, at the same time, toughly persistent inequalities of class and opportunity which resisted the leveling of society and that free play of democratic evolution which the future inevitably demanded. Behind its beneficent parliamentary constitution there was entrenched a mediaeval, feudal organization, powerful and protected by custom and law, and constantly reënforced from the ranks of a financial "parvenu-cracy" — the two groups, between them, controlling political and economic life. Englishmen were not equal and, what is almost worse, seemed proud of traditional inequalities which froze the British system into a pattern — fine and useful in its day, but too rigidly congealed for change without conflict.

In his own country and in France, democracy had developed as a result of struggles for principles that had penetrated deeply into the consciousness of all their citizens and had established, even among the lowest economic orders, that sense of equality and human dignity that is the motive force of democratic progress. To our own liberalism — as Walter Lippmann has pointed out — something had happened which began in the 1870's with the development of powerful monopolies and their legal protection by the government. This had begun to drive us in the British direction. The prodigious influx of European proletariat and their industrial exploitation, the urbanization of the population, and financial concentration had done their part. Our democracy was sick, but not beyond redemption — in fact, beginning to convalesce.

In France, in spite of governmental inefficiency and corruption, R.S. thought he perceived a deep sense of social solidarity, an unshakable consciousness of equality among all classes (except the politically negligible Camelots du roi) which he felt was the *sine qua non* without which future democracy could not be solidly built. He felt with Heine: "Let us cherish the French! They have provided mankind with its two most important achievements, good food and human equality. In cooking and in liberty they have made the greatest progress." It was this invincible spirit of equality and liberty, even somewhat more than *sole Marguery, boeuf à la mode*, and Burgundy, which made France dear to him. And France, whenever revisited, kept him steadfast in his faith in the eventual triumph of democratic principles in a world returned to normal.

R.S., it will be seen from this, believed that no system of government could solve the evils of the world unless developed from below by the free consent of the governed — an opinion which ten years before would have been the tritest of platitudes, but now appeared again almost original. And since this renewal of old convictions was kept alive largely by his admiring observation of the French, he liked to dwell upon the type of experiences on which it was based. In the course of such narratives, as was his habit, he indulged in many digressions — some of them quite irrelevant.

1

Plato says somewhere in his *Protagoras* — I have not taken the trouble to verify the passage — that even though a man be a good flute player, this is no reason to consider him an authority on politics.[1] I may have garbled the phraseology, but the sense is that of Plato's thought. But like so many platitudes set down by great philosophers, often quoted and too simple to be misunderstood, this one has had little or no influence on human action; and the world, still waiting for the disciplined and trained governing class recommended in the *Republic*, is being guided, as always, by what may be broadly referred to as "flute players." We have apparently again reached that phase in the cycle of political history at which, as Aristotle foretold and Polybius described, democracy — having developed *ad absurdum* — is destroying itself and is forcing the pendulum back into the swing of autocracy — "Fascism" or "Bolshevism."

[1] Apropos of this, it was interesting that just before these notes went to press the papers were alive with public discussions of foreign policy by Colonel Lindbergh and Gene Tunney.

At any rate, as one of the French leading writers (Was it that clever Gallic Aryan, Jules Sauerwein? Or Leon Bailby of *Le Jour?*) said, "The time has come at which no citizen of any country can afford to remain indifferent." But what good does it do not to remain indifferent?

I resented deeply not being allowed to remain indifferent, when it made no difference whatever whether I was or was not; especially when this interference with my indifference distracted me from concentration on those interests in which by nature and training I was alone capable of rendering some little service to my generation.

Accordingly I made up my mind, though I did not succeed, to remain indifferent, and I welcomed the chance to make a quick trip to Geneva to a League of Nations conference on epidemic control. And though I was reluctantly beginning to approve of much that our government was doing, I wanted to get away from all the New Deal business and the headlines about Messrs. Wallace and Ickes and Eccles, Madame Perkins, the CIO, the WPA, PWA, SEC, TVA, etc., etc. Also, I hadn't voted for the whole Roosevelt family. I was sick of Sistie and Buzzie and Jimmie and Elliott and John, of "My Day," and of the everlasting smile on the Presidential countenance — which glowed like an Eno's Fruit Salts advertisement or the face over a Lifebuoy bath, in every picture, however serious the issue or however disturbing the speech. I thought it would be nice to get away from politics, economics, and class consciousness. A few months without politics! I will seek the quiet byroads where there are peasants and mountains, fields, streams, *poulet rôti*, *soupe à l'oignon*, and Pernod.

I had looked forward to the voyage as eight days of happy stupor; and under ordinary circumstances, with sufficient deter-

mination, such coma can still be achieved — in spite of the
fact that ships are now hotels for the new plutocracy, with
everything going on except bullfights to give the first cabin the
illusion of having achieved the high life.

There wasn't a vacant table in the smoking room the first
night out. I hesitated between two remaining empty seats.
One was at a table with a lady whom I sized up at first sight
as, possibly, a snake charmer. She was tall and thin and dusky;
quite high in front, but almost naked behind; with a pre-
hensile face and large green earrings. The protruding sandaled
feet revealed gilded toenails. Later, she turned out to be the
very intelligent wife of the cousin of a former acquaintance
from the North Shore of Long Island. But the toenails scared
me off. I turned to the remaining vacant seat, at a table for
three — the other places occupied by a Catholic priest and a
distinguished-looking gentleman with sideburns, who looked
like the Hollywood idea of a Russian general. I sat down, and
then asked them whether I might do so; to which they amiably
acquiesced.

"We were speaking," said the general, "of the deplorable
corruption of American politics."

"Do you mean Republican or Democratic?" I asked.

"Both," said the Catholic Father. "While nothing too severe can be said of the Harding administration, who will claim
that the use made of government money for political purposes
by the present administration is any better? Now, I was speaking with the Honorable Alfred Smith not long ago . . ."

"Excuse me," I said, rising. "I think that I have just seen a
friend."

My impulse was to escape from political discussion, but since
I knew no one in the room, my only recourse was to walk over

to the empty seat opposite the snake charmer. With great care to avoid stepping on the gilded feet, I sat down and addressed her.

"Be good enough," I whispered, "to receive me as an old friend."

I was a little afraid she might overdo it; but as she fixed me with a stern gaze, I hurriedly continued.

"I have been dodging conversation about Mr. Roosevelt for a number of months. I am completely indifferent. But I was just about to be involved in an ardent debate on the things that I care least about, with a Catholic priest and a Russian general, and to escape I pretended to know you. Just talk to me for a few moments, and I'll promise to leave you alone for the rest of the voyage."

At that she smiled and said, with a face as amiable as nature permitted, — which now, in its forced cordiality, reminded me of a horse of which I had once been very fond, — "How do you do?"

"I'm quite well, thanks, if I can only steer clear of politics for a few days longer, until I get among professional friends in England who care about them as little as I do."

"Well, as far as that's concerned," she replied, "you've come to the wrong address. I'm running for the School Board on the Republican ticket in my own town, back in Long Island. Now, if you political slackers would only realize that another four years like the last ones will land the country in the poorhouse, you'd wake up. Do you know, for instance, how many people in the United States are at this moment supported by the government?"

"Thanks for helping me out," I said. "I think that my two

friends are now satisfied that I knew you. I feel a little seasick anyway. Will you excuse me?"

I went to my cabin, and got the steward to bring me a double
brandy and soda. The steward was a nice-looking, stocky young
Breton, who would have seemed more natural in a striped
jersey and rubber boots.

"And where are you from?" I asked, as a sort of stock
gesture of good nature, while he was pouring the soda.

"Saint-Malo," he said. "Has Monsieur ever been there?"

"Oh, God," I replied, "how seasick I've been on the Folk-
stone–Saint-Malo boat! A lovely spot, Saint-Malo, with the old
sea wall. But the hotel was dirty, and a lot of poor people, I
thought."

"You would find it much changed now, *monsieur*. Our government is at last being forced to wake up to the social in-
justice of the old capitalistic régime." He waved the empty
soda bottle over his head.

"Here is a dollar," I said. "Go up and get me a couple of
packs of Lucky Strikes or Camels or something, and lay them
outside my door. Your government may be waking up, but I
want to go to sleep."

He came out of his stance and went out, leaving me to the
brandy and the last copy of the *New Yorker*.

2

As I passed through Paris, it happened that a distinguished
Belgian scientist was giving lectures at the Pasteur Institute.
I had long known and admired this man, and hearing from
one of our mutual Parisian friends that I was passing through,
he invited me to dine with him at M. Cholot's *Âne Rouge*.

There were twelve at table, four of them among the most distinguished scientists in France. The conversation, when it became serious, was largely political. Everyone there was "Front Populaire" and the opinions that were expressed were of a type which in America would have been labeled "red." One of the men (there were two women present, one of them a physicist of high standing) was in Blum's cabinet. Deceived by the tone of the conversation into believing that these people whom I so admired were convinced communists, I made a remark which indicated that I hoped France would be spared the fate of Russia. Right then and there I received an education in French psychology which should have been unnecessary.

"You quite misunderstand," said the physicist. "What happened in Russia will never happen in France. We are not internationalists. We want social justice for France. We are and will remain a democracy, and the tricolor, not the red flag, will remain our emblem. We would oppose a dictatorship of the proletariat as vigorously as we are now opposed to a dictatorship of the financiers. But only liberalism toward labor and reform in our industrial and economic life can save for France the solidarity and the national pride which the Revolution gave her and which the Commune consolidated as the French Republic."

Frenchmen may quarrel among themselves, but conservative and radical together agree with Renan that *"la France est charmante comme elle est."* A German, E. R. Curtius, who has performed a noble but so far futile task in attempting to explain the French to the German nation, knew long ago what I learned on that — to me — memorable evening on Montmartre. In his *"Essai sur la France"* (1932) he said: "Justice is not, for the French, a mere theoretical virtue; its power over the French spirit is considerable. . . . It [sense of justice] is a reaction [of this people] with which politicians of all parties are familiar. . . . We have seen generals of the Third Republic proclaim to their troops: 'You will impose respect for justice because, more even than liberty, equality and fraternity, it is the sentiment to which the French will adhere above all others.' "

France can be conservative and radical at the same time. Radicalism in France is as much an intellectual as a political movement and is not, except in certain industrial centres, determined — as so largely with us — by economic condition. The past is strong in France, and in all classes there is the powerful influence of what Barrès has called "*la terre et les morts.*" As Montégut said: "*La vérité est que la France, pays des contradictions, est à la fois novatrice avec audace et conservatrice avec entêtement, révolutionnaire et traditionnelle, utopiste et routinière.*" France may go far to the left in the sense of adjustment to the new social order. She will not do it as Russia did, with destruction of all the heritage of the great past. She has had her great revolution, but, violent as it was, the real France survived it.

It is a great pity that all those wise foreign correspondents who write our books about European conditions so rarely are competent to dive below the surface of the superficial political storms into the deep and powerful ground swells of national character and tradition.

3

One warm and sunny day I accepted an invitation from a friend to visit a fishing club which meets in a region of *étangs* and river overflows not far from Paris. Fishing in France, it should be observed, is an occupation not in any way comparable to the same sport in Anglo-Saxon countries. When an American or an Englishman — especially an Englishman — speaks of going fishing, he is alluding to an upper-class accomplishment which necessitates a highly specialized and expensive equipment, — such as hip boots and cloth hats draped with half-concealed fish hooks, — involves a technical vernacular concerning pink hackles, green widows, and so forth, and an air of sportsmanly superiority not unlike that of those who play polo and ride to hounds. Fishing in France is quite another thing. It is a democratic occupation that requires only the simplest equipment, very little knowledge, not much water, and, in most cases, seems able even to dispense with the fish. I once knew a man who had met someone who had seen a friend catch a fish in the Seine. I have taken this story on hearsay. But as far as my own experience over the course of a great many years is concerned, I have seen many thousands of French fishermen holding anywhere from one to four long bamboo poles over the waters of almost all the French rivers, — the Seine, the Marne, the Loire, the Doubs, the Oise, the Indre, etc., etc., — over an incredible number of *étangs*, ponds, and even puddles; I have watched them for hours on end (one of the great charms of France has always been the fact that one can watch people do things or doing nothing for hours on end and not feel that one is losing time), and never have I seen any one of them catch a fish. It is all very well for gentlemen like Izaak Walton, Bliss Perry, Stephen Leacock, and others to expound upon fishing as the occupation of philosophers. But when the Anglo-Saxon fishes, he takes the whole thing unphilosophically; he travels long distances, he climbs hills or "carries" between lakes, he "whips" streams and "plays" fish, and whatever else is necessary; his fishing involves thought, aptitude, effort, and attention. Now it may well be that I have had bad luck, and that occasionally in the history of *faire-ing la pêche* in France a perch or a *brochet* has been actually caught. A great many Frenchmen have fished for many centuries. But even so, I assert that catching fish is not the primary purpose of fishing in France. The French fisherman with a day off takes his wife and his one or two children, his mother and father, or his wife's mother and father if they are living with him, a large basket of provisions, — sausages, bread, brioches, and wine, — a little bait, and five or six long and cheap bamboo rods; and, on foot, by bicycle, tramcar, or omnibus, — rarely by motor, — he goes to the nearest body of water in which a fish might reasonably live. Going to such a body of water is about the only concession made to the ostensible purpose of fishing. On his arrival here, the hooks receive each a bit of worm or of yesterday's veal or pork, and are dropped into the water with cork floats to hold them at the right depth. The rods are then fixed on shore, the children start a game of some kind, and their elders begin to converse with each other or with neighboring groups — for the chances are that there are similarly fishing households ten or fifteen yards away on either side. Or, again, if the fisherman is alone, when the rods are in place their owner will stretch out and go to sleep until it is time for lunch. There are many ways of doing it, but the principle remains the same. The French fisherman is the real philosopher. He fishes because the quiet, the peaceful scenery, the soothing swish of the waters, rest mind and body and give him time to think about the destiny of France.

Leaving my friends to their poles and flat-bottom boats, I walked along the banks of the Marne Canal. I came upon a solitary fisherman.

"What luck?" I asked.

He roused himself from a lethargic concentration on three corks bobbing on the muddy water, and ignored my question.

"*Les anglais* like to walk in the sun. Me, I like to sit in the shade."

"How about a little Calvados?" I asked, pulling a flask out of my pocket.

This broke the ice. I gave him a sturdy dose in the metal screw-cap. I sat down and had one myself. He had another. I had another. We each had two more. I became interested in the corks.

"Do you ever catch anything?" I queried.

"Once in a while," he replied, "but it doesn't matter. What is a fish or two? They aren't very big anyway. It's the calm. No wife, no children, no *patrons*, no politics. Here I am — alone in France."

This gave me my cue.

"What do you think of the state of affairs? Is France approaching an economic revolution?"

"*Je m'en fiche*," he said. "Me, I am a mechanic. My friends work in factories and shops. We are making poor livings, but we live. Our children get educated — the schools are free. We have enough to eat. Our wives are working at one thing or another. Mine keeps an *épicerie*. Her father is a *fermier*. We get butter and eggs when he has them to spare. And if there are no fish in the Marne, it is still a restful pleasure to go fishing — nevertheless." He laughed. "Is there another little drop in your flask, *monsieur?*"

I stretched out on the slope beside him. Here was a kindred spirit. He "en-fiched" himself. We might have become firm friends in the solidarity of convinced "en-fichism," but we both went to sleep, and when I woke up the sun was setting and he was gone.

4

When I returned to my hotel that night I found a note from an old friend, asking me to spend a few days at his place in Touraine. I of course accepted, because I am very fond of him and his children. Moreover, there is no part of France more delightful than the little section near Tours where the Vouvray grows.

On the next day, my friend Michel and I were standing close under a footbridge, where the sluggish Cisse, muddily flowing out of the meadows, broadened into a pool which held out promise of a swim. It was hot, with a grape-ripening sun beating down on the vine-burdened hills of Vouvray. The water was dirty. It is amazing how a relatively small population can contaminate such immense quantities of water in a country where wide-flowing rivers give their names to the provinces. Thanks to my medical training, it was possible for me to determine that cows had recently wandered over the places where we stood. Flies buzzed over these, to my professional eyes, unquestionable indications of "recent" cattle. Yet it was hot, and we sought intervening patches of clover to shed our clothes, determined to swim with our mouths closed and our noses above our Plimsoll lines.

As we sat with our feet appraising the temperature of the water, nakedly exposed to the wide landscape, a peasant with one of those triangular, dangerous-looking French hoes in his hand emerged from behind a willow bush. His face was hairy and seamed, and his eyes watery with the slightly intoxicated expression of one whose six-o'clock breakfast consists of a half litre of new wine and a large roll of bread and who, throughout the working day, remains aware of the dangers lurking in natural waters.

It is an old tradition, this fear of the water. There is a passage somewhere in Froissart that tells about an army of ten thousand men, sick with dysentery only because the wine gave out and they were forced to drink water. There is even a suspicion, at the present time, that the wine interests are surreptitiously opposing the sanitary protection of rural water supplies. But this is only a rumor, and to one who has lived in the Vouvray region there are ample and more logical reasons to account for a reluctance to drink water.

The peasant looked friendly enough, though slightly tight. Yet we could not help being startled into momentary fear at his approach. There is a peculiar "conditioning," the physiological psychologists would call it, among civilized men in regard to nakedness and courage. I remember one time having taken off my clothes (the first time for a number of nights), and being thus rolled in my blanket, when the Germans began to bombard the village in which I was stationed. I still think of my utter demoralization and panic, which lasted until I had my breeches on again, when my *sang-froid* — such as it was — came back. It was not the gas mask or the helmet or any other possibly protective part of my accoutrement. I remember distinctly, it was the breeches. Sometimes it works in the opposite manner — that is, panic may be so extreme that it becomes berserk. A good friend, a tramp whom I knew in my ambulance days, once told me that he had entered an empty apartment one summer's day and, finding circumstances convenient after rifling the pantry, had decided to take a bath. While he was completely undressed the janitor, or some neighbor, came in, fussed around in the hall, and went out again. So nothing happened. I asked my friend whether he was frightened. He said that he was so scared that if the man had come in he would most likely have killed him. "What chance has a janitor against a naked man?" he asked. "If I'd had my pants on, I'd probably have given myself up and taken thirty days, like the lamb I really am." The subject is an alluring one, especially in connection with the growing interest in nudism.

However this may be, the sudden appearance of the peasant gave us a start which sent our hands nervously toward our clothing, but we relaxed with his "*B'jou', messieurs.*"

"And how is the wine coming along?" I asked as — not being a confirmed nudist — I slipped into the water to cover my embarrassment.

"So-so. *Ca laisse à désirer,*" he replied. "We've had too much water. A little sun and heat like to-day, and it will be well enough."

My companion, a young French lawyer, less modest than I, stood up and shook hands. I realized that I should have done the same, for courtesy in France transcends social barriers. They chatted about the wine, the wife, and the children. Bouchard — that was the peasant's name — had a bright boy who had been recommended for the *Lycée* at Tours. My friend Michel had taught the boy mathematics during a vacation. There was the charming lack of any consciousness of class distinction in their conversation, testimony — often confirmed

— to the instinctive democracy of the French. Indeed, the French peasantry is the group most respected by the intellectuals.

"I hear there's been a lot of excitement in Paris, M'sieur Michel," said Bouchard.

"Well — moderate," answered Michel. "It isn't serious, though. They carry a lot of red flags on the Fourteenth and sing the 'Internationale'; but they carry the *tricolore* too, in the same parade."

"Ah! *Je m'en fous*," replied Bouchard, scratching his foot with the hoe. "There was a fellow in Vernon the other night who talked about Russia — old Casimir's boy, who's been working in Tours. A lot of rot, I call it. He was talking about this community farming. Let 'em try it! I've got my ten hectares, and my father had 'em before me. And the Hairlip, my neighbor, has got his. He can keep his and I'll keep mine, and not a *poil* on the *queue* of my cow will I give him — or any of them!"

"No one has any such ideas," said Michel.

"Well, *tant mieux* — but just let 'em try it," said Bouchard. "Let 'em try it — not a *poil de la queue de ma vache*," he kept repeating as he ambled back to the field. He was growing angrier and angrier, muttering to himself. He walked into the neighboring field to look at a sick mare that was lying in the sun with hardly enough strength to do more than swish at flies with her tail.

"Why doesn't he shoot the poor beast?" I asked my friend.

"Oh, he's sorry for it, and goes there every day to feed and water it. Besides, if it gets a little more weight on its bones, the butcher will give more for it when it eventually dies. He's fond of the old horse, and we French are a tender-hearted people. But did you notice how little he cares about what happens in Paris?"

I went to bed happy that night. Here I'd stay a while — for they didn't care about politics.

The next day at breakfast I got papers with accounts of the sit-down strikes. The *Journal de Vernon* — the paper in use in the village to wrap up the butter — said that a deputy was going to make a speech there that night about the "Front Populaire." I left for Paris.

CHAPTER XXII

A continuation of the preceding. R.S. made a new
chapter only because the last one was
growing too long

1

At the conference at Geneva under the auspices of the Health
Commission of the League of Nations I met a group of old
friends, directors of typhus laboratories from all corners of
the world, and, incidentally, the Minister of Health of the
Spanish Republican Government — a bouncing, attractive,
and intelligent lady, a lawyer by profession, who described her
political faith to me by saying: "Je suis une anarchiste idéa-
liste." It left me in the dark, but I did not inquire further.
Our discussions were technical, carried on in three languages,
and presided over by a great gentleman — Dr. Sergent of the
Pasteur Institute of Algiers. The substance of our conferences
would be uninteresting to lay readers. I need only say that
whatever other faults and failures one may lay at the door of
the League of Nations, its Commission d'Hygiène has from the
beginning consistently carried out a policy of international
health information, statistical research, and epidemic relief
which cannot be overestimated. Ludvik Reijchmann, the
Director of this Commission, had built up an organization
which, whatever happens to the purely political activities of

the League, cannot be abandoned without inestimable loss to Europe. And, as I have so often remarked, while nations will refuse to coöperate on almost any other issue, they can be brought into the most friendly intercourse by common interest in matters of health. They will tear each other to pieces with high explosives, teach their young boys to rip each other's bellies with bayonets, and then take the tenderest care of each other's wounded. The situation is as inconsistent as the recent republication in a widely distributed American magazine — during the week of the President's appeal to Italy and Germany — of some of the most brutal and hate-inspiring war posters of 1917. Yet in this paradoxical behavior in regard to the wounded — I believe truly — lies the influence of the medical profession in all countries of the world, who — whatever their minor faults and weaknesses — are conditioned from earliest training to the complete disregard of the race, religion, political belief, personal virtue, or baseness of those needing their help. Such artificial differentiations are reduced to the common denominator of human suffering and pain, and a sick Arab is much the same, in medical eyes, as a sick Jew, Nazi, Marxist, financier, or tramp — all stripped by the fear of death of the tinseled harlequinade of worldly things. It sounds a little exalted to say so, but I think that there is a little of the spirit of Saint Francis in every good doctor.

There was, of course, at the Geneva Conference, a good deal of political talk. After the meetings were over I bethought myself of the one corner of Europe where I felt that I should be entirely isolated from politics — Liechtenstein.

From the lovely old Austrian town of Feldkirch, the road runs upward into the hills of Liechtenstein. At the border station, one passes from the hands of the comfortably *gemütlich* Austrians into those of the solemnly practical Swiss. One used to be sorry to leave Austria. Even the customs guards accentuated this regret. Smilingly, they examined nothing but the passports — and this only casually. They were different now, looked scared, and tried to be businesslike. But their native good nature was not entirely suppressed.

"We won't give you any trouble. We Austrians have had so much taken away from us already, we don't worry about a little more filched across the border. *Grüss Gott. Auf Wiedersehen.*"

The Swiss across the street were more businesslike. The Liechtensteiners have turned over their customs affairs to their guardians, the *Schweizers*. They don't want to be bothered. It's like appointing a 4 per cent (now a 2½ per cent) trustee in Boston.

Oh, Liechtenstein — happy landlet! Its capital is Vaduz, a village spreading among green, well-watered meadows under moderate mountains, on the most proximate ones of which is the *Schloss* of the *Fürst* — to which he never comes. He lives in Vienna and, with a wisdom almost sublime for a ruler, stays away from his principality. Thus he remains, — even more than the King of England, — because never present, a symbol of government rather than an active force.

Happy Liechtenstein! Its business is done by the hard-headed *Schweizers*, who probably make a penny or two, like all good trustees, but who can be relied on to pay honest interest on their trusts. They — the Liechtensteiners — are so little and, in modern terms, so poor that nobody wants to take anything away from them. Besides, they lie off the main highways of international conflicts, a bit like New Jersey. Who would want to conquer New Jersey? They have no army at all, and only seven policemen, who lead a comfortable existence riding bicycles from one village *Gasthof* to the other, and sit in the sun drinking the wine of Vaduz with their relations. Can it last? Oh, to be a policeman in Liechtenstein! The dream of a pacifist. And the wine of Vaduz! . . . It is red, and a little sour, and has a faint aroma of onions. But, as the labels say, if you drink it every day for a century, you are sure to live a hundred years. And the fleas of Liechtenstein. . . . Even the fleas are friendly. One of them stayed with me as far as Besançon. He was not exacting. A meal or so every day, and he was satisfied. When I took a bath, he hopped off into the cracks of the floorboards, and came back to me when I was dressed again. It worried me considerably how he was ever going to get back to Liechtenstein, where he belonged and spoke the language, and I hated to turn him loose so far from home among a Francophile flea population and a human blood nourished on the sour wine of the Doubs.

The *Gasthof* was kept by a one-legged veteran from Munich. He had no — or at least expressed no — political opinions.

"We have no politics here," he said. "The *Fürst* appoints a locum tenens who is confirmed by the *Landtag*. Nothing ever happens here, and I keep my mouth shut. So many people like you come through, one doesn't know whom one is talking to. It's bad for business to talk politics, and it doesn't matter here anyway. And there are no Jews. But," and he slapped the table, "they are soft here. What they need is discipline. Now in Germany under Hitler we have discipline and — " I reminded him that it was dangerous not to keep his mouth shut, paid for my drink, and wandered up the street.

The village was asleep and dark by nine-thirty. In only one

café was there a light. There I found a table surrounded by a gay party: men and women in mountain dress, who greeted my entrance like that of an old friend. The landlady, a fine young matron of the buxom mountain type, with dark braids wound around her head like a Defregger, shook hands with me and ordered a bottle of Vaduzzer wine — at my expense. They were friendly, they were loud, they were *weinselig* — a trifle "lit." But it turned out they were *Schweizers*.

"I came to see Liechtensteiners," I said. "Where are they?"

"They are up in the mountains in bed by this time," they answered. "They'll show up about six to-morrow morning. Let them sleep in peace. They go to bed early to save candles and produce twins. So it's not a real economy."

I couldn't sleep very well that night; the flea had something to do with it, though I am sure there was only one, and a good-natured one, as I have said — my Liechtenstein flea. But he did have me leaning out of the window at six the next morning in search of Liechtensteiners, looking up the road where, from Feldkirch, it turns south toward the Swiss border. Two geese were waddling down the middle of the street, and a cock was herding his harem out of a barnyard into a neighboring garden. The faintly pleasant fragrance of cow manure hung warmly on the early morning air. (Oh, cow manure! How nostalgically thy aroma calls forth bittersweet memories of the first girl I saw after the Armistice. She was *caissier* at the Café de la Comédie in Toul. It was not, of course, the girl herself. She was sweet and fresh as a jasmine. It was the general atmosphere of the town. She was blonde as Hebe, but had a dreadful voice when she shouted orders through a little door behind her desk.)

I dodged my head into the window in time to avoid a

shower of soft bread and milk which a lady from above threw down as a morning offering to the gander and his consort.

A door opened across the street and a comely servant maid, loosely pinned together, in bare legs and slippers, came to fill a large pitcher at the *Brunnen* on the corner. She disappeared, and out of the *Hof* opposite emerged a small troop of cows, followed by a little boy in leather shorts and an undershirt — no shoes — still rubbing the sand grains of sleep from his eyes. He passed down the street followed by a big yellow mongrel, who wagged his stump of a tail, pleading to be allowed to come. But he was sent home, and sat in the gutter — still wagging his tail and, sadly now, looking after the departing master.

Up the street, two men drove out of a *Thor* with a hay wagon. Gradually, the town woke up. Liechtenstein — happy Liechtenstein, where there are no politics! — resumed its daily round of simple toil and contentment.

This time, I said to myself, I have really escaped. I have found the only place in the world where they don't talk politics. How long will it last, I sorrowfully asked myself, as I got out my car and started back toward the Swiss border.

2

I was back in Paris during the following winter, this time to take part in the teaching at the Faculté de Médecine. It turned out to be one of the happiest experiences of my checkered career. I was among colleagues, many of whom were old friends and acquaintances, and the French medical students were as responsive a lot of youngsters as it has ever been my good luck to teach — displaying, incidentally, a great deal of courteous patience with my difficulties with the subjunctives and *passé défenis* in my lectures. By courtesy of my friends of the Pasteur Institute, I was given a laboratory in that institution, so that my own work could be carried on without interruption. The genial and kind-hearted Charles Martin, one of the few survivors of the old guard, was then Director. Roux, the discoverer of diphtheria toxin, had died the year before — but fortunately I had had the good fortune to know him for some years before his death. He was the last of that small group of Pasteur's intimate disciples whose names are inscribed, with that of his teacher, on the permanent rolls of our profession. Small, frail, and shrunken with age, Roux remained until the very end keen, alert, and almost fanatically devoted to science. The *Institut* was his life and he expected from others the same exclusive concentration on the work which had governed his own existence. For years, and I suspect always, he had lived the life of a recluse, almost that of a saint — frugal, asking nothing of the world but to be left undisturbed in the rue Dutot, now the rue du Docteur Roux. As he grew more feeble and less able to work, his mind turned — as so often happens in old age — to the past, to memories of the great master and the glories of those days when, with Chamberland, Duclaux, Metchnikoff, — all of them now gone, — he had "assisted" at the birth of a new science. It was a strange experience meeting him, for it was hard to realize that one was actually speaking to a person who had known and worked with the legendary figure which Pasteur has become to those of us who are his disciples. So much has happened in our subject since he founded it that one forgets how relatively short the space of years, and seeing and talking to Roux was like meeting someone who had known Saint Francis.

That anyone privileged to work in medicine could have other interests was incomprehensible to Roux. A friend of mine, Dr. Plotz, now a *chef-de-service* at the Pasteur, has told me that when he was first beginning to work there he used to go out on spring afternoons to play tennis. One day, on his way to the courts, he ran into Roux, who was wandering about in the yard in his long cape and little black skullcap. According to custom, Dr. Plotz doffed his hat and paid his respects. Roux looked him over with his bright, appraising eye and, pointing to the tennis equipment, shook his head in sorrow and said: *"Un homme de science qui joue avec de petites balles!"*

During my winter of teaching at the University of Paris I had occasion to make comparisons between French students and those of other nations with whom I had associated. In France the educated classes — a definition which, less than in other countries, corresponds with the economically affluent — move forward largely as a result of competitive examination. Education being free throughout, the leaders of national life, whether political or otherwise, are composed more than elsewhere of the most industrious and intelligent of whatever social layer. It is not unlikely, therefore, that the peculiar qualities of French academic youth may be of considerable significance in the determination of the nature of national life in general.

I can speak from experience only of the medical students, but this group at the École de Médecine in Paris is in sharp contrast to the pupils in our American medical schools because of its extreme, perhaps exaggeratedly critical, attitude toward its teachers. In France, until he graduates from the *Lycée*, the boy is under the most rigid personal and intellectual discipline; but after he enters the university he enjoys a degree of freedom which is limited only by the necessity of eventual success in the competitive examinations which will largely determine his future career. In America, we have come to carry the regimentation of the students from the college into the professional school — indeed, we control the older professional groups even more rigidly than we do the undergraduates. The pupils in our medical schools are so completely dependent upon faculty control that they have become entirely docile and critically inarticulate. Once accepted by a first-class school, an American boy must follow a carefully prescribed sequence, with step-by-step appraisal from which there is no individual variation. He must meet certain standards in a large number of short courses given by specialists, in order to move forward, and must follow this curriculum in a prescribed order, without choice of his own. If he falls below the standard, even in a few subjects, there is only a very limited opportunity for repetition or recovery. He must start his work within a narrow range of age and finish it as prescribed, whatever his particular mental predilections may be for incidental pursuits like, let us say, philosophy, chemistry, physics, and such — all the students doing the same things at the same time, in the same order, and with the same requirements. Dropped from one institution, a would-be doctor may find it difficult or perhaps impossible to be accepted in another Class A school, and may, in consequence, be forced to abandon the medical career entirely. He therefore submits docilely to whatever is offered him and may even, year after year, accept, without protest, courses inadequately given or poorly organized, feeling that he is helplessly a part of a machine which in most cases, to be sure, is an excellent one, but which allows him no leeway or personal judgments on his intellectual career.

In France, the students may be of a wide range of ages, some of them having decided upon medicine relatively late in life, others coming straight from the *Lycée*. Since their eventual standing depends upon actual capacity for success in the *concours* more than upon pleasing any individual professor, they adopt a critical attitude toward their courses. To lecture to a group of these French pupils is an amusing, though at times harassing, experience to a teacher accustomed to American conditions. He is greeted at each meeting of the class with considerable applause, but a poor lecture is sure to result in the departure of large numbers of students and, at the end, may earn as much stamping as clapping from those who are left.

During my short incumbency of the Visiting Professorship at the University of Paris, there was a disagreement between the medical students and the academic administration. Apparently for political purposes, the government had allowed certain foreign students to gain admission to the Faculté de Médecine on a basis somewhat less rigid than that demanded of native applicants. The student body had given the administration one month in which to remedy this. When, at the end of this time, nothing had been done, they called a strike. I was to lecture on the first day of this strike, and in the morning was called on the telephone by the Dean of the School and informed that my class would have to be postponed. I went to the Medical School to see what was going on, and found a situation which would be inconceivable in any American institution.

The short street of the rue de l'École-de-Médecine was barred at the open end on the Boulevard Saint-Germain by a double row of *agents*, and in the street itself, between the old Medical-School building on the one side and the laboratory buildings on the other, there was a milling crowd of about a thousand students. The buildings had been thickly placarded with large signs: "*La France pour les Français,*" "*A Bas les Metéques,*" and so forth, and with the names of professors of whom the strikers did not approve. Whenever a non-striking student tried to enter the buildings, he was taken by the scruff of the neck and literally thrown at the *agents,* who received him with open arms and passed him through their lines, grinning and enjoying the fun. Faculty members were allowed to pass in and out, in many cases with a respectful greeting or cheers.

This went on for three days. During that time no classes of any kind were held. On the fourth day the Dean came out, harangued the picketing crowd, and invited a committee of students to his office to talk the matter over. It was amicably settled by due concession on the part of the administration, and we all went happily back to work, trying to make up for lost time.

The French system has many defects in its purely academic and intellectual aspects, most of these being due to tradition and to the historical concentration of intellectual life in Paris. With some of the best talent in the world, and a scientific intelligence that has proved itself again and again in the course of the centuries, the French medical system will not be as efficient as our own until decentralization occurs, the provincial universities are brought to a point of distinction at least comparable with that of Paris, and the students are distributed to the provinces in groups sufficiently small to be handled in the individual manner which is necessary for sound medical teaching. But the independent spirit and the unwillingness to be entirely docile which the French student displays are qualities which, inculcated in some manner upon our own student groups, might contribute in a very important way to the proper growth of the American academic system, and might often act as a corrective of the ever-recurring stodginess that inevitably develops here and there. Incidentally, it would add considerably to the color and picturesqueness of our university life.

The ideal system, of course, was that which prevailed in German universities before they were ruined by the present disaster. The Germans I knew only as a fellow student, and not as a teacher. Before 1914 they had a freedom and independence quite equal, and in some respects superior, to that enjoyed by the French to-day. Until they entered the universities, in the *Gymnasium* and the *Realschulen*, they were under the same kind of regimentation which prevails in the *Lycées*, but when they were matriculated into the universities they were absolutely free, and became personally responsible for their own intellectual development. Unlike France, there were in Germany, scattered all over the country, a large number of historically important and well-organized small universities. Between these institutions there was a free exchange of professors, and the courses — while similar in content — varied considerably according to the eminence of the respective men giving them. A student was not held to more than a very loose curriculum, nor was he constrained to finish a given number of courses in a rigidly prescribed period of time. He could take his medicine in a leisurely manner if he had money and other intellectual tastes, delaying his professional progress, if he cared to, by taking extra courses in chemistry, philosophy, or even classical literature, if this appealed to him. He could move from university to university, taking his pathology in one place, his chemistry in another, his hygiene, medicine, or surgery wherever he was attracted by the place, the professor, or the quality of the beer. All that was required of him was that he pay his matriculation fees and eventually complete a certain group of courses in qualified and accepted institutions before offering himself as — in his own judgment — ready for either the preliminary, preclinical examination or *Physikum*, or that for the final doctor's degree. He was in consequence forced to consider his training maturely, make his own choices, and stand or fall according to the intelligence which he had used. There was some waste in this, and many students did very little work in their first semesters, but the system made for a freedom and intellectual maturity which are rarely found among our own supervised student bodies.

It is the eventual development of some such system for which I hope in America — not only because I believe that our upper student bodies could make contributions to educational method which are now entirely suppressed, but because an intellectual freedom which implies self-determination would, in itself, broaden the sense of responsibility of our educated classes.

3

In the restaurant on the big square in Versailles, I met my friend Vallery-Radot. It was a rainy Sunday, and I had been wandering about in the stately gardens that one is accustomed to see in their summer glory, with flowers blooming, fountains in full play, and happy groups strolling along the paths. The paths were empty that day, gray, quenched in sleet, and melancholy as one of Verlaine's poems. I was glad to be among people again and to see a friendly face; for nothing is more saddening than to wander alone and a little homesick in the emptiness of a wintry park where one has spent happy summer days in gay company. Vallery-Radot, with the sensitiveness for the mood of others that I found so common among my French friends, seemed to notice that I wanted companionship.

After lunch he invited me to come with him to his mother's apartment in one of the old houses of the square, to see some personal effects of his grandfather's that had not been shown to the public. His mother had recently died, and Vallery-Radot was dismantling the apartment, trying to decide what to do with pictures, papers, and so forth, many of which had more than sentimental family value. He showed me pastel portraits done by Pasteur in his youth, writing utensils used by him, clothing, ornaments, furniture; letters written by men who had played important rôles in the golden age of French bacteriology. Among all the things that he showed me there was one that moved me deeply and that testifies, more than anything that has been said or written, to the infinite goodness and tenderness of heart of the man whose brain created a new era in the history of medicine. It is Pasteur's Testament. Vallery-Radot allowed me to copy it and has given me permission to publish it in this book.

> Ceci est mon testament.
> Je laisse à ma femme tout ce que la loi permet de lui laisser. Puissent mes enfants ne jamais s'écarter de la voie du devoir et garder toujours pour leur mère la tendresse qu'elle mérite.
>
> Paris, ce 29 mars 1877
> Arbois, ce 25 aôut 1880

CHAPTER XXIII

Unsentimental journey to Japan and China. R.S. learns once again that "plus ça change, plus c'est la même chose"

1

WHEN I was a little boy, my friend Art Crawford, the blacksmith of Shruboak, told me that if one could dig a hole on the boundary of Westchester and Putnam counties and keep on digging, one would eventually stick out one's head in China; and that, there, everything was just the opposite from the way it was with us. The men wore pigtails and the women trousers; armies ran away from each other instead of fighting; farmers and blacksmiths were more highly esteemed than bank presidents and generals; and children honored their grandmothers and grandfathers instead of putting firecrackers under their rocking chairs. From the things he told me — and he had once been a machinist in the navy and had had shore leave in Shanghai — I shouldn't have been surprised, had I been able to do the digging experiment, if I had found the Chinese walking on their hands and the dogs wagging their heads instead of their tails.

By the time that, many years later, I got to the Orient, many of these superficial differences, which were the only ones obvious to a simple mind like that of Art Crawford, had been changed. But fundamentally, if one can believe, as one most surely can, such an informed commentator as Lin Yutang, there are still distinctions far more deeply significant than male pigtails and female trousers. For, apart from the important cultural fact that the Chinese have developed a "glorious art but a contemptible science," there is the still more profound distinction that, as a nation, the Chinese take life thoughtfully and are "more philosophic than efficient." Now of course no intelligent observer could, by any standards, accuse the Western World of being philosophical in the conduct of life. And it is quite apparent that, while we possess a treasure of recorded philosophical thought both sacred and profane, of which we are justly proud, our commercial and scientific efficiency has driven it quite out of the minds and lives of the masses of our peoples; and even our political and intellectual leaders are quite uninfluenced by it in the practical conduct of affairs; so that it survives only in the libraries of scholars and, to a lesser extent, in a few churches. The contrast between two civilizations, in one of which philosophy and art have been ascendant over science and efficiency, in the other of which the applied benefits of science have run away with philosophical balance and art, could furnish a theme for a wiser pen than my own. Moreover, since the Chinese and Japanese are rapidly learning from us while we are learning little if anything from them, there is an opportunity for much interesting speculation regarding the future.

However, God forbid that I should try to contribute to these problems, or even to write about the Japanese and Chinese with any pretense of authoritative knowledge. There have been, for many years, both in China and in Japan, colonies of Western residents, — diplomats, soldiers, missionaries, businessmen, and so on, — many of whom have been scholars and have written of the various aspects of Oriental civilization with knowledge and intelligently. Moreover, in response to the recently increased Western interest in these countries there have come such readable books as those of Lin Yutang, Crow's amusingly affectionate accounts of Chinese business habits, and the excellent political studies of Gunther. It would be silly to add a mere travelogue. Of course I could write about the country in the manner in which British lecturers and Dr. Duhamel have written of America, but I was a little too long in China to do this sort of thing with the happy assurance of confident misinformation. For when I went there at the invitation of the Peiping Union Medical College, I was actually not a stranger to the Chinese. I had had long and close associations with a considerable number of Chinese medical students and colleagues, many of whom had become and remain intimate and affectionate friends. These were, to be sure, all of the upper intellectual tiers, but none the less able interpreters of the mentality and customs of their people. Yet I am keenly alive to my limitations, and make no claim to profundity of understanding. If, therefore, any opinions I express are at variance with those of others, I should advise the reader to accept the other fellow's views without giving the matter too much thought. On the other hand, as will be seen, some of the things that I record were told to me by those more well-informed. These I am inclined to take seriously myself.

For upward of twenty years I have had Chinese students in the various laboratories in which I have worked, and I have come to understand much about them which has saved me from the patronizing sense of superiority which has characterized so much of the Western writings on their country. From

Tsen, Chu, Wu, Tang, Zia, Yü, Huang, Wang, Lim, Wei, and Liu, I learned that the capacity of the cultured Chinese for comprehension, affection, friendship, and the appreciation of moral and artistic values is, at its best, quite equal to anything the West has produced. Missionary-educated and conditioned by a preliminary training in Asiatic philosophy for the reception of the best that Christianity has to offer, these boys differed from their American fellow students largely in the fact that they were Christians in the spiritual sense of the word, actually, and, to a Westerner, naïvely, guided in their behavior by what are colloquially spoken of as "Christian principles." This, as I have said, the work of earnest missionaries, has contributed materially to the development among the earlier Chinese converts of that pious docility which constitutes such an ideal soil for commercial exploitation when, in the usual course of events, business follows the Cross.

If only we had succeeded in similarly Christianizing the Japanese before they learned some of our other tricks, we should probably now control treaty ports in Yokohama and Kobe, with millionaires, unlimited markets, and cheap labor; and the present disgraceful cutting in on our natural rights over the Asiatic continent might never have come to pass.

2

On the steamer across the Pacific I was still tired as a result of my hurried departure from a busy laboratory, and perhaps this influenced the opinions I gathered of my fellow travelers. More than that, however, my impressions were guided by my friend Polisson, whom I encountered unexpectedly in the smoking room on the first night out. The last time I had seen Polisson had been about five years before, when we had met in a café on the Cannebière in Marseilles and had together crossed to Tunis on the Messageries boat. He was one of those postwar wanderers who, for one reason or another, found themselves unable to readjust to the humdrum of civilian life after discharge from the armies in 1918. One met that kind all over the strange places of the world during the temporary outbreak of peace between 1918 and now. Some of them, like Polisson, had no personal obligations, a little money, and much intellectual curiosity. Others, disgusted with the trend of European civilization, had wandered merely to get away from it. Some were voluntary political refugees, hating the developments at home. Others, again, were just restless adventurers, in the intellectual rather than the merely physical sense. I ran into many of these "denaturalized" ones on different occasions, and found them often among the most charming and intelligent types of their respective nations. There was the anti-Nazi German scientist who had abandoned a distinguished place at home to eke out a precarious living by practising first-class medicine in the native quarter of Mukden; there was the German ex-professor of philosophy whom I met in the poorest quarters of a Chinese city where he was frugally living and becoming daily more learned in Chinese philosophy and art; another, an Englishman, one of the most cultivated men I have ever met, had been walking and hitch-hiking through China for several years, living on a pittance from home, collecting photographs and sketches of frescoes and statuary in out-of-the-way Chinese temples. There were others — but we must get on.

Polisson had lived in China since I had last seen him, had learned Chinese and had become deeply interested in ceramics and jade carvings — a natural development since, before the war, he had kept a little art shop in the rue St.-Augustin. Here he was, on his way back to Peking after a visit home, looking just as comfortably dilapidated and ungroomed as in Marseilles. His good-natured, round face was framed in a moth-eaten, untrimmed beard; his hair was uncut and unbrushed, and he wore what appeared to be the same black, badly cut suit he had had on five years before, except that there were new leather patches over the elbows. We were happy to meet again and sat drinking Canadian beer while the smoking room began to fill up with our fellow travelers.

These were troubled times and, except for the passengers for Honolulu, the first cabin consisted almost entirely of oil promoters, machinery and automobile salesmen, and others engaged in some variety of profitable enterprise in the East, much disturbed because they were seeing the handwriting on the walls of commerce. For it was the general opinion that, whoever might be victorious in the present "incident," the easy pickings for the Western merchants were gone; either the Japanese would take over or, more amazingly insolent still, the Chinese themselves might desire to profit from their own markets and resources. Polisson, who spoke English like a native New Yorker, having lived there for a year, began to explain to me the species "Western merchant in the Orient." "There is a slightly ridiculous arrogance in these mostly halfbaked commercial employees," he said, "toward the race they are engaged in exploiting. They all have a little of the White God complex. Observe that group of red-faced men behind us who are drinking 'gimlets.' They enjoy shouting 'Boy!' in severe voices, whether it is a drink — which it usually is — or any other service they desire; and when the drink arrives you may notice the often painful contrast between the common-place appearance and ordinary manners of the 'masters' and the spiritual faces and gentle courtesy of the servants. I have rarely seen a brutal Chinese face.

"American dollars and English pounds," he continued, "at prevailing rates of exchange go a long way in China; and business agents, salesmen, and clerks who, at home, would live quite commonplace lives are able there to surround themselves with servants, assume the grand manner, and feel altogether like conquerors lording it over docile helots. The English set the standards, and the Americans ape them and are all very Kipling — writing 'chits,' having 'tiffin,' and so on. The middle layer, who, in their native environments, might progress as far as the local country club, are quite horsy over there about the races and the feeble type of polo you will see them playing on Mongolian ponies. They all 'love' the Chinese with the same amused condescension with which your Cincinnati Virginian who has settled in the Piedmont loves his 'niggras.' (I met some of those when I visited a cousin a few years ago.) As to friendship with educated Chinese, interest in Oriental art, culture, literature, and the incalculable treasure of their intellectual history — these you will find only among American, French, and German scholars, permanent residents, missionaries, doctors, and members of the diplomatic corps. In contrast to these, the commercial crowd still cling to an attitude toward the Chinese which was exemplified by the Opium War of 1839 and has been kept alive by the 'treaty port situation,' which permits foreign powers to establish their own governments and jurisdictions on Chinese soil, collect customs, set up police and garrisons, and disenfranchise the natives in their own cities. One of my student friends once told me with indignation of

the exclusion of 'Chinese and dogs' from a park in an important Chinese city."

Thus Polisson. He may have been a little too bitter, because
the beer was bad and, besides, he had become so "native"
in his feelings that he seemed to resent the European "superiority" almost as strongly as some of my Chinese friends.

3

No, I cannot "hate" the Japanese. On the contrary, though
I have taken *Bushido* with a large grain of salt, I have found
much that I like and admire about them. Of course I hate
what they are doing to China, and I hope sincerely that they
will singe their tails thoroughly and conclusively before they
get through with it — as I believe they will. But it would be
silly to ignore the fact that the things they are doing are exactly
of a kind with those that built up the British Empire, the
French colonial possessions, and gave us New Mexico, Arizona,
and California. In actual fact, considering the area of their
arable land in relation to their population, the increasing barriers opposed by the Western World to their trade and racial
expansion, and lessons of militarism learned from Europe, their
actions are no more cynical and brutal and are far more excus-
able than the Opium War, our own Mexican War, and —
above all — the British annexation of South Africa. It is all
very well to say that "times have changed," but have they?
No, they don't seem to have, if one looks around in this year
of our Lord 1940.

The Japanese are following strictly Western patterns, and I
venture to say that the universal indignation against the Japanese would not be half as intense as it is were their actions in
China increasing business for the Western nations instead of

destroying it, or if they were doing to Russia what they are now doing to China. However, such considerations do not alter the fact that the Japanese are following the very worst Western standards, and, having unwisely undertaken a job which is infinitely more dangerous and difficult than the conquest of small and impoverished people like South African farmers, naked natives with trade guns, or spear-brandishing Abyssinians, they are probably going to rue the day on which their military caste constrained them to stick out their necks. And most of us will be pleased. But meanwhile some of us, who have known men like Nitobe and others, know that there are in Japan — as there are in Germany and in Italy and as there were in England and America at various times in their histories — many thousands who, unhappy and helpless, are carried along by force against their better judgments or, excusably, by a patriotic reaction against world disapproval.

On the dock at Yokohama stood little Tamiya, waving his hat at me. He was rounder and fatter than I had known him, and he bubbled over with cordiality. At the Imperial Hotel, three other Japanese professors, all young, trained at Harvard and Johns Hopkins, were waiting. They were the men in charge of the new School of Hygiene which Rockefeller donations were building in Tokyo — a foundation probably superior in material equipment to anything of a similar nature in the United States. We spent the afternoon at the Institute for Infectious Diseases. They gave me everything I needed to transfer my cultures, and all the time I was working I was being photographed. Little spectacled assistants and even technicians were snapping kodaks in every corner. It is extraordinary how many Japanese wear spectacles. Is it a racial defect or is it the desire to appear learned? I did not venture to inquire. Then I was taken the rounds of Japanese colleagues. In every office there was first a tea party, before we talked business. They requested transfers of my cultures and the demonstration of methods, but asked no embarrassing questions about my work for the Chinese. Indeed, the pose of the Japanese was that the "incident" in China is something analogous to the English euphemism of the "white man's burden." They only wish to confer the blessings of peace and friendship upon the Chinese, and are going to see that they get it if they have to kill them to do so. In the language of the woodshed, it hurts them more than it does the Chinese. That may be more true, in the end, than they now suspect.

At the invitation of the lovable and wise Nagayo, I lectured to the medical students of the Imperial University. The contrast of these students with our own and with the French ones was striking. Of course they understood little of what I was saying, though they are all taught English, but they were so courteously attentive that I almost believed they fully understood. In America, the students would have laughed or gone to sleep; in France, they would have stamped their feet and walked out.

Pierre Loti was right. The Japanese girls are charming. During a delightful but gastronomically trying dinner I caught Mitamura, the jolly professor of pathology, winking at me in genuinely American fashion. "Later," he said, "we go to a geisha party." It was in a guest house, a place of entertainment where parties are arranged and the landlady summons girls of the type and number required by the host. It was as jolly and innocent as a children's party. Tamiya did card and sleight-of-hand tricks. The girls sang and danced. Mitamura had procured as my special companion a little geisha who looked as I had always imagined Madame Chrysanthème. She spoke English — strange, but comprehensible. "Do many geisha girls speak English?" I asked her. "Not many yet," she replied, "but we are getting ready for the Olympic Games." If this had been generally known, Japan might not have lost the Games last year. The evening was one of laughter and child-like gayety, and was altogether charming.

I had lunch with the Harvard Club of Tokyo. There were present, aside from American residents, a Japanese admiral, several Japanese professors, and merchants. I sat next to a lieutenant commander of the Japanese Navy who had taken a degree at Harvard under Professor Kittredge and now, in addition to his naval duties, was the most distinguished scholar and translator of Shakespeare in Japan.

At lunch at the Kitasato Institute I was the guest of Dr. Shiga. There is among the older generation of my profession no one more distinguished or nobly exemplifying the best standards of the medical scientist than he. With much reverence he showed me a little shrine which Kitasato had erected in the Institute garden to his teacher, Koch. There was in this, as in some other Japanese customs, something attractively simple and childlike. I saw another example of the same thing at Osaka, where little Dr. Ito showed me a temple in which, each year, teachers and students of medicine devote a day of thanksgiving worship in honor of the laboratory animals sacrificed "to knowledge" during the previous twelve months. Can one imagine the faculty and students of the Harvard Medical School going to King's Chapel once a year for a guinea-pig service?

My friend, a Swiss parasitologist, left his hotel room in Kyoto looking for the dining room. In the hall on the first floor he came face to face with a flowerlike Japanese beauty wearing the obi of an unmarried woman. She smiled, sucked in her breath politely, and bowed. He bowed. Thereupon she bowed again. Not to be outdone, my friend repeated his bow. She smiled some more and this time bowed twice. My friend was just about to bend again when a polite little Japanese behind him said, "Why don't you go into the dining room? She's the waitress."

I, of course, did not dare to embarrass my hosts by political questions. They knew how I felt since they were familiar with the nature of my mission. But this did not modify their friendliness. I left with the conviction that there are many in Japan — silent by necessity — who look at the situation just about as we do.

4

Western science in all its branches is thoroughly established in Japan. As far as medicine is concerned, hospitals and research institutes are in no essentials inferior to our own, or to those of Europe. Their organization is, in most cases, modeled on the government-controlled plan of pre-Nazi Germany, although there are a few institutions — like the celebrated Kitasato Institute in Tokyo, Kayo University, and the new Rockefeller-donated Hygienic Institute — which have been founded entirely or partially by private benevolence. Japan began, in the latter half of the nineteenth century, to send intelligent young men for prolonged tours of study to Germany, France, and England. Later, many came to the United States. Unlike the scattered early efforts in China, which will be referred to below, the absorption of Western knowledge soon became a state policy, systematically pursued. In consequence progress was rapid and Japan began, almost immediately, to contribute as well as to absorb. The great Kitasato helped Behring to develop tetanus antitoxin in 1892. Shiga, still active, and a perfect type of the kindly, distinguished scientist, discovered the dysentery bacillus. Hata, Nagayo, Takaki, Inada, Ogata, — to mention a few of the older men only, — have become important figures in the history of discovery, and it should be remembered that the Japanese Army medical service was the first to demonstrate — in the Russo-Japanese War — that typhoid fever in troops can be prevented. There is in general, at present, no fundamental difference between Western and Japanese medical teaching or method.

It is erroneously assumed that all Western ideas came to Japan after Perry's visit in 1853. This is not strictly true, since, long before that, Japanese thought was profoundly influenced by information picked up from sea captains and travelers on the ships of nations permitted to carry on a limited trade. Professor Nagayo, the distinguished investigator of tsutsugamushi or river-valley fever, a disease which is a first cousin to typhus, published some years ago an entertaining account of the dawn of Western medicine in Japan.[1] His narrative is based on a novel of Kan Kikuchi's which records the life of Sugito Gempaku, a Japanese physician who lived in the latter half of the eighteenth century.

There was, in those days, an inn on Honokucho Street in Yedo (Tokyo) in which a group of Japanese court physicians, a samurai, a monk, a scholar, several interpreters, and some other more convivial than learned companions were in the habit of gathering to drink wine and to meet a jolly Dutch sea

[1] I am permitted to quote from this article by the editor of the *Scientific Monthly*.

captain, Karance by name, who delighted in entertaining them with accounts of Dutch customs and manners; apparently enjoying himself mightily by laughing at their questions and stumping them with mechanical puzzles which he carried in his pockets. In the end, as a rule, the good captain appears to have taken the edge off his legpulling by setting up his visitors to a very good wine called Chinda.

Most of the questions he was asked were trivial ones formulated largely for amusement, but Gempaku and a rival physician called Ryotaku — serious fellows — were eagerly curious about the state of Western medicine and science. And the captain, a well-informed mariner, showed them barometers, thermometers, and instruments of navigation, and told them a good deal about Dutch medicine and physics. By a fortunate coincidence, at this time both Gempaku and Ryotaku independently obtained, from one of the interpreters, copies of Kulm's *Tabulae Anatomicae*, published in Holland in 1731, with a multitude of pictures of the organs of the human body colored in red and green. Gempaku had to borrow the price — the equivalent of three dollars — from his patron lord, through the good offices of a samurai, Ogura Saemon.

Now Gempaku and Ryotaku were eager to learn Dutch, so that they could read the legends under the pictures. And, further, they wanted to find out, by actual observation, whether these diagrams — so different from the classical opinions of the Chinese doctors whom the Japanese had heretofore followed — were true descriptions of body structure. The opportunity for this study soon presented itself, since there was to be an execution of a woman who had murdered her foster children. She was still beautiful, though over fifty, and was known as the "Greentea Hag." Ryotaku was so excited on the night before the promised dissection that he could not sleep a wink, and left his house at 2 A.M. in order to be on time. When, in great excitement, the party arrived at the execution grounds, they saw the severed head of the woman on an "exposure stand."

The executioner, Toramatsu, did the dissecting, with much boasting of his skill, and the little group of scholars eagerly compared the corpse with the pictures in Kulm's book. "Deep feeling formed a lump in every throat" — I quote from Dr. Nagayo. It was all exactly like the illustrations. "They were stirred by the excitement of the demonstration." For the first half hour they "kept a deep silence, full of emotion." But on the way home, they determined that they must study every detail of the human body after the model of this wonderful Dutch science. Ryotaku and Gempaku translated the book. There were difficulties for want of adequate instruction in the Dutch language. It took four years, during which Gempaku rewrote the translation twelve times, and there were still five points which they could not make out at all, and seventeen doubtful ones. Finally, however, against the pedantic Ryotaku's advice, Gempaku published the work.

This was the real beginning of Western medicine in Japan.

5

The Japanese were formerly largely under the intellectual influence of Germany. Now in their daily and business life they admiringly imitate the United States. Throughout the cities they do their daily dozen to the radio. They speak American rather than British English. And baseball! . . . On a little packet coming back across the Yellow Sea, with two Americans, Japanese soldiers escorting boxes with the ashes of comrades, and a few Japanese civilians, one afternoon I found all the crew that could be spared from the bridge and engine room standing about the radio in the dining saloon. They were all, from captain to cabin boy, as excited as school children. I could not understand a word that came out of the machine, but I recognized a baseball game by the cheering and the tone of the announcer. It was Tokyo playing Kayo University.

The newspaper reporters are obviously brought up on our model. They pop up everywhere and at the most unexpected moments. Coming into Shimonoseki late at night, to catch the boat to Fusan in Korea, I thought I was all through after I had passed the secret service, the military police, the passport people, and the ship's special police agent. I had just slipped into a berth in a cabin I shared with the fattest Japanese I have ever seen, when the door was burst inward by three tough-looking sportsmen with pads and pencils in their hands.

Who was I? Where was I going? What was I there for? What did I think of the "Sino-Japanese incident"?

When that question came, I thought of the lad with a bayonet who was walking up and down the corridor, and I grinned. They saw the point, and grinned back.

The train through Manchuria was so crowded that there was hardly a place for sitting — no chance whatever for lying down. There were a few officers, a delegation of the Domei news service en route to record "victories" at the Manchurian front, and the rest carpetbaggers going into conquered territory. They were just like the analogous class elsewhere — with bad manners, cocky and ill-natured. I was the only foreigner on the train, got many a sour look, and had a row with a little catfish-like man who had taken my seat while I had gone off to the observation car. In that place the progressive railroad management supplied and kept refilled a decanter of cognac for the pleasure of the passengers. The Japanese like liquor but can't stand much — it generally makes them sentimental and harmless.

There was no sleeping on the train. The newspaper boys were out for a good time, carrying banners up and down the corridors and drinking beer, and at every station at least three or four local, military, and civilian spy-detectors went through my papers. In one place I showed them four times within ten minutes. We got over the frontier at 2 A.M. — and I lost my trunk.

I walked into the Consul's office in Mukden and saw a nice-looking young American sitting behind a desk.

"Well, what have you done?" he asked me.

"I've lost my trunk," I replied.

"Oh, is that all!" He seemed relieved. "I thought you might have photographed a farmhouse or slugged a sentry."

He set things going to find my luggage and took me home to lunch. His name was Gludden, he had a charming New England wife, was only about thirty-five, and made me proud of our foreign representation. Here he sat, isolated in a frontier town in Asia, merrily doing his job, learning the languages, and keenly studying local conditions. By reason of some papers I carried for him to the Peking Embassy, I promptly got to know Salisbury and his assistant, Clubb, who kept that station going while the Ambassador was in Hankow. They engendered in me a feeling of pride not unmixed with surprise that a country like ours, largely run by demagogues at home, could command the services of this type of American in foreign posts. It was the old story that, however incompetent and opportunistic may be the temporary rulers and politicians, the technical services keep our country running by a superb pride of profession and *esprit de corps*. The men whom I have mentioned were all cultivated, ambitious American youngsters who spoke Chinese or Japanese, kept in close touch with the political and military situation, and altogether gave the impression of being competent gentlemen of a high class of breeding and intelligence who represented us with dignity and sagacity.

The young Consul in Mukden, with his courtesy, efficiency, and scholarly attitude toward his work, presented a heartening contrast to the American consuls I had run into in former years, in the Levant and other parts of the world. In those days, they were chiefly peddlers of American business, with no ambition to know anything about the people among whom they worked, their language, their civilization, and their political trends. Now these officials are career men of high quality — perhaps a consequence of the recent consolidation of the consular with the diplomatic service.

While we are on the subject of government services in foreign countries, I may say that it was pleasant again to come in contact with the army, represented by the company of marines still stationed in the American Embassy grounds in Peking. These, it will be remembered, were traditionally the only horse marines in existence, but they have recently sold their mounts. The genial colonel of these 250 youngsters, Marston, was like the headmaster of a boarding school. There were infinite opportunities for getting into trouble with the Japanese military authorities in Peking, especially on nights off, when these high-spirited boys scattered over the city in groups, sharing the amusements provided for the Japanese garrison. They were healthy, mischievous, and full of vitality, and frequently had to be helped out of difficulties by the colonel. For in such matters the Japanese have no sense of humor. A sock in the jaw or the temporary borrowing of a girl becomes a diplomatic incident. The colonel knew how to heal the injured feelings of the officials, and to deal with his charges with paternal severity and considerable secret amusement. It was a relationship of humorous common sense, without relaxation of strict discipline, which caused me to wonder whether a year in the marines might not be a good training for most American boys.

CHAPTER XXIV

*More about the Orient. If R.S. had not been so
exasperatingly discursive, all this would have gone
into one chapter*

1

"You will find," wrote my friend Dr. Zia, "that the Chinese
world is completely different from your own. Yours was made
in six days, and then the Creator rested. It was a rush job. He
couldn't have had much time for speculation about the rattles
that might develop after the driving power that He put into
your brains had gathered speed. P'an Ku, the Chinese Creator,
took 18,000 years with a chisel and a mallet, fashioning our
world out of chaos. Then Sui Jên, our Prometheus, by watching a woodpecker, got the idea of making fire with a stick
and invented cooked meat. Charles Lamb's story of the much
later accidental discovery of roast pig is one of those superior
British witticisms. When the Great Flood came in 2297 B.C.,
or thereabout, there was no panic, wholesale drowning, or
hasty loading of lizards and snakes, pandas and dragons, and
so forth, into a Noah's Ark; but the learned Yü, with no fuss
or excitement, quite sensibly built a few canals and sent the
waters back into the Pacific. Then he devised practical mathematics with a knotted string, and the Chinese were all set for
their simple wants in a permanent order which satisfied them.

P'an Ku, being in less of a hurry, took time to consider consequences and thought it better to leave out of the human experiment any of the Western Adam's genius for scientific invention — perhaps because he questioned his ability to balance this by supplying brains enough to have such ingenuity used for wise purposes. P'an Ku must have felt that not even a great creating Deity could control the brains of men once he had let them loose on one of his planets. He thought that the capacity for metaphysical speculation was adequate to keep men occupied and harmless. Your Western Adam was given inventive genius without sufficient moral control.

"Well, it was possibly an experimental Creation; it is being thoroughly observed, and when the divine Experimenters have drawn Their conclusions, just as we do when an honestly conceived experiment turns out wrong, They will perhaps let this creation blow itself up, leave a few unspoiled chimpanzees with Professor Yerkes as caretaker, and try over again on a different young constellation, either leaving out the capacity for invention or supplying an adequate equipment of moral sense to control it within reasonable purposes. With the suggested setup established on our disappointing planet, moreover, They might even give Professor Yerkes carte blanche and see whether, starting from scratch with a population of apes, he might not rebuild a world motivated by instincts and the spinal centres rather than by intellectual complexities, and eventually achieve something harmlessly amusing on the model of Southern California.

"The two civilizations of the East and the West might have learned so much from each other for the benefit of both," Zia continued. "But your Western conceit translated your greater material efficiency into a sense of superiority and utilized it for purposes of subjugation and exploitation, instead of bringing it as a gift for strength and plenty to your Eastern fellows. The time is past for the amicable correction of your ways. The East has learned that it can save itself only by imitating you; and it is rapidly proving an adept pupil. It can learn to play your game when it sets its mind to it."

Nothing could have expressed the awakening of the East to the necessity of self-defense more clearly than this letter, and I wondered to what extent this enforced Westernization might destroy the ancient philosophical heritage of Asiatic thought which, sweeping across the passes from India, enriched by Confucius, Lao Tzǔ, Chuang Tzǔ, and Meng Tzǔ, had given them their highest qualities, but — at the same time — had rendered them helpless to resist Western aggression. I remembered the final paragraph of a thoughtful book by L. Adams Beck, who cites the hopes of an India sage that eventually the world might unite "the vigor of European action with the serenity of Asiatic thought."

2

At Shan-hai-kwan one passes the Great Wall. Once within its grim, majestic reaches, which lie across the desolate landscape like a sleeping serpent, coils closely weaving across hills and down valleys, one feels that one has entered the old and mysteriously strange world of the China of which one has heard and read.

If one stops over at Tientsin, this spell is partly broken. The splendor of the treaty ports has been quenched by the heavy hand of war. Victoria Road in Tientsin, with its great business houses and bank buildings, — reminding one in places of lower Broadway, — is like a street that has become drowsy and is slowly going to sleep. Many of the great mansions stand empty, and the deserted racecourse with its magnificent club-house seems doubly desolate as one imagines past scenes of holiday crowds and colorful gayety. One has the feeling that here, in this outpost of commercial conquest, there reigned until recently an opulence, a Victorian solidity of secure wealth, and an elegance of living that have been disappearing from the Western World itself these thirty years past. And when one speaks with any of the remaining representatives of this, incidentally, attractive type of merchant prince, one of those staying on of necessity to conserve what may still be rescuable, one senses in them the discouraged acceptance of the end of an era, the sad conviction that the old days will never return, irrespective of who may win the war. And if one were sure that the Chinese rather than the Japanese would profit by the change, one would not be so easily moved to sentimental sympathy after the third brandy and soda. As it is, one is depressed — as one always is by the spectacle of passing magnificence. I felt somewhat as I had when, after the war, I first saw the curtainless and "blind" windows of the great empty palaces of Vienna, their cobbled courts with grass between the stones.

Peking is different. It is still China as it has always been, in spite of foreign invasion, and as it will always remain, whatever the Japanese may do. I often walked at dusk upon the great city wall, gazing out at the Winter Palace and the Temple of Heaven and over the wide expanse of endless alleys lined with low walls and houses; and I reflected that in these crowded compounds, as in those of many other cities and villages, the life of China, strong in patience and resistance, was marking time until the forces of disturbance had worn them-

selves out against its mighty inertia. China is changing. But
her ultimate destiny will be determined not by external pressure, even pressure as powerful as that which Japan is now
exerting, but by the ground swell that will rise from the
depths of her racial solidarity and latent power; and when
these waves roll in they will sweep her clean of the surface
disturbances of foreign ambitions. And this I venture to say
on the basis of the quiet, inexhaustible capacity for taking
beatings without feeling licked that is still undiminished after
almost three years of disastrous warfare. No Chinese friend
with whom I spoke during long evenings of intimate conversation ever seemed to have the slightest idea of ultimate defeat or surrender, and every Japanese victory — however exaggerated in the despatches — was to them a victory of Pyrrhus
which weakened the invader more than the vanquished. The
Japanese Hercules has tackled a Hydra without an Iolaus to
help him cauterize the wound wherever he knocks off a head.
And two heads will keep growing where he removes one, until
his strength will be spent. Writing this makes me almost sorry
for the Japanese, for that's the way one writes oneself into
emotional jams.

Could I borrow the pen of a Loti or a Gide, I should be
tempted to describe Peking, its noises and its smells, the
evening crowds on Hatemen Street, the files of long-haired,
coal-laden camels threading their way along a street that might
be a Paris boulevard, among automobiles and rickshaws; its
children and beggars; the strange, mysterious silences of its
twisted alleys after dark; the surprise of passing through gates
from sordid lanes into quiet and charming courts and gardens;
and the majesty of its palaces (for, truly, the Winter Palace
with its symmetric immensity is more impressive than Ver-

sailles). This would make a better book if I could write with grace and originality of these things; but it has been done before, and better than I could do it. I can only summarize that Peking had a charm that no other city except Paris has ever held for me. Outwardly strange, as of another world or even another planet, I felt immediately and happily at home, and could quite understand how those of my Western friends who had once been settled there for a year or two had no desire to leave.

I have said many admiring and appreciative things about the Japanese, but in Japan I felt that, as a foreigner, I was being courteously treated by a race whose surface good manners are proverbial. But still I remained — except with a few old friends — essentially a stranger; and I suspected that I was being "convinced" that Japan was not as bad as she is painted. And truly I don't think she is. But in China — was it the reunion with a group of my old pupils, the immediate association with a student body that differed from our own only in greater eagerness and appreciation, or the friendly hospitality of American, French, and English residents who understood and liked the Chinese? All these things helped. Yet, pleasant as all this was, I do not believe that these circumstances alone gave me the contented sense of at-homeness. It was so easy to like my amiable and patient rickshaw cooly, my doorman, my houseman and cook. There was an indefinable something that attracted me to the people in the streets and in the shops. Perhaps I had been psychologically prepared to like and understand them by the friends who had, in an almost uninterrupted succession of over twenty years, worked with me in the intimate companionship of the laboratory and had removed from my mind all sense of "differentness." At any rate, I felt as though I understood these people as I did my own countrymen, and that in spite of dress, language, and complete strangeness of habits and traditions, the intimate texture of heart and spirit was essentially like our own.

3

It is not impossible that the difference between the Chinese and Japanese attitudes toward women and family life may be responsible for the greater ease with which the Westerner can fit himself into Chinese than into Japanese society. This is an important matter in the association between races. Nicolle once told me that while, during his twenty-five years in Tunis, he had established relations of mutual regard and friendship with many cultured Arabs, any development of personal intimacy was impeded by the impassable barriers of social customs governing family life.

In Japan, though there begin to be signs of change, the position of women is still one of considerable subservience to the male; the geisha still fulfills an important function in the lighter moments of social habit. In China, on the other hand, though concubinage still exists among the conservative, woman appears to exert a strong and often even dominating family influence. And this situation is not of recent Western importation. It seems to have been so for centuries and rests on the family ideal and husband-wife relationship which Lin Yutang ascribes to the teachings of Confucius. Ancient China had her poetesses, her women artists, and, if we can credit some of her writers, even her Xanthippes. (Incidentally, it is an historical tribute to the amiability of women that this last heroine should have achieved immortality only because, two thousand years ago, she made the life of a great philosopher miserable.) One meets the wives of one's Chinese friends on the same basis as one meets those of one's friends at home. There is no intention in all this to imply that one race is more "moral" than the other. The points of view of both toward matters of sex are quite wholesome and robust. A psychoanalyst would starve in either country. People go crazy in China and Japan as they do with us, but they do so for other reasons than ours. Moreover, it would be difficult to imagine the need for a lady doctor — like Dr. Stopes in England — to write a book to tell Chinese or Japanese gentlemen how to make love. (Of course the Stopes book has probably not been a best seller in France or Italy, either.) Moreover, in bringing out these differences between China and Japan, there is no purpose whatever of contrasting "moralities." Such comparisons are always unsatisfactory unless based on searching studies of the historical evolution of codes, taboos, religious, social, economic, and other influences for a treatment of which I possess neither the aptitude nor the training. Otherwise they become mere anecdotal indecency *pour épater les yokels* and are classifiable as "anthropology." What is a natural reaction in one place may be quite dreadful in another, without implying fundamental immorality. An African traveler once told me, for instance, that he had lived with a tribe in the southern Soudan among whom promiscuity was quite *de rigueur* and everyone went almost naked. Yet he heard a chief severely admonish his sixteen-year-old daughter because, not being able to find her "G" string that morning, she had put a finer "E" string around her waist. "Indecent exposure," he called it.

But all this is merely by the way to indicate that one of the things that made life natural and easily familiar was the fundamental similarity between their attitudes and our own toward their wives and families — a fact which facilitates sympathetic intercourse and goes far to bridge the minor differences between hamburger and birds' nests, forks and chopsticks, etc., etc.

4

After these digressions I suppose it would be in order to say something about the medical work I did in China. But that will all come out when Sam Zia, Pang, and little Liu finish it and get results in the field. The thing that I want to and can write about with the confidence of information gained from reliable sources and personal observation, a subject which, moreover, is close to my sympathies and interests, is the attitude of educated Chinese youth to the present national crisis. Few people fully appreciate the extent of the intellectual progress which was being made in China during the years immediately preceding the beginnings of Japan's benevolent decision to bring order and culture to China. Under Wang Shih-chieh, in the early 1930's, $29,000,000 was appropriated for educational purposes in one year, and 49,000 primary schools were established. In 1935, $37,000,000 was spent for similar purposes. Under the program initiated, Chinese factories in large centres were ordered to establish primary schools for employees; in the so-called "primary schools" the pupils ranged from six to sixty years. In 1912 there were 2,790,000 school children in China; in 1935 there were 12,000,000. In 1912 there were 4 universities; in 1935 there were 82 universities and 29 special colleges with an aggregate of 44,000 students. Even after the outbreak of hostilities the Chinese were able to add 5 further universities to the 82 previously established. In the "Special Education Movements" in Kiangsi, Hupeh, and other provinces, four-month courses were set up to prepare young teachers for distribution to villages all over the provinces in an attempt at mass education. An effort was made to teach reading, simple principles of hygiene, and enough military training to stimulate national feeling. With this went the wide distribution of pamphlets and an effort to develop local newspapers. The "New Life" movement initiated by Madame Chiang Kai-shek had a similar purpose, and is still making headway in spite of the disorganizing effects of war.

In all these energetic and very practically conceived innovations, the students of China played a leading rôle. Academic and educated youth in China to-day is taking part in political and social reform much as similar groups did in the Europe of the early nineteenth century. Revolution seems to call out the latent idealism and sacrificial enthusiasms of the young, or it did in Europe formerly as it does in China to-day.

It is perhaps one of the great misfortunes of the modern Western World that movements for change in economic and political organization are so exclusively initiated by pressure from below, with a leadership developed entirely out of the revolting oppressed or by professional and cynical theorists of revolution. The millions of the young, intelligent, and eager, whose eyes should be clear and pointed upward and from whom future leaders of idealism and vision should develop, have been with us in some unintelligible manner kept in swaddling clothes; and in the turmoils of the last twenty years have remained silent and passive. One wonders what might be the present conditions in Russia, in Germany, in Italy, and even in England and in our own country, had our college and university populations played parts in molding public opinion and forcing issues to which their ages and importance entitled them. Revolutions should not come entirely from below.

China's students are playing heroic and enormously important parts in the evolution of their nation. It was they who early organized a movement to arouse national consciousness. In 1923 they led the strikes in Hong Kong. It was they who started the defensive boycott of the Japanese. In 1927, when General Chiang was marching on Nanking, they joined his colors in large numbers. It was they who made possible the mass educational movements of which I have spoken. At the time of the battle at the Marco Polo Bridge in 1937, they enlisted by hundreds in the 29th Army. They are now, unless still in training, performing the professional and technical services and furnishing the officers for the armies of defense. It is they to a large extent who see ahead, who arouse the spirit of resistance and the national pride of the masses who, as is generally the case, would see no further than their own noses. This, to me, makes the Chinese one what I should like to call a "healthy revolution." The students believe in ultimate victory and I have yet to meet one of them who feels that China should make peace as long as there is a Japanese soldier in North China or even Manchuria. Numerically, of course, they are a mere handful compared with the masses who must do most of the fighting. But they are the yeast. And we all know what a handful of yeast will do to the most placid and uncombative barrel of cider.

5

The contact of China with Western medicine is an ancient one, but the legendary accounts of the very earliest penetration of Western physicians into China are not easily substantiated. A scholarly effort to collect the facts on these matters has been made by K. C. Wong and my friend Wu Lien-teh in their *History of Chinese Medicine*. A number of physicians from various parts of Europe came to Asia in pre-Christian days, but these had little or no influence on Chinese medical thought. The same may be said of the staff of Western doctors attached to the courts of the Mongol conquerors in the thirteenth century. After 1600, a more effective introduction of Western medicine was accomplished by Catholic missionaries, notable among whom were Matteo Ricci (about 1600) and Father Terrentius, a Swiss whose real name was Schreck, who practised medicine and published a small treatise on human anatomy in the Chinese language between 1618 and 1630. An interesting tale is told by Wong and Wu of the cure, in 1692, of a malignant fever at the court of the Emperor K'ang by Jesuit missionaries who had imported a small supply of cinchona bark from India. At about this time, also, a translation into Chinese of an eight-volume French work on anatomy, chemistry, toxicology, and pharmacology was made by Father Parrenin, but this — for reasons not very well known — was never published, though it is said to exist in manuscript copy, in the library of the French Academy and in the Dudgeon Library in China.

The first Western dispensary was probably that opened in Peking about 1700, by a French Jesuit, Brother Rhodes. Rhodes won the confidence of the Emperor by curing him of a boil on the lip, but narrowly escaped great displeasure when the Emperor discovered that four of the hairs of his sacred moustache had been clipped, when three might have been enough. The now traditional association of missionaries with medical service was firmly established by these noble friars, and was worthily continued by Franciscans and by the physicians attached to Russian missions into the eighteenth century.

These scattered efforts of the Catholic orders could not, however, influence more than a small fraction of the population — chiefly the upper-class, intelligent Chinese in a few of the large cities. The mass of the population still favored the devil exorcisers, the dispensers of powders made of dragons' teeth and snakes' skins, and physicians like the renowned Tu Fu, who cured malaria by reading his own poems to the sufferer.

It was the introduction of Jennerian vaccination in the nineteenth century which spread the renown of Western methods widely through coastal China. It is peculiarly appropriate that Jennerian vaccination should have had so fundamental an influence on the medicine of Asia, whence smallpox inoculation had first reached the Western World. Wong and Wu quote a legend in which the first performance of smallpox inoculation is attributed to a nun living on a mountain, Omei, near Tibet. The great courtier Wang Tan had lost several children from smallpox and when, in his old age, another son was born, he sought methods by which this child might be protected from the disease. He was directed to the nun, who successfully carried out the inoculation. This was about 1000 A.D., and the practice had probably come to China from India. The method of "Chan-na," or Jenner, was first used in China in 1803 by officers of the East India Company. It made slow progress, however, until large-scale vaccination was organized by another East India Company surgeon, Alexander Pearson, at Macao. Pearson began to train Chinese assistants, in order to reach large numbers. Vaccine departments were then established in various places, and the method made freely accessible to the poor. It was this successful campaign for the prevention of smallpox — the disease most dreaded by the Chinese people — which gave European methods their permanent foothold.

In 1820 an East India Company surgeon, John Livingston, with the help of the Reverend Mr. Morrison, opened a dispensary for Chinese at Macao. This was the first institution of its kind in South China, and when the founders retired, their work was taken up by Dr. Thomas R. Colledge, an English physician, who was popularly known as "the Chinaman's Friend." It was the work of these pioneers which attracted the attention of missionary societies in America and England and was responsible for the persistent and effective policy of sending to China, as practising missionaries, chiefly men trained in medicine. This plan was officially adopted by the American Board of Commissioners for Foreign Missions, who sent the first Protestant medical mission to Canton in 1830. In this group was Dr. Peter Parker, — born in Framingham, Massachusetts, graduate of Yale in both theology and medicine, — who first settled in Singapore, where he studied Chinese and opened a dispensary, eventually founding a hospital in Canton. His undertaking was so successful in gaining the confidence of the Chinese that the rich Canton merchants liberally subscribed and enabled Dr. Parker to engage both European and Chinese assistants. Although other medical missionaries arrived in considerable numbers, the movement was delayed by the unsettled conditions produced by the first Anglo-Chinese War of 1839, but in 1842 the Canton hospital was reopened by Parker.

It is quite impossible to follow in detail the adventurous and distinguished careers of the many medical missionaries who were sent out, chiefly from the United States and England, during the latter half of the nineteenth century. There were, in addition to these, some German, French, and Russian missions, both Catholic and Protestant, which did similar work. As a consequence, hospitals were founded in many of the larger cities, and these soon began to fulfill educational as well as purely practical functions. Young Chinese became interested, were employed as assistants, and many of them took up the practice either of Western medicine alone or of a combination of Western methods with the old, traditional Chinese teachings, carrying the missionary influence far and wide through the country. A few young Chinese, such as Dr. Wong Fun, then began to seek medical education in Europe.

The times during which these early missionary hospitals were developed were turbulent with political disorders and war, and the work was often delayed and hampered by the forced abandonment of well-organized and usefully functioning institutions. However, the fervor and self-sacrifice with which all obstacles were overcome by men who seem to have been both heroic and intelligent constitute the one bright chapter of Western penetration of the Orient, and one of which there is much reason to be proud.

According to Wong and Wu Lien-teh, the first properly organized medical school was that of the Canton Missionary Hospital, installed in 1866. This institution both systematically trained young Chinese in Western methods and co-operated with individual missionary-physicians who ran hospitals in other parts of China — not, however, being able to give instruction in the fundamental, preclinical subjects. These small hospitals were numerous and began to penetrate into the interior. One of the most interesting of the centres of instruction was that at Amoy, which in 1871 was taken over by Patrick Manson. It was here that Manson, with two Chinese assistants, carried out his classical studies on human filariasis. By 1890, medical schools of various degrees of efficiency had been opened in many other Chinese cities. There was the Viceroy's Medical School in Tientsin, St. Luke's at Shanghai, and another in Soochow.

In 1886, Dr. Sun Yat-sen, the great organizer of the League of Revolutionary Union, became a student in the Canton Medical School, and later in the Hong Kong Medical College. In the latter he came under the influence of Patrick Manson, and graduated in medicine and surgery in 1892. He actually practised medicine for a while, but his heart was in the organization of the future Chinese Republic, which — strange to record — was first conceived by him in the city of Tokyo.

It was in the late eighties and nineties of the last century, too, that public-health supervision, water-supply control, and Western sanitary methods in general made their first appearance along the Chinese coast, and a notable feature in this development is the rapidity with which important functions were taken over by trained Chinese. From that time on through the early twentieth century the development was one of expansion and consolidation of the beginnings made by the missionaries. The growth of the Peking Union Medical College, which has become the most important centre for the teaching of medicine in China, exemplifies the increasing receptiveness of the Chinese public and of the Chinese Government to Western standards.

In 1903 the North China Educational Union was formed by three missionary societies — one from London, the American Presbyterian, and the American "Board Mission." This educational union was joined by the Methodist-Episcopal Society and by another English medical missionary association. The Methodists, who had taught medicine in their Peking hospital, gave up their educational activities, and the new Union undertook to create a medical college under Dr. Thomas Cochrane of the London Missionary Society. The college was opened in 1906 and recognized by the Chinese Government.

In 1914, the Rockefeller Foundation established a commission to study and report on conditions of public health and medicine in China, and in 1915 the China Medical Board assumed full support of the college.

Thus a school started by missionaries and partly supported by the Chinese Government was taken over financially by an American foundation, under which it has attained a standing second to few medical institutions in the world. Meanwhile, other schools were growing up in the interior, partly with American support, notable among which are the Hunan-Yale College of Medicine at Changsha, the Yünnan Army Medical School, the Nantung School, the West China Union School, and the Shantung Christian University.

At the beginning of the outbreak of the present war, medical development had achieved extraordinary efficiency and had begun to react upon Chinese conditions and habits. The ultimate credit belongs to the large group of devoted missionaries who loyally labored for a century against great odds and often in peril of their lives. Much of their success, however, is due to the extraordinary intellectual receptivity of the Chinese people. If one is familiar with the type of purely metaphysical and Asiatic humanistic education which, until very recently, dominated the training of upper-class Chinese, it is little less than amazing how rapidly the younger generation (most of them, of course, of the upper, wealthy, often merchant classes, but the general group distributed over all layers of economic levels) have been able to adjust themselves to Western standards and have — practically in one generation — developed men and women who are now taking over independently the responsibility for the development of Western science in China.

I have often said many unkind things about missionaries and, if reports are to be believed, it is more than likely that, in many places where they have interfered with habits of food, customs of dress, housing, and the moral standards developed by primitive races through ages of local adaptation, they have done a great deal of harm. Until I went to China, the only missionaries who had elicited my complete admiration were those Catholic orders like the White Fathers of Tunis, whose young men were annually sent into Equatoria with the statistical prospects of an approximate 50 per cent mortality. I had seen isolated, devoted, medical missionaries like my friend Sam Cochran, who carried on through years of work in the interior of China at the expense of health and economic safety. Having thought of missionaries more as theologians than as medical men, I was apt to wonder whether it was not largely ignorance which gave these Westerners the arrogant confidence to believe that Christianity could contribute to the spiritual enlightenment of a nation which had lived for centuries under the teachings of Buddha and had modeled itself on the ideals of Confucius and his disciples. Indeed, if one compares the shrewd immorality of Machiavelli's *Prince* with the noble *Guide of Princes* of Meng Tsŭ, one cannot help realizing how much more deeply the lives of Eastern nations have been influenced by the spirit of their great philosophers than have those of the Western races. But these China missionaries were no bigoted evangelists. They were of the blood and spirit of the friars and, in the history of Western avarice and exploitation in China, theirs is the consoling note.

CHAPTER XXV

A chapter which sets forth a record of philosophical confusion tempered by long-range optimism

MEMOIRS and diaries of the relatively undistinguished are of value in recording the reactions which important events of any period call forth in the daily lives, habits, and thoughts of the average, intelligent contemporary. They are Lenotre's *Petite Histoire*. But since no one person can see the whole, the clear apprehension of any particular period requires the study of the reactions of many types, selected from a variety of temperaments and occupations. Realizing this, I never took these fragmentary records of R.S. as seriously as he feared I might take them. Yet on reading over what I had written about him so far, it seemed to me that he was a particularly interesting specimen for the *petite histoire* of our times, since he represented that growing class of the scientifically trained who began to suspect — toward the later years of the interval between the two last wars — that scientific progress was so far outstripping other forms of social development that it was endangering our civilization almost as much as it was benefiting it. Unlike that analogous period of scientific energy which occurred in the seventeenth century, our own age has lacked the balance of a parallel aesthetic intelligence. The seventeenth century, as Whitehead says, "provided intellectual genius adequate for the greatness of its occasions." Bacon, Galileo, Kepler, Harvey, Newton, Leibnitz, were preceded by Leonardo and were, culturally considered, contemporaries of Rabelais, Cervantes, Montaigne, Shakespeare, and Descartes. Moreover, the science of that epoch, exerting its influence almost purely in intellectual and philosophical directions, had not begun to transform the existence of man by its offspring, technology and industrialism. But now the accelerated pace of material progress, which had begun in the early nineteenth century with the substitution of coal for human hands, was beginning to outstrip the capacity of man to direct its velocity.

Distrust of the recent preponderance of science over aesthetic development has been voiced from time to time by serious critics — Brunetière, Lasserre, Babbitt, Henry Adams, Benda, Brooks, and many others who, in one way or another, preached the earlier doctrine of Boutroux, a follower of Comte, that "*la science doit être soumise au sentiment.*" But, coming from men largely preoccupied with letters, it usually amounted to little more than a quite justified but ineffective scolding of scientists for their neglect of values other than those of the material world. The weakness of such criticism was always the lack of sufficient knowledge on the part of the critics, who surveyed the scene quite as one-sidedly as did the scientists of whom they were complaining. We are living in an age in which the sciences not only are transforming the structure of society and the habits of men, but are equally confirming an orderliness of natural forces vaguely suspected, hitherto, by philosophers and great artists. Goethe recognized this orderliness and put his finger on the eternal quandary of the philosophers — that the creative force, whatever it might be, was powerless to modify the course of its own creation — when he said: "*Die Natur wirkt nach ewigen, notwendigen, dergestalt göttlichen Gesetzen, dass die Gottheit selbst daran nichts ändern könnte.*" The criticism of the future, therefore, to have any value, will demand a fundamental comprehension at least of the effects of the new understanding of nature upon human thoughts and affairs. For, after all, it is awareness of the scene as a whole which must form the equipment of the critic.

In response to such a need, there has arisen a literature largely contributed by distinguished physicists — Eddington, Jeans, Dingle, and Millikan among them — who began to contemplate the modern world in its broader relations from a base-line of deep scientific wisdom. But, as has ever been the case with physicists, they soon gave the poor earth little thought in their preoccupations with the universe. Yet some of them, notably Dingle, have tried to apply the logical processes of scientific method to the criticism of art; and a more than usually well-informed literary critic, I. A. Richards, made an attempt to meet these efforts halfway by approaching the scientific point of view from literature as a base. From none of these did R.S. gain much comfort. He became, however, a profound admirer of Whitehead, who, it seemed to him, combined — in the wide horizon of his mature wisdom — deep erudition of the sciences with sensitiveness to aesthetic values, appearing in this regard to possess some of the qualities, less creative but perhaps more contemporaneously sound, of a Goethe. It was in Whitehead's diagnosis of the sick world that R.S. recognized his own, less learnedly arrived at, to the effect that, with the rapid development of industrialism and urbanization (both consequences of the scientific control of natural forces) there was a neglect of the "aesthetic qualities of the new material environment"; there was a limitation of the "moral outlook" at a time when it was most needed. The "moral pace of progress," says Whitehead, "requires a greater force of direction," but a grooved professionalism (also a consequence of the headlong rush of science) has brought it about that "the leading intellects lack balance" and "the task of coördination is left to those who lack either the force or the character to succeed in some definite career." The corrective, therefore, it seemed to R.S., should lie not in the checking of science, but rather in catching up with it.

Thus, with Whitehead's assistance, R.S. thought he understood the general diagnosis. But that is as far as he got before he died. He stood before the problem as he often stood at the bedside of a dangerously sick patient, helplessly hoping for greater physicians to point a way of cure. He looked to art, literature, and criticism as the instruments through which this might come. For it seemed to him that what had happened was that mankind had been so busy planting the potatoes and corn and turnips of life that it had forgotten to tend the gardens. And now it had no gardens in the enjoyment of which it could find the reasons for which it had planted the potatoes and the turnips. For the arts and the spiritual values which they represent (and this was the pathology of the disease) had come to be regarded as trivial and not worthy of the efforts of serious men, a speculative commodity like stocks or postage stamps for rich collectors or a plaything for amateurs and eccentric incompetents; at best, a civilized amusement or a hobby.

It was this, the reënthronement of art in its broadest significance as an important, vital guardian and guide of the objectives of progress, which alone could cure. Sociology, economics, and political science in their present perplexed and experimental quandaries seemed merely "placebos" which could correct this or that pain and make the world feel temporarily better. For as fast as they could be applied, the disease would catch up with them. Santayana has said somewhere that there is a "high breathlessness about beauty that cancels lust and superstition." Might it not cancel materialism gone wild as well? And might it not — if it could move arm in arm with science — give direction and harmonious dignity to the new powers for happiness that science provides? For there is, in the discoveries of science, a harmony and beauty which has yet to be assimilated by the artist of our time.

It is one thing to make a diagnosis, quite another to devise an operation or a remedy. Whitehead was by no means the only diagnostician who put his finger on the modern world's McBurney's point. But he was the particular one who, standing, in the tranquillity of his wisdom, "*au dessus de la mêlée*," seemed to make the situation objectively clear to R.S. There was in many other critics, especially those like Babbitt and other lesser humanists, in writers, poets, and artists generally, a feebly masked resentment against the scientists who seemed to them to usurp too much of the modern world's attention. They appeared to feel toward science somewhat as the Church did in the sixteenth century.

To R.S. this was confusing, since with his own profound distrust of mere fact accumulated without philosophical and aesthetic coördination, the philosopher and the great artist were to him the architects who must build the cultural edifice of the future, using science — among other things — as an indispensable part of their equipment. But he found among most of his friends little or no appreciation of the fact that the last forty years had witnessed an era of enlightenment in man's understanding both of nature and of himself which was not incomparable to the epoch beginning with Galileo.

And yet the specific developments of the modern period, in their correlation of matter and energy and in the application of the exact sciences to biology, appeared to R.S. to bring scientific thought and its effects much closer than ever before to the everyday lives of men. Some of the landmarks of this era he pointed out to me as follows.

In 1895, Roentgen observed the clouding of photographic

plates which, thoroughly protected from light, had been placed near vacuum tubes through which electric discharges were passed. From this came the discovery of X-rays. Within a year, J. J. Thomson and Rutherford found that such X-rays, when passed through a gas, ionized the gas so that it became a conductor of electricity, and thus established for gases the same ionic principles that van't Hoff had demonstrated for liquids. Now it had been known for some time that when electrical discharges were passed from a platinum electrode through tubes evacuated of air, these discharges produced phosphorescence on the opposite wall of the tube, or on interposed bodies, preferably tungsten or platinum, and in this manner generated X-rays. These "cathode rays," which were the responsible forces, could be deflected in a magnetic field and in an electrical field — facts which gave Thomson the idea that they were particulate and made up of what he called "corpuscles," streams of rapidly moving particles which he believed smaller than atoms. Out of this grew the conception of electrons, which, even then, Thomson conceived as the possible elements of which matter of all kinds was composed.

At about the same time, Becquerel observed the action, on photographic plates, of potassium-uranium sulphate, and proved that the "rays" or "emanations" from the uranium salts can pass through black paper. This observation led directly to the discovery of radium by the Curies. Regarding this, Rutherford, in a posthumous article recently published, tells a story which is pleasant to read in these days when science and art themselves are, for the time being, corrupted by nationalism. He says that the first preparations of nearly pure radium were put on the market by a Dr. Giesel of the Braunschweig Chemie-Fabrik, and that, although Dr. Giesel was said to have separated radium somewhat earlier than the Curies, yet — having used the Curie methods — he refused to claim priority. Professor Rutherford does not vouch for the truth of this story, yet it is the kind of thing one likes to believe.

Next, and as direct consequences, came the modern theories of atomic structure. By Moseley's association of atomic numbers with charges on the nuclei of atoms, and the replacement of atomic weights by atomic numbers in the periodic system, the alchemist's dream of the transmutation of elements had come true in a sense; for instance, that uranium, with an atomic number of 92, — that is, 92 electrons in its periphery, — in giving off radiations "degenerates" through ionium to radium and, eventually, into entirely inactive lead, with an atomic number of 82. The profound influence of such conceptions on chemical theory is obvious.

For biology the new physics served to stimulate the development of the science of "biophysics." Many of the simpler methods of the physical laboratory became valuable assets in medical investigation. The potentiometer, the electrocardiogram, the encephalogram, diathermy, electrophoresis, ultraviolet photography, the study of membrane potentials, X-ray analysis of organic compounds, ultracentrifugation, ultrafiltration, and, lately, Langmuir's monomolecular surface-film technique — these and many other things began to find application in biological investigation, guided usually by preliminary advances in biochemistry.

Chemistry itself was meanwhile penetrating more deeply into the structure of living matter. In 1901, Hopkins and Cole discovered tryptophan, and in 1906, Fischer, from the single amino-acid, glycine, formed a series of peptides, dipeptides, and so forth. Protein became a chemical as well as a morphological entity. Its constitution of linked amino-acids, the nature of the linkages and the molecular weights, were being determined. Quantitative techniques were being developed for investigations of animal metabolism and microanalyses were made available in medical laboratories. Then came the study of the hormones, those internal secretions of the ductless glands and of organs like the ovaries and testes which regulate the chemical economy of the body and, when deficient or overactive, are responsible for many abnormalities and diseases. In these matters the organic chemist became the clarifier and converted what was loose, empirical guesswork into precise, quantitative knowledge.

Next, in 1912, came the discovery of the accessory food factors or vitamins, some of which can now be synthetized. The common sources of these in food materials were determined and a new group of "deficiency diseases" — among them rickets, pellagra, beriberi, and scurvy — were segregated. Subsequently, a biological link between physics and chemistry, it was found that sunlight or radiation with ultraviolet light may, like vitamin D, prevent rickets and that ergosterol, the responsible substance, can be isolated and converted into vitamin by ultraviolet radiation.

Turning to another problem, protein chemists succeeded in isolating and crystallizing enzymes, thus giving chemical incarnation to the previously mysterious initiators of body metabolism.

New understanding was coming from all directions, often from the least expected sources of supposedly "pure academic" investigation. The beauty of the situation was this growing integration of all the sciences in biological research.

But at the same time similar things were happening in biology itself. Up to 1900, the Darwinian conceptions of evolution by continuous natural selection and Weismann's ideas of heredity had remained virtually unchanged. Almost simultaneously, in 1900, Bateson and De Vries rediscovered the work of Mendel. The laws deduced by Mendel in his experiments with sweet peas, the conception of the dominance or recessive nature of certain qualities, and a numerical relationship between the appearance of the dominant and the recessive in hybrids became the basis of the modern knowledge of heredity. When the effects of the Mendelian theory of unit characteristics were correlated with microscopic studies of cell cleavage, the carriers of hereditary qualities were sought in the chromosomes of the nuclei of the germ cells, and work such as that of Edmund B. Wilson, on the manner in which chromosomes divide before cell cleavage and are united in pairs in the new cells, strengthened the growing belief that there was some connection between the two. The idea was formulated by Sutton, and in 1910 Thomas H. Morgan brought the matter to a definite conception by his work on the fruit fly, Drosophila. From these studies originated the idea of genes within the chromosomes — the linkage of numerous hereditary factors in one chromosome. Modern genetics became a logical, if not entirely a precise, science. And soon these principles found application in medicine. A large number of human qualities, ailments, and deformities could now be traced to genetic origin and, for some of them, it has already been possible to determine which are "dominant" and which "recessive." Such knowledge made it possible to differentiate many physical and physiological defects into those which are hereditary and those which are due to extraneous causes. It may establish certain principles of human breeding in extreme cases where physical defects are known to be "dominant." (Yet there is no rational basis for immediately embarking on a totalitarian regulation of marriage on a eugenic basis. That is an old story, tried out — as Castle has indicated — in Sparta, and advocated in the Darwinian period by Galton. But social instincts, cultural struggle, and emotional factors are too complex and strong to be even temporarily overcome by a far-seeing plan of man-husbandry which cannot be expected to take hold effectively in less than many generations of a control abhorrent to the strongest physiological urge. Moreover, there may be much justifiable difference of opinion concerning the desirable traits toward which such breeding might aim. A six-toed or hunchbacked critic might be judged a more desirable citizen than a morally defective Adonis; or a tuberculous Chopin or a neurotic Shelley than a normal delicatessen merchant. And as far as the socially valuable characteristics are concerned, J. B. S. Haldane holds out the hopeful suggestion that since the virtuous are often rewarded by poverty and since the poor breed quicker than the rich, we may possibly expect some slight, though slow improvement. His mathematical treatment of the subject does not, at any rate, support the kind of eventual system which, one imagines, some eugenists might approve — that is, limiting procreation to those holding a "fornication license" from the Statehouse, with number plates appropriately attached. Even science must leave some things to what Ehrlich called *"Die Uralte Proto-plasma-Weisheit."*

To this incomplete thumbnail sketch of the great scientific era through which he had lived, R.S. refused to add illustrations from his own specialty, above all because he did not want this to be a "doctor book," but partly because he thought it was sufficient to make his point — to wit, that the fundamental sciences had in a short forty years revolutionized understanding of the nature of matter, inanimate and living, and of the forces which regulated it. It seemed only reasonable to hope that this formidable enrichment of our intellectual capital should work considerable improvement in the wisdom and well-being of mankind, both by the influence of its philosophical implications and because of the consequences in invention and industry by which health, comfort, and plenty would seem assured. Yet it seemed to make no difference at all; or, if any, it appeared rather to speed up the *"Sieg des Blutes"* which the cheerful Spengler had predicted. The only mistake this male Cassandra seemed to have made was that he limited his woeful prediction to the *Abendland*, whereas, at the present writing, the east or *Morgenland* appears to be going the same way.

Now what was happening in the short space between the 1890's and the present day was nothing new. It was merely an immense acceleration of the tempo of scientific understanding which had begun with Bacon. In its earlier stages, mighty as was the intellectual impact of Galileo, Newton, and others of that great period, the immediate effects were only to confuse the philosophers and arouse the theologians to self-defense. The Church itself was too strongly organized, too deeply rooted in the consciousness of the people, perhaps too necessary for the maintenance of a moral equilibrium, to be easily disturbed. Its second line of defense, however, the philosophers, continued to be progressively confused. The havoc which the struggle for understanding could play with philosophy can best, perhaps, be illustrated by what Haeckel spoke of as the "two Kants." Kant No. 1 was the critical protagonist of pure reason, who maintained that the conceptions of God and immortality were not amenable to proof by reason; and Kant No. 2 was the metaphysician who was convinced that these two concepts were indispensable to a reasonable understanding of the universe.

Science, as we have seen, has developed exponentially since Kant's day. Yet the position of the informed philosophers has hardly changed in regard to the ultimate quandary. And now those who have followed this modern acceleration of scientific discovery are growing in the conviction that, however far it may progress, this philosophical confusion is the permanent lot of man. For, as R.S. put it, even those great modern physicists who alone among us can justly be dignified as "experts" on God's handiwork, having come to the end of their scientific rope, are left dangling in mid-air without the strength to climb back up to a comfortable mechanistic foothold or the courage to let go and trust that the metaphysical ether will float them gently into the arms of the "super-mathematician" who "invented the electron" and then washed his hands of the whole affair.

The philosophical quandary was obviously a permanent one and the hope of achieving a physicochemical basis for human morality was as far off now as it was in Kant's time, or, for that matter, as it was when our ancestors gnawed bones in Neanderthal. And though the power of man over his material environment had been infinitely enriched, the very understanding which had brought this about was threatening to take away something without which his painfully achieved civilization was in danger of perishing. Science had made it impossible for the intelligent man and woman — and therefore eventually for the mass of the people — to fall back for their ethical codes upon the supernatural and miraculous authority which had served so long and so well (with certain well-known lapses) to maintain a reasonable moral equilibrium. Thoughtful theologians, recognizing this, were beginning to transmute much that was once doctrine into symbolism, though the process was hard sledding and had its definite limitations. R.S. never questioned the usefulness of, even the necessity for, some sort of an organized guardianship of spiritual values; but the Church, he thought, had need of a modern Thomas Aquinas who could redefine God as the atomic physicists had redefined matter and force. Yet, he thought, it was highly important to consider that Christianity was really losing relatively little in being forced away from its supernatural and miraculous elements. After all, Christ remained, and it seemed a challenge to the Church to find a way consistent with modern understanding of keeping Him vivid and alive by the sheer spiritual strength that was in Him.

Thus, thought R.S., science, instead of helping to release mankind from toil, poverty, and war, actually seemed to be accelerating materialism, hatred, and the forces of destruction. And in its fundamental aspects science was demonstrating that however deeply it might penetrate into the mechanisms of nature and the universe, it would never — alone — solve the ultimate problems or appease that hunger of the spirit, that yearning toward an ethical ideal which, in one form or another, he believed to be an inherent, biological attribute of human beings, as strong as the hungers of the body. For its existence, what more convincing scientific proof could be desired than the irresistible force with which the teachings of Buddha and of the New Testament had swept across the world and had conquered the imaginations of men, often to the disadvantage of their material interests and racial supremacies. R.S. had seen many of his most admired and distinguished scientific contemporaries, despairing of the powers of reason alone, seek spiritual sanctuary either — acknowledgedly *faute de mieux* — in the arms of the established Church, or, more deplorably, in some form of mysticism.

Both the desire for and the guidance toward such "aesthetic apprehension," as Whitehead calls it, were apparent. Yet less and less were they effective in arresting the downward course of our civilization. Some regulating force was needed, something of the heart; and "the heart," says Anatole France, "*n'est jamais tout à fait philosophe.*" Was recourse to supernatural authority the only alternative for this "apprehension" of the higher values of existence, he asked himself. If so, it appeared to him, the outlook was dark. For the masses of the people, once lured away from a weakening religious control, would be more and more delivered, spiritually hog-tied, to the mercy of pure material forces. It seemed to him that the sole hope lay in a powerful development of the arts.

Now there were times — for a while in Athens, later, in the Renaissance, and possibly among the Elizabethans (when, as Theodore Spencer has said, Shakespeare reduced to poetic order and made recognizable the common experience of his age) — when art was a living influence in the lives of people. But those were simpler days, without newspapers, cinema, or radio. Then the taste of the average man was formed by the sincere artists of his time. The artist was a hero, was close to earth, close to man, and comprehensible in this "common experience."

It was too much to expect, of course, that in times as complex as our own, with huge populations of widely diverse interests and educational backgrounds, the best in art could find its way, unaided, into the hearts and minds of the people. The output of artistic endeavor, good, bad, and terrible, sincere and insincere, was too overwhelming, and too strong the temptation for commercial exploitation of the spurious and the corruption of taste. Here, thought R.S., was a situation which called desperately for the development of sound criticism in its broadest sense; in which the art of criticism might become one of the most important factors in civilization. Critics were needed to interpret, to segregate, to create judgment, to come out of their ivory towers and carry the battle for aesthetic standards into the market places of the world.

Never before was there such an important function for great critics, thought R.S., critics who — like Goethe, Coleridge, Sainte-Beuve, or Taine — could lead the intelligent and sensitive up hills whence they could see many things to gladden their hearts and enrich their spirits, which, unguided, they might never have beheld. Then, filtering downward, from the few to the many, standards and taste might eventually emerge. At any rate, art might regain the dignity to which it is entitled by man's need of it.

But a great critic, said Voltaire, is "an artist who possesses great knowledge and taste without prejudice and without envy," and he adds: *"Cela est difficile à trouver."*

In spite of Voltaire's definition of a critic, R.S. wanted to air his own views on modern art and, incidentally, on the critics who — he thought — were more and more devoting their talents to an almost scientific defense of the obscure, incomprehensible, and psychologically aberrant performances of modernistic experimenters — valuable, perhaps, in developing innovations of expression and breaking down time-worn conventions, but, as Archibald MacLeish has put it, incapable of the "construction which must be done to make recognizable to us our experience of our time." R.S. had little sympathy or appreciation of much that was obscure, incomprehensible, and erratic in the productions of the ultra-experimenters. He held to the old-fashioned opinion of Boileau: —

> Avant donc que d'écrire, apprenez à penser
> Quelque sujet qu'on traite, ou plaisant ou sublime,
> Que toujours le bon sens s'accorde avec le rime.

Yet even in many of the most extreme he could see a vitality of effort born of an increased pressure for artistic expression. Moreover, there began in 1900, especially in America, an era of productivity in verse and prose — satire and fiction — which, however far from the mark some of it may have fallen, still indicated that the need for artistic interpretation of the modern world was beginning to assert itself. And with it there developed a parallel new energy in architecture, in painting, in sculpture, and in the appreciation of music. Best of all, much of this was good, strong, and sincere, and some of it beginning actually to penetrate increasingly into the population. And though one can rarely certify a great critic until the passage of time has confirmed his judgment, R.S. thought that men like Brooks, Wilson, Canby, De Voto, MacLeish, and some others, were trying to do an honest and increasingly effective job.

R.S. was optimistic. He believed that the tide was turning; that, in America at least, the creative artist would play an increasing rôle in the development of culture; and that this was the strength of our future even more than our gold reserves — the significance of which, by the way, he could never understand.

I was a little nervous about letting R.S. — who was, in my opinion, artistically quite naïve — stick out his neck any further in his self-imposed rôle as a critic. Since his own preoccupation, outside of science, had been chiefly with poetry, I asked him, instead of criticizing the poetry of contemporaries, to tell me what it was that gave him satisfaction in the poetry he read and which he tried to write himself. I add his reply more from the desire to give a complete picture of the man than from any idea that his views were either original or profound.

"Poetry," he said, "has been to me much like horses. Though I was often cheated in consequence, I never enjoyed critically appraising a horse, walking around it, feeling its hocks, looking at its teeth, and then seeing other people ride it. A horse meant little to me until I could feel it under me, between my thighs, swing with the rhythm of its gaits, rise over fences with it, and lean over its neck in the exhilaration of its galloping vigor.

"And so a poem means nothing to me unless it can carry me away with the gentle or passionate pace of its emotion, over obstacles of reality into meadows and covers of illusion. Nor is it the material that matters — whether it be the old stirrings of nature and love, or war, or whether it deals with the tragedies and complexities of human fate. The sole criterion for me is whether it can sweep me with it into emotion or illusion of beauty, terror, tranquillity, or even (Herder to the contrary) disgust, — as in Baudelaire, — so long as it arouses fundamental feelings or reflections which, encountered without the poet, might have passed half realized, like a tongue of flame or a flying leaf. For the poet arrests emotions at their points of greatest supportable heat, just short of the melting point as it were, and can hold in that perfect state, permanent in his words and metres, those feelings and comprehensions which pass too quickly to be held through the minds of ordinary men. The poet imprisons them in words or color or marble, so that we lesser men can contemplate them and recognize in them their own hearts and minds."

This was the last serious conversation I had with R.S.

CHAPTER XXVI

In which death is met adagio and allegro instead of, as often, maestoso or largo sostenuto

R.S. returned from his last professional journey badly damaged. On the steamer he was humiliated by the fact that not only occasional youngsters but even a British general of approximately his own age could outlast him at deck tennis. Also the sun, instead of tinging his skin a healthy brown, turned him the lemon yellow of the sunburned anaemic. He made a tentative diagnosis on himself before arrival in port.

So when he got home, he went to see an old friend, a doctor, who had pulled him through a nasty infection a few years before. This friend to whom he had gone was one of those precious individuals whom nature had meant to be physicians. He was fond of R.S. and showed it most helpfully by his affectionate abstinence from any expression of sympathy. And R.S. told me that, together, this good friend and he stood for a long time at the office window, looking out at the Charles River Basin. It was one of Lowell's June days, in the early afternoon. Bright sunshine was reflected from the water and from dozens of little white sails on the dinghies that were racing along the Cambridge shore. The Esplanade was alive with contented men and women, strolling and sitting on the benches; and the sounds of playing children came up through the open window like the voices of many birds. The world looked a bright and attractive place.

But in those few minutes, R.S. told me, something took place in his mind that he regarded as a sort of compensatory adjustment to the thought that he would soon be dead. In the prospect of death, life seemed to be given new meaning and fresh poignancy. It seemed, he said, from that moment, as though all that his heart felt and his senses perceived were taking on a "deep autumnal tone" and an increased vividness. From now on, instead of being saddened, he found — to his own delighted astonishment — that his sensitiveness to the simplest experiences, even for things that in other years he might hardly have noticed, was infinitely enhanced. When he awoke in the mornings, the early sun striking across the bed, the light on the branches of the trees outside his window, the noise of his sparrows, and all the sounds of the awakening street aroused in him all kinds of gentle and pleasing memories of days long past which had left their imprints — indelible but, until now, not consciously realized — of contentment and happiness. It was quite the opposite of the "woe of the remembering of happy times" in Canto V of the *Inferno*, beginning: "*Nessun maggior dolore*" and so on. R.S. felt a deeper tenderness for the people whom he loved, and a warmer sympathy and understanding for many whose friendship he had lost in one way or another. Each moment of the day, every prospect on meadow or hill or sea, every change of light from dawn to dusk, excited him emotionally with an unexpected clarity of perception and a new suggestiveness of association. Thinking of the shortness of the time still left him, he reread — as though for a sort of P.P.C. conversation — the books that had meant much to him at the various stages of his life, and found them more moving, more deeply wise, or more hilariously robust, according to their natures. Everything that went on about him or within him struck upon his heart and mind with a new and powerful resonance. So, on the whole, he was far from either meriting or desiring sympathy. The only thing that depressed him at all in those days was the thought of horses. He couldn't stand the sight of his saddles, his bridles, and the various bits that hung about his bedroom — and which he now packed out of sight in the cellar.

As his malady progressed, he had another variety of experience which, to some others more conditioned to religious belief than he was, might have signified an intimation of the separateness of body and soul.

He said to me: "Here I am, me as always. My mind more alive and vivid than ever before; my sensitiveness keener; my affections stronger. I seem for the first time to see the world in clear perspective; I love people more deeply and more comprehensively; I seem to be just beginning to learn my business and see my work in its proper relationship to science as a whole; I seem to myself to have entered into a period of stronger feelings and saner understanding. And yet here am I — essentially unchanged except for a sort of distillation into a more concentrated me — held in a damaged body which will extinguish me with it when it dies. If it were a horse I was riding that went lame or broke its neck, or a ship on which I was traveling that sprang a leak, I could transfer to another one and leave the old vehicle behind. As it is, my mind and my spirit, my thoughts and my love, all that I really am, is inseparably tied up with the failing capacities of these outworn organs.

"Yet," he continued, apostrophizing in a serio-comic mood, "poor viscera, I can hardly blame you! You have done your best, and have served me better than could be expected of organs so abused. When I think of the things that have flowed over and through you! Innumerable varieties of fermented hops and malt and of the grapes of all countries and climates: Vouvray, Anjou, Chablis, Haut Sauternes, Chambertin, Nuits-

Saint-Georges, Riesling, Lachryma Christi, Johannisthaler, Berncastler, Saint-Julien, Clos de Mouche, Liebfrauenmilch; endless amounts of *pinard* and *vin du pays*; the sour wines of Alsace, of North Africa, and of the Pyrenees; the stronger ones of Spain — Oporto, Sherry Madeira, Malaga; the Tokay of Hungary; sparkling vintages of Burgundy and of Champagne; Veuve Cliquot and her brothers Mumm and Pommery; and the California brews bought in demijohns; to say nothing of the distillates — flavored and unflavored; cognac, Three-Star Hennessy; whiskeys — Scotch, Irish, Canadian, rye, bourbon, and the yellowish moonshine, colored with chicken droppings, from the Blue Hills; and gin — genuine and synthetic; Schlibovitz from the Balkans, Starka from Poland, and the vodka of the Steppes; crème de menthe and cacao, Marie Brizard, Cointreau, and Calvados.

"No, no, my organs! I cannot feel that you have let me down. It is quite the other way round. Only now it seems so silly that you must take me with you when I am just beginning to get dry behind the ears."

Though he had these spells of half-humorous revolt against the idea that his personality and his increasing joy of living should be so helplessly at the mercy of his deteriorating body, he was still grateful that, in his case, it was this and not the mind that was going to pieces first. He was not, at any time, tempted to seek strength in wishful surrender to a religious faith in which far greater men than he had taken refuge just before death. When this had, astonishingly, happened in the cases of several of his intimate friends, he regarded it as a capitulation of the mind to the fatigue of suffering. Indeed, he became more firm in his determination to see things out consistently along his own lines of resignation to agnostic uncertainty — as his father had done before him. Moving further away, therefore, from faith in any comprehensible conception of God, he yet grew closer in conviction of the wisdom and guiding integrity of the compassionate philosophy of Christ.

As his disease caught up with him, R.S. felt increasingly grateful for the fact that death was coming to him with due warning, and gradually. So many times in his active life he had been near sudden death by accident, violence, or acute disease; and always he had thought that rapid and unexpected extinction would be most merciful. But now he was thankful that he had time to compose his spirit, and to spend a last year in affectionate and actually merry association with those dear to him. He set down this feeling in his last sonnet: —

> Now is death merciful. He calls me hence
> Gently, with friendly soothing of my fears
> Of ugly age and feeble impotence
> And cruel disintegration of slow years.
> Nor does he leap upon me unaware
> Like some wild beast that hungers for its prey,
> But gives me kindly warning to prepare:
> Before I go, to kiss your tears away.
>
> How sweet the summer! And the autumn shone
> Late warmth within our hearts as in the sky,
> Ripening rich harvests that our love had sown.
> How good that 'ere the winter comes, I die!
> Then, ageless, in your heart I'll come to rest
> Serene and proud, as when you loved me best.[1]

It is apparent, therefore, that in his last months R.S. achieved a certain degree of philosophical tranquillity and resignation. It would be a mistake, however, to suppose that, apart from his purely personal reactions to his own fate and his immediate environment, he was less confused at the time

---

[1] Reprinted by permission of the *Atlantic Monthly*.

of his death than I have described him in my introductory chapter. When he gazed beyond the circle of his own work, his family and friends, into the rushing world about him, he was completely bewildered. He had a little the same resentful feeling that he remembered having when, as a boy, he had walked through Normandy and had to jump into the ditch to let one of the recently invented automobiles rattle by — knowing that its passengers would have dinner at the town where he expected to arrive two days later. It was all moving too fast for him. Indeed, he was not sure whether the world that was rushing by was going forward or backward. He wondered whether he had not, perhaps, been born a little too soon and remained unable to catch up with his time. The world to which he had been born had not alone speeded up with that acceleration of which Henry Adams complained, but it had actually seemed to change direction. Scientific progress had brought as much sorrow as happiness. With immensely enhanced powers of production, millions were out of work and starving. Ideas of democracy and individual freedom which he had accepted as the gradually evolved goals of centuries of struggle were not only being denied, but entire nations were frantically intent on destroying them. Great racial masses seemed willing to fight and perish, if necessary, for their own enslavement. New so-called "ideologies" were tearing up the foundations of all that men had thought firm and permanently established. Something had cracked in the old Western civilization, and its walls and lofty towers — cemented with the sweat and blood of their forefathers — were tumbling about men's ears. And the intellectual calamity seemed to be that no one could say whether the turmoil was the result of avoidable stupidity or of the operation of laws of economic and social evolution that were acting on mankind as other laws had acted on the dinosaur and the sabre-toothed tiger.

But in all these things he could never tell, before he died, whether the fault was in him or in the trends he disliked. He didn't admit this, of course, and remained, to the last, argumentatively arrogant. But I knew that at the time of his death he was as thoroughly bewildered as any thoughtful individual of our time is bound to be.

All of which goes to prove that, as I pointed out in the first chapter, R.S. was really a quite ordinary person about whom it was hardly worth while to write a book.